*"Let us, each of us, now embrace with solemn duty
and awesome joy what is our lasting birthright. With
common effort and common purpose, with passion and
dedication, let us answer the call of history and carry
into an uncertain future that precious light of freedom."*

PRESIDENT BARACK OBAMA
Second Inaugural Address
January 21, 2013

PETER BAKER

OBAMA

THE CALL OF HISTORY

Foreword by Jon Meacham

author of *The Soul of America*

Expanded and updated text

The New York Times

Callaway

The New York Times

CALLAWAY

Published by
CALLAWAY ARTS & ENTERTAINMENT
Bryant Park Studios
Penthouse East
80 West 40th Street
New York, New York 10018

Visit The New York Times at www.nytimes.com
Visit Callaway at www.callaway.com

ISBN 978-0-935112-78-8

First text edition, second printing
Printed and bound in the USA
Distributed in the U. S. by Ingram Publisher Services
www.ingramcontent.com

TABLE OF CONTENTS

Michelle Obama, it turned out, was ahead of the curve. At 10 p.m. on Election Night 2016, as her husband, the forty-fourth president of the United States, turned on the television in the White House residence to watch the returns from the race between Hillary Clinton and Donald Trump, the first lady bailed and went to bed. "She may have had the right idea," Peter Baker writes in the following pages. "For Democrats, the stress levels climbed higher and higher as the results were announced." The end was nigh, and soon enough, Baker writes, "the unthinkable had happened": the New York real-estate and reality-TV impresario had been elected to succeed Barack Obama. "This stings," Obama said. "This hurts." Of course Trump's victory did more than that, and it was Mrs. Obama, who'd had the foresight to rest up for the coming storms, who had perhaps put the stakes of the moment best. "Being president doesn't change who you are," the first lady had said on the campaign trail, "it reveals who you are."

The book you are holding is testament to the truth of Mrs. Obama's observation. (Interestingly, Richard Nixon, a man not known for self-awareness, once made a similar point, writing: "The presidency is not a finishing school. It is a magnifying glass.") Drawing on his eight years of first-hand observation as chief White House correspondent for *The New York Times*, Peter Baker, who is also the author of landmark books about the Bill Clinton impeachment and about the presidency of George W. Bush, has given us a thorough and insightful account of how Barack Obama's years in power revealed who the forty-fourth president really was—and what the first African-American to hold the office meant to the nation and to the world he led.

In the eye of history, the Obama presidency ended only a moment ago, but the tumult of the Age of Trump—and its contrast with Obama's reign—has already consigned the 2009-2017 period to a distant, seemingly mythic era in which presidents tended to tell the truth, lived in a fact-based universe, and conducted themselves with equanimity and with grace. "His person, countenance, character, and actions are made the daily contemplation and conversation of the whole people," John Adams wrote in 1790, later, after his own presidency, adding: "The people cannot be too careful in the choice of their Presidents." In the late 19th century the English diplomat and historian James Bryce observed: "The President has a position of immense dignity, an unrivalled platform from which to impress his ideas (if he has any) upon the people." In a series of 1906 lectures, Woodrow Wilson of Princeton argued that the president "is at liberty, both in law and conscience, to be as big a man as he can." Wilson was the epitome of the educated man; one of his successors, the self-taught Harry Truman, came to the same conclusion, writing: "Every hope and every fear of his fellow citizens, almost every aspect of their wealth and activity, falls within the scope of his concern—indeed, within the scope of his duty."

Baker's account of Obama's embrace of this sense of presidential duty offers readers and historians an essential cartography of the geography of power in these years. The forty-fourth president came to office amid the greatest financial crisis since the Great Depression, and it fell to him to manage the ongoing war on terror that had resulted from Al Qaeda's devastating attack on the U.S. homeland in 2001. He presided, too, over a nation undergoing significant demographic shifts and changing opinions about the nature of sexual identity; a country that endured far too many school shootings; a political culture that grew ever more tribal and reflexively partisan; and a world still trying to find its way

8

in a geopolitical ethos of multiple rising military and economic powers without the defining struggle of the Cold War.

Experience teaches us that the character and the temperament of the American president is often decisive in the great public affairs of the Republic. George Washington's probity and prudence were essential to the founding of the constitutional order; Andrew Jackson's single-minded devotion to the Union saved us from armed strife in the 1830s; Abraham Lincoln's political savvy and tragic sensibility rescued the nation; Franklin D. Roosevelt's dexterity saw us through depression and a world war; John F. Kennedy's cool realism and sense of history brought the Cuban Missile Crisis to a successful conclusion; Ronald Reagan's sunny disposition restored our confidence after Vietnam, Watergate, and the drift of the late 1970s; George H.W. Bush's empathy and care enabled him to end the Cold War peaceably and quietly.

And it was Barack Obama's intriguing combination of passion and distance that gave him the ability to break seemingly insuperable racial barriers in his rise and to govern in a complicated time with a sense of balance and of proportion. The son of a white woman from Kansas and a black man from Kenya, Obama was raised, largely by his white grandparents, in Hawaii. Always straddling between different racial worlds, he met his father just once, in 1971; the elder Obama had chosen to leave his wife and child in Honolulu in order to attend graduate school at Harvard. (He turned down New York University, where a scholarship would have enabled him to have taken his family.)

"Something's got to be driving you, and in my case if you have somebody that is absent, maybe you feel like you've got something to prove when you're young, and that pattern sets itself up over time," Obama told me in an interview in 2008. "But also because, again in my case, the stories I heard about my father painted him as larger than life, which also meant that I felt I had something to live up to. You could argue that if you're too well adjusted, you don't end up running for president."

A fair, funny, honest point—and it's clear that the Obama who governed America for eight years had reacted to his unusual, even chaotic, childhood by learning to mask his feelings and to present a calm demeanor to the world whatever emotional currents may have been swirling beneath the surface. Anger at his missing father would have been understandable, but unproductive. Surliness was no path to success, much less greatness, and Obama was born with an intelligence that gave him the capacity to see problems in all their complexity—a gift, honed over the years, that enabled him to have the confidence that he could compete in the most contentious of arenas. Best, then, to take the long view, to make his own way, to look before he leapt.

And that in many ways defined how he conducted his presidency. He could seem aloof and unemotional, the Mr. Spock of American politics, entranced by logic more than he was driven by emotion. (I asked him once if he could do the Vulcan hand signal. He smiled, split his fingers, and said "Live long and prosper.") Yet the country, in 2009, after the difficult post-9/11 years and the gutsy presidency of George W. Bush, was ready to trade swagger for a bit more Spock.

American history is often marked by such reactions in our choice of presidents. We veer from guardrail to guardrail. In just the last three decades, voters have moved from George H.W. Bush, a hero of World War II, to Bill Clinton, a Baby Boomer who took pains to avoid military service in Vietnam. We then replaced the licentious Clinton with the highly disciplined George W. Bush, only to choose the professorial Obama to succeed Bush, who eschewed second-guessing and called himself "the Decider."

Which brings us to Donald Trump, the ultimate antithesis of Barack Obama. Reading Baker's history of Obama's careful decision-making, of his thoughtful weighing of pros and cons, of his triumphs and of his inevitable mistakes, is to explore a presidency that could not be more different from that of the incumbent's. This is not a partisan point; it's a self-evident one. The long-term decision facing the American people is which nation—Trump's or Obama's—we wish to be.

After the results became clear on that November night in 2016, West Wing staffers were said to be in tears at the prospect—the reality, now—that a man who had risen to prominence in right-wing politics by promulgating conspiracy theories about Obama's birth (Trump trafficked in discredited rumors that Obama had been born in Kenya, which would have made him ineligible to be president under the "native-born" clause in the Constitution) would soon be sitting in the Oval Office.

Unsurprisingly, it was Obama himself who offered words of reassurance. "I always say," Obama has remarked, "that things are never as good as we think when they're going well, and never as bad as we think when they aren't." It was the voice of a man who'd seen it all—the good and the bad, the hopeful and the fearful, the best and the worst. What follows is the story of what he saw, and what he did, when he encountered all those inescapable realities, often all at once, when he stood at the pinnacle of power.

Jon Meacham is a Pulitzer Prize-winning biographer whose latest book is 'The Soul of America: The Battle for Our Better Angels.'

PROLOGUE 'Riding the Wave'

Only a few dozen people were still lingering around the White House that night in January 2017 in the twilight hours of Barack Obama's presidency. Most of his aides had turned in their badges, packed their boxes and left to begin a new chapter. With his lease on the building expiring at noon the next day, Obama invited those left to the State Dining Room, where hors d'oeuvres and drinks were served.

He was at the end of a momentous journey, full of triumph and tribulation, success and setback. He was grayer than on that heady day at Grant Park in Chicago when he first won the presidency, scarred from the many battles that had followed. The lofty expectations, both his own and those he generated, had long since faded into grinding reality. And so, on this, his last evening before leaving office, Obama was in a contemplative mood, ruminating on the meaning of his presidency.

"I have had an ongoing debate with Ben about whether individuals change the course of history or if structural changes happen on their own and people are just riding the wave," he told the last remnants of the team that had ridden the wave with him, including Ben Rhodes, the speechwriter and national security aide who had become one of his closest confidants. "What I know after working with this team and with our Cabinet is that in fact it is *teams* that change history."

More than just a final attaboy for his crew, Obama's observation on the way out the door touched on essential questions of his time in office. How much did he drive events and how much did they drive him? How much did he write his story and how much was it written by forces of history far greater than he? Obama was propelled to power on a tide of yes-we-can determination in a moment of existential crisis for the country, by a hunger for something new and different after years of struggle and a palpable desire on the part of many Americans to turn the page on an ugly racial past. But he left office with the nation still deeply unsettled and bitterly split. While initially a figure of inspiration, Obama could not overcome the demons of division and, however unintentionally, may even have played a part in empowering them.

His landmark presidency ended with an election that anointed Donald J. Trump as his successor, a devastating blow to Obama elevating the very man who had spent years promoting the racially charged lie that the first African-American president was not actually born in the country. How much Trump's victory could be reasonably interpreted as a repudiation of Obama given the vagaries of the Electoral College and the popular vote will be debated for years, but it was certainly not a validation and, after eight trying years, it was a humbling climax to his time in office.

For many of Obama's conservative critics, it was the welcome culmination of a grass-roots revolt against an elitist, big-government presidency that had pushed the boundaries of the law and had already cost Democrats scores of seats in Congress, many governorships and nearly a thousand state legislative seats across the nation. For many of his supporters, on the other hand, it was hard not to look at the results as a racial backlash. Campaign rhetoric like "take our country back," in this view, was thinly veiled code for white Americans who felt threatened by the nation's rapidly changing demographics. Trump appealed to racial resentment more overtly than any major party presidential nominee in generations, barely even maintaining any pretense about it.

It was not just that the country opted to replace Obama with someone who was his polar opposite in temperament, style, philosophy and goals. It was that his successor would make it his mission to take a sledgehammer to Obama's legacy and tear it down brick by brick. In some cases, that would prove harder than Trump had imagined. While some of what Obama accomplished could be reversed, much of it was already cemented into the system and, indeed, he handed off a growing economy that benefited Trump. It would take years to evaluate how much of Obama's work would endure. But much as he might hate to admit it, Obama was now paired in the history books with Trump, his place to be measured to some extent against his successor, two archetypes representing conflicting strains in the American identity. As a matter of policy, that would be discouraging to the forty-fourth president and his admirers. But as a personal contrast, Obama left office looking better than while he was president, finishing his presidency near the peak of his popularity and admired for his steady dignity juxtaposed against his voluble and impulsive successor. A year after leaving office, Obama was viewed favorably by 66 percent of Americans, some twenty percentage points ahead of the incumbent president, making him by some measures the most admired living American.

Barack Hussein Obama had promised hope and change and indeed his presidency was all about hopes – those that were realized and those that were dashed. He took the oath of office at a time when the country was perched on the edge of an economic abyss while fighting two foreign wars and still facing a potent terrorist threat. He righted the economic ship that was in danger of capsizing, brought home the vast majority of the 180,000 troops deployed in overseas war zones, authorized the mission that dispatched Osama bin Laden, enacted policies to stem climate change, imposed new regulations on Wall Street banks, rescued the auto industry and created a new health care system that provided coverage to 20 million Americans. But his health care program was seen by many Americans as intrusive and ineffectual, helping trigger a conservative Tea Party revolt that cost him both houses of Congress in successive midterm elections and helped undermine his ability to install a chosen successor. Rather than bringing peace to a raucous Middle East, Obama washed his hands of a region even more turbulent than he found it. The progressive, post-racial, bridge-building society he had promised gave way to an angry, jeering, us-against-them nation to be led by a new president who relished reality-show name calling with racial overtones.

The country was in a sour mood even before Obama arrived and remained so for his entire presidency – the last time a majority of Americans in Gallup polls was satisfied with the way things were going in the country was in 2004. At one point during Obama's first term, only 11 percent of Americans were happy with the country's direction. It said something about our times that even an unvarnished triumph like the commando raid that finally caught up to and killed bin Laden lifted public spirits only briefly. An economic recovery that produced millions of jobs, cut unemployment in half and vaulted stock markets beyond even their pre-crash heights nonetheless had many Americans feeling left behind and resentful. And so the candidate of hope and change ended up presiding over an era of paralysis and polarization.

Eloquent yet didactic, engaging yet remote, Obama was something of an enigma even to those around him. Historians and commentators constantly tried to categorize him. When he took office, he self-consciously emulated Abraham Lincoln, arriving in Washington along the same route and using the old rail-splitter's Bible to take the oath. He was depicted in those early days as a latter-day Franklin D. Roosevelt, George Washington or John F. Kennedy. As the years passed, and the hardships piled up and the poll numbers fell and the hope faded into gridlock, other comparisons came to mind. Some likened him to Lyndon B. Johnson for temporarily sending more troops to the sink hole of Afghanistan or Jimmy Carter for seeming feckless in the face of threats like Russia and Iran or even George W. Bush for his embrace of drone warfare and certain counterterrorism tactics. There were times he resembled Woodrow Wilson in his haughty certainty that he was more principled than his adversaries or Dwight D. Eisenhower for his hidden-hand approach to governance. "Sometimes I think the only president we haven't been compared to is Franklin Pierce," one aide noted wryly.

As it happened, the difficulty in defining Barack Obama stemmed in part from the fact that he was not really like any of his predecessors, at least not precisely. As Obama himself noted during the 2008 campaign, he did not "look like all the presidents on the dollar bills." A breaker of racial barriers, he knew his first line in the history books was written the day he won office, but he was determined to offer more than simply a new complexion in the Oval Office. He managed to captivate and confuse his nation simultaneously, presenting himself as a champion of the progressive idea that government could be a force for good in society while at the same time promising to be a non-ideological consensus builder who would reach across the aisle. "I am like a Rorschach test," he told *The New York Times* at one point. People saw in him what they wanted to see.

He was just as opaque to those of us in the White House press corps who covered him day in and day out. While many politicians lay it all out there, like his famously unfiltered vice president, Joe Biden, Obama was as reserved in private as he was in public. He could flash that famous smile that stretched from one side of his face to the other, but it would disappear an instant later, replaced by a grim visage that revealed little. He did not shoot the breeze with us. He did not let his guard down even off the record. He did not dispense playful nicknames as Bush did or spin out colorful Ozark yarns as Bill Clinton did. If Obama came back to the press cabin on Air Force One, it was to deliver a message or to meditate out loud about the serious, substantive issues confronting him or perhaps to chide a reporter whose story he did not like. There was a *purpose*. Where other pols might put a hand on the shoulder or ask after the kids, he saw that as frivolous or fake. When he sat down for an interview with a reporter, he started with a matter of fact, "All right, fire away." No small talk in this Oval Office.

Not that he was necessarily cold, or at least not always. While Maureen Dowd famously compared him to Mr. Spock, the hyper-logical half-Vulcan from *Star Trek*, Obama had a human side. He was a fierce, trash-talking competitor on the basketball court and golf course, enjoyed an eclectic range of music on his iPad and stayed up late watching ESPN's *SportsCenter*. He could deliver a one-liner with impeccable timing. He was a family man who made sure to leave the Oval Office by 6:30 p.m. in time for dinner at home. He doted on his two daughters and took his motorcade, complete with the ever-present ambulance and press vans, to watch their school basketball games. At his most emotional moments, we watched him cry in the White House briefing room over the shooting massacre of school children in Newtown, Connecticut, and sing *Amazing Grace* from the pulpit of a church in Charleston, South Carolina, where African-American worshipers had been gunned down by a white supremacist.

Obama arrived in office with great faith in the power of his oratory to inspire and in the power of his good sense to solve problems, only to discover the limits of both. The speeches that he scrawled out by hand on yellow legal pads may have thrilled supporters on the campaign trail, but in too many instances they failed to move entrenched forces at home or abroad and, indeed, gave way over time to professorial lectures from the White House podium. The notion that reasonable people could settle their disputes if only he could get them to the table seemed contradicted everywhere from Capitol Hill to the Kremlin to Jerusalem.

Haunted by the devastation in Syria and frustrated by his inability to fully extricate from Iraq and Afghanistan, Obama set about transforming America's relationships with two longstanding enemies, Iran and Cuba, an effort to show that diplomacy really does work. But he gave up trying to transform Washington. After a while, he did not even try to disguise his contempt for the capital and its denizens, disdaining its rhythms and customs to the point that it curtailed his ability to get what he wanted. He had little interest in spending time with lawmakers, even from his own party, and never understood why he should. If his policies made sense, and he was sure they did, then the rest of Washington should naturally see them the way he did.

Like his predecessors, Obama regularly noted that the easy issues never made it to his desk, only the difficult ones. On his desk he kept a plaque that said, "Hard things are hard." Exasperated by all the tough choices that had to be made, he and his first White House chief of staff, Rahm Emanuel, joked that they should move to Hawaii and open a T-shirt shack with only one size and one color (medium, white) so they would not ever have to make another decision. It became such a running joke that during meetings on especially thorny issues with no good options, Emanuel would turn to Obama.

"White," he would say.

"Medium," Obama would reply.

Picking between shirts of different colors and sizes could be vexing. Obama never met a policy decision that could not benefit from another meeting or another memo. Aides would brief him and send him documents only to have to do it again as he came up with more and more questions. He was a second-order thinker constantly searching for the unintended consequences of any possible decision, sometimes to the point that no decision became the path of least resistance. After the from-the-gut style of his predecessor, the thoughtful, almost scholarly approach struck some as a welcome tonic, but it also could aggravate advisers anxious for a final decision that they could implement.

If the trials of his time took a personal toll, Obama did not show it. Through all manner of challenges, he carried himself with calm poise and grace under pressure. A night owl, he sat alone late in the White House residence after the rest of the family had retired, reading briefing papers, watching sports or playing Words With Friends. The only indulgence he permitted himself during these solitary hours was a handful of almonds – the president's chef joked to Michael Shear of *The New York Times* that it was exactly seven almonds each night, no more, no less. Obama felt compelled to deny such robotic exactitude after it became public, but it seemed all too plausible. Either way, it was a self-discipline that, for all the controversies, allowed him to emerge from eight years in office without a hint of personal scandal.

Still, it was a sobering experience. Supremely confident to the point of hubris, Obama started out promising that his election would be the moment "when the rise of the oceans began to slow and our planet began to heal." By the low point of his second term, he had radically revised his expectations. Perhaps there were no more Lincolns. "I'm leader of the free world," he said once in frustration, "but I can't seem to make anything happen." He came to believe that maybe even a president could not single-handedly change the world – that at most he could just push it in the right direction.

After riding the waves, he told the writer David Remnick, he had learned that as president "you are essentially a relay swimmer in a river full of rapids, and that river is history." Switching metaphors, Obama said, "At the end of the day, we're part of a long-running story. We just try to get our paragraph right."

This is his paragraph.

CHAPTER ONE
'This Winter of Our Hardship'

For all intents and purposes, Barack Obama's presidency got under way more than a month before he actually took the oath of office on the steps of the United States Capitol. It was a bitterly cold Chicago day just a little more than a week before Christmas of 2008. A storm enveloped the city and made for an arduous journey for a team of economic advisers trudging through nine inches of snow to a meeting with the president-elect. Gathering in a generic government office being used for the transition, they sat with Obama around a set of sectional tables pushed together. A video screen on the wall beamed in other advisers from Washington.

The economists delivered to the incoming president the sort of sobering news that would make anyone wonder why he wanted the job in the first place. Not only was the economy in free fall, which Obama already knew, it was much, much worse than anyone had realized – and quite likely to get even worse. As in another Great Depression. As in massive unemployment. As in a banking system on the verge of collapse. As in an auto industry falling apart, businesses folding, homes being seized, savings disappearing. Actually, the advisers told Obama, it could turn out to be even grimmer than the Depression. More American families were tied to the markets than in 1929. Household wealth was falling faster than ever before. The American business sector was more dependent on the financial system. "Is it too late to ask for a recount?" Obama asked aides.

In any White House, certain moments become transformed into a creation myth, part of the narrative told again and again to explain a presidency. For Obama, the meeting on December 16,

2008, was one such moment. In the space of a couple of hours, any residual feelings of euphoria over his historic election quickly vanished in a haze of statistics and forecasts that, when added up, spelled potential calamity for millions of Americans. In the years that followed, Obama's closest aides would look back at that meeting both to underscore the gravity of the situation that he faced coming into office and to understand the decisions that would flow from it. Even before putting his hand on Abraham Lincoln's Bible, Obama was forced to make critical choices about how he would respond to the crisis and what kind of presidency he wanted to have.

Little had prepared him for this moment. He might have been a former president of the *Harvard Law Review* and one-time community organizer with a compelling personal story, but Obama was then just four years out of the Illinois state legislature with no executive experience to speak of and little exposure to the sorts of monumental issues that cross the desk in the Oval Office every day of the week. Now he had the fate of the world's last superpower resting on his forty-seven-year old shoulders.

Calm and cerebral, he gave no indication to advisers that day of feeling overwhelmed, but some of them later felt that way themselves and were convinced it left a mark on their leader. "That was a formative event," said David Axelrod, Obama's senior adviser. "Here's the incoming president with his economic team essentially being confronted with as bleak a report as anyone has gotten in generations." As Rahm Emanuel later put it, "This was not your father's or my father's recession. This was our grandfather's Depression."

The country was frightened. The crisis was triggered by the unraveling of a housing market artificially inflated by risky subprime mortgages and profit-seeking speculation. Over-leveraged and swimming in bad debt, some of the nation's largest and most storied Wall Street investment firms suddenly found themselves on the brink of disaster, including Bear Stearns, which was rescued thanks to the intervention of the government, and Lehman Brothers, which was not. American International Group, ostensibly an insurance company known as AIG but really a corporate behemoth with its tentacles reaching far and wide throughout the economy, had to be bailed out with more than $170 billion in taxpayer funds. Stock markets were in free fall, dropping by more than 36 percent. Oil prices fell by 55 percent. In the days before the meeting in Chicago, Dow Chemical closed twenty plants. Bank of America announced that it would shed at least 30,000 jobs, following Citibank, which had already said it would lay off 52,000.

None of this was what Obama anticipated when he first set out on his path to the White House. As he kicked off his campaign in February 2007, he was running as the anti-Iraq war candidate, the apostle of hope and change, the unifier of Blue America and Red America, the antidote to eight years of George W. Bush. At the time Obama announced his candidacy, the economy was humming along, its fatal flaws unnoticed by most policymakers. But by the time he prevailed over John McCain in November 2008, Obama was confronted with an economic emergency the likes of which had not occurred since before he was born. He had no time for anything but on-the-job training.

In that fateful December meeting, he was presented with proposals for an economic stimulus package intended to jump-start the economy. This was a page out of John Maynard Keynes's book, pumping government money into the economy to promote growth, a mainstay of Democratic economic theory for decades. Bush had already pushed through Congress a $152 billion package of tax breaks to fuel the economy at the beginning of the year. During the campaign, Obama promised another $175 billion. Soon after the election, it had grown to $500 billion.

But now Christina Romer, tapped to chair the President's Council of Economic Advisers, told him the job could require far more. Realistically, she said, the economy needed a jolt of $1.2 trillion in government spending and tax cuts, a jaw-dropping figure that was so inconceivable politically that Lawrence Summers, a former Treasury secretary now advising Obama, had talked her out of even putting it in a memo listing options. Instead, she, Summers and the other economic advisers recommended an $800 billion package – even so, the largest in the nation's history. The stimulus would come on top of the hundreds of billions of dollars that Bush had already committed to save the banks in his final weeks in office and the billions more that would be required to keep the auto industry afloat. Romer, who wrote her dissertation on Franklin Roosevelt, understood how daunting this would be for a newly elected president who had yet to even move his belongings into the White House. "Mr. President-elect," she told him, "this is your holy shit moment."

The crisis would force Obama to contemplate the larger questions of the government's role in the economy – at what point should the state step in to rescue private enterprise, how far should politicians go in regulating business, when should taxpayers bear the burden? But Obama did not want to simply be reactive. He had a long agenda of ambitious initiatives. He wanted to overhaul the health care system to cover millions of Americans without insurance coverage. He wanted to rewrite the nation's immigration rules to provide a path to citizenship for many of those in the country illegally. And he wanted to put in place a new market-oriented system of pollution limits called cap-and-trade designed to curb the greenhouse gas emissions blamed for climate change while allowing cleaner industries to sell credits to dirtier ones.

The theory was that the country would be more open to radical change at a time when it seemed to be teetering on the brink of disaster, rather than during moments of stability when it might be more wary of upsetting the status quo. Roosevelt effectively reinvented the American domestic system with his New Deal during the Depression. Emanuel summed up the imperative in typically pithy fashion: "You never want a serious crisis to go to waste."

Rebuilding the economy while doing all of that would be a tall order for any president and not everyone thought he should dilute his focus, given the scope of the threat confronting the economy. In a conference call earlier in the transition, Obama brought up his desire to use his presidency to accomplish big things and asked advisers what he should try to get done in his first term.

"Your accomplishment is going to be preventing a second Great Depression," said Timothy Geithner, his incoming Treasury secretary.

"That's not enough for me," Obama replied. "I'm not going to be defined by what I've prevented."

"If you don't prevent a depression," Geithner pushed back, "you won't be able to do anything else."

"I know," he said. "But it's not enough."

The same tension came now in the meeting at the Chicago transition office. Obama had just been told that the crisis was even worse than anticipated and that he might have to convince Congress to spent hundreds of billions of dollars to keep the country from falling off the cliff. Clean energy, education improvements, health care access – all of those were fine priorities that advisers like Geithner shared. But with the immediate threat looming, aides wondered whether Obama would be willing to scale back some of his aspirations just to focus on the crisis at hand and then at some later point return to these other initiatives. After all, there was only so much bandwidth in the Washington political system.

No, Obama said. "I want to pull the Band-Aid off quickly, not delay the pain."

If nothing else, there would be plenty of pain.

*

The magnitude of the challenge facing him was evident a month later when he stood before as many as 2 million Americans gathered on a frigid day on Washington's National Mall on January 20, 2009, to be sworn in as the forty-fourth president of the United States. As he waited to stride down the platform on the West Front of the Capitol, Obama shivered in the frosty air. "How cold do you think it will be by the time I actually deliver the speech?" he asked his trusted personal aide, Reggie Love, a young former Duke University basketball star who had been with him throughout the long and arduous campaign. "Not as cold as Springfield," Love responded, harkening back to the day Obama first announced his candidacy. Obama warmed to the recollection even as he observed that it was colder now. "Colder and a little more crowded," Love joked, as the two fist-bumped.

As extraordinary as it was for Obama to be there, at this moment, facing this crowd, about to be sworn in to the most powerful position on the planet, it also marked an extraordinary moment for the nation. The son of a black man from Kenya and a white woman from Kansas, Obama inherited a White House built partly by slaves. The ceremony captured the imagination of much of the world as Obama recited the oath with his hand on the same Bible that Abraham Lincoln used at his first inauguration 148 years earlier, held by his statuesque, Harvard Law School-educated wife, Michelle. The sight of a black man climbing the highest peak electrified people across racial, generational and partisan lines. "For people that look like me, for my race, to be there and to have witnessed that – I just kept thinking about my grandfather and how he would feel to have lived to see this day," said Desirée

Rogers, a longtime friend of the Obamas and herself a trailblazing African-American corporate executive who was joining them in Washington as the White House social secretary.

But in his eighteen-minute Inaugural Address, Obama offered a grim assessment of "this winter of our hardship," a nation rocked by home foreclosures, shuttered businesses, lost jobs, costly health care, failing schools, energy dependence, climate change, two overseas wars and the threat of Islamic terrorism. It was time, he said, to "begin again the work of remaking America."

"Now there are some who question the scale of our ambitions, who suggest that our system cannot tolerate too many big plans," he acknowledged. "Their memories are short, for they have forgotten what this country has already done, what free men and women can achieve when imagination is joined to common purpose and necessity to courage."

Barack Obama was an unlikely avatar for that national purpose for all sorts of reasons beyond the color of his skin. Tall and thin, he had probing eyes that seemed to see everything and the diffident, detached demeanor of a college professor. For a man with relatively little experience at the highest echelons of public life, he projected a preternatural self-assurance that even aides thought bordered on cockiness. When he first met David Plouffe prior to his 2004 race for Senate, he told him, "I think I could probably do every job on the campaign better than the people I'll hire to do it." He later told another new adviser something similar. "I think I'm a better speechwriter than my speechwriters," he said. "I know more about policies on any particular issue than my policy directors. And I'll tell you right now that I'm going to think I'm a better political director than my political director." It was a confidence that served him well through the ordeals of a marathon campaign in which he managed to take down two of the biggest names in American politics, first Hillary Clinton and then John McCain. But it would also prove a drawback at times while in the Oval Office.

Born in Hawaii and abandoned by his father, Obama grew up far removed from the American mainland and the core American experiences of his generation. He was too young and geographically distant to undergo the traumas of the Vietnam and civil rights eras that left their marks on Clinton, McCain, Bush and other modern political leaders. Indeed, Obama was the first American president born too late to have served in the killing fields of Southeast Asia, and yet he spent a formative period of his own childhood living in Indonesia with his white mother, Ann Dunham, an anthropologist, as she moved to Jakarta to build a new life with a new husband. "Eccentric in many ways" and "hungry for adventure and skeptical of convention," in her son's words, Dunham sent him back home to Hawaii to live with her parents. Barry, as he was known then, attended Punahou Academy, the island's premier prep school. He played basketball, earned academic honors, smoked marijuana with his friends and could not help but notice he was one of just a handful of black students in class.

A little aimless and unsure of his place in the universe, he headed to the mainland for an education, first at Occidental College in Los Angeles and then as a transfer student at Columbia University in New York. After a period as a community organizer in Chicago, he earned his way into Harvard Law School, where he won election as the first African-American president of the prestigious law review in 1990 by assembling an odd-bedfellows coalition of liberals and conservatives and convincing both sides that he would listen to their views with respect – the first but not the last time he would land on the pages of *The New York Times*. He went on to briefly work at a law firm and teach law part time at the University of Chicago, but a legal career was not in the offing as he was drawn to an exploration of race and his roots that generated an acclaimed early memoir, *Dreams from My Father.* His election to the Illinois State Senate led to an improbable candidacy for the United States Senate, propelled by a star turn at the Democratic National Convention of 2004 with his call for "a single American family," as he put it memorably in his keynote address in Boston's FleetCenter before the nomination of Senator John Kerry for president:

There's not a liberal America and a conservative America – there's the United States of America. There's not a black America and white America and Latino America and Asian America – there's the United States of America. The pundits like to slice and dice our country into red states and blue states – red states for Republicans, blue states for Democrats. But I've got news for them too. We worship an awesome God in the blue states and we don't like federal agents poking around our liberties in the red states. We coach Little League in the blue states and have gay friends in the red states. There are patriots who opposed the war in Iraq and patriots who supported it. We are one people, all of us pledging allegiance to the stars and stripes, all of us defending the United States of America.

That speech, more than any other single moment, embodied the inspiration that catapulted Obama to the national stage and eventually the presidency, the idea of unity in an era of division, common purpose in an atmosphere of partisanship. It helped propel him first to the United States Senate and then to the White House as the unknown former community organizer rallied crowds of tens of thousands with a yes-we-can, change-we-can-believe-in message. Yet Obama's stirring oratory then and later underscored the key conundrums about his political identity. He could move audiences of tens of thousands in a football stadium to tears with his rhetoric, yet in news conferences or policy talks come across as plodding and even patronizing. He could galvanize strangers en masse but did not seem to especially enjoy them as individuals. He flashed an incandescent smile but was not a natural backslapper. He was "a solitude-loving individualist," as Michelle Obama put it, an introvert who was drained after a public event to the point that some aides tried to make sure he had a few minutes alone to recharge before heading into his next appointment. He generated gales of anger among his many critics and yet was rarely roused to demonstrations of passion himself. He saw governance as the rational calculation of benefits and drawbacks in which different players could ultimately find mutual agreement, only to repeatedly discover that Washington did not always bend to his logic.

If Obama hoped to usher in a new era of bipartisanship as he took the oath that day in January 2009, it would not last out the night. Even as he raced around town to ten inaugural balls that evening, about fifteen top Republicans, including rising stars like Representatives Eric Cantor of Virginia, Kevin McCarthy of California and Paul Ryan of Wisconsin, gathered for dinner at the Caucus Room, a well-known Washington watering hole, to talk about how to rebound from their defeat. Central to their strategy would be standing against Obama's plans to expand government. The thinking was straightforward if calculating: Going along with Obama's plan, in addition to betraying their own conservative principles, would only ensure that Republicans remained the minority party. Opposing him, on the other hand, would pay off at the polls if he failed. And if he succeeded, the country would move on to other issues and not dwell on votes that did not matter.

For four hours, the Republican insurgents mapped out a campaign of resistance, according to the author Robert Draper, who writes for *The New York Times Magazine*. "The only way we'll succeed is if we're united," Ryan told the group. "If we tear ourselves apart, we're finished."

McCarthy urged relentless opposition. "If you act like you're the minority, you're going to stay in the minority," he said. "We've got to challenge them on every single bill and challenge them on every single campaign."

*

As historic as that day was, Obama's presidency got off to an oddly uncertain start. During the ceremony, Chief Justice John Roberts Jr. mangled the order of the thirty-five word oath as he administered it to Obama, and in the hours that followed, lawyers began to worry that someone somewhere would make the claim that he was not legitimately the president.

The goof was about as minor as it could get. As Roberts began reciting the oath for Obama to repeat, the two got slightly out of rhythm. Obama interrupted Roberts before he finished the first phrase, which may have thrown the chief justice off. Roberts then said the phrase, "that I will execute the office of president to the United States faithfully," even though the oath as proscribed by the Constitution says the new president "will *faithfully* execute the office of president *of* the United States." Obama recognized that it was out of order and paused, then said "that I will execute." Roberts tried it again, but this time left out the word "execute."

At a luncheon following the ceremony, a chagrined Roberts took the blame, telling Obama it was "my fault." The crossed circuits caused some smirks in the audience but in a town of lawyers some began to get nervous. Given that the Constitution lays out the words in an exact order, was it possible that Obama was not really the president? Could anyone go to court to challenge some presidential decision down the road citing that as a justification? Far-fetched as that seemed, Greg Craig, Obama's new White House counsel, did not want to take any chances. So he tracked down Obama at the White House a few hours after the ceremony and pulled him away from a receiving line. Despite his you've-got-to-be-kidding-me reaction, Obama agreed to a do-over just to be safe.

The next evening, Roberts arrived at the White House to try again. He brought his robes to make it seem more formal, even though they simply gathered by themselves with just a few witnesses in the Map Room on the ground floor of the main part of the mansion.

"Are you ready to take the oath?" Roberts asked.

"I am," Obama replied. "And we're going to do it very slowly."

The second time was executed flawlessly. But if the mix-up left open even the theoretical possibility that some might not consider Obama the legitimate president, he soon found that many opponents would not be assuaged simply by a correctly recited oath. In the months and years to come, Obama and his advisers would complain that many of his adversaries were not content to simply stand against his policies but seemed never to genuinely accept him as the leader of the country. The eight years of trench warfare that would follow, he came to believe, represented more than the clash of ideas but a fundamental struggle over his very presidency.

As he embarked on his term, Obama assembled a team that blended his own most trusted advisers with veterans of Bill Clinton's administration as well as a few Republicans in search of that elusive spirit of bipartisanship. He hoped to forge the same No Drama Obama ethos that his campaign became known for, a goal that would prove exponentially harder given the different factions he was seeking to blend into a single team. Most prominent among his selections was none other than his Democratic primary rival, Hillary Clinton, tapped for secretary of state. Obama also convinced Robert Gates, George W. Bush's widely respected defense secretary, to stay on. While Timothy Geithner, the Federal Reserve governor from New York who had been instrumental in fashioning the response to the financial crisis under Bush, would now become Treasury secretary, Obama convinced Larry Summers, who had served as Bill Clinton's Treasury secretary, to accept the far less prestigious position of national economic adviser, joining the new chief of staff, Rahm Emanuel, another veteran of the Clinton White House who had gone on to serve in Congress.

While the team would also include loyalists like David Axelrod, the mustachioed strategist universally known as "Axe," the choices left some from the Obama campaign grumbling. They had just mounted one of the most extraordinary revolutions against the political establishment of both parties in modern American history, only to bring in the candidate they beat in the primaries and veterans of both Clinton and Bush administrations? Somehow that felt like a betrayal of the spirit of the Obama campaign. And yet it said something about Obama that he considered the economic crisis and two wars he inherited so serious that he was willing to overlook the verities of a campaign to enlist a team with the experience he hoped would guide him through perilous times.

Not all of Obama's choices worked out well. He nominated Tom Daschle, the former Senate majority leader and a mentor, to be secretary of health and human services, a post he was to use to shepherd through the new president's health care program. But reports that Daschle had failed to pay $128,000 in taxes for the use of a car and driver as he advised clients about how to influence government actions exemplified the very cashing-in culture that Obama had vowed to dismantle. Daschle withdrew and Obama admitted that he "screwed up" by thinking he could exempt someone from his standards just because he trusted him.

As it happened, Daschle was not the only tax scofflaw on the Obama team. Geithner owed more than $34,000 in back taxes, leaving Obama in the position of nominating a tax evader to be chief tax collector. But Geithner still managed to win confirmation, perhaps because of the urgency of the economic situation. And an analyst Obama had hired from the McKinsey & Company management consultant firm dropped out after disclosing that she had failed to pay taxes for a nanny. Asked later what surprised him most about becoming president, Obama said sardonically, "The number of people who don't pay their taxes."

It also took three tries to find a commerce secretary. His first choice, Governor Bill Richardson of New Mexico, was dropped because of an investigation into state contracts given to a political donor. The probe resulted in no indictments, but not before derailing Richardson's trip to the Cabinet. Obama's second choice, Senator Judd Gregg, a Republican from New Hampshire, accepted in the name of bipartisanship, but then quickly reversed himself and withdrew, citing "irresolvable conflicts" with the president's approach to the stimulus. Frustrated, Obama turned back to a Democrat, Gary Locke, the former governor of Washington State. The third time finally worked out and Locke was confirmed. But a ridiculous amount of political energy had to be expended to fill a second-tier post. Nothing, it seemed, was going to be easy. "Where the fuck is our honeymoon?" Jim Messina, a campaign adviser tapped as deputy chief of staff, kept asking.

Assembling a team was hardly the only challenge in store for Obama in those early days. Whatever he had imagined life in the White House would be like when he moved in, he quickly discovered it was more controlled and suffocating than anyone could have expected. He and the new first lady, Michelle Obama, settled their two daughters, Malia, age ten, and Sasha, age seven, in the residence and enrolled them in Sidwell Friends School, a private Quaker academy attended by Chelsea Clinton and Joe Biden's grandchildren. Michelle's mother, Marian Robinson, moved into the mansion to help with the children, taking a room on the third floor, one story above the president and first lady. Robinson was not exactly enthusiastic about the move – her son Craig said she was dragged "kicking and screaming" – but her presence helped provide a little stability for the youngest children to live in the White House in decades.

One benefit the president found about life in the White House was that "we live above the store," as he put it. Unlike his years in the state legislature or on the campaign trail, when he was on the road much of the year, he actually found more time to spend with his family. He made a point in those early days of leaving the Oval Office early enough to have dinner with the children most nights before picking up work again in the residence, a practice that he would keep through much of his presidency. He also made a point of taking Michelle out to dinner in Washington and even flew her up to New York for a Broadway show, all an effort not to let the presidency change them too much. But they quickly found that the disruption of a motorcade and security made such outings a burden on many others, and fairly or not, taking a night on the town while the rest of the country was on the edge of financial collapse sent a damaging political message. Their stated intention to return to their home in Chicago every six weeks quickly vanished after their first trip back resulted in street closures, barricaded sidewalks and identification checks of neighbors. No matter how much they wanted life to remain the same, it never would.

*

It did not take long for the first collision between the new president and his Republican opposition. With the economy bleeding 700,000 jobs a month and unemployment climbing to 7.6 percent, Obama would focus first on a massive stimulus package along the lines that Christina Romer outlined, composed of public works spending, aid to beleaguered states, extended unemployment benefits and temporary tax breaks. Obama, who during the transition read Jonathan Alter's *The Defining Moment* about Franklin Roosevelt's frenetic first months in office, would attempt to do in a single package what FDR did in a series of separate measures that ultimately would add up to his New Deal. Obama's version of the New Deal was put together at what counts as lightning speed in the world of legislation, the urgency of the crisis propelling the incoming team to action for fear that the bottom could fall out of the economy at any moment.

The immediate goal was to quickly inject money into the system, massive amounts of money in a sort of economic electric-shock therapy. While liberals were pushing Obama for astronomical sums, he stuck by the compromise $800 billion figure put forth by his advisers, still a mind-boggling amount by any measure. A study by Romer and Jared Bernstein, the economic adviser to Joe Biden, concluded that without the stimulus plan, unemployment would rise to 9 percent but if it passed, the jobless rate would fall to 7 percent by the end of 2010 – a prediction that would prove wildly optimistic and come back to haunt the new president. Unemployment benefits were considered among the most effective stimulus because recipients nearly always spent them right away; tax cuts would put more cash in the pockets of middle-class families, although they were deemed not quite as effective since some would save the money. "Shovel-ready" public works projects would put people back to work but no matter how they were advertised they often took time to get under way.

As Obama and his Democratic allies in Congress fashioned their plan, they also resolved to use it to accomplish other policy goals – to encourage the development of more clean energy, jump-start high-speed rail, extend broadband Internet access, expand health clinic services, weatherize homes, modernize federal buildings, upgrade electronic medical records and repair and re-build the nation's creaking roads, bridges and schools. In effect, the package became a grab-bag of liberal policy priorities, not just an emergency rescue measure.

Obama assumed that at least some Republicans in Congress would embrace the plan since it included tax cuts in the form of breaks for college tuition payers, car purchasers and first-time homebuyers plus $400 for individuals and $800 for families. But he overestimated their appeal – and his own. Three days after taking the oath, he invited to the White House Congressional leaders from both parties, including Representative John Boehner of Ohio, the House Republican minority leader, and Eric Cantor, his whip, to talk about the recession.

Cantor came prepared and handed out a Republican plan. Obama preferred his own. The two exchanged words. Finally, Obama pulled out his trump card.

"Elections have consequences," he said, in Cantor's recollection, "and Eric, I won."

Aides insisted Obama was being lighthearted and recalled the exchange differently. "We just have a difference here and I'm president," Obama said in this version.

Either way, the message was clear – Obama was in charge and he expected Republicans to defer to him, at least in a moment of national crisis like this. The Republicans, however, did not see it that way. Four days later, as Obama prepared to go to Capitol Hill to meet with the entire House Republican conference, Robert Gibbs, his press secretary, showed him an Associated Press dispatch reporting that Boehner had just urged the conference to reject Obama's stimulus plan, without even waiting for him to make his case. Indeed, what the story did not say was that Cantor had gone so far as to vow not to lose a single Republican vote. Obama was miffed. "This shit's not on the level, is it?" he asked as he walked out the door to head to the meeting. In the years that would follow, that moment would be recalled again and again as the point of realization for the new president and his team that the game was "not on the level," a favorite Obama phrase meaning that the opposition was all about politics and not serious about policy or interested in compromise.

For their part, beyond any disinclination to give Obama a bipartisan political victory, Republicans also harbored real doubts about a massive spending package crafted by liberals taking advantage of the crisis to expand government. The deficit had already grown through George W. Bush's tenure, in part because of his tax cuts, the wars in Afghanistan and Iraq, his expansion of Medicare and the collapse of the economy that sapped revenues to the government. Conservatives had to swallow hard when it was a Republican driving up the deficit. Now that it was a Democrat, they were liberated to finally protest.

There was also plenty of doubt among Republicans about Keynesian theory. While Obama was studying Jonathan Alter's book on FDR, the Republicans were devouring Amity Shlaes's *The Forgotten Man*, a conservative take on the New Deal arguing that Roosevelt's spending actually exacerbated the Depression. Plenty of economists took issue with Shlaes's analysis, blaming FDR for reversing gears on fiscal stimulus in his second term to focus unwisely on curbing the federal deficit. But many scholars have concluded that, whatever benefits of the New Deal, the Depression was really ended by World War II.

Obama's assumption that he could win over Republicans with tax cuts proved a miscalculation. He thought that they should happily accept the package because he had included one of their priorities. But the package was not negotiated with Republicans; it was handed to them as a fait accompli. Not only did they resent being left out, they had no investment in the plan as it was unveiled because they had had nothing to do with drafting it. Rather than taking credit for bargaining with Obama to get tax cuts included in the plan, they bristled at Democrats telling them what they should like and what they should not.

At this point, Obama and the Democrats decided to push ahead without Republicans, reasoning that with the economy on the edge of a precipice, speed was more important than across-the-aisle consensus. Republicans mocked the 1,073-page bill as "Porkulus" and singled out easily ridiculed items like water safety mascots, a brain chemistry study of cocaine-addicted monkeys and $200 million to revitalize the National Mall. Focusing on money for family-planning services for lower-income women, Republican critics said the stimulus produced by contraceptives was not the kind that would help the economy.

On February 13, just twenty-four days after the inauguration, the House passed the American Recovery and Reinvestment Act, a $787 billion package, without a single Republican voting for it, just as Eric Cantor had vowed. The Senate concurred with just three Republicans in favor. It was a remarkable achievement for a new president, passing the largest such economic package in American history in barely three weeks. Adjusted for inflation, the Obama stimulus was more than 50 percent bigger than the entire New Deal and, as Michael Grunwald wrote in *The New New Deal*, twice as big as the expense of the Louisiana Purchase and the Marshall Plan combined.

It also set the tone for the next eight years, poisoning relations between the president and his Republican opponents from the start. To Obama, it was an illustration of bad faith. The Republicans never intended to even consider working with him. To Republicans, it was a case study in a liberal "I won" president shoving his agenda down their throats. Neither side would forget.

CHAPTER TWO

'The Hardest Option'

"Why can't the American car company make a Corolla?" Obama asked. It was a simple question without a simple answer, but went right to the heart of the next challenge confronting the new president. Even with the stimulus in place, Obama was facing the imminent collapse of the auto industry. The Big Three automakers reported their worst monthly sales in a quarter-century the same week that Obama was elected. Two of the three, Chrysler and General Motors, were running on the fumes of last-minute government loans issued by George W. Bush meant to tide them over until Obama could take office and decide what to do. And Obama was trying to get his head around the question of why the American firms seemed unable to produce a safe and reliable car that consumers wanted to buy.

The auto industry crisis would test the boundaries of Obama's activist approach and the acuity of his political instincts. When was it appropriate for the federal government to come to the rescue of private businesses? Did the auto sector play a critical too-big-to-fail role in the economy and therefore demand federal intervention as the banks had in the final days of Bush's presidency? What sort of conditions could the administration impose on the companies in exchange for assistance? How far did the government want to get into the business of making cars anyway? As it was, thanks to the broader bailout program initiated by Bush and continued by Obama, the government already owned a fair share of the nation's banking and insurance sectors.

Once the industrial backbone of the United States economy, the American auto industry had been struggling to compete with the Japanese and Germans for years, long before the financial crisis that hit in 2008. But the collapse in credit made it more difficult for consumers to buy new vehicles. Sales of cars and light trucks in the United States fell from 16.2 million in 2007 to 13.5 million in 2008 and 10.1 million in 2009, the most precipitous decline since World War II. The fall was steeper for the Big Three automakers in Detroit, whose combined sales plunged from 8.1 million in 2007 to 4.6 million in 2009. Showrooms sat empty without customers. Assembly plants were idled or put on reduced shifts. Buyout plans were put into place to trim the work forces even as the car companies were saddled with costly pension and health care plans guaranteed by union contracts.

Obama had little sympathy for the troubled automakers, seeing their troubles as a function of their own "failure to adapt to changing times," as he put it, but the industry occupied a distinctive place in the American identity and the prospect of its downfall seemed almost unthinkable. Advisers warned the president that letting Chrysler and GM slide into an unstructured bankruptcy would set off a cascade effect through the whole chain of suppliers and vendors, leaving tens of thousands, or even more, out of work and undercutting the impact of the stimulus program he had just worked so hard to pass. Obama recruited Steven Rattner, a New York financier and Democratic fundraiser close to Hillary Clinton with no real auto industry experience, to lead a task force that would formulate a rescue plan. Under pressure from labor, the president added Ron Bloom, a longtime adviser to the United Steelworkers, to the task force leadership. Within weeks, Team Auto, as they called themselves, was ready to present findings to Obama.

Despite representing Illinois, a state with assembly plants affected by the crisis, Obama did not know much about the industry. But he was a quick study and he demonstrated early on how he would approach complex problems like this one. Unlike his predecessor, who fancied himself a chief executive officer who made big decisions and delegated the rest, Obama liked diving deep into the details. He did his homework and then often went in search of information beyond what his briefers were providing him. To Obama, every complex problem had a solution; the only question was how to find it and what the tradeoffs would be once he did.

He had little patience for repetition. When Larry Summers, his national economic adviser, began running through the numbers in a meeting in the Oval Office one morning in late March, Obama cut him off. "I know that," he said curtly. "I read that memo." That would be a trademark Obama move all too familiar to advisers in the months and years to come. He read the briefing papers and he did not like advisers to recite things he had already absorbed. He wanted crisp discussions and pushed for more. He also wanted a range of views and did not want his team protecting him from recommendations they did not favor.

As he sorted through the decisions on the auto industry that morning, he noticed that one of his top economic advisers, Austan Goolsbee, was missing. Goolsbee opposed rescuing Chrysler, and while Summers had not invited him because of the protocol of this particular meeting, others suspected his absence was a not terribly subtle way of steering the decision. Obama did not care for such gamesmanship. "Where's Goolsbee?" he asked, directing an aide to summon him to join the discussion.

The choices were complicated but one decision that Obama found easy to make as he reviewed the recommendations of his task force that day was forcing GM's chief executive, Rick Wagoner, out of the job and ordering a new leadership to produce more aggressive plans to save the company. After nine years in his post, Wagoner had presided over the collapse of one of America's most fabled companies, with its share price plummeting from $70 a share to $3 a share, making his dismissal an obvious move. If the government was going to step in to keep the firm afloat, it had every right to demand a different chief executive. But if GM was clear, Obama was still struggling over what to do about Chrysler when an aide slipped into the office and handed him a note informing him another meeting was set to begin.

Obama told the advisers that he needed more time and directed them to return for another session later in the day. Then he headed off for a day that would be consumed by the war in Afghanistan, a threatened missile launch by North Korea and the evacuation of a flooded Fargo, North Dakota. ("What is this, a *West Wing* episode?" a flabbergasted David Axelrod asked Rahm Emanuel.)

At 6 p.m., Obama reconvened his auto advisers in the Roosevelt Room. The real question was whether to let Chrysler slip into bankruptcy or give it another month to pursue a life-saving alliance with Fiat, the Italian carmaker. Some like Goolsbee argued to let Chrysler go. With a contracting market and finite resources, bailing out Chrysler might make it harder to salvage GM and potentially even threaten Ford. Better to focus on saving GM. Others maintained that abandoning Chrysler would ripple through the region, affecting a whole supply chain of businesses and workers. Robert Gibbs, the White House press secretary, pointed to a map showing areas that already had unemployment of 18 percent, even 24 percent, communities that would suffer even more if Chrysler went under.

"You're always explaining that things are bad, but it's not like the Great Depression," Gibbs told Obama. "Well, in some of these counties – "

"I know what you're going to say," Obama cut in. "In some of these counties, it *will* be like the Great Depression."

Yet Axelrod cited poll numbers showing how unpopular the idea of a government bailout would be. The public was already unhappy about rescuing the bankers who helped cause the crisis; now taxpayers would have to foot the bill for automakers who had run their businesses into the ground?

Scratching notes on briefing papers, Obama fired off question after question about the costs and tradeoffs. And just as he would cut off anyone who repeated the memos, he demonstrated another typical technique, going around the room calling on everyone to give an opinion, even those who sat in the back hoping not to be noticed.

After seventy-five minutes, Obama decided to give both companies one last chance to come up with viable plans to overhaul themselves and return to profitability, but he would make clear that bankruptcy awaited should they fail. Chrysler would get thirty days and GM sixty days to reorganize or face the cutoff of government aid. "All the advisers were divided; the public was absolutely against it," Emanuel said later. "Nobody is giving you consensus; there is no consensus. Nobody had ever done what we were about to do. And he picks the hardest option."

Among those unhappy about the president's approach were his fellow Democrats from Michigan. In a conference call previewing his decision, they erupted at the idea that Obama would even broach the possibility of bankruptcy, fearing the mere discussion of it would sink the companies.

"Whatever you do, sir, don't use the word *bankruptcy*," one of the congressmen said.

"You know I can't do that," Obama replied.

Obama did not shrink from the tough reality. Where other presidents might have worried about the politics of what he was about to do or try to finesse it to avoid openly acknowledging the reality of his plan, Obama was willing to call the situation what it was and take his chances. It was not that he did not care about politics – in some ways, he was more attuned to domestic politics than his predecessors, perhaps at times too much so – but he nursed a sense of himself as a leader capable of making difficult decisions. That would not always be true over the next eight years, but in the opening months of his presidency, he had little choice but to act. The consequences were too great.

Eventually, the government would take over GM and push Chrysler into the merger with Fiat, forcing both firms into a planned bankruptcy to restructure their operations, reduce debt and lower labor costs. Then the government would back out, concluding one of the most expansive interventions in a major industry in modern times but saving two of the country's most iconic enterprises. And in the end, the rejuvenated automakers would pay back the vast majority of the $80 billion that the government spent to save them.

*

As he sat in the conference room on Air Force One heading back from an event in Ohio one day in the spring of that first year, Obama reflected on the tasks in front of him. Even as he was dealing with the auto industry and the economy, he faced decisions on Iraq and Afghanistan. He was busy building an administration, filling hundreds of sub-cabinet jobs and ambassador posts and United States attorney positions. He was rethinking the war on terrorism and pondering what to do about Wall Street regulations. And on top of that, he was crafting a new health care system in hopes of finally achieving universal coverage or something close to it. "Look, I wish I had the luxury of just dealing with energy or just dealing with Iraq or just dealing with Afghanistan," he told *New York Times* reporters traveling with him that day. "We've got to use this moment to solve some big problems once and for all so that the next generation is not saddled with even worse problems than we have right now."

All of those plans were fueling concerns about the growth of government, a perennial dividing line in American politics but one increasingly at the center of the debate as Obama moved to assert a greater role in the nation's economy. The Republican complaints of socialism were hardly surprising, but Obama bristled at the charge. Asked by the *Times* reporters if he was a socialist, he said, "The answer would be no," then laughed for a moment. He said he was "making some very tough choices" on the budget.

But the question clearly nettled him, because less than ninety minutes after Air Force One landed, he called Jeff Zeleny of *The Times* to expand on his answer. "It was hard for me to believe that you were entirely serious about that socialist question," he said. He then noted that large-scale intervention in the markets and expansion of social welfare programs began under George W. Bush. "It wasn't under me that we started buying a bunch of shares of banks," he said. "And it wasn't on my watch that we passed a massive new entitlement, the prescription drug plan, without a source of funding." He was not done. "We've actually been operating in a way that has been entirely consistent with free-market principles and some of the same folks who are throwing the word 'socialist' around can't say the same."

He had a point. Bush had expanded government rather than contracted it and some of Obama's policies were being built around market ideas. But the accumulation of everything Obama was attempting at once seemed overwhelming and gave the impression of an ever-expanding reach of government. Because of the financial crash, the government essentially now owned much of the nation's banking, insurance and auto sectors, it was spending hundreds of billions of dollars on new infrastructure projects, it was aiming to reshape the energy industry and if Obama had his way it would take a much larger role in health care, which represented about one-sixth of the American economy. For many Americans, genetically suspicious of government, this was all pretty head-spinning.

And yet Obama was under enormous pressure to do even more. Constituent groups on the left, anxious to finally advance their priorities after eight years of frustration under Bush, were lobbying for further action on a wide array of fronts. Activists were pushing Obama to tackle climate change, liberalize immigration laws, improve education and expand gay rights. They wanted more spending on their favorite programs. They thought he should do more for African-Americans and other often-disadvantaged minority groups. Obama, of course, was sympathetic to all of these causes, but as much as he had raised expectations for far-reaching change during the campaign, Washington was still a place deeply resistant to swift or sweeping action.

Among those unhappy that he was not focused enough on their issues were members of the Congressional Hispanic Caucus, who arrived at the White House one day that spring to press their case. While Bush had supported a comprehensive overhaul of the nation's immigration laws, to no avail, they were counting on Obama to pick up the mantle and fulfill the mission. Representative Luis Gutiérrez, a Democrat from Illinois and chairman of the caucus's immigration task force, brought with him three boxes filled with petitions signed in Atlanta, Boston, Chicago and elsewhere, essentially calling on Obama to keep his promise of immigration reform.

To Gutiérrez, Obama did not seem particularly happy to be put on the spot by members of his own political coalition. "Luis, I'm going to assign that to Rahm Emanuel," the president told him. Gutiérrez was not impressed. That "basically meant, 'This is bullshit to me,'" he said later.

In the cold calculations of the moment, immigration reform was not the top goal. Obama had too much else to do first, no matter how committed he was to the goal. But he found himself with an opportunity to satisfy disgruntled Hispanic leaders in another way a few weeks later when Justice David Souter, an anchor of the liberal wing of the Supreme Court, suddenly retired, opening a seat for Obama to fill. After culling through forty possible candidates and interviewing the top four finalists, Obama in May nominated Sonia Sotomayor, a federal appeals judge from New York who would become the first Hispanic member of the high court and only the third woman to sit on the bench in the history of the nation.

Obama was impressed by Sotomayor's life story. She grew up the daughter of Puerto Rican parents living in a Bronx public housing project, worked her way up to Princeton and Yale and served as a prosecutor, corporate litigator and federal district judge before joining the United States Court of Appeals for the Second Circuit in New York. Casting her as the embodiment of the American dream, Obama opened a Senate confirmation campaign that he intended to wage over biography more than ideology.

If the president assumed that Senate Republicans would be loath to oppose a Hispanic candidate for fear of alienating a growing voter bloc, he misjudged. Sotomayor, known for bracing candor and lively wit, found her past words coming back to haunt her. Republican senators focused on a lecture she delivered in 2001 describing how her background shaped her jurisprudence. "I would hope that a wise Latina woman with the richness of her experiences would more often than not reach a better conclusion than a white male who hasn't lived that life," she said then. At a conference four years later, she said that a "court of appeals is where policy is made." Taken together, the comments were interpreted by critics as evidence that she would try to impose her values and make policy from the bench rather than follow the letter of the law.

Given that Sotomayor would replace Souter, her appointment would not significantly shift the balance of power on the divided court, and she ultimately performed well at her confirmation hearings, explaining away her statements by insisting they did not mean she would put her thumb on the scale of justice. After a ten-week battle fueled by well-funded interest groups on both sides, the Senate confirmed Sotomayor, 68 to 31, on August 6, with nine Republicans joining every Democrat who participated in voting for her.

It was late in the day when word of the vote arrived at the White House, where most officials had already begun to clear out. Obama strode out of the Oval Office and down the hall looking for someone with whom to savor the victory. He found David Axelrod and gave him a fist bump.

"We just put the first Latina on the Supreme Court," Obama exulted. "Pretty cool, huh?"

Still, he was a little disappointed not to find more aides. "He was frustrated because there weren't enough of us around," Axelrod said later. "He was seeking out people to celebrate with."

*

By that summer, there was little else to celebrate. Not content to simply put out economic fires, Obama was pressing ahead with his far-reaching initiatives to fundamentally restructure American society. But progress had been slower than he had imagined. His theory of the case was that the country was trapped in a bubble-and-bust cycle, careening from one artificial, unsustainable boom to the inevitable crash to the next fake high. He wanted not just to apply a short-term patch but to erect a more durable system with a stronger set of rules. He and his team even came up with a name for his program – the New Foundation, a rather awkward and self-conscious takeoff of Franklin Roosevelt's New Deal. Nearly every president since FDR had tried to devise a pithy term to describe his collective ideas, some more successfully than others (think Lyndon Johnson's enduring Great Society versus Bill Clinton's quickly forgotten New Covenant). The New Foundation did not trip off the tongue any better than George W. Bush's Ownership Society, and it also quickly disappeared as a failed branding effort.

But the notions underlying it did not. Obama wanted to overhaul the country's health care, energy, education and immigration systems and he wanted to move ahead while he still had political momentum. The White House pushed on several fronts as part of a "big-bang" strategy, but the area where it applied the most muscle was health care. More than 45 million Americans had no health insurance, costs were rising far faster than inflation and even many of those who did have coverage were frustrated by policies that left them on their own for their particular ailments.

For more than a century, presidents from Theodore Roosevelt and Harry Truman to Richard Nixon and Bill Clinton had unsuccessfully sought to redesign the health care system with the ambition of universal coverage. Obama was determined to succeed where they had not. "I understand the risks," he told Axelrod. "But what are we going to do? Are we going to put our approval ratings on the shelf and admire them for eight years? Or are we going to spend down on them and try to get some important things done for the future?"

The crafting of a health care plan would reflect Obama's approach to politics and policy. He was a committed liberal without being especially ideological. He was dedicated to the goals of the left without being wedded to its orthodoxy about how to achieve them. In thinking about how to extend coverage to the uninsured, he eschewed a full-scale government takeover of health care along the lines of Britain or Canada. If he were starting from scratch and designing an ideal health care system, Obama reasoned, then a government-run program for all might be the way to go. But he was dealing with a long-established, entrenched system and it made sense to build on it rather than tear it down entirely.

With that in mind, he and his team drew on ideas once promoted by the conservative Heritage Foundation and designed a market-oriented program to help working families pay for private insurance. Insurance marketplaces would be set up in each state so that Americans could compare plans and purchase policies that met certain minimum standards. Those with less income would get government subsidies to help afford these private sector plans. Insurers would be required to cover pre-existing conditions, allow adult children to be covered on their parents' plans and set other minimum standards. At the same time, Medicaid would be expanded dramatically to cover millions of Americans who were too poor to purchase insurance even with help, but not destitute enough to qualify for the government program under existing rules.

For policy and political reasons, Obama jettisoned some of the promises he had made during the campaign. On the trail, he had castigated Hillary Clinton for proposing a mandate requiring everyone to have insurance, only to conclude now that he was in office that she was right after all. The only way to pay for expanded coverage of the sick was to force the young and healthy to contribute into the system. He had likewise criticized John McCain for proposing to tax high-value insurance plans provided by employers, only to reverse course and adopt just such a tax as part of his program. Obama's vow to provide a "public option" – that is, a government-sponsored alternative health plan to compete with private plans, in theory forcing everyone to lower costs – sounded like too much government for the moderates he was wooing, like Senator Joseph Lieberman of Connecticut, so he dropped it, much to the consternation of liberals. And to win over powerful opponents, Obama cut a deal with pharmaceutical giants, agreeing to block the import of cheaper medicine from Canada in exchange for an $80 billion industry commitment to expand coverage, a tradeoff that upset reformers.

Rather than force the plan through Congress right away on the strength of his Democratic majorities, as he had done with the stimulus package, Obama let lawmakers take their time in hopes of attracting Republican support. He got some help when Senator Arlen Specter, the longtime moderate Republican from Pennsylvania, switched parties. But the delay waiting for more GOP allies nearly proved fatal. Conservatives like Senator Jim DeMint of South Carolina were determined to block the health care plan, seeing it as critical to stopping what they saw as the president's assault on the private sector. "If we're able to stop Obama on this, it will be his Waterloo," DeMint said that summer. "It will break him." When Republican lawmakers like Senator Charles Grassley of Iowa, who had been negotiating with the White House on a health care bill, returned home for the August recess, they found themselves under siege from conservative constituents livid that they might go along with such a major government intrusion.

Obama's chances were not helped by distortions of the plan, such as the widely spread myth that it would create "death panels" to decide which patients would receive treatment and which would be left to die. But the heat at those summer town hall meetings reflected a growing libertarian uprising against Obama's expansion of government that was dubbed the Tea Party movement after the Boston Tea Party. Suddenly Republicans like Grassley were taking a harder line on cooperation. In a memo to Obama, David Axelrod fretted that they had lost the public argument because too many Americans were leery of spending even more money in a crisis. "They suspect that this is about spending and taxing more to take care of someone else," he wrote. "And even if they see universal coverage as a laudable goal, they think it's irresponsible to undertake it now – a liberal indulgence we can't afford."

The Tea Party revolt got under way under Obama but it had its roots in George W. Bush's administration. For years, conservatives had simmered about Bush's spending policies, including the expansion of Medicare to cover prescription drugs and the construction of an elaborate counterterrorism and domestic security infrastructure. They had also resisted his efforts to liberalize immigration laws, efforts that ultimately collapsed in his second term. They were hardly mollified when Bush left behind a sky-high deficit, fueled by the cost of two wars, tax cuts, the collapse in revenues due to the economic crisis and the bank bailouts. But their rebellion was muted as long as it was a Republican in the White House. When a Democrat took over, they were finally liberated to vent their aggravation at what seemed like an explosion of big government. The fact that he was African-American added a toxic racial element to the unrest. To the extent that the grass-root resentment was organic, it was nonetheless channeled by well-financed professional conservative groups like Freedom-Works that stepped in to harness the grievance and weaponize it against Obama.

The uprising on the right was amplified and magnified by Fox News, which covered it extensively amid nonstop reports and commentaries criticizing Obama and his every move. To the president and his team, Fox had morphed beyond a conservative news outlet into a hand-in-glove adjunct of the Republican Party. "I've got one television station that is entirely devoted to attacking my administration," Obama told John Harwood of CNBC that summer. "That's a pretty big megaphone. And you'd be hard pressed if you watched the entire day to find a positive story about me on that front."

He had cause for unhappiness. During the campaign, Fox had reported falsely that Obama had been educated in a madrassa while growing up in Indonesia, suggesting he was secretly really a Muslim, and had suggested that his congratulatory fist bump with his wife at the Democratic convention might be a "terrorist fist jab." Since arriving in the White House, Obama had been regularly denounced in often-racial terms. Glenn Beck, the network's most incendiary nighttime host, said Obama "has a deep-seated hatred for white people or the white culture," never mind that he was raised by a white mother and white grandparents and surrounded by mostly white advisers. Beck aired a series of reports on Van Jones, a White House aide, linking him to radical leftists and reporting that he had signed a letter suggesting that George W. Bush might have allowed the terrorist attacks of September 11, 2001, to happen as a pretext to go to war. Jones resigned on September 5, which Fox took as a major victory.

A week later, an organization founded by Beck helped organize a massive Tea Party march on Washington, filling the West Lawn of the Capitol and beyond with voters upset at what they saw as the nation's drift toward socialism. "Obammunism is Communism," read one sign. Others went further. "TREASON," said one. "Parasite-in-Chief," said another. A popular theme among some signs showed Obama made up as Heath Ledger's wicked and maniacal Joker from a recent Batman movie.

Egged on by Dan Pfeiffer, the deputy communications director who by his own later account was "young and pissed and looking for a fight," Obama authorized his aides to declare war on Fox. "We're going to treat them the way we would treat an opponent," Anita Dunn, the White House communications director, told *The New York Times*. Both Rahm Emanuel and David Axelrod then went on Sunday shows of other networks and amplified the message in almost identical words; Fox was "not really a news station," Axelrod declared, while Emanuel said it was "not a news organization so much as it has a perspective." Indeed, Beck and some of his evening colleagues were going well beyond the role of media commentators by directly organizing or promoting political groups. But the ones who would be punished were the network's news correspondents who, during daytime programming, labored to present traditional, even-handed coverage.

The White House excluded Fox from pool events that included their competitors and refused to give it an interview with the president when he made a round of all four other networks to pitch his health care plan. "I am putting some dead fish in the fox cubby – just cause," Jen Psaki, the deputy communications director, wrote another aide in an email. Ultimately, however, the move backfired. When the administration tried to exclude Fox from a briefing on executive pay, the other networks balked and refused to participate. An attack on one was an attack on all. The White House relented. "In the end," Pfeiffer reflected after leaving office, "this fight was a mistake of hubris."

Even as Obama was on the defensive that summer, he lost his most important Congressional ally. Senator Edward Kennedy of Massachusetts, the longtime liberal stalwart, died of a brain tumor on August 25, just shy of his goal of finally passing universal health care legislation. Kennedy had written Obama a letter to be delivered after his death thanking the president for his commitment to the cause. "And while I will not see the victory," he wrote, "I was able to look forward and know that we will – yes, we will – fulfill the promise of health care in America as a right and not a privilege."

Before Congress even returned to Washington, though, Obama's health care program seemed to be on life support. Rahm Emanuel went to the president day after day in August urging him to pull back and narrow his goals. Rather than push for a comprehensive plan that might go down to defeat, Emanuel advised, try instead for a "skinny" bill that focused on covering low-income children and families and would be easier to pass. Bill Clinton had adopted such an incremental strategy after his own sweeping health care proposal failed in the 1990s and by the time he left office he had made important progress in providing medical services for children. If Obama insisted on pressing for the whole program, Emanuel warned, it would be at a cost to his other priorities. "That means a lot of this other stuff is going to get sidelined in the process," he said.

Obama met with the rest of his team to discuss the matter. He went around the room and, one by one, his advisers listed all of the obstacles to passing the more expansive health care plan. Finally, Obama came back to his legislative director, Phil Schiliro.

"So can we do this?" Obama asked.

"There's a path," Schiliro said. "But it's like the Clint Eastwood movie. Do you feel lucky?"

"My name is Barack Obama, I'm a black man and I'm president of the United States," he answered. "Of course, I feel lucky."

*

Having decided to press ahead for the full plan, Obama and his allies spent the fall of 2009 grinding it out on Capitol Hill. Obama rallied Democrats and all but gave up on Republicans. He made it the central test of his presidency – and let Democrats know that they could not afford to let him fail. Emotions ran so high that when he delivered an address to a joint session of Congress pitching his health care plan in September, a backbench Republican representative, Joe Wilson of South Carolina, shouted out, "You lie!" in the middle of the speech.

In November, House Democrats muscled through the bill, 220 to 215, just two votes more than a majority. Seven weeks later, on Christmas Eve, Senate Democrats followed suit with their own version, garnering the bare-minimum sixty votes needed to overcome a Republican filibuster. It was not always pretty. The deal with the pharmaceutical industry was followed by deals with individual senators, including an advantage on Medicaid financing for Nebraska to win the vote of a fellow Democrat, Senator Ben Nelson, a sweetener that Republicans branded the "cornhusker kickback."

For another president, that would just be business as usual. But for Obama, who promised to end business as usual, the means cheapened the ends. Suddenly, he no longer looked like the reformer who would slay the dragons of Washington but just another deal-making pol who would cut whatever corners were necessary to get what he wanted. He had not conquered the system. The system had conquered him. "There's a constant tension between the need to get things done within the system as it is and the commitment to change the system," David Axelrod reflected. "Finding that line at any given moment is really, really difficult."

In this case, all the horse-trading had not even finished the matter. The House and Senate versions of the bill were different, meaning they had to be reconciled into a single final measure and voted on again before the program could become law. But after a grueling few months, Obama was satisfied that he was getting to where he wanted to go. As he headed off to spend the holidays in his home state of Hawaii, he had no idea that the whole thing would come unraveled thanks to a former underwear model in a pickup truck.

The unexpected hitch came, of all places, in the deep-blue liberal bastion of Massachusetts, where a special election in January 2010 to fill Edward Kennedy's Senate seat took a surprise turn. Scott Brown, a Republican state senator who once posed nude for *Cosmopolitan* magazine, pulled off an upset after traveling around the state in his GMC Canyon assailing Obama's big-government health care plan, beating a hapless Democrat who took a vacation shortly before the election, scorned the idea of campaigning outside Fenway Park and suggested that the former Boston Red Sox star Curt Schilling was a New York Yankees fan. Not only was Brown's triumph seen as the first voter repudiation of Obama since his election, it also cost the Democrats their sixtieth vote in the Senate, depriving them of the unilateral power to break a filibuster and pass legislation at will.

Obama was furious. "We were this close on health care," he told David Plouffe, holding his thumb and forefinger just an inch apart, as they waited for the inevitable results a few hours before the polls closed on the day of the special election. He sighed. "It's hard to believe that all of that may unravel because we lose what should have been a sure thing."

This was not where he was supposed to be at this point. By the end of his first year in office, he had expected not only to have overhauled the health care system but also to have restructured the energy industry to fight climate change, reined in Wall Street with a new regulatory structure, closed the prison at Guantánamo Bay, Cuba, and at least made some progress on liberalizing immigration policy. None of that had happened. Instead, the president's approval ratings had fallen by more than twenty percentage points, unemployment remained higher than even the worst initial White House forecast and Obama's legislative agenda had stalled.

Somehow Obama's message of hope and change had been muddied by the messy reality of governance. After a year in office, inspiration had turned to exasperation. His soaring rhetoric now seemed to come with asterisks and fine print.

While he tried to explain complex positions and rationalize old-school Washington deal-making, the Republicans enjoyed the simpler position of simply rejecting Obama's policies without having to offer a plausible alternative. "Their bumper sticker has one word: 'No,'" noted Senator Al Franken, a Democrat from

Minnesota. "Our bumper sticker has – it's just way too many words. And it says: 'Continued on next bumper sticker.'"

The day after Brown's victory, Obama seemed resigned to retreat. Maybe it was time to return to the "core elements" of the health care plan, he mused publicly, channeling the advice that Rahm Emanuel had been giving him for months. But he quickly stiffened again, authorizing aides to walk back his comments and insist he did not necessarily want a scaled-back program. A week later, he went before Congress again for his State of the Union address and vowed to press on. "I don't quit," he said. But he pleaded for patience from disappointed supporters. "I campaigned on the promise of change – 'change we can believe in,' the slogan went," he said. "And right now, I know there are many Americans who aren't sure if they still believe we can change – or that I can deliver it. But remember this. I never suggested that change would be easy or that I can do it alone. Democracy in a nation of 300 million people can be noisy and messy and complicated. And when you try to do big things and make big changes, it stirs passions and controversy. That's just how it is."

In traditional Washington fashion, the setbacks demanded a scalp and the most obvious target was Emanuel, whose high-octane style had generated as much resentment as admiration in the White House. Emanuel had cultivated a ferocious, profanity-spewing, send-a-dead-fish-to-a-rival, Rambo reputation since his days as a young White House aide to Bill Clinton. He had gotten on the bad side of Hillary Clinton and had nearly been fired. He earned his way back into President Clinton's good graces by helping pass the North American Free Trade Agreement, or NAFTA, but his centrist instincts had long earned him enemies on the left. After a stint in investment banking back in his home of Chicago, he ran for Congress and quickly made himself into a force among House Democrats with his eye on the speakership before giving that up to join Obama's White House.

Now fifty years old, he still had the coiled energy of aides half his age, still as wiry thin as he was during his hard-to-imagine days as a ballet dancer, still as determined to impose his will on a system that defied taming. He met with Obama at the beginning of each day and again at the end, in between dipping his hands into virtually everything the White House did, from economic policy to national security. He worked the phone and email in staccato fashion, staying in touch with a dizzying array of law-makers, officials, lobbyists, journalists and political operatives with one-minute calls or one-word messages. Descriptions of his style almost invariably included some sort of martial reference. "Hand-to-hand combat," his Chicago friend Bill Daley put it. "A heat-seeking missile," said David Axelrod. Emanuel's four-letter tirades left a lot of bruises but he did not seem to care. On his credenza was a name plate: "Undersecretary for Go Fuck Yourself."

Where Obama was about inspiration, Emanuel was about getting things done, far less concerned with the details of a bill than whether he could find the 218 votes in the House and sixty votes in the Senate to pass it. He pushed for as much as he could and when he judged that he had gotten as much as the system would bear, he cut a deal. "He's a Malcolm X Democrat – by any means necessary," said his longtime friend Paul Begala. But Emanuel's willingness to get in bed with the pharmaceutical industry, dispense with the public option and make other compromises in the health care bill had made him a target. A *Financial Times* article questioning Emanuel's team was followed by a slam by the blogger Steve Clemons on his well-read Washington Note, which was followed by a column in *The Daily Beast* by Leslie Gelb titled, "Replace Rahm." Even a public defense of Emanuel worked against him. When Dana Milbank, a *Washington Post* columnist, wrote that the real problem was not Emanuel but other aides or even the president himself, critics accused Emanuel of orchestrating the column, which he and Milbank denied.

Emanuel felt compelled to offer the president his resignation.

"Oh no," Obama replied. "You're not resigning. Your punishment is that you have to pass health care."

With Republicans emboldened, Obama and Emanuel concluded that they had no choice but to lean on their Democratic majorities. In the end, they came up with a bit of legislative legerdemain to push the health care program through. Since Republicans could now filibuster any revised plan in the Senate, Obama convinced House Democrats to simply approve the version already passed by the Senate without changes. That would send it immediately to the president's desk without another vote in the Senate. Then they could pass changes to the program that House Democrats wanted by inserting them into a separate spending bill that under Senate rules could not be filibustered and therefore needed only fifty-one votes instead of sixty. The Democrats would grease passage of that separate measure by bootstrapping onto it an unrelated but popular reform of the student loan system, cutting out the middlemen lenders and saving the federal government $60 billion, some of which would be used to pay for health care.

Republicans cried foul. "The American people are angry," John Boehner declared. The bill was a "fiscal Frankenstein," said Representative Paul Ryan of Wisconsin. Representative Virginia Foxx of North Carolina called it "one of the most offensive pieces of social-engineering legislation in the history of the United States." The path to passage relied on the sort of gamesmanship that Candidate Obama might have decried if he were on the other side of the issue but one that President Obama chose to accept.

When the votes were taken late on the night of Sunday, March 21, 2010, Obama gathered in the Roosevelt Room with top aides.

Among those on hand to watch on television with him was Hillary Clinton, who had made health care her big push as first lady more than fifteen years earlier. Obama now was finally realizing the dream she had tried so hard to fulfill. After the final tally was called and health care was passed, the president rose to his feet and led a standing ovation, then hugged Clinton to celebrate the culmination of their mutual efforts. "This is what change looks like," he said a few minutes later to cameras gathered in the East Room.

With the hour just passing midnight, Obama invited his team over to the residence for a champagne toast on the Truman Balcony overlooking the South Lawn and, in the distance, the Washington Monument. The mood was loose and happy. All the hard work, all the ups and downs, the near-death experiences and the comebacks—it had finally paid off.

Obama seemed more relaxed and cheerful than aides had seen him since the election. This was better than Election Day, he told them.

Why? someone asked.

Because the whole point of the election was to get to do things like this, he answered.

Still, he knew that his success in passing the Patient Protection and Affordable Care Act would only drive his opposition to distraction. He anticipated only rough days ahead. "You know," he told an aide as they savored the moment on the balcony, "they're going to kick our asses over this."

Obama signed the bill a couple of days later, using twenty-two pens so that he could give them away as keepsakes to key players in the fight. Joe Biden summed it up in an aside to the president that, unknown to him, was picked up by a microphone and broadcast for everyone to hear.

"Mr. President," he told Obama, "this is a big fucking deal."

*

With health care in hand, Obama looked for one more victory while he still had political capital. The cap-and-trade climate change program had passed the House but was mired in the Senate. No one seemed ready to move on an immigration plan. The biggest opportunity seemed to be new regulations governing the financial institutions that had plunged the country into the Great Recession.

What to do with the banks had been one of the most vexing questions for Obama when he arrived in office. FDR closed the banks after his inauguration in order to calm the waters before eventually reopening them. What many of Obama's more liberal advisers and supporters wanted him to consider was closing at least some of the big banks permanently or breaking up the biggest ones. After all, the behemoths on Wall Street, the too-big-to-fail institutions, had sent the world economy into a tailspin through catastrophically bad judgment and irresponsible behavior. Someone had to pay the price.

If Obama did not fully recognize the wellspring of popular anger at the banks before taking the oath, he got a searing lesson soon afterward. When news outlets reported that AIG, the insurance company bailed out by taxpayers, planned to issue about $165 million in bonuses to some of the same senior executives who had nearly driven it into the ground, the president faced a powerful bipartisan backlash. Even though nearly 80 percent of the company was now owned by the federal government, Obama administration lawyers concluded that they could not stop the bonuses because they had been promised in binding contracts before the bailout. Obama's advisers were so deferential to the executives' position that they had even previously talked Democratic allies out of putting a provision in the Recovery Act that would have empowered the government to claw back existing bonuses because, they reasoned, it would undercut faith in the inviolability of contracts.

The national uproar nonetheless prompted the president to respond by ordering the Treasury Department to find a way to stop the bonuses. This was the sort of reactive, stuck-in-the-news-cycle brand of politics that Obama disdained. His intellectual approach to issues somewhat disconnected with popular sentiment. Even though he said the words, the outrage he expressed publicly somehow came across as muted. He did not reflect the visceral grievances felt by taxpayers watching their money go to well-fed, tailor-dressed corporate executives who had sent the economy into a tailspin.

The criticism aggravated Obama, and he bristled when Andrew Cuomo, the attorney general of New York, got more credit for forcing AIG executives to return some of the bonuses than his own administration did. Pressed on why he did not express outrage immediately upon learning of the bonuses, Obama snapped, "Well, it took us a couple of days because I like to know what I'm talking about before I speak."

It was a telling moment, one that would foreshadow more such episodes in the years to come. Thoughtful and analytical, Obama often reached the place where politics insisted he go, but he sometimes took his time getting there and he resented being pushed. He did not fully grasp the importance of a president channeling public sentiment. He dismissed the demands for a public show of emotion as political fakery. And it would cost him.

Moreover, he was not inherently built for populist class warfare. While his policies undoubtedly targeted the rich in favor of the poor and his politics certainly played on economic resentments, it was not natural for him to crusade against "malefactors of great wealth," as Theodore Roosevelt did, or to declare that the wealthy were "unanimous in their hate for me – and I welcome their hatred," as FDR did. At one point when Obama lashed out in an interview at "fat cat bankers" on Wall Street who had not shown "a lot of shame," he was accused of demonizing those who worked in the investment sector, and he largely backed off using such language.

As it was, the AIG furor only exposed the surface of the real debate consuming the Obama administration. George W. Bush had stabilized the crashing banks before leaving office with the Troubled Asset Relief Program, or TARP, a $700 billion bailout initially voted down in Congress until petrified lawmakers reversed themselves and approved it lest they be blamed for another stock market crash. As a senator, Obama had supported TARP and by and large it seemed to have stopped the economy from teetering over the cliff into another Depression. But some of the nation's largest banks were still on the edge and it was now up to Obama to decide what to do about it.

Advocates of a hard and unforgiving approach – what Rahm Emanuel called Old Testament policy – pushed to nationalize or break up the banks. Given what their reckless behavior had done to the country, that seemed only fair and would presumably stop it from ever happening again. Others suggested creating what was called a "bad bank" financed by the federal government to take the riskiest assets off the books of the banks, leaving them in stronger financial shape while leaving the taxpayers on the hook.

But Timothy Geithner, the Treasury secretary, resisted going that far. Slight, relaxed and confident, prone to using words like "cool" to describe esoteric economic ideas, Geithner at age forty-seven was well liked within the new Obama team, so much so that he was universally known simply as Tim. Many assumed that he had once worked in the banking sector because of his remarkable fluidity with the world of Wall Street, but he had actually spent a lifetime in public service managing the nation's finances. Despite that, he thought it would be a mistake to insert the government into the banking sector more than necessary, much less nationalize the banks. He was strictly New Testament.

Instead, Geithner proposed imposing what became called "stress tests" on the biggest banks, an examination crafted by the Federal Reserve to determine what would happen to each institution in case of another downturn comparable to the Great Depression. The idea was to introduce more transparency to the system, expose vulnerabilities that could then be addressed and reduce some of the uncertainty that was terrifying the markets. Those banks that were not capitalized enough to weather a catastrophic scenario would have to either raise more funds privately or the Treasury Department would inject whatever was needed and, depending on the size of the investment, potentially take over management.

At the same time the AIG bonuses were coming to light, Obama was deciding what to do if the stress tests came back poorly and the government had to take a majority stake in one of the big banks. Geithner favored a "conservatorship approach," in which the government would have the discretion to wind down investments to minimize shock to the system. Larry Summers favored a "rapid resolution exit," which meant an immediate restructuring of the bank, possibly even carving it up and diluting the stakes of its shareholders. When they were initially portrayed as championing a dovish approach versus a hawkish one, Geithner heatedly objected. "You can't say we're dove and he's hawk," he shouted into a phone during a conference call. "There's no dove. You've got to make it Hawk One and Hawk Two!"

Obama was presented with Hawk One and Hawk Two during a Sunday meeting just before the AIG revelation and there was plenty of sentiment for the sharpest talons. After hours of contentious discussion went nowhere, Obama finally lost his patience and stood up. "I'm going to get a haircut and have dinner with my family," he said. "I'll be back at seven. When I get back, I want a consensus."

After he left, as David Axelrod remembered it, "all hell broke loose." The advisers went back and forth, with Summers pressing for more aggressive action. But when it became clear that Summers's option could require another $200 billion to $400 billion of taxpayer money, Rahm Emanuel practically leapt out of his chair.

"What are you talking about?" he snapped. "There's no more fucking money!"

Summers was nonplussed. "Well, that's no good," he said.

"Well, welcome to my world, Larry!" Geithner erupted.

By the time Obama returned, Geithner's plan became the default consensus. They would give it a try if for no other reason than no one could come up with a better, more plausible idea.

Nearly two weeks later, Obama invited the chief executives of the thirteen largest banks to the White House to discuss the plan for restoring stability to the financial industry. In what they took as a message of frugal resentment, the bankers were served only flat water with no ice and no refills.

The executives were still resistant, chafing at the conditions that had come with the government aid. The limits on bonuses and other compensation were strangling their ability to recruit candidates for top jobs, they complained.

Obama had no sympathy. "Be careful how you make those statements, gentlemen," he said. "The public isn't buying that. My administration is the only thing between you and the pitchforks."

When the results of the stress tests came back in May, the news was better than expected. Of the nineteen biggest banks, nine were in such good shape that they did not need any additional capital even in the case of an economic disaster. The other ten, including Citibank, needed a combined total of $185 billion in capital as of January 1, but since they had already increased their equity by $110 billion on their own since then, that meant they only needed to raise another $75 billion. Most if that could come from private funds, meaning the government would not have to make another unpopular investment. Moreover, the results of the stress tests finally eased the jitters on Wall Street. The banks seemed to be on the path to stability again.

Obama then turned attention to figuring out how to prevent such a crash from ever happening again. Once again, he assumed that Republicans would join him in a consensus effort to rewrite the rules of Wall Street only to spend months chasing after votes that would not come his way, either because they were always committed to obstruction (his view) or he was too intent on doing things his way (their view). Even some Obama administration officials thought the White House traded away its chances of a bipartisan bill by turning up the volume and making it a public issue to use against the Republicans.

Crafted by the two Democratic banking committee chairmen, Senator Christopher Dodd of Connecticut and Representative Barney Frank of Massachusetts, the legislation envisioned the most sweeping crackdown on the banks since the New Deal. The same banks that survived due to government intervention now assembled an army of lobbyists to keep the government from intervening in their business. The House passed the bill by the end of 2009 but as with health care, Scott Brown's election in Massachusetts in early 2010 put its chances in the Senate in doubt. Geithner tried to strengthen its prospects by introducing an additional provision championed by Paul Volcker, the tall, balding former Federal Reserve chairman who helped beat inflation in the 1980s and maintained an enormous reservoir of credibility, especially among liberals looking to be tougher on the banks. The provision would prohibit banks from trading with depositors' money, in effect barring some of the risky practices that might lead to trouble. Obama agreed and announced the proposal the day after Brown's election. David Axelrod came up with the idea of calling it the Volcker Rule, to trade on its author's standing.

A final version of the overall bill passed Congress in July 2010 with the support of just three Republicans in the House and three in the Senate – including Brown. The Dodd-Frank Wall Street Reform and Consumer Protection Act expanded federal regulations to cover more financial institutions and cracked down on derivatives, the complex form of securities that helped trigger the crash of 2008. It created a new federal Consumer Financial Protection Bureau to keep watch on the banks and other financial firms and a council of federal regulators to monitor risks to the financial system. The government would have new powers to limit and even break up troubled firms.

Banks and other businesses complained that Dodd-Frank went too far; liberal activists complained it did not go nearly far enough. But Obama took what he could get. "Because of this law, the American people will never again be asked to foot the bill for Wall Street's mistakes," he said as he signed it into law. "There will be no more taxpayer-funded bailouts. Period."

The Bush era was now over. For better or worse, it was now definitively the Obama era.

CHAPTER THREE
'Bring Our Troops Home'

On the first Veterans Day he marked as commander in chief, Obama visited Arlington National Cemetery and wandered among the chalky white tombstones commemorating those who had fallen in the rugged mountains of Central Asia and the scorching deserts of the Middle East. Stern and silent, he kept his thoughts to himself as he stared at the simple markers representing the sacrifices of eight years of war. But he was aware that these would not be the last.

After he was done, Obama headed back to the White House and marched into the Situation Room for the eighth meeting of a long, torturous review in which he was weighing whether to send thousands more young men and women into harm's way. He had come to office determined to end what he called the "dumb war" in Iraq but vowing to make a renewed effort to win the "good war" in Afghanistan. This would be the critical meeting where he shaped the course of his presidency as a wartime commander, essentially settling on a plan to send reinforcements to Afghanistan while setting a limit on how long they would stay.

It was an audacious decision, one that fully pleased neither side in the long-running national debate about security in the wake of the September 11 attacks. The left objected to doubling down on a guerrilla war with no visible end on the horizon. The right complained that setting a deadline for the additional troops allowed the enemy to simply wait them out. But on Obama's mind were the costs, including those at Arlington and the injured troops he had met at Walter Reed National Military Medical Center in Washington. "I don't want to be going to Walter Reed for another eight years," he had told aides when visiting wounded soldiers a few weeks earlier.

Obama was an implausible wartime president, a onetime community organizer whose rise was powered in large part by his opposition to the invasion of Iraq. He was the first president in four decades to inherit a shooting war already raging the day he took office – two, in fact, plus subsidiaries in far-flung corners of the global struggle with terrorism. Along the way, he confronted some of the biggest decisions a president has to make, even as he gave every impression of being a reluctant warrior. He demonstrated in the opening period of his presidency that he was willing to use force to advance national interests, tripling forces in Afghanistan, authorizing secret operations in Yemen and Somalia and escalating drone strikes in Pakistan.

But Obama did not see himself as a wartime president the way his predecessor did. He rarely talked about the conflicts in public in any extended way, determined not to let them define his presidency. While George W. Bush saw the wars in Iraq and Afghanistan as his central mission as well as opportunities to transform critical regions of the world, Obama saw them as "problems that need managing," as one adviser put it, just some of many, in fact, that needed to be weighed against each other on the scale of national priorities. The result was an uneasy balance between a president wary of endless overseas commitments and a military worried that he was not fully invested in the cause. "He's got a very full plate of very big issues," said Defense Secretary Robert Gates, "and I think he does not want to create the impression that he's so preoccupied with these two wars that he's not addressing the domestic issues that are uppermost in people's minds."

Obama was an eleven-year-old boy in Hawaii when the last American combat troops left Vietnam, too young to have participated in the polarizing clashes of that era or to have faced the choices Bush and Bill Clinton did about serving in the military. "He's really the first generation of recent presidents who didn't live through that," said David Axelrod. "The whole debate on Vietnam, that was not part of his life experience."

Taking over as president of a country at war, Obama had a steep learning curve. He was taught basics like military titles and ceremonial rules. He surfed the Internet at night to research the toll on troops. His campaign recruited retired generals to advise him. He learned how to salute. But it still took time to adjust when he became president. The first time he walked into a room of generals as commander in chief, he was taken back when they stood. "Come on, guys, you don't have to do that," he said.

Perhaps his most important tutor was Gates, the first defense secretary ever kept on by a president of another party. They were a political odd couple, a forty-seven-year-old Harvard-trained lawyer and a sixty-five-year-old veteran of Cold War spy intrigues and Republican administrations. But they were both known for unassuming discipline, and they bonded in the many hours spent huddling over battlefield maps and deployment plans. Gates had served eight presidents and cycled in and out of the Situation Room since the days when it was served by a battery of fax machines. A former CIA officer who rose to head the agency under George H.W. Bush, Gates was hardly a natural fit in the Obama team, a diminutive Republican gray-haired "geezer," in his own word, surrounded by basketball-playing, new-generation Democrats twenty years younger. But Gates commanded so much respect that the Obama aides began calling him Yoda after the wise and wizened if tiny Jedi master from *Star Wars*. His low-wattage exterior masked a wily inside player.

Obama relied on Gates as his ambassador to the military and deferred to him repeatedly in the opening months of his presidency. When Gates wanted to force out General David McKiernan as commander in Afghanistan in favor of General Stanley McChrystal, Obama signed off. Likewise, cognizant of Clinton's ill-fated effort to end the ban on gay and lesbian soldiers, Obama let Gates set a slow pace in overturning the "don't ask, don't tell" policy that barred them from serving openly, even though he disappointed gay rights advocates by not being more aggressive.

Keeping Gates not only ensured continuity in a time of war, it also provided political cover against the Democrats' historically weak-on-defense image. Indeed, Obama surrounded himself with uniformed officers. He kept Bush's war coordinator, Lieutenant General Douglas Lute, and tapped General James Jones, a former Marine Corps commandant and NATO commander, as his national security adviser, Admiral Dennis Blair as director of national intelligence and Lieutenant General Karl Eikenberry as ambassador to Afghanistan.

Obama had little time to even figure out where the Situation Room was before he was asked to make two huge war-and-peace decisions. Bush left behind a request from General McKiernan to send 30,000 more troops to Afghanistan, deferring to the new president to decide whether to follow through. After a quick review, Obama agreed just four weeks after taking office to send 17,000 troops as reinforcements. Ten days after that, he flew to Camp Lejeune in North Carolina to announce that he would pull combat forces out of Iraq by August 2010 and the rest of American troops by the end of 2011.

The president's priorities were clear in how he announced the two decisions. The Afghan reinforcement was disclosed in a written statement and not treated as a seismic event, generating relatively modest news coverage and little public debate. Obama made no speech or public appearance to explain why he was sending more troops or what he hoped they would accomplish. He offered no explanation of his strategy or his thinking when it came to the nearly eight-year-old war. The Iraq withdrawal, on the other hand, was presented as a historic turning point with television-friendly pictures of the president addressing a crowd of impassive Marines clad in camouflage. "We will complete this transition to Iraqi responsibility, and we will bring our troops home with the honor that they have earned," Obama said.

Although Obama did not acknowledge it, his Iraq withdrawal plan essentially followed the blueprint left behind by Bush. Before he left office, Bush signed a strategic pact with Iraq agreeing to pull American troops out of major cities by June 2009 and leave the country entirely by the end of 2011. Obama retained both of those targets and simply added an intermediate step for combat forces. Even on that, he compromised on the sixteen-month withdrawal of combat troops he had promised on the campaign trail, accepting a nineteen-month time frame instead in deference to Gates and the generals, who wanted more time.

In announcing the Iraq withdrawal, Obama hailed General David Petraeus, the former Iraq commander, and the military for turning the war around without mentioning the Bush surge of troops and strategy change from 2007 that many credited – and that Obama had opposed as a senator. Nor did he mention that he was about to follow a similar strategy in Afghanistan.

*

If Obama thought his quick dispatch of extra forces to Afghanistan in February would buy him time, he soon realized how wrong he was. Within weeks, the military was back, asking for 4,000 more troops. Obama approved the request, bringing the total new forces he had sent to 21,000. But he became wary of mission creep and suspicious of a military hierarchy that he thought was trying to manipulate him.

By the summer of 2009, Stanley McChrystal, now installed as commander in Afghanistan, was back pressing for even more troops. If the United States hoped to repeat the counterinsurgency strategy used by Petraeus in Iraq, McChrystal argued, he would need a substantial increase in combat firepower. He developed three options, one for an additional 10,000 troops, a second for 40,000 troops and a final one for 85,000 troops – in keeping with the classic Washington technique of giving an upper recommendation that is clearly untenable and a lower one that is palpably insufficient, effectively making a middle alternative, the so-called "Goldilocks option," the only real proposal.

Under Bush, the war effort in Afghanistan had always been a small-footprint affair, with just 15,000 to 30,000 American troops at any one time, aided by small numbers of NATO forces in support of a rudimentary Afghan army whose soldiers seemed to run away more than they fought. After the Taliban government fell in the months after September 11, the presumption of victory in Afghanistan led the Bush administration to siphon American resources and attention to Iraq, and the low-grade guerrilla war petered along without resolution until late in his presidency, when it appeared the enemy had taken the upper hand.

With McChrystal now seeking more forces, Obama decided he wanted a more comprehensive assessment than the rushed process in his first weeks in office. In the meantime, Gates asked for 5,000 more troops, "enablers" like medevac units and specialists in countering the improvised explosive devices, or IEDs, that were so damaging. But Obama reacted angrily to the request. Why do you need more enablers? he asked. Is this mission creep? In the end, Obama grudgingly went along – what choice did he really have? But Gates was deeply disturbed, worried that the president did not fully appreciate the inherent unpredictability of war. "I came closer to resigning that day than at any other time in my tenure, though no one knew it," Gates wrote in his memoir.

To consider the larger McChrystal request, Obama launched a

review that would involve a far deeper study of both Afghanistan and Pakistan, aided by the Pentagon, State Department and intelligence agencies. If he was going to be asked to invest so many more forces to the conflict, he wanted to think about whether it was worth it and what could be accomplished. He faced enormous political pressure at home from liberals in his own party who thought Afghanistan was becoming a quagmire just like Iraq and from conservatives who feared he was not truly committed to victory or even knew what that would look like.

Just as the review got started, though, McChrystal's sixty-six-page memo detailing the critical condition on the ground that he argued justified more troops was slipped to Bob Woodward of *The Washington Post*, a bombshell leak that infuriated Obama, who suspected that the military was trying to force his hand. He summoned Gates and Admiral Mike Mullen, the chairman of the Joint Chiefs of Staff, for a dressing down.

"I can only conclude one of two things, Mike," Obama said. "Either you don't respect me as commander in chief or you all have been very sloppy. Neither is justifiable."

The room grew deadly silent. After a tense pause, Gates spoke up. "We respect you, Mr. President," he said. "The mistakes are ours."

With that strained beginning, the three-month review that followed proved a case study in decision-making in the Obama presidency – intense, methodical, rigorous, earnest and at times deeply frustrating for nearly all involved. It was a virtual seminar in Afghanistan and Pakistan, led by a president described by one participant as something "between a college professor and a gentle cross-examiner." Obama peppered advisers with questions and showed an insatiable appetite for information, taxing analysts who prepared three dozen intelligence reports for him and Pentagon staff members who churned out thousands of pages of documents. He demanded a "proof of concept" to back up the counterinsurgency strategy the generals were pursuing. He invited competing voices to debate in front of him and guarded his own thoughts until near the end of the process. Obama devoted so much time to the Afghan decision in the fall of his first year – nearly eleven hours on the day after Thanksgiving alone – that he joked, "I've got more deeply in the woods than a president should, and now you guys need to solve this."

The outsize personalities on his team vied for his favor, sometimes sharply disagreeing as they made their arguments. Gates and Hillary Clinton pressed in favor of more troops, while Joe Biden, James Jones and Rahm Emanuel, as well as Tom Donilon and Denis McDonough, both deputy national security advisers, were more dubious. Still seething over the leak of the McChrystal memo, Obama came to feel that the military, led by Mullen, McChrystal and Petraeus, who was now the head of the United States Central Command, were trying to game the process – "box in the president," in the parlance used in the White House – by leaking other details of the review as it proceeded and exaggerating the dangers of not sending more troops. Gates and Mullen, for their part, suspected Emanuel, McDonough and other White House aides of leaking themselves to undercut the case for more troops.

The review was a profound test of the new partnership between Obama and Clinton, whose epic battle for their party's nomination had divided Democrats into camps that, a year later, remained wary of each other. Obama's White House saw Clinton's State Department as a rival power center. Team Hillary watched the new president's stumbles with a quiet told-you-so satisfaction. Team Barack made a point of blocking Clinton from bringing its least favorite partisan gunslinger, Sidney Blumenthal, into the administration. Clinton, who nonetheless stayed in touch with Blumenthal, was insecure in those early months. She was deferential to an extreme, trying to show she was a loyal member of the administration. One assistant secretary of state told the author Jonathan Alter that it was like a teenager trying too hard on a date. Clinton herself used the same metaphor, saying their first meeting after he beat her for the nomination, was "like two teenagers on an awkward first date." Trying to find her place at the head of a cabinet run by the man who had beaten her, she nursed concerns about whether she was in the right meetings and whether the president or his people were holding grudges against those who had supported her during their primary contest. She traded messages with political advisers who sent her sometimes-scathing assessments of the president she now served, although she was careful not to respond in writing.

"I heard on the radio that there is a Cabinet mtg this am," Clinton emailed aides one day in the early months of the administration. "Is there? Can I go?" (It turned out to be a meeting for lower-level officials.)

Four days later, she showed up for a White House meeting that had been canceled without her knowledge. "This is the second time this has happened," she wrote aides. "What's up???"

While Obama's advisers managed to block Blumenthal, Clinton did insist on a place for one of her close friends, Richard Holbrooke, the architect of the Dayton Accords that ended the war in Bosnia during her husband's administration in the 1990s. He was a diplomat of rare skill, a dominating personality who managed to impose order out of chaos. Called "the Bulldozer," he essentially locked the major players in the Balkans war in a room and would not let them out until they settled the war. Had Clinton won the presidency, Holbrooke might very well have been her secretary of state. Instead, Clinton made him special representative for Afghanistan and Pakistan, hoping he could replicate his success in the Balkans.

Brimming with ambition and a larger-than-life self-confidence that masked a deep insecurity, Holbrooke was relentless in pursuit of what he thought was the right approach. When Clinton rejected a suggestion of his, he would simply wait a few days and try again, and if that did not work, try again later. "Richard, I've said no," she once exclaimed. "Why do you keep asking me?" He replied, "I just assumed at some point you would recognize that you were wrong and I was right." What amused and impressed Clinton, however, grated on Obama and others. The running joke among some officials when he arrived for a meeting was, "The ego has landed." When Clinton fell and injured her elbow, Colin Powell, the former secretary of state, and John Podesta, her husband's former chief of staff, each emailed her separately to joke that Holbrooke must have tripped her in hopes of taking her job. Obama made a similar joke at Holbrooke's expense at a black-tie Washington dinner, quipping that right before Clinton fell, "Secret Service spotted Richard Holbrooke spraying WD40 all over the driveway." Biden at one point called Holbrooke "the most egotistical bastard I've ever met," while adding that as a result, he "may be the right guy for the job." As the Afghan review got started, Holbrooke expected to play a central role, only to discover that this president did not have the same vision.

"Not since Clark Clifford counseled Lyndon Johnson on the Vietnam War has a commander in chief faced such a momentous decision," Holbrooke said pompously during an early meeting, reading from notes as he joined the discussion on a video linkup from Kabul.

"Richard," Obama cut in. "Do people really *talk* like that?"

The internal divisions grew more corrosive as the review dragged on. Many White House officials harbored scorn for James Jones, who seemed oddly detached for a retired four-star Marine general. Jones did not feel the need to brief the president personally, leaving it to Tom Donilon, and he made a point of leaving work to bicycle home in the early evening, long before the president's workaholic aides. The feelings were mutual; Jones referred to the aides as "the water bugs" or "the Politburo." Mike Mullen thought his vice chairman, General James Cartwright, was going behind his back to assist Obama and his political advisers in deflecting the military hierarchy, while Cartwright dismissed Mullen because he had never been a war fighter. Gates worried that Jones would be pushed out and succeeded by the lawyerly, methodical and exceedingly cautious Donilon, who the defense secretary thought would be a "disaster" in the post. As for Petraeus, he complained when he had to talk with David Axelrod, whom he viewed as "a complete spin doctor." Petraeus, viewed warily by Obama's team as a Bush holdover and a political threat, potentially even a Republican challenger in 2012, was effectively banned by the White House from the Sunday talk shows, but he worked private channels with Congress and the news media. And Dennis Blair, the national intelligence director, was fighting with Rahm Emanuel, John Brennan and Leon Panetta.

Prodded by his staff, Obama started the review skeptical of McChrystal's request and resentful that it was being set up as a test of his manhood. "Why is this whole thing being framed around whether I have any balls?" he asked a small group of aides in the Oval Office one day. "I think it's clear I care about Afghanistan because I'm spending all this time trying to get it right."

*

Having dinner at Donilon's house one night, Emanuel wandered into the library and asked what he should be reading as they deliberated about what to do in Afghanistan. Donilon showed him a copy of *Lessons in Disaster*, Gordon Goldstein's book about McGeorge Bundy and the slow, disastrous slide into Vietnam. Emanuel read it and later made sure others in the White House did as well, including Obama. The conclusion they drew from the book was that John Kennedy and Lyndon Johnson failed to question the underlying assumptions about monolithic Communism and the domino theory. Obama and his advisers resolved not to make the same mistake with Al Qaeda and the Taliban.

Biden encouraged this re-examination as he led the opposition to McChrystal's proposed troop buildup, arguing that while Al Qaeda was a threat to the United States, the Taliban really was not. While Al Qaeda was a foreign body, the Taliban could not be wholly removed from Afghanistan because it was too ingrained in the country. Moreover, forces often described as Taliban were actually an amalgamation of militants that included local warlords like Gulbuddin Hekmatyar and the Haqqani network or others driven by local grievances or ambitions rather than jihadist ideology. Treating them as the same as Al Qaeda, in this view, was to inflate their importance. The Taliban could be contained while American forces focused on destroying Al Qaeda. With this in mind, Biden offered an alternative to a major influx of forces that would focus on counterterrorism and training Afghan forces rather than the broader mission of population protection and nation building envisioned by McChrystal.

Fueling the skepticism of a large troop deployment was the economic cost. The Office of Management and Budget predicted that a surge of 40,000 troops on top of existing forces, plus commitments to nation-building projects like electricity and schools, would push the expense of the American venture in Afghanistan to $1 trillion over the following ten years. Obama found himself in sticker shock, watching his domestic agenda vanish in front of him.

Adding to his worries was the mercurial leadership of President Hamid Karzai, who often seemed overtly hostile to his American allies and flirted with Taliban leaders in a way that led some in Washington to wonder whose side he was really on. Richard Holbrooke wanted Karzai out and without much subtlety sought to help his opponent in Afghanistan's election. Karzai prevailed anyway in a campaign marred by widespread corruption and he refused to deal with Holbrooke.

David Petraeus described the Karzai government as "a crime syndicate." Karl Eikenberry, the ambassador, said in a classified cable that Karzai "is not an adequate strategic partner" and "continues to shun responsibility for any sovereign burden." Holbrooke saw little chance for a good outcome. "There are ten ways this can turn out," he told David Sanger of *The New York Times*, "and nine of them are messy."

But McChrystal had the most important advocate in the Situation Room in Gates, a longtime veteran of such reviews who knew how to play the system. Gates kept his counsel early in the process to let it play out. He had a strong ally in Clinton, who if anything seemed even more hawkish than the defense secretary did. Recognizing that it would be politically difficult for Obama to agree to the entire request for 40,000 troops, Gates developed an option that would send 30,000 instead, reasoning that NATO could make up most of the difference.

Warned that anything less would risk the success of the project, Obama was inclined to accept the compromise, but was frustrated that the Pentagon was projecting a long timetable for the deployment. He wanted the extra troops to arrive within six months, just as they had for Bush's Iraq buildup.

"The Petraeus surge was much quicker than that," Obama said. "This has to be a surge like that."

Biden seconded it. "That's goddamn right."

Never mind that Obama, Biden and Clinton had all opposed the Bush surge – now conveniently labeled the Petraeus surge – it had now become the model for what the new administration was trying to do. Indeed, Gates was shocked to hear both Obama and Clinton acknowledge privately during their deliberations that they had opposed the Iraq surge out of presidential primary politics, neither one of them wanting to let the other get to the left of them before the kickoff Iowa caucuses in 2008. Obama would never publicly give Bush credit for turning the Iraq war around, but he now hoped to do the same thing in Afghanistan with a similar concentrated burst of military power and strategy change, only this president would not do so with what he saw as the blank check his predecessor gave the Pentagon.

Obama gathered his team at 8:15 p.m. three days before Thanksgiving in a Situation Room strewn with coffee cups and soda cans. The late hour added to the momentous feeling. Obama presented a revised version of Gates's plan titled "Max Leverage" calling for 30,000 more troops to arrive by mid-2010. When combined with earlier troop increases, he would be tripling the total force in Afghanistan. But unlike Bush, he was not making an open-ended commitment. He wanted to start withdrawing the surge troops by July 2011 – two years after the arrival of the first reinforcements he dispatched shortly after taking office. His theory was that if the effort was not working after two years, it probably was not going to work at all.

A few days later, he told his advisers that he was ready to approve the plan. He went around the room one last time to let anyone voice dissent.

"I'm not asking you to change what you believe," he said. "But if you do not agree with me, say so now."

No one said anything.

"Tell me now," Obama repeated.

The advisers fell in line.

"Fully support, sir," Mike Mullen said.

"Ditto," added David Petraeus.

With the decision made, Obama wanted to announce it at an appropriate setting. He flew to West Point in New York on December 1, 2009, to address 4,000 cadets at the United States Military Academy. As he waited to go on stage, he looked out at the crowd of fresh-faced, scrubbed cadets. "They're so young," he noticed. At least some of them could be sent into harm's way by his new war plan, perhaps even killed.

"If I did not think that the security of the United States and the safety of the American people were at stake in Afghanistan, I would gladly order every single one of our troops home tomorrow," Obama told the cadets in a prime-time address televised to the nation. "So no, I do not make this decision lightly." But he argued that the comparison to Vietnam was "a false reading of history."

"Let me be clear: None of this will be easy," he added. "The struggle against violent extremism will not be finished quickly and it extends well beyond Afghanistan and Pakistan. It will be an enduring test of our free society and our leadership in the world."

But he also sent a signal that his commitment was not unlimited. He had instructed his speechwriters to include a quote from Dwight Eisenhower, the hero of World War II, to make the point that the Afghanistan operation would have to compete with other national priorities, presumably like health care and economic stimulus – a balancing that only he, as president, could make. "I must weigh all of the challenges that our nation faces," Obama said. "I don't have the luxury of committing to just one. Indeed, I'm mindful of the words of President Eisenhower, who, in discussing our national security, said, 'Each proposal must be weighed in the light of a broader consideration, the need to maintain balance in and among national programs.'"

No one was particularly thrilled with his decision. Antiwar liberals thought it was a mistake to double down in a losing war. Some of Obama's own advisers agreed. Richard Holbrooke thought the strategy "can't work" and Douglas Lute likewise thought the long review did not "add up" to the decision the president had made. On the other side, Republican hawks welcomed the additional forces but complained that the timetable would handcuff commanders on the front end. The enemy knew it had only to wait out the Americans for another eighteen months. At one point, Senator Lindsey Graham, a Republican from South Carolina, asked Obama how firm he was about the withdrawal deadline. "I have to say that," Obama replied. "I can't let this be a war without end and I can't lose the whole Democratic Party."

*

Barely a week after the West Point address, Obama boarded Air Force One again, this time to deliver a speech in a very different setting. On an overnight flight to Oslo, the president who had just escalated his nation's eight-year-old war in Afghanistan figured out what he wanted to say when he collected the Nobel Peace Prize.

The juxtaposition could hardly have been more powerful or perplexing. In addition to pouring more troops into Afghanistan, Obama had also ordered a dramatic surge of unmanned drones into the skies over Pakistan to launch missiles at presumed terrorist targets and had retained some other controversial national security policies of his predecessor. Somehow he had to reconcile those decisions with the world's most prestigious honor for peacemaking.

The night before leaving for Oslo, Obama stayed up till three in the morning scratching out thirty pages of handwritten passages. He arrived at the Oval Office and handed them to his speechwriters, Jon Favreau and Ben Rhodes, and asked them to merge them with their own drafts. The two worked all day, along with Samantha Power, a presidential adviser known for her book, *The Problem From Hell*, a chronicle of America's failure to stop genocide in Bosnia and elsewhere. By the time they got on Air Force One, they still did not have a finished speech. While most of the other staff members slept during the flight, the three stayed up with Obama, rewriting and rewriting. The president handed Favreau his last edits in the elevator on the way to the ceremony, leaving the harried aides to rush the final changes into the teleprompter even as Obama was walking onto stage.

As Obama was greeted by trumpets and presented to the king and queen of Norway for the honor, his challenge was explaining how a commander in chief could be a champion of peace, how a president prosecuting war could practice diplomacy, how a man who signed deployment orders for soldiers could follow in the footsteps of the Reverend Dr. Martin Luther King Jr. and Mohandas Gandhi. For Obama, it was a chance to explore the concept of a "just war" as debated through the ages:

> As someone who stands here as a direct consequence of Dr. King's life work, I am living testimony to the moral force of nonviolence. I know there's nothing weak, nothing passive, nothing naïve in the creed and lives of Gandhi and King. But as a head of state sworn to protect and defend my nation, I cannot be guided by their examples alone. I face the world as it is, and cannot stand idle in the face of threats to the American people. For make no mistake, evil does exist in the world. A nonviolent movement could not have halted Hitler's armies. Negotiations cannot convince Al Qaeda's leaders to lay down their arms. To say that force may sometimes be necessary is not a call to cynicism – it is a recognition of history, the imperfections of man and the limits of reason."

Obama was only the third sitting president awarded the Nobel Peace Prize, after Theodore Roosevelt, who won for brokering an end to the Russo-Japanese War, and Woodrow Wilson, who won for negotiating the Versailles Treaty after World War I. The difference was that Obama's prize was more of a promissory note than a reward for past service. The committee gave him the prize for "extraordinary efforts to strengthen international diplomacy and cooperation between peoples," but even Obama did not think he had done enough to merit it in just the first few months of his presidency. "To be honest," he said in the Rose Garden on the day the committee made its announcement, "I do not feel that I deserve to be in the company of so many of the transformative figures who have been honored by this prize, men and women who've inspired me and inspired the entire world through their courageous pursuit of peace."

If anything, the prize was a reminder of the gap between the ambitious promise of his words and his actual accomplishments to that point. It drew attention to the fact that while much of the world was celebrating him as the anti-Bush, he had not broken from the previous administration's national security policies as fully as he had once implied he would. And it set off another round of mocking criticism from opponents who chafed at what they saw as Obama's charmed and entitled rise. "The real question Americans are asking is, 'What has President Obama actually accomplished?'" Michael Steele, the chairman of the Republican National Committee, said after the announcement.

Even Obama's advisers did not have a persuasive answer to that question. No one at the White House had so much as thought to prepare for the prize. Word of it arrived at the White House in the form of an email message from the Situation Room at 5:09 a.m., Friday, October 9, 2009, with the subject line, "item of interest." Shortly before 6 a.m., Robert Gibbs, the White House press secretary, telephoned Obama, awakening him with the news.

"Gibbs, what the hell are you talking about?" the president asked.

"You won the Nobel Peace Prize," Gibbs repeated.

"Are you kidding me?"

"I promise you, sir, that I wouldn't wake you up to play a joke. You've won the Nobel Peace Prize."

"Gee. All I want to do is pass health care."

The White House had no idea how to handle what was a decidedly mixed blessing. Some thought Obama should turn it down in recognition that he had not yet earned it. Others thought that would be rude and inappropriate, that the prize could be a spur to achieving what it set out to honor. "I'd like to believe that winning the Nobel Peace Prize is not a political liability," David Axelrod said shortly after the announcement. "But this isn't something I gave a moment of thought to until today." In the end, on that October day, Obama chose to cast it as an honor to America more than him. But it was lost on no one that he ended the day closeted with his national security team talking about intensifying the war in Afghanistan.

*

Obama's three-month Afghan review became a demonstration project, in effect, for a new commander in chief coming to grips with the office. For Obama, like most of his predecessors, the presidency was learned one day at a time. The complexities of policy, the nuances of politics, the clashing interests of competing factions, the trade-offs of any decision — all that took time to master. As he settled into the job, Obama developed his own style and rhythm, yet there were unconscious parallels to those who had occupied the office before him.

In some ways, he seemed like a cross between his two most immediate predecessors. Like Bill Clinton, he enjoyed digging into the details of policy, consumed long memos and books on issues confronting him and solicited views from around the table, as he did during the Afghan review. As he had shown during the auto-bailout debate, he had little patience when briefers recited what had already been presented to him on paper. He would zero in on the one aide sitting in the back of the room who had remained quiet during a discussion, insisting that he or she give a view.

Yet like Clinton, he could also be slow to make decisions, often to the point of exasperating advisers. Any choices that did not come with a hard-and-fast deadline invariably got pushed off. Every possible ramification of a policy option had to be examined and then examined again. The torturous decision-making process became an inside joke among his staff. At key moments in his presidency, when it really counted, Obama could be remarkably decisive, but the rest of the time he wrestled with uncertainty and did not always come out on top. "He was deliberate to a fault," a sometimes frustrated Joe Biden said later.

Like George W. Bush, Obama preferred a disciplined operation and prized order. In his early days in office, he even tried to overcome his own struggles with punctuality, although the longer his presidency went on the more his fidelity to starting and finishing on time seemed to slip. While he often took his time to make a decision, Obama was like Bush in that once it was made, he rarely looked back. He did not revisit policies after they were set, he did not second-guess himself and he did not invite appeals from the losing side of any internal debate.

While Clinton's mind ranged widely and creatively, often seeing connections that others did not, Obama was a linear thinker, logical and clear-headed if not especially innovative or imaginative. Much like Bush, Obama relied mainly on a close-knit circle of advisers he trusted, like Valerie Jarrett, David Axelrod, David Plouffe, Denis McDonough and Ben Rhodes; he was not one to make midnight calls around Washington seeking input from outsiders as Clinton did.

If the people around him learned a lot about Obama from the Afghan review, the president took away his own lessons that would shape the rest of his time in office. In the end, he gave the military most of what it wanted but it left a bitter taste in the

Oval Office. Already convinced that Bush had given the military too much latitude, Obama came away from his first year in office believing that the generals were playing politics with him. Robert Gates sought to reassure Obama that the various leaks and public comments that had stirred the president's ire were happenstance with no ulterior motive. But Gates understood the suspicions. "My position was this is not a deliberate attempt to jam the president," he said later. "It's indiscipline."

Still, Gates bristled at what he thought were untoward efforts by White House officials to dictate to commanders. He resented it when Obama dispatched Denis McDonough to Haiti after a 2010 earthquake to monitor military rescue efforts. "That was a degree of micromanagement I found intolerable," Gates said later. The defense secretary grew so annoyed at White House officials bypassing him to call combatant commanders directly that he ordered a dedicated line at military headquarters in Afghanistan pulled out. He instructed commanders to refer presidential aides to him. "And by the way, they were to say go to hell," Gates said.

He thought Obama did not show enough passion and commitment to the wars he was overseeing and that the president's staff did not show enough respect for the military. "I'm really disgusted with this process," Gates wrote in a note to himself after the West Point speech. "I'm tired of politics overriding the national interest, the White House staff outweighing the national security team, and NSS (Donilon and Lute) micromanagement." He was thinking about leaving earlier than his two-year commitment. "May 2010 is looking a lot more likely than January 2011," he wrote. "I'm fed up."

He did not leave in May 2010, but it was against this backdrop that Robert Gibbs walked over to the private quarters of the White House one evening in June 2010. He had with him a copy of an article by Michael Hastings in *Rolling Stone* magazine profiling General McChrystal. "Stanley McChrystal, Obama's top commander in Afghanistan, has seized control of the war by never taking his eye off the real enemy: the wimps in the White House," read the magazine's summary of the article. The text quoted McChrystal aides disparaging Obama ("didn't seem very engaged"), Biden ("Did you say: Bite Me?"), James Jones ("a clown") and others. McChrystal himself was, by and large, not the author of the offensive statements, but he clearly had assembled a team that openly showed disrespect to the commander in chief and his advisers.

The article set off anger in the White House. McChrystal tried to head off the furor by calling Biden on Air Force Two and, in a brief and confusing conversation over a scratchy connection, warned the vice president that there would be an article coming out that he might not like. Biden was baffled until his staff managed to find a copy. McChrystal also called Gates to apologize.

"What the fuck were you thinking?" Gates asked.

"No excuses, sir," McChrystal answered.

Aides to the president thought the general should be fired. Obama, inclined to agree, ordered McChrystal to fly back from Afghanistan to explain himself. He told his speechwriter, Ben Rhodes, to write two statements for the next day, one declaring that he would keep McChrystal in the interest of a stable military leadership in a war zone and the other announcing that he had fired him to preserve military discipline and reinforce the tradition of civilian control over the armed forces.

While McChrystal made the fourteen-hour flight home, a series of meetings at the White House sealed his fate. "Joe is over the top about this," Obama told Gates. The defense secretary appealed to the president to spare McChrystal, afraid that sacking the Afghan war commander at this stage of the surge operation would undercut the mission. "I believe if we lose McChrystal, we lose the war," he said. But when Obama suggested that he might replace McChrystal with David Petraeus, Gates accepted the decision.

McChrystal arrived at the White House on June 23 with a resignation letter in hand. During a twenty-minute conversation with Obama that McChrystal later called a "short, professional meeting," the general apologized and offered to step down. The president accepted. Then he summoned Petraeus, who happened to be in the building for a separate meeting anyway, and offered him the job. Petraeus took it without taking time out to call his wife first.

Not since President Harry S. Truman fired General Douglas MacArthur during the Korean War had a commander in chief cashiered a top general in the field for insubordinate behavior. The dramatic clash set the tone for Obama's relationship with the military for years to come.

"I welcome debate," he said, "but I won't tolerate division."

Tolerate it or not, his team would continue to have plenty of both. The decision on Afghanistan fully satisfied none of the factions and tension over policy and personality would continue to define his national security team deep into his presidency. McChrystal was not the only one pushed out as Obama struggled to build a cohesive foreign policy. Dennis Blair, his director of national intelligence, was forced out shortly before McChrystal after losing a turf battle with Leon Panetta, a black-belt bureaucratic infighter, over who would control appointment of CIA station chiefs around the world. James Jones resigned as national security adviser in October 2010 after a book by Bob Woodward, *Obama's Wars*, quoted him deriding the president's closest political advisers. Douglas Lute found himself regularly at odds with Gates, Clinton and others who thought he was micromanaging the war efforts from his basement office in the White House. And Karl Eikenberry ran afoul of Clinton and Gates over how to handle Afghanistan.

The case of Richard Holbrooke was perhaps the most poignant, and one that divided Washington between those who found the special envoy for Afghanistan and Pakistan to be an insufferable blowhard who represented all that was wrong with the capital's know-it-all dinner-party circuit and those who saw him as a unique talent wasted by Obama and his team out of petty rivalries at the expense of possibly bringing peace to Afghanistan. The architect of Dayton put together an impressive team of advisers who labored away in their State Department offices trying to repeat history in Kabul, all to no avail. He had been so open about his opposition to Hamid Karzai that he was effectively ostracized by the Afghan government just as he was by the White House. He wanted to launch a full-scale diplomatic initiative with the Taliban, but the White House, dominated by political advisers rather than policy experts, seemed wholly uninterested. "The primary concern of these advisers was how any action in Afghanistan or the Middle East would play on the nightly news, or which talking point it would give the Republicans in the relentless war they were waging against Obama," said Vali Nasr, Holbrooke's deputy.

It did not help when a long piece by George Packer in *The New Yorker* that was originally expected to be a profile of the president's national security team centered instead on Holbrooke, much to the consternation of Obama and his closest advisers. White House aides kept him out of briefings for Obama on Afghanistan and even tried to stop him from attending a meeting between the president and Karzai. When White House aides told Holbrooke that he should step down, Clinton intervened and said that if Obama wanted him out, "he needs to tell me himself." She then told the president directly that if Holbrooke were to be fired it would be "over the objection of your secretary of state."

But even with her protection, Holbrooke could not get Obama's attention no matter what he did. He tried to go see David Axelrod, figuring that was a way of getting to the president, only to be ignored, so one day he followed Axelrod's young assistant into the bathroom in the West Wing to ask why his requests for a meeting had not been granted. In December 2010, when Obama made a secret trip to Afghanistan, Holbrooke was left behind. Spotted at a Washington restaurant that weekend, he seemed glum but tried to spin away the snub, saying he had to stay in the capital to meet with his counterparts from other countries, an excuse that no one bought.

A few days later, Holbrooke met with Clinton at the State Department, clearly frustrated. As he sank down into his seat, she noticed his face and neck turning scarlet red, his chest heaving. An ambulance was summoned and he was raced to George Washington University Hospital, where doctors discovered that he had a ruptured aorta. When one of the doctors asked what she could do to make him more comfortable, he joked, "Ending the war in Afghanistan, that would relax me." That would not happen, of course, nor would twenty-one hours of surgery save him. Two days later, he was dead at sixty-nine, felled before he could pull off another geopolitical miracle, his deathbed words to the doctor taken, rightly or wrongly, as a final rebuke of an indifferent White House.

His memorial service at the Kennedy Center was an all-star Washington affair, attended by presidents, generals, cabinet secretaries, ambassadors, journalists, lawmakers and power brokers of all stripes. Obama came and spoke, delivering antiseptic remarks that expressed no genuine warmth toward his deceased envoy. Holbrooke's many friends in the room sat stone-faced, seeming to hold Obama responsible for his isolation if not his death. When Bill Clinton told the crowd that "I never did understand how people would let the little rough edges" mean that they "didn't appreciate him," everyone understood whom he had in mind.

Fairly or not, Holbrooke's demise became an indictment of an incumbent president too blinkered to use the resources he had available to him and too unwilling to commit to anything other than a temporary military surge to finally resolve the nation's longest-running war.

A few weeks after the service, Obama was still simmering about the narrative. "I'm sick of people writing about how I killed Richard Holbrooke," he groused to aides.

CHAPTER FOUR
'Time to Turn the Page'

Obama was singing Christmas carols with his family at a lavish rental house in Hawaii, celebrating the end of his first year in office, when a military aide arrived with head-snapping news. Someone had just tried to blow up a plane over Detroit, the aide reported. Breaking away from his yuletide respite, Obama got on the telephone with his counterterrorism adviser back in Washington, who told him that a twenty-three-year-old Nigerian man aboard Northwest Airlines Flight 253 had attempted to ignite chemicals hidden in his underwear, only to have passengers and crew members jump him before the improvised bomb could go off.

If not for the quick thinking and instinctive courage of a group of civilians, America would have endured another devastating airborne terrorist attack in the opening year of another presidency. Beyond the nearly 300 people on board, hundreds more on the ground could easily have been killed by an airliner plunging into a big city. More than eight years, two overseas wars, millions of airport pat-downs and hundreds of billions of dollars after the crucible of September 11, the near-miss in the skies over Michigan brought home the grim reality that Islamic radicals determined to wage holy war on America and its allies were not only undefeated but were branching out in dangerous and unpredictable ways.

The initial public response by Obama and his team was less than sure-footed. While the president conducted regular conference calls with his national security team, it took him three days to emerge from seclusion in his island vacation to address the matter in public and, when he did, he was typically cool and dispassionate rather than visceral and reassuring. Obama deemed Umar Farouk Abdulmutallab, the Nigerian by then universally called the underwear bomber, an "isolated extremist," and Janet Napolitano, his secretary of homeland security, declared that "the system worked." Neither assertion was true. Abdulmutallab was affiliated with Al Qaeda in the Arabian Peninsula, a branch of the original terror group operating in Yemen, and the young man's own father had warned American officials about him. Worse, despite all the post-September 11 reforms, the government possessed conversations intercepted by the National Security Agency that it had failed to distribute widely enough to stop him. He was foiled not by the system but by observant and brave people on the plane.

In private, Obama was angry at the breakdown. "Let me make this very clear to you," he told advisers on the phone. "While I understand intelligence is hard and I'll never fault anybody for not having full intelligence, what I will fault is when we have full intelligence that's not shared."

After hanging up, aides scrambled to organize a fresh statement to reporters. Denis McDonough typed out a draft on the president's laptop in Hawaii as an impatient Obama hovered over his shoulder.

"What's the deal?" Obama asked, agitated at the delay.

"I'm just about done," McDonough said.

"Well, just move over," Obama said.

The president sat down and finished it himself. His eventual statement acknowledged a "systemic failure" but it did not quell the political furor that followed and Obama and his team were caught off guard by the intensity of the criticism. The Christmas bombing attempt proved a painful experience, forcing Obama to re-examine his assumptions about the nation's security. "The fact that this guy came as close as he did – basically the detonator didn't work – and the fact that we hadn't detected it in advance really came as a shock to them," said John McLaughlin, a former deputy CIA director who later participated in a review of the incident for the administration.

Obama was the first president to take office in the Age of Terror ushered in by September 11, and he inherited two struggles from George W. Bush – one with Al Qaeda and its ideological allies and another that divided his own country over issues like torture, prosecutions and what it meant to be an American. The first had proved complicated and daunting. The second made the first look easy.

Where Bush saw black and white, Obama saw gray. Where Bush felt the threat of terrorism in his gut, Obama thought about it in his head. Where Bush favored swagger, Obama was searching for a more supple blend of force and intellect. Where Bush saw Islamic extremism as an existential threat akin to Nazism or Communism, Obama believed that overstated the danger and played into terrorists' hands by elevating their stature and allowing them to alter the nature of American society even without another successful attack. Rather than seeing terrorism as the challenge of his time, Obama rejected the phrase "war on terror" altogether, hoping to recast the struggle as only one of a number of vital challenges confronting America much as he did with the war in Afghanistan. The nation was at war with Al Qaeda, he would say, but not with terrorism, which, after all, was a tactic, not an enemy. Perhaps the biggest change Obama made at first was what one adviser called the "mood music" – the choice of language, outreach to Muslims, rhetorical fidelity to the rule of law and a shift in tone from the with-us-or-against-us days of the Bush administration.

As a matter of emphasis and atmospherics, if not policy, the shift was stark. "You've got almost two extremes," reflected

Henry Crumpton, who led the CIA's operation in Afghanistan after September 11 and later served as the State Department's counterterrorism chief under Bush. "You've got Bush 43 who aspired to have a warrior's ethos. He was driven, I think, by that, and in some ways it hurt us with the lack of rigor and examination of some of the consequences of our actions, Iraq being the most horrible example. Obama comes at it from the other extreme. He comes at it like a lawyer would, someone who may not accept and may even reject this idea of a warrior's ethos. And it is a war. You've got guys out there who want to kill us."

*

Obama was a state senator in Illinois when hijacked planes smashed into the World Trade Center, the Pentagon and a field in Pennsylvania. He was driving to a legislative hearing in Chicago as he heard early reports on the radio. When he arrived, he found tall buildings in Chicago being evacuated out of fear of further attacks. "Up and down the streets, people gathered, staring at the sky and at the Sears Tower," he recalled in a memoir.

That day instilled in Bush a sense of unwavering purpose, but Obama's support for the pursuit of Al Qaeda in Afghanistan gave way to doubts about the circumvention of legal structures at home in the name of security. As a Harvard Law School graduate who taught constitutional law and spent part of his childhood growing up in Indonesia, the world's most populous Muslim nation, Obama saw the emerging global campaign through a different lens. By the time he won his Senate seat in Washington and set his sights on the White House, Obama was calling for a new paradigm. "It is time to turn the page," the candidate said.

His own inauguration offered an eye-opening example about just how hard that would be. In the days before his swearing-in ceremony, intelligence agencies picked up reports that a group of Somali extremists was planning to cross the border from Canada to detonate explosives on the National Mall in Washington as the new president took the oath of office. With more than a million onlookers on hand and hundreds of millions more watching on television around the world, what could be a more inviting target? Obama's incoming team sat in the Situation Room with Bush's outgoing team as they evaluated the threat and tried to figure out how to prevent it.

As it happened, the supposed attack turned out to be a "poison pen" case, when one group of radicals ratted out another to get the Americans to take out rivals. For a fledgling president, it was what David Axelrod called a "welcome-to-the-NBA moment before the first game," not to mention a lesson in the fluid, murky nature of terrorism. The challenge, as the episode made clear, was more than just hunting down bad guys; it was distinguishing between what was real and what was illusion – and determining the balance between acknowledging danger and projecting confidence.

For Obama, finding that balance would be a challenge throughout his presidency. He came in promising to correct what he considered the excesses of his predecessor, signing executive orders drafted by his new White House counsel, Greg Craig, banning interrogation techniques like waterboarding and ordering the closure of the prison at Guantánamo Bay, Cuba, within a year. While Craig and others argued that it was important to send a signal of change from the start, other aides, like John Podesta, the new president's transition chief, worried about taking on such fights at the risk of distracting from larger priorities, like fixing the economy.

To change the dialogue with the Muslim world, Obama made a point of giving an interview to Al Arabiya television network a week after taking office and delivered a much-touted speech in Cairo in June 2009 reaching out to those who believed in Islam. To break with the past and demonstrate transparency, he authorized the release of secret Justice Department memos from the

Bush era detailing the use of waterboarding and other techniques that Obama had now banned. Even the words he would use were meant to signal a new day. He would informally banish the rhetoric of the Bush administration. Not only was "war on terror" out, so too were "radical Islam," "Islamofascism" and "evildoers." As he told Al Arabiya, "The language we use matters." At points, however, this would be taken to extremes; when Janet Napolitano used the phrase "man-caused disasters" instead of terrorism, she was roasted by Republicans. Even some Democrats worried that Obama was so focused on political correctness that it might blind him to the very real threat that existed, whatever it was called.

But there were limits to how far Obama would go. When Craig and others wanted to release photographs of abuses by American interrogators in response to a court challenge, Robert Gates and the military objected on the grounds that they would inflame radicals and endanger American troops. General Ray Odierno, the top commander in Iraq, made a personal appeal to Obama during a visit to Washington. Obama sided with the commanders and ordered the photos kept secret.

Small wonder that the debate was more vigorous than Obama's liberal supporters might have expected. In addition to Gates, Odierno, David Petraeus, Mike Mullen and Doug Lute, Obama was still surrounded by veterans of the Bush era, including Michael Vickers, the assistant defense secretary for special operations; Stephen Kappes, the deputy CIA director; Michael Leiter, the director of the National Counterterrorism Center; Daniel Fried, an assistant secretary of state under Bush now tapped to manage the effort to close Guantánamo; Stuart Levey, the under secretary of the Treasury in charge of chasing terrorist financing; Brett McGurk, a White House adviser on Iraq; and Nick Rasmussen, the National Security Council's senior director for combating terrorism at the White House.

Perhaps most important was John Brennan, a career CIA official and former station chief in Saudi Arabia known for setting up the National Counterterrorism Center for Bush. Obama had originally eyed Brennan to be CIA director, but his chances were sunk by liberal protests over his ties to the old order, so instead he was made assistant to the president for homeland security and counterterrorism, a position that did not require Senate confirmation. Solidly built, with a weathered face and close-cropped, retreating hair, Brennan looked the part of a terrorist fighter. And he soon became one of Obama's most trusted advisers, hoping to correct what he saw as the excesses of the Bush administration while defending his old agency against what he considered an overreaction by its critics.

He and Obama were helped in this by none other than Bush, who had pulled back some of the more radical tactics used in the terror war before leaving office. Long before Obama showed up at the White House, Bush had halted waterboarding, emptied the secret CIA black site prisons where terror suspects had been held incommunicado overseas and secured bipartisan Congressional approval for restructured versions of his warrantless surveillance program and military commission system. Bush had even declared that he wanted to close Guantánamo and, while he did not succeed, his team released or transferred about 500 detainees in pursuing that goal.

Obama built on those changes without overturning the whole security apparatus he inherited. He left the surveillance program intact, embraced the Patriot Act, retained authority to use renditions to spirit suspected terrorists out of other countries and embraced some of Bush's claims to state secrets. Obama preserved the military commissions and national security letters he criticized during the campaign, albeit with more due-process safeguards. While he once decried the indefinite detention of terror suspects without charges, he now felt compelled to approve the continued and essentially permanent imprisonment of about fifty Guantánamo inmates deemed most dangerous without ever bringing them to trial. And he dramatically expanded Bush's campaign of unmanned drone strikes against suspected Al Qaeda targets in the tribal areas of Pakistan, authorizing more in his first year in office than his predecessor did in his entire eight-year administration. "The CIA gets what it needs," Obama said during an early meeting in the Situation Room.

In an assessment that Obama the candidate might not have made on the campaign trail, Obama the commander in chief acknowledged that he had inherited from Bush a more measured set of security policies than commonly perceived. "I would distinguish between some of the steps that were taken immediately after 9/11 and where we were by the time I took office," he told *New York Times* reporters one day on Air Force One. "I think the CIA, for example, and some of the controversial programs that have been a focus of a lot of attention, took steps to correct certain policies and procedures after those first couple of years."

Obama was seeking the space where he felt most comfortable, splitting the difference on a tough issue and presenting it as the course of reasoned judgment rather than dogmatic ideology. To the partisans in the long-running national debate over terrorism, Obama's approach had been either a dangerous reversal of the Bush years or a consolidation of them, depending on who was talking. Obama managed the unusual trick of angering both former Vice President Dick Cheney and the American Civil Liberties Union at the same time.

At a private meeting with civil libertarians and liberal activists, Obama got an earful. "Look, you're the only politician I've ever believed in," Anthony Romero, the director of the ACLU, told him, according to others in the room. "When I was a gay Puerto

Rican growing up in New York, I never thought I could identify with a political leader the way I identify with you. But this stuff really pains me."

Obama pushed back, bristling at the comparisons with Bush. But Romero circled back before the meeting broke up, urging the president to prosecute at least a single Bush administration official to make a point about the rule of law.

"Hunt one head and hunt it famously and bring it down to ensure we don't make the same mistakes again," Romero said.

Obama dismissed the notion. "That's one man's perspective," he said.

To some Republicans and veterans of the Bush administration, Obama's approach was something of a validation after so many years of being criticized by armchair terrorist hunters. "The administration came in determined to undo a lot of the policies of the prior administration," said Senator Susan Collins of Maine, the top Republican on the homeland security committee at the time, "but in fact is finding that many of those policies were better thought out than they realized – or that doing away with them is a far more complex task."

Still, others on the right took no solace from Obama's mixed strategy, choosing to focus on the change rather than the continuity. No one was more vocal than Cheney, who had quietly fought a rear-guard action against Bush's own moves toward moderation while the two were still in office. Now that he was a private citizen watching a Democratic president further tempering the counter-terrorism program, Cheney felt free to voice his discontent publicly. Cheney was most agitated at Attorney General Eric Holder's decision to re-investigate whether CIA officers violated anti-torture laws in their interrogations of terror suspects, even though a previous investigation had been closed without charges. To Holder, this was a straightforward matter of accountability and rule of law. To Cheney, it was selling out loyal soldiers who followed orders in the interest of protecting the country at a precarious time.

The debate between Obama and Cheney played out one day in split-screen fashion as the former vice president delivered a speech excoriating the new president's strategy even as Obama was speaking elsewhere in Washington defending his actions. "In the fight against terrorism," Cheney declared, "There is no middle ground."

That was a proposition Obama was determined to test.

*

The test would play out, at least at first, at Guantánamo, the notorious Caribbean prison that had so come to symbolize the Bush-Cheney war on terror. Obama planned to release or send to other countries as many of the detainees as could safely be dispatched and then transfer the remaining inmates to an American prison in Illinois so that the island facility could finally be closed in what he hoped would be a demonstration of change to the world.

Yet even a relatively modest, preliminary move provoked a furor underscoring the difficulty facing Obama. Greg Craig and others decided to start with seventeen Chinese Uighurs who were not affiliated with Al Qaeda or the Taliban and had been swept up by mistake, but could not be sent home to China, where they might be persecuted. When Craig proposed resettling them in the United States, Congressional Republicans revolted and, with Democratic support, voted in May 2009 to ban the administration from transferring prisoners from Guantánamo to American shores.

Craig's adversaries were not only outside the White House. As far as Rahm Emanuel and other top Obama aides were concerned, closing Guantánamo was not a top priority and hardly worth expending the president's limited political capital. With an economy still on the edge, with health care legislation foundering in Congress, with priorities like climate change and immigration eluding Obama, the prison slipped lower and lower on the list. A year came and went and still Guantánamo had not been closed as promised; indeed, a plan by Eric Holder to bring Khalid Sheikh Mohammed, the mastermind of the September 11 attacks, to New York for trial collapsed amid vociferous complaints about security and precedent. Obama's failure to shutter Guantánamo and resolve the cases of its inmates became a sore point not only for him but for many liberals who blamed him for lack of commitment to the values he ostensibly advocated. By the end of the year, Craig, their favorite champion inside the White House, stepped down in frustration.

The debate over how to handle terrorism came at the same time that the nature of the threat seemed to be evolving. On November 5, 2009, a United States Army officer with extreme Muslim beliefs opened fire on fellow troops at Fort Hood in Texas, gunning down dozens of people in a rampage that left twelve soldiers and a civilian dead. The officer, Major Nidal Malik Hasan, an Army psychiatrist, later told authorities that he was trying to protect Taliban leaders in Afghanistan from American troops before they were sent to the war zone to fight "against the Islamic Empire." It was a shocking turn of events – soldiers mowed down not on a foreign battlefield but on their home post by one of their own.

Obama flew to Texas to lead an outdoor memorial service, standing in front of thirteen sets of boots, rifles, helmets and photographs to symbolize the thirteen victims. One by one, he listed the names of those killed and described their hopes and dreams and the families they left behind. "It may be hard to comprehend the twisted logic that led to this tragedy," he told thousands of soldiers and relatives gathered at the nation's largest Army post.

"But this much we do know: No faith justifies these murderous and craven acts. No just and loving God looks upon them with favor. For what he has done, we know that the killer will be met with justice, in this world and the next."

Yet while he linked the massacre to a twisted interpretation of faith, Obama did not use the words "terrorism" or "Islam" in his speech, nor did he address the larger questions raised by the tragedy: How did an American soldier become so radicalized in the first place? Did this count as an international terrorist attack? And if so, what could the country do to protect itself against enemies within?

The danger of terrorism seemed more insidious as a new generation of homegrown extremists emerged. During the first year of Obama's presidency, authorities arrested a number of American citizens and legal residents plotting attacks. Among them was Najibullah Zazi, an airport-shuttle driver trained in Pakistan who went to New York near the anniversary of the September 11 attacks intent on mounting what he called a "martyrdom operation" by blowing up himself and others on the subway with a homemade bomb. Authorities also arrested David Coleman Headley, a Pakistani-American who had aided terrorist attacks in Mumbai, India; a group of Somali-Americans from Minnesota who wanted to fight in Somalia; and five American Muslims from Virginia who traveled to Pakistan to join the jihad there.

Tying together several of the threats was a single American-born radical cleric named Anwar al-Awlaki, who after September 11 initially preached moderation and then left the United States for Yemen, where he became a leading figure in Al Qaeda in the Arabian Peninsula. Awlaki was an increasingly powerful voice in extremist circles, attracting a large following with audio-taped lectures, a Facebook page and web site, particularly in the English-speaking world, where he was that rare Al Qaeda figure with fluent and even colloquial command of the language. Acolytes made the pilgrimage to Yemen to meet with him. Authorities in the United States, Britain and Canada found Awlaki's calls for violence on the laptops of nearly every suspected terrorist they arrested.

Abdulmutallab, the underwear bomber, told the FBI that his attempted plot was approved and partly directed by Awlaki. Hasan, the Fort Hood shooter, was inspired by the radical cleric and sent him email messages asking his views on the religious justification for killing American soldiers, although Awlaki was noncommittal in his responses. Zazi, the would-be subway suicide bomber, testified that he was radicalized by Awlaki's message, listening to more than 100 hours of taped lectures by the American cleric and another extremist imam. Clearly, Awlaki and his disciples with blue passports or green cards were going to be a recurring threat for Obama's presidency.

Obama was still determined to put that threat in perspective and not let it consume his administration, but he emerged from the string of events all too aware of how serious they were. After the attempted Christmas bombing, Robert Gibbs, consciously or not, used the term "war on terror." And Obama made almost as many statements about terrorism in the two weeks following the foiled plot as he had in the eleven months preceding it.

"Our nation is at war," he declared the day after New Year's.

"We are at war," he said again five days later.

*

For all of that, Obama preferred to think of himself as a peacemaker rather than a warrior and even as he confronted the country's new-generation enemy he was concentrating on forging a better relationship with the country's old-generation enemy. When he arrived in office, ties between the America and Russia had deteriorated to their lowest point since the Cold War. Vladimir Putin had spent the last nine years rebuilding his country after its post-Soviet economic and geopolitical collapse, increasingly challenging what he saw as the illegitimate, unipolar hegemony of the United States.

Putin grew up in a communal apartment in Leningrad, an undersized boy chasing rats in the hallways and picking fights with bigger kids to prove he was tough. As a mid-level KGB officer stationed for a time in East Germany, he resented the demise of the Soviet Union, which he later called the "biggest geopolitical catastrophe" of the twentieth century. He rose to power in the post-Soviet Russia by playing loyal functionary to a series of powerful figures and since his ascension at the turn of the century, he had set about reconsolidating power in the Kremlin and rebuilding the great state he believed Russia should be.

In the latter years of George W. Bush's presidency, Putin grew increasingly aggressive in the international arena, especially in the so-called near-abroad states around Russia that had previously been ruled by Moscow until the collapse of Soviet power. He bitterly opposed America's war in Iraq and was convinced that the United States intelligence apparatus was behind what came to be called the color revolutions in former Soviet republics – the Rose Revolution in Georgia in 2003, the Orange Revolution in Ukraine in 2004 and the Tulip Revolution in Kyrgyzstan in 2005. With each passing year, Putin became more convinced that Washington was secretly bent on regime change not just in places like Kiev and Tbilisi but even in Moscow. In the months before the 2008 election that brought Obama to power, Russia invaded Georgia, flexing its muscles and making clear that it expected to remain the dominant power in its own neighborhood.

Obama had no stake in the old rivalries and thought it was counterproductive to be at odds with Russia in this new era. He resolved to "reset" the relationship and seek out areas where the two could work together, even as they continued to disagree on major points of dispute. He and Putin would never see eye to eye; the master of the Kremlin still had "one foot in the old ways," Obama observed shortly before they met. When they sat down for the first time in Moscow in the summer of 2009, Obama made the mistake of opening their discussion by noting that he understood that the Russians had some grievances; Putin then launched into an uninterrupted monologue outlining them in great detail. Obama did not get a word in for fifty-five minutes. While he was perfectly comfortable delivering lectures, Obama did not especially enjoy being on the receiving end. But he was patient and made his case for the reset. "When Putin ranted about the stupidity of invading Iraq, Obama responded calmly that he agreed," said Michael McFaul, the president's Russia adviser. After all, Obama had opposed the war too. Putin seemed surprised.

But while the two had not exactly made a personal connection, Obama held out hope that he could make progress with Russia. His real plan was to work around Putin. The Russian had officially stepped down as president in 2008 in theoretical compliance with Russia's constitutional two-term limit, but he set up his protégé, Dmitri Medvedev, as a caretaker replacement and took for himself the role of prime minister. Everyone understood that Putin was still the paramount leader regardless of title, but Obama embarked on a strategy aimed at forging a friendship with Medvedev, a young, Western-oriented lawyer, in the hopes that they could see eye to eye. Perhaps by working together, Obama could elevate Medvedev's profile on the world stage and build him up as a genuine power center of his own in Russia.

The initiative got off to an embarrassing start when Hillary Clinton presented her Russian counterpart, Sergey Lavrov, with a button marked with the Russian word *peregruzka*, which she had been told meant "reset." Actually, it translated to "overcharge."

When Lavrov explained the error, Clinton laughed. "We won't let you do that to us, I promise," she told him.

Despite the gaffe, Obama and Medvedev went on to collaborate in several areas, striking an agreement allowing American troops bound for Afghanistan to travel through Russian air space and securing Moscow's support for tougher sanctions against Iran in hopes of pressuring it to give up its nuclear program.

Most important to Obama was a new arms control treaty to replace the expiring Strategic Arms Reduction Treaty, or START, agreement of 1991. Obama saw such a treaty as the opening bid on a broader drive to eventually eliminate nuclear weapons around the globe, a goal that would prove more elusive.

Treaty talks leapt from London to Moscow to Geneva to Singapore to Copenhagen to Washington with twists and turns that extended months beyond the original deadline and required ten rounds of talks by full-time negotiators in Geneva. Ultimately, it kept coming around to intense personal interventions between Obama and Medvedev, who met or talked by telephone fourteen times to hash through the disputes. It came close to falling apart when Medvedev suddenly reintroduced the idea of limiting missile defense into the discussions at the last minute, which was a nonstarter with the Americans. At the end of that conversation, as Obama hung up the phone, he was steaming. "I saw him genuinely angry for the first time," said McFaul.

Ultimately, Medvedev backed down and the two agreed to the final terms. Under the New Start treaty they fashioned, both countries would pare back their nuclear arsenals within seven years to their lowest levels in decades, with no more than 1,550 strategic warheads and 700 deployed launchers each. While those represented relatively small reductions compared to previous treaties, the agreement provided for the resumption of on-site inspections, which had halted when the original START treaty expired the year before.

In April 2010, Obama flew to Prague to sign the new pact with Medvedev in the majestic, gilded hall of Prague Castle. "Today is an important milestone for nuclear security and nonproliferation, and for U.S.-Russia relations," Obama declared. Medvedev, adopting an American phrase from Obama, called it a "win-win."

Back in Moscow, Putin acquiesced to Medvedev's collaboration with Obama for the time being. But his was a zero-sum worldview. There was no win-win, as far as he was concerned, only win-lose. The competition, in his mind, was not over.

*

Obama's days were never focused just on one issue. Like any president, he had to juggle a myriad set of problems, domestic and international, simultaneously. In that second year of his presidency, there were natural disasters and man-made disasters, opportunities and setbacks, sometimes all in the same day.

In January 2010, a monster earthquake ravaged Haiti, collapsing buildings and killing as many as 300,000 people in what was already one of the most impoverished nations on the planet. The killer quake measured 7.0 on the Richter scale, making it the most powerful to hit Haiti since the eighteenth century and leaving in its wake unfathomable scenes of destruction and death. Obama responded as American presidents do, with expressions of grief and promises of aid. He dispatched an aircraft carrier and thousands of American troops to help with relief efforts and committed the first of what would become $4 billion for humanitarian relief and longer-term reconstruction. And he tapped two predecessors, George W. Bush and Bill Clinton, to lead a fund-raising drive.

No sooner had Obama put a response in place for Haiti than he faced another seismic event, this one at the intersection of politics and the law. A year after Obama appointed Sonia Sotomayor to the Supreme Court, Justice John Paul Stevens announced his retirement, opening a second seat for the president to fill. The president did not have to search far for his candidate. He picked Elena Kagan, his own solicitor general, naming a second woman in a span of two years. Kagan had never been a judge herself and would be the first new justice without prior experience on the bench in nearly forty years, breaking the hold of what some called the judicial monastery on the high court. On the other hand, she preserved the Ivy League monopoly on the court. A graduate of Princeton and Harvard, she had worked as a policy aide in Clinton's White House before becoming the first woman to serve as dean of Harvard Law School. The Senate confirmed her after only a modest fight, in part because, like Sotomayor, her appointment effectively replaced a liberal with a liberal and did not shift the balance on the court.

That victory for Obama, though, was overshadowed by another disaster on America's southern flank. An explosion on an oil rig in the Gulf of Mexico in April 2010 killed eleven workers and unleashed a gusher of oil and methane gas from an uncapped wellhead a mile beneath the surface. What started as a human tragedy soon transformed into an environmental catastrophe as millions of gallons of oil spread through the area and washed up on the shores of Louisiana and elsewhere along the coast.

For eighty-seven days, the spill at BP's Deepwater Horizon platform seemed to confound Obama, defying his best efforts to stanch the leak and appear in command. As powerful as a president may be, the spill demonstrated that there were limits, and many compared Obama's uncertain response to Bush's handling of Hurricane Katrina. Eventually, he dispatched his energy secretary, Steven Chu, a Nobel Prize-winning physicist, to take a hands-on role in directing the effort. But even the president's eleven-year-old daughter, Malia, seemed baffled by his inability to quickly fix the problem. "Did you plug the hole yet, Daddy?"

she asked him one morning in the bathroom while he was shaving. It would not be until July, nearly three months later, that he would be able to tell her yes.

Critics in both parties piled on. A web video posted by the National Republican Senatorial Committee spliced Obama's own "never again" words about Katrina together with liberal commentators demanding that he do something about the oil spill. Among them was James Carville, the flamboyant Democratic strategist and television pundit who had a home in Louisiana. "He just looks like he is not involved in this," Carville groused. "Man, you got to get down here and take control of this and put somebody in charge of this thing and get this thing moving. We're about to die down here." It got so bad that David Axelrod one day fielded a call from none other than Donald Trump, the real estate mogul and reality television star, offering to help. "I know how to run big projects," Trump told him. "Put me in charge of this thing and I'll get that leak shut down and the damage repaired." Axelrod politely brushed him off.

Obama employed most of the tools of his office to respond. He imposed a deep-water drilling moratorium, traveled repeatedly to the region to demonstrate his commitment, fired the director of an ineffectual regulatory agency and appointed a commission to study what had happened. He held a news conference to acknowledge responsibility, saying he "was wrong" to assume that oil companies were prepared for the worst as he authorized expanded offshore drilling. He conceded that his administration did not move with "sufficient urgency" to reform regulation of the industry, that in the case of the BP spill it "should have pushed them sooner" to provide images of the leak, and that "it took too long for us" to measure the size of the spill.

Finally, on June 15, nearly two months after the explosion, Obama summoned cameras to make the first prime-time Oval

Office address of his presidency, reassuring the nation that he was fully engaged in the crisis and vowing to hold accountable those responsible. He asked for prayers to "guide us through the storm towards a brighter day."

But he knew that if he got through this one, there would be another storm. "The oil spill," he said, "is not the last crisis America will face."

Nor the last one Obama would.

CHAPTER FIVE
'Sleepless Nights'

For all the burdens of life in the White House, there were moments when it was pretty fabulous being president. For Obama, one such moment came during his second birthday while living in the executive mansion. The birthday boy wanted to play a little pickup basketball – so he gathered some of the game's all-time greats for a tournament that he would personally organize.

Among the players he brought to a court at Fort McNair near the White House that day in the summer of 2010 was a stunning list of legendary hoopsters, including Alonzo Mourning, Bill Russell, Grant Hill, Magic Johnson, Chris Paul and LeBron James. With the glee of a fantasy fan setting up his own personal all-star game, Obama personally divided the players into four teams, taking care to even them out by skills. "I didn't get picked?" an astonished James asked when he did not make the first two teams. "I'm on Team C? How'd I get on Team C?"

Now forty-nine, Obama was among the youngest presidents, still energetic, trim and fit. He loved basketball and played frequently, the first president to shoot hoops on a regular basis. Indeed, he had the White House tennis court retrofitted so it could be used as a regulation-sized basketball court. He was famous for his intense play, trash talking aides he did not think were carrying their weight. He had "this instinct of being a killer" on the court, said Education Secretary Arne Duncan, a friend from Chicago who regularly suited up. "At the end of the game, Barack always wants the ball." At one early game, he was playing physical defense when a young official from the Congressional Hispanic Caucus accidentally slammed his right elbow into Obama's mouth, inflicting an injury requiring twelve stitches. In a show of forgiveness, Obama sent him a three-photograph sequence of the episode framed and signed to "the only guy who ever hit the president and never got arrested." Still, there was a limit to amnesty; the man with the sharp elbow was never invited back.

The bro culture on the court spilled over into the testosterone-filled White House, which was populated by fist-bumping young men. While there were women in Obama's orbit who wielded considerable clout, most prominently Hillary Clinton and Valerie Jarrett, the West Wing at times had the feel of a men's college dominated by such large personalities as Rahm Emanuel, Larry Summers, David Axelrod, Robert Gibbs and the president himself. When Mark Leibovich of *The New York Times* set out to write about the boys' club, Obama personally managed the efforts to influence the story, asking Jarrett to call the reporter and, in an awkward and patently transparent move, he invited Melody Barnes, his domestic policy adviser, to join his golf foursome for an outing, the first time any woman had been included. Ten days after the article ran, he had dinner with senior women in the White House and listened to their concerns.

But sports was a way for Obama to break out of the sometimes suffocating bubble that constrained any president. Harry Truman once called the White House the crown jewel of the American penal system. Like others who followed Truman, Obama was determined not to be imprisoned. While he had to give up privacy, anonymity and a personal life, one thing he was not willing to give up was his BlackBerry – his one small connection to the outside world. Never mind the security concerns, he insisted that after taking office he still be allowed to carry a smart telephone that he could use for email. So the Secret Service and other government agencies developed a specially designed device that, they hoped, would at least keep the president's communications secure. The messages were designed so that they could not be forwarded and only a handful of selected confidants would have his email address, suddenly becoming the most exclusive list in Washington. Most members of his Cabinet did not have it; neither did leaders of his own party in Congress.

Another way to fight off isolation were the letters from everyday Americans that came into the White House each day. On his second day as president, Obama established a habit of reading ten each day selected by his staff and delivered to the residence around 8 p.m. in a purple folder tucked within his nightly briefing binder six days a week. They commented on the momentous issues of the day or described their own struggles with life. Some asked for help finding a job or getting health care or resolving a dispute. Others asked for nothing other than to be heard by the most powerful person on the planet. For Obama, the letters were a way of staying in touch, however remotely, with the more than 300 million people whose lives were in his care. He generally responded to one or two a day and noticed when the tone became darker as his presidency progressed, with the early thank-you notes and letters of admiration giving way to angrier screeds that started, "Dear Jackass" or "Dear Socialist." As he once put it with a laugh, "I will tell you, my staff is very even-handed because about half of these letters call me an idiot."

For Obama and his family, the White House may have felt like an incongruous home at first, but one they came to appreciate over time. Until just a few years earlier, when sales of his old book took off along with his fame, Obama was still paying off student loans. Now he and his wife and daughters lived in perhaps the most famous house in the world, complete with 132 rooms, thirty-five bathrooms, twenty-eight fireplaces, eight staircases, three elevators and the ghosts of nearly forty prior presidents.

As parents, the president and first lady sought to create a home life that, for all the grandeur, would bear some resemblance to a normal upbringing for Malia and Sasha. Obama, who grew up without a father and had been an absentee dad himself while in the Senate and on the campaign trail, pressed his staff not to schedule out-of-town trips or evening events that would take him away more than two nights a week. He made as many parent-teacher conferences and sports outings at Sidwell Friends School as he could.

Moving into the White House at age forty-five, Michelle Obama told her staff she would devote two or three days a week to official activities, but she considered her primary role to be "mom in chief." She laid down the rules for their daughters: Television only on weekends. Bedtimes initially at 8 p.m. Take up two sports, one of their choosing and one selected by their mother. "I want them to understand what it feels like to do something you don't like and to improve," she explained. At first, she made them write reports about the special visits they took to places like Monticello and Mount Vernon until they protested and she let the idea go. Marian Robinson's decision to move into the mansion to help take care of her grandchildren went a long way toward creating something akin to a functional family. Robinson, however, did what she could to give her daughter and son-in-law space, excusing herself rather than joining them for dinner. "I'm going home," she would say, meaning her bedroom on the third floor.

The Obamas' marriage was a public selling point, seemingly a model match without the psychodramas of the Clintons or the Kennedys – so much so that a movie would eventually be made about their first date. Michelle LaVaughn Robinson was raised in a small apartment on the South Side of Chicago, the rent paid by her father, a water pump operator for the city who struggled with multiple sclerosis, while her mother stayed home to sew the clothes and tend to their daughter and son. Her father, Fraser Robinson III, refused to see a doctor even as his illness eventually stole his vitality. Marian Robinson was calm and unflappable, eventually going to work as a bank secretary to help put Michelle and her brother Craig through Princeton University. After earning a degree from Harvard Law School, Michelle joined a blue-chip law firm in Chicago, where she was assigned to mentor a promising young recruit named Barack Obama, who was two and a half years older than her. She was a check-the-box control freak who color-coded her notes in college; he was a laconic never-in-a-hurry Hawaiian who did not bother to fold his clothes. To her, he was "like a wind that threatened to unsettle everything." He proposed the night he finished his bar exams and they were later married at Chicago's Trinity United Church of Christ by the Reverend Jeremiah Wright, whose fiery sermons would later come to haunt Obama. With the help of in vitro fertilization, they welcomed Malia and Sasha to the family.

By most accounts, Barack and Michelle genuinely admired and loved each other. But theirs was a relationship that had been strained over time as well. She did not care for his career choice or the tradeoffs that came with it. When he was in the Illinois State Senate, away from home from Monday through Thursday night or Friday each week, she felt abandoned and the friction between them was thick and growing. "You only think about yourself," Michelle told him at one point. "I never thought I'd have to raise a family alone." They underwent couples counseling to save the marriage. "It was if at the center of our relationship there were suddenly a knot we couldn't loosen," she later wrote in her memoir. After the counseling, "the knot began to loosen." Even so, she went along with his campaigns only reluctantly. "Each one had put a little dent in my soul and also in our marriage," she said. When he set his eyes on the presidency, the conversations turned "angry and tearful" and she finally signed off in part because she did not think he could actually win.

The White House meant that the separations were no longer quite so constant; not only did he work in the same building where they lived, Air Force One made it a whole lot easier to get back home from a work trip the same day. But there were small, telltale signs of tension. The two did not always spend Valentine's Day or birthdays together and she was away the night of his biggest legislative victory, the passage of his health care program. He would crack little jokes making himself out as a henpecked husband – how she would nag him to hang up his clothes, how she hardly revered him the way others did. At one point, he joked to reporters that had he not been able to pass a child-nutrition bill she favored, "I would be sleeping on the couch." At another point, he was caught on a live microphone joking that he quit smoking "because I'm scared of my wife." These were probably coping mechanisms as much as anything else, but they hinted at a marriage that was more real and more complicated than the storybook fairy tale version.

The "mom in chief" title never fully captured Michelle Obama's actual role in her husband's presidency. In front of the cameras, she could be a dazzling saleswoman for the president's campaigns, certainly the most popular member of his team. Behind the scenes, she was a formidable guardian of the values that animated Barack's run for the White House in the first place. She watched *Morning Joe* on MSNBC after getting up each day and reacted to any criticisms of her husband by sending emails to Valerie Jarrett with her thoughts. She was aggravated by Scott Brown's victory in Massachusetts, seeing it as a sign that Barack was relying on the wrong team of advisers.

For public consumption, Michelle Obama chose safe causes like fighting childhood obesity. She planted the first White House garden since World War II, complete with arugula, fennel, broccoli, carrots, collard greens, onions and shell peas. To promote her healthy eating lessons, her Let's Move! exercise program and her education priorities, she cheerfully "mom-danced" with a wig-wearing Jimmy Fallon, Nerf-dunked on LeBron James and rapped "Go to College" with Jay Pharoah. Although sometimes cast as the "finger-wagging embodiment of the nanny state," as she put it, she took it with good humor, playing along through guest appearances on television shows like *NCIS*, *iCarly* and *Parks and Recreation* and smiling when her husband used her eat-your-broccoli message as a political punch line.

Michelle also played surrogate mom for some of the younger aides, checking with them to make sure they were balancing their lives with all the hours they were devoting to her husband's success. "Who are you dating? Is it serious?" she would ask Reggie Love, the president's personal assistant. "Do you think she's a good person?"

That did not, however, define the extent of Michelle's interests. She did not want to involve herself in policy the way some of her predecessors had – "I don't want to be Hillary Clinton," she said. "I can't be that person" – and she resisted being scheduled. When her husband's staff committed her to an appearance without checking with her first, she refused for nearly a year to agree to any campaign events for the 2010 midterm elections and even when she did only accepted a relative handful. Her East Wing office was so isolated from the rest of the operation that one White House official dubbed it Guam – "pleasant but powerless," as Jodi Kantor of *The New York Times* put it in her book, *The Obamas*.

But behind the scenes, Michelle expressed her views to the one person who mattered most and at times those views filtered into the West Wing. She was not afraid to say when she thought her husband's team was steering him astray and at times even urged him to make personnel changes. She cherished the idea of him as a transformational figure and bristled whenever she thought his staff was turning him into just another politician. That was the last thing she wanted him to be.

"If we can't do this being ourselves," she told Marty Nesbitt, the founder of an airport parking lot company and a close friend, during the campaign, "I don't want to win."

*

For Michelle, life in the White House was a compromise, not a goal. She won raves for her toned arms and her stylish wardrobe. She made a point of supporting new American designers who produced clothes with a back story. But she did not care for the harsh glare of the klieg lights. Her unguarded moments on the campaign trail during the 2008 campaign had put her in the crosshairs in ways she had never imagined. At one point, as her husband's bid to become the first African-American president caught fire, she said, "For the first time in my adult life, I am really proud of my country." She later explained she meant that she was proud to see so many people turning out to vote, but to her husband's opponents it sounded as if she was not sufficiently appreciative of American exceptionalism. She felt burned by the cascade of criticism.

As the first African-American first lady, Michelle Obama traced her roots to a more traditional experience with race in the United States than her multicultural husband. As Kantor and her *New York Times* colleague Rachel Swarns discovered, Michelle was descended from a slave who was impregnated by a white man shortly before the Civil War. Growing up in Chicago's South Side, Michelle earned her way to Princeton University, where she struggled to find her place in a predominantly white environment even as she excelled academically to win a place at Harvard Law School.

In the national spotlight, she found herself accused of "uppity-ism" and called one of her husband's "cronies of color." A cable television network, she noted, "once charmingly referred to me as 'Obama's baby mama.'" (Three guesses which one.) When she took a politically ill-timed, five-star vacation with her daughters to Spain in the early recession days of the administration, a *New York Daily News* columnist dubbed her a "modern-day Marie Antoinette." She bristled at her husband's staff, believing that they both micromanaged her and did not do enough to support her. When she wanted to throw a Halloween party in her first year at the White House, they objected, saying "the optics are just bad." (She went ahead anyway, dressed in a leopard outfit.) She hated that when she wanted to have her hair cut into bangs, it was first run by the West Wing staff to make sure it would not be a problem.

No wonder it seemed perfectly plausible when Carla Bruni, the first lady of France, wrote in a book that Michelle had told her that she loathed life in the White House. "It's hell," she was quoted saying. "I can't stand it." The White House quickly worked to squelch the story. Robert Gibbs contacted the French government to get it to issue a denial and by the end of the day he had managed to keep the story from exploding in the American media.

But at Rahm Emanuel's 7:30 a.m. senior staff meeting the next morning, Valerie Jarrett announced that the first lady was dissatisfied with the way the White House had handled the episode.

Emanuel could see that Gibbs was about to explode. "Don't go there, Robert, don't do it," he said.

But Gibbs could not hold back. He had worked his ass off to protect the first lady and now he was being criticized for it? "Fuck this, that's not right," he snapped. "I've been killing myself on this. Where's this coming from?"

Jarrett did not give any details and Gibbs pressed some more with additional four-letter insistence.

"You shouldn't talk that way," Jarrett said.

"You don't know what the fuck you're talking about," he fired back.

"The first lady would not believe you're speaking this way," she said.

"Then fuck her too!" he shouted and stormed out.

Gibbs later spoke with the first lady's chief of staff, who said Michelle actually had no complaint about his handling of the Bruni book. Gibbs concluded that Jarrett had made it all up and would never treat her seriously again. But whether Jarrett really was venting her own views or the first lady's was never really clear. And Gibbs would leave the White House soon. Crossing the first lady was never healthy in any White House – but in this White House, it was not a good idea to cross Jarrett either.

Jarrett, fifty-three, was more than a White House official; she was practically a member of the Obama family, a fellow transplant from Chicago with no national political experience but a bond that allowed her to anticipate where they wanted to go and nudge them where she wanted them to go. While she held the nondescript title of senior adviser and director of public engagement and intergovernmental affairs, she wielded the unrivaled power of being able to say "the president wants this" or "the first lady wants that." She was the gatekeeper, the protector, the messenger, the enforcer. She weighed in on any issue that interested her and staff memos were regularly marked with telltale "VJ thinks" or "VJ says." She stiffened Obama's spine on issues she considered "first principles," particularly with regard to civil rights.

A single mother with a grown daughter, she was the one who would cross the Colonnade to join the Obamas for dinner in the residence, prompting some rivals to dub her "the night stalker," and she traveled with them to Camp David for the weekend. In private conversations, she still called the president Barack. He used her to stay connected to his old life. "We gossip all the time," Jarrett said. "He's always interested in good stories, particularly stories from back home, because I think we're both homesick and so he'll always say, 'What's going on? Tell me what I'm missing,' because he doesn't watch television, so he doesn't hear a lot of stuff."

Jarrett's influence stemmed in part from longevity and loyalty. She had known the Obamas longer than anyone else in the West Wing, even before they were married. She hailed from one of Chicago's most prominent African-American families – her grandfather built much of the city's public housing, her father was a prominent physician whose work took the family to live for a time in Iran and her mother's efforts in early childhood education were so well regarded that a street was named after her. While working as deputy chief of staff for the mayor, Jarrett offered a young lawyer named Michelle Robinson a job. When Michelle was advised against it by her boyfriend, Jarrett joined the two of them for dinner to make the pitch, thus meeting Barack Obama. Nearly five years older than him, Jarrett became "practically a sister," as Obama later put it, introducing him to the people he needed to know to succeed in Chicago politics. By the time he ran for president, he said, "I don't make any major decisions without asking her about them first."

But Jarrett was the source of enormous enmity – some would say jealousy – within the West Wing. Emanuel detested her so much he tried to steer her toward taking Obama's seat in the Senate after he won the presidency just to keep her out of the White House. Obama was the one to talk her out of that. "Why on earth would you want to be in the Senate?" he asked. But her presence in the West Wing in a second-floor office once occupied by Karl Rove proved to be the challenge Emanuel anticipated. Gibbs, David Axelrod and later Bill Daley, who would become Obama's chief of staff after Emanuel's departure, all clashed with her at times. They doubted her political acumen and felt she was an unchecked force who led the president down the wrong path at times. She had alienated many in the business community to whom she was supposed to be the president's liaison. But Obama would never listen when the others complained. He trusted Jarrett. He could relax around her. He was certain she had only his interests at heart. She was the one non-negotiable member of his team. Everyone else would have to adjust to that or leave. Some did better than others.

Jarrett persevered even as other aides fell by the wayside. Michelle had a way of burning through her own team at first, trading in chiefs of staff several times in the opening couple of years. Her relationship with Desirée Rogers, her friend from Chicago who came to Washington to be the White House social secretary, tattered amid tension over Rogers's high-profile magazine covers and penchant for attending fashion shows, which seemed tone-deaf amid the economic hardship. The friction came to a head after two wannabe reality television stars named Michaele and Tareq Salahi gate-crashed the first state dinner of the Obama presidency being organized by Rogers – not that she was in charge of security.

As the nation's first African-American first lady, Michelle felt the burden of history weighing on her and Barack. It was not enough to set a good example and avoid mistakes – they had to be *perfect*. If a white president's family got in trouble for some misjudgment, that would be par for the course. But if the first black family in the White House screwed up, it felt like it would set back African-Americans for years, even decades. Obama wanted to be the first black president, not the only black president. The pressure was enormous. "We know that everything we do and say can either confirm the myths about folks like us," Michelle said, "or it can change those myths."

By her own telling, even living at the world's most prominent address did not erase the sting of racial misunderstanding. The "insults and slights" directed at her and her husband "used to really get to me," she reflected in the second term. There were "a lot of sleepless nights," she said. "But eventually, I realized that if I wanted to keep my sanity and not let others define me, there was only one thing I could do – and that was to have faith in God's plan for me. I had to ignore all of the noise and be true to myself."

The threats to the family sometimes went beyond politics or misunderstanding. One winter night in the first term, a gunman pointed a semiautomatic rifle out the window of a car parked south of the White House and opened fire. At least seven bullets hit the upstairs residence of the mansion, one smashing into the ballistic glass window in the Yellow Oval Room, where Michelle Obama liked to sit and have tea. The president and first lady were not home at the time, but Sasha Obama and Marian Robinson were. No one realized the building had actually been struck until four days later when a housekeeper noticed broken glass and a chunk of cement. Michelle Obama learned from an usher.

When she and the president met with the director of the Secret Service, her angry voice could be heard through the closed door. Replacing the window took weeks and she often found herself staring at the crater left in the glass, "reminded of how vulnerable we were," as she put it. It was just one of a series of Secret Service mishaps during their time in the White House.

But Michelle, like Barack, was determined not to be trapped in Harry Truman's prison. More than her husband, she got out and about in Washington, dropping in for dinner with friends at BLT Steak a couple blocks from the White House or heading to a Soul-Cycle studio for candlelit workouts that blended the meditative aura of a yoga class with the rhythmic music pulsing of a nightclub.

That was her escape. That was her time outside the bubble. And then she would head back to the big white mansion and the life that she did not ask for.

★

Malia and Sasha arrived at the White House as little girls, smiling, nervous, shy and precocious. Malia was ten when their father took office and Sasha seven, and they would grow up in front of America's eyes. More seen than heard, they survived those awkward years without really making themselves known to the public. Unlike other presidential children, they stayed out of trouble, at least the kind that would land them in the gossip columns. But in political terms, they humanized their emotionally distant father, reinforcing the image of a loving family man with a stable home life.

"I want them to be normal kids, just like you guys, polite and respectful and kind," Michelle Obama once told a group of students. By all accounts, they seemed to be. They loved iPhones and laptops, hung out with friends, played tennis and basketball. They watched *Modern Family* even if their own was anything but typical. Their parents got them two Portuguese water dogs, who pretty much had free run of the building, wandering into the rooms around the Oval Office, sometimes chased by the head groundskeeper, who looked after them when the first family was not around. And they needled their famous father, keeping him grounded in that way that children do. Shortly before his first Inaugural Address, Malia teased him. "First African-American president," she said. "Better be good." Afterward, Sasha let him off the hook. "That was a pretty good speech, Dad."

If the unparalleled opportunities of living in the White House or the unique stresses of having a Secret Service detail in the seventh grade had warped their upbringing, they were adept at hiding it. The girls were taken to the Grand Canyon and Carlsbad Caverns, toured the Eiffel Tower and the slave port in Ghana, strolled down the streets of Havana and boated on Lake Nahuel Huapi in Argentina. There were few celebrities they did not get to meet, including their favorite Jonas Brothers – though not without a tongue-in-cheek warning from the father in chief. "Sasha and Malia are huge fans," he said. "But boys, don't get any ideas. I have two words for you: Predator drones. You will never see it coming."

The girls were shielded in less violent ways. When a toymaker began selling Marvelous Malia and Sweet Sasha dolls, the parents expressed displeasure and the company pulled them. When a Republican Congressional aide berated the girls on Facebook for appearing antsy at the annual Thanksgiving turkey pardon – "try showing a little class" – a backlash forced her to apologize and resign.

The girls were not identical, though. "We have one who generally stays here," the first lady told an interviewer, indicating an even keel. "And then we have one we call our grumpy cat, our salty biscuit. You just never know what you're going to get from that one." Which was which? "I'm not saying – they could be watching."

The Obamas came to town with a no-new-friends philosophy. Wary of the Washington archetypes – the lobbyists and politicians and fundraisers who cozy up to people in power, especially a president, the people who *want* something – they resolved to not fall into the fake-friends trap that ensnared so many other tenants at 1600 Pennsylvania Avenue. And indeed, they remained steadfastly loyal to the friends they already had from Chicago, the ones they were truly close with, who had been there before and would be there afterward. Every Christmas, when they vacationed in Hawaii, their friends would join them, especially Marty Nesbitt and Eric Whittaker, a physician and health care investor, and their families.

Yet if they resisted the celebrity of Washington, they found themselves entranced by the celebrity of Hollywood. For a president who was normally so rational, so self-contained, so un-needy, Obama proved surprisingly eager to socialize with the nation's leading singers and actors and entertainers. After the early-to-bed presidency of George W. Bush, the Obamas brought entertaining back to the White House in a big way, both openly and behind closed doors. Over their eight years, they would give the White House stage to Irish fiddlers, mariachi bands, pop stars and jazz singers. They sponsored the first White House poetry jam featuring James Earl Jones as Othello. They started an annual tradition of hosting a Passover seder. They held dinners for thinkers and filmmakers like Ken Burns. They even brought the cast of the Broadway hit *Hamilton* to perform at the White House.

At one point in the second term, the Obamas secretly gathered 500 people for a star-studded party at the White House where Prince and Stevie Wonder performed. On hand were professional athletes, Wall Street executives, Washington lobbyists, movie stars, members of the Cabinet and plenty of others. The White House called it a private affair paid for by the Obamas and declined to give details. White House veterans dating to the Lyndon Johnson administration could not remember such a large party being held at 1600 Pennsylvania Avenue in secret.

Most of this was for fun, or to highlight the arts, not so much for political schmoozing or high diplomacy. Obama did not bother to use such events to curry favor with the potentates of the capital, nor did he care for formal, black-tie state dinners for visiting foreign leaders any more than Bush did – and not just because of the gate-crashing incident at the first one. Obama held only a few more state dinners than his predecessor did and far fewer than Ronald Reagan, Bill Clinton or George H.W. Bush did.

Instead, Obama preferred to hang out with celebrities and enjoy an eclectic blend of music and art. The list of those who performed at the White House during the Obama era amounted to a who's who of American entertainment. Among them: Burt Bacharach, Joan Baez, Joshua Bell, Tony Bennett, Leon Bridges, Natalie Cole, Sheryl Crow, Gloria Estefan, Aretha Franklin, Jennifer Hudson, Mick Jagger, Booker T. Jones, B.B. King, Nathan Lane, Queen Latifah, Cyndi Lauper, John Legend, Lyle Lovett, John Mellencamp, Smokey Robinson, Paul Simon, Jordin Sparks, Mavis Staples, James Taylor and Justin Timberlake. And of course, Stevie Wonder, an Obama family favorite.

The Obamas seemed to be especially fond of Beyoncé and her husband, Jay-Z, and the president often enlisted celebrities for political causes, discussing Sudan with George Clooney and climate change with Leonardo di Caprio. But he was sensitive about how their presence would be perceived, saying he knew that "somehow it'll be tagged as Obama hanging out with Hollywood stars."

There were moments of tension with some of those Hollywood stars who, like other liberals, grew disenchanted with the president. After the actor Matt Damon criticized him over drone strikes and secret surveillance, Obama fired back with a joke at a black-tie dinner. "Matt Damon said he was disappointed in my performance," Obama said. "Well, Matt, I just saw *The Adjustment Bureau*, so right back at you, buddy."

But Obama was an eager consumer and promoter of popular culture. He released his playlists on Spotify, including songs like *Ain't Too Proud to Beg* by the Temptations, *Paradise* by Coldplay, *Boozophilia* by Low Cut Connie and, of course, *Another Star* by Stevie Wonder. The lists had impact. Streams of Low Cut Connie jumped nearly 3,000 percent overnight. The professionals were impressed. Rarely had there been a president as attuned to popular culture as Obama. As the spokesman for Spotify said, "If he wants a job curating music when this presidential gig is over, we'd take him in a second."

When he was not hanging out with celebrities, Obama could just as likely be found on the golf course. As his presidency wore on and his hair turned gray, Obama had increasingly turned to the links instead of basketball. He still loved hoops – he stayed up late to catch ESPN's *SportsCenter* and made a point of releasing his own NCAA March Madness tournament brackets every spring (although he only picked one champion correctly in his eight years in office). When his hometown Chicago Bulls fired their coach, Obama took to Twitter to lament the move.

But by his own admission, he slowed down as the years wore on. "I used to play basketball more," he told the comedian Marc Maron in his second term. "But these days, I've gotten to the point where it's not as much fun because I'm not as good as I used to be and I get frustrated." He added: "Now I'm one of these old guys who's running around. The guys I play with – who are all a lot younger – they sort of pity me and sympathize with me. They tolerate me, but we all know I'm the weak link on the court and I don't like being the weak link."

So golf became his leisure time preoccupation. He did not especially like Camp David, with its woodsy isolation – Michelle told dinner guests that he was an urban guy – so most weekends he was in town, and if the weather was even passable, he headed to the links, usually at the Secret Service facility in Beltsville, Maryland, where security was as tight as could be. Like most of his modern predecessors, Obama found release on the tees, a chance to escape the confines of his admittedly grand white home, spend a few hours outdoors and even put out of mind, however briefly, the troubles of the nation and the world. He usually played with a set of younger aides or old friends, staying away from other politicians who would pepper him with unwanted requests or advice. But he was relentlessly honest, unlike Bill Clinton, who regularly took mulligans. He counted all his strokes and even played for money. He did not like to talk politics. Over all, he was a fair, not excellent, duffer, generally shooting in the nineties or low one-hundreds, respectable but hardly remarkable.

By his last summer in office, Obama had played his 300th round, making him the most avid presidential duffer since Dwight Eisenhower. Whereas George W. Bush gave up golf in office to avoid looking insensitive to troops fighting overseas, Obama ignored critics who mocked what they presented as his golfing-while-Rome-burns pastime. "Can you believe that, with all the problems and difficulties facing the U.S., President Obama spent the day playing golf," Donald Trump wrote on Twitter at one point, a tweet that would some day seem ironic given his own proclivity for the sport while in office.

Others jabbed him about his performance. Michael Jordan publicly said he preferred not to play with him. "He's a hack, man. It'd be all day playing with him." But Obama reportedly brought his score down into the eighties. As he talked one day with Thomas Friedman of *The New York Times*, he prefaced his perorations on the Middle East to crow that he had just played his best game ever.

"Had an eighty last week," Obama said. He had "a fifteen-foot putt for seventy-nine. I was feeling pretty good. I missed it by about that much."

CHAPTER SIX
'A Shellacking'

On Election Night in November 2010, Obama sat in the White House working the telephones as his secretary fed him number after number to call defeated Democrats. There were a lot of calls to make, nearly one hundred in all. He stayed up until 2 in the morning offering condolences and then started again the next day. One of those he reached was a young freshman Democrat from Virginia named Tom Perriello. There were few stronger supporters of Obama's economic and health care programs than Perriello, despite his conservative-leaning district in the largely rural rolling fields of Virginia, and Obama made a special point of trying to rescue him with a rally the Friday before the election. It did not help. Perriello fell along with dozens of his colleagues. "Brutal," Obama wrote in an email to David Axelrod around midnight.

The midterm elections of 2010 proved to be a painful rejection for Obama, a repudiation by voters of a president they had elected with such enthusiasm just two years earlier. Republicans picked up a whopping sixty-three seats in the House, the biggest swing between parties in a midterm election since 1938, yielding the largest G.O.P. majority since 1948. Although Democrats hung onto the Senate, they lost six seats there too, narrowing their control of the chamber. Overnight, the gauzy hope of 2009 had faded into the stark reality of divided government. "I'm not recommending for every future president that they take a shellacking like I did last night," Obama said ruefully. "I'm sure there are easier ways to learn these lessons."

The shellacking was particularly painful for Obama because he realized that many of the losing Democrats, like Perriello, went down because of their support for him or his programs. It was his "responsibility," to use the word he repeated in front of reporters ten times the day after the vote. "We didn't realize how deep the loss was going to be," Pete Rouse, the president's senior adviser, said later. "The president felt for a number of House Democrats, in particular, who lost in part because of sticking with him on some tough votes, and how many of them, had they voted differently, might have still been there. That was really weighing heavily on him."

The president who muscled through Congress perhaps the most ambitious domestic agenda in a generation now found himself vilified by the right, castigated by the left and abandoned by the middle. He presided over a White House that felt shell-shocked, where aides were busy wondering whether the best days of the Obama presidency were now behind them. Some advisers who had been ready to carve a new spot on Mount Rushmore for their boss two years earlier privately conceded that he would never be another Abraham Lincoln after all. In the toxic environment of Washington, they concluded, the deck may be so stacked against a president that any of them were doomed to be, at best, average. "'Arrogance' isn't the right word," said one, "but we were overconfident."

They were not helped by an economy that stubbornly resisted Obama's most fervent efforts to jump-start it. By the end of his first year in office, it looked like the economy was beginning to turn around, but it hit the skids by the spring of his second year. Rahm Emanuel blamed the stall on a series of factors that he called the "G-force" – the gulf explosion, the financial collapse of Greece, the latest conflict in Gaza and a Germany reluctant to bail out its irresponsible European partners. The markets gyrated with unsettling ferocity. "You felt like you were finally getting everything moving and then, boom," Emanuel said.

In a fit of optimism, or perhaps self-delusion, the White House then began promoting what it called "Recovery Summer." Except that it wasn't. The early forecast by the White House economists Christina Romer and Jared Bernstein that had confidently predicted that unemployment would top out at 7 percent in 2010 if Congress passed the stimulus package proved ludicrously rosy; the jobless rate actually hit 10 percent in October 2009 and was still stuck at 9.6 percent as "Recovery Summer" opened in 2010. In theory, an explosion of stimulus-financed, job-creating public works projects was due that season – repairing old highways and building new ones, weatherizing homes, cleaning water sources. But it would not be enough to be felt by voters in the fall and the cost of Obama's initiatives was piling more debt onto the nation's balance sheet. His approval rating slid to 43 percent in August, the lowest level of his presidency to that point.

As he sorted through the wreckage, Obama mulled the lessons of the past and examined his decisions. "History never precisely repeats itself," he mused one day during an interview in the Oval Office with *The New York Times*. "But there is a pattern in American presidencies – at least modern presidencies. You come in with excitement and fanfare. The other party initially, having been beaten, says it wants to cooperate with you. You start implementing your program as you promised during the campaign. The other party pushes back very hard. It causes a lot of consternation and drama in Washington. People who are already cynical and skeptical about Washington generally look at it and say, This is the same old mess we've seen before. The president's poll numbers drop. And you have to then sort of wrestle back the confidence of the people as the programs that you've put in place start bearing fruit."

The easy thing, of course, would be to blame the Republicans for waging a nonstop campaign of obstruction against him, and Obama certainly subscribed to this view. But even while he expressed no regrets about the broad direction of his presidency, he did identify what he called "tactical lessons." He had let himself look too much like "the same old tax-and-spend liberal Democrat," he said. He realized too late that "there's no such thing as shovel-ready projects" when it comes to public works. Perhaps he should not have proposed tax breaks as part of his stimulus and instead "let the Republicans insist on the tax cuts" so they would have some ownership over the final package and it could be seen as a bipartisan compromise.

Still, Obama did not disguise his disdain for Washington and the conventions of modern politics. He thought of the capital as a staged show, filled with too much fakery and not enough substance. When he emerged from the Oval Office during the day, he sometimes paused before the split-screen television in the outer reception area, soaked in the cable news babble, then shook his head and walked away. He had little patience for what Valerie Jarrett called "the inevitable theater of Washington."

But in politics, theater mattered, a rule of life that Obama kept relearning, however grudgingly. Symbols told stories. Narrative defined politics. Small things he did not think important took on disproportionate meaning. His decision to redecorate the Oval Office, for instance, was criticized as an unnecessary luxury in a time of austerity, no matter that it was paid for by private funds. On the campaign trail, he thought it was silly to wear a flag pin, as if that were a measure of his patriotism, until his refusal generated distracting criticism and one day he showed up wearing one. Likewise, he thought it was enough to pray in private while living in the White House, and then a poll showed that most Americans were not sure he was a Christian; sure enough, a few weeks later, he attended services at St. John's Church across from Lafayette Square, photographers in tow.

Obama's supreme faith in his own judgment left little room for doubt. One prominent Democratic senator concluded that

Obama's biggest problem was that he was not insecure – he always believed that he was the smartest person in any room and never felt the sense of panic that made a good politician run scared all the time, frenetically wooing lawmakers, power brokers, adversaries and voters as if the next election were just a week away.

Perhaps not surprisingly then, Obama chose to attribute most of his problems in that fall of 2010 to a failure to communicate the merits of his policies, not the policies themselves. "Given how much stuff was coming at us," he said, "we probably spent much more time trying to get the policy right than trying to get the politics right." He and his team took "a perverse pride" in doing what they thought was the right thing even if it was unpopular. "And I think anybody who's occupied this office has to remember that success is determined by an intersection in policy and politics, and that you can't be neglecting of marketing and PR and public opinion."

That presumed that what he had done was the right thing, of course, a matter of considerable debate. At that point, the left thought he had done too little and the right too much. But what was striking about Obama's self-diagnosis in that moment of defeat was that, by his own rendering, the figure of inspiration from 2008 neglected the inspiration after his election. He did not stay connected to the people who put him in office in the first place. Instead, he simultaneously disappointed those who considered him the embodiment of a new progressive movement and those who expected him to reach across the aisle to usher in a postpartisan era. On the campaign trail throughout that fall of 2010, he confronted that disillusionment – the woman who told him she was "exhausted" defending him, the mother whose son campaigned for him but was now looking for reaffirmation. Even the artist who made the iconic multi-hued "Hope" poster said he was losing hope.

The policy criticism of Obama, of course, was confusing and

deeply contradictory at the same time – he was a liberal zealot, in the view of the right, or a weak accommodator, in the view of the left. He was seen by some as an anti-capitalist socialist and by others as too cozy with Wall Street. He was somehow both a weak-on-defense apologist for America and the validator of George W. Bush's unrelenting anti-terror tactics at the expense of civil liberties. Pummeled from both sides, Obama was frustrated and, at times, defensive. At a Labor Day event in Milwaukee, he complained that the special interests treated him badly. "They're not always happy with me," he told supporters. "They talk about me like a dog – that's not in my prepared remarks, but it's true."

The friendly fire bothered him the most. "Democrats just congenitally tend to see the glass as half-empty," he groused at a fund-raiser in Greenwich, Connecticut, where he mocked the bellyachers in his party. "If we get an historic health care bill passed – oh, well, the public option wasn't there. If you get the financial reform bill passed – then, well, I don't know about this particular derivatives rule, I'm not sure that I'm satisfied with that. And, gosh, we haven't yet brought about world peace. I thought that was going to happen quicker."

In some ways, of course, Obama had no one to blame for inflated expectations but himself. Not only did he benefit from them in 2008, he consciously lifted them, promising grandiloquently to do no less than heal the planet. "I make no apologies for having set high expectations for myself and for the country because I think we can meet those expectations," he reflected that day in the Oval Office. "Now, the one thing that I will say – which I anticipated and can be tough – is the fact that in a big, messy democracy like this, everything takes time. And we're not a culture that's built on patience." Now he faced two years in which he had to skillfully lower expectations again so that he could rebound from defeat and win a second term.

For comeback lessons, Obama turned to the so-called Comeback Kid himself, Bill Clinton. The shellacking Obama had taken echoed powerfully the Republican Revolution of 1994 that left Clinton with both houses of Congress in opposition hands. Fitfully at first, deftly after a while, Clinton managed to pivot away from that defeat to handily prevail in his re-election bid just two years later.

That Obama was turning to Clinton for advice was remarkable. Just two years earlier, as a candidate, Obama had scorned the forty-second president, deriding his small-ball politics and triangulation maneuvering while comparing him unfavorably to Ronald Reagan, a more transformative leader. Running against the former president's wife, Obama had been the anti-Clinton. Now he was hoping to be the second coming of Bill Clinton – because, in the end, of course, it was better than being the second coming of Jimmy Carter.

To Obama, Clinton had been everything that was wrong about the Democrats of the 1990s, the exemplar of the self-indulgent baby boomers constantly playing out their dramas in public. Clinton was famously undisciplined and loquacious, a whirling dervish of energy, ambition and raw politics, all traits that tended to turn off Obama, who saw himself as more high-minded. To Clinton, Obama had not paid his dues in some backwater like Little Rock, instead rocketing to the top on star power and little else. Clinton, after all, was competitive and perhaps even a little jealous; it rankled that this upstart could eclipse him. And so, for the two most dominant Democrats of their era, Obama and Clinton were not exactly friends. When their two staffs finally arranged for a bury-the-hatchet golf game between the two, Clinton's non-stop chatter and constant mulligans wore out the younger man. Asked by aides how it went, Obama said, "I like him – in doses."

Within weeks of the midterm election, though, Obama developed a new appreciation for Clinton. He came to recognize the native skill that had taken Clinton so far and helped him endure so many setbacks only to bounce back again. He was reading books on Clinton's time in office and cut a Clintonian-style deal with Republicans on tax cuts. At one point, it even looked as if Obama had actually outsourced his presidency to Clinton. On a quiet Friday afternoon that fall, the two were meeting in the Oval Office to discuss Obama's post-midterm recovery plans when suddenly they decided to go talk with the reporters hanging out in the briefing room. Rarely a spontaneous man, Obama found he could not even open the door to the briefing room because it had been locked and he had to ask someone how to get through. Then after talking with reporters for a few minutes, Obama excused himself to head to another obligation, but Clinton stayed behind, happily holding forth on the state of politics and answering questions as if it were a decade earlier and he were still the commander in chief.

Clinton had recovered from his own midterm debacle through a mix of conciliation and confrontation. He tacked to the political center by cutting deals with Newt Gingrich's Republicans on issues like welfare reform, but he relished fighting with them over budget issues that led to a partial government shutdown. Whether Obama could duplicate the feat remained uncertain. He was not as nimble a politician as Clinton, and while he was more of a pragmatist than his critics wanted to admit, he was not instinctively the centrist Clinton was.

"There's a lot to learn from what the Clinton White House did in 1994 forward with a similar situation," said Dan Pfeiffer, who had been promoted to White House communications director. "But it's also important to understand we're not in the exact same situation." Indeed, Gingrich's Republicans, while profiting off public discontent with Clinton, came to office with a set of ideas they wanted to advance, some of which happened to coincide with the president's. The Republicans now taking over the House were animated far more deeply by public opposition to Obama than by any particular policy prescriptions. Moreover, Clinton presided over fundamentally better times – unemployment was at 5.6 percent then, compared with 9.8 percent at that point under Obama, and the country was at peace under Clinton, while the wars in Iraq and Afghanistan still consumed the American military in Obama's time.

The first decision Obama had to make after the shellacking was how much political capital to invest in trying to pass leftover legislation in the post-election lame duck session of a Democratic Congress before the House gavel was handed to the Republicans. Obama focused right from the start on an ambitious agenda for the departing Congress, to the point of disregarding the election results in favor of lame-duck legislating. "The next day he came into the office and said, 'We got our butts kicked, but we've got a lame-duck session here, and I've got a lot I want to get done,'" David Axelrod recalled. "He recited a lengthy list. And everybody kind of looked at each other and thought, 'What disaster does he not get?'"

The list included restructuring the Bush-era tax cuts, which were due to expire at the end of the year; ending the Clinton-era "don't ask, don't tell" ban on gays and lesbians serving openly in the military; overhauling the immigration system to allow the children of illegal immigrants to stay in the country; and ratifying his New Start arms-control treaty with Russia. The idea of addressing so many big issues in the lame-duck session seemed fanciful if not defiant – after all, the voters had just served eviction notices on the House Democratic majority. But Obama and his Congressional allies decided to press ahead before surrendering control, realizing that the next two years under Republican rule would be enormously frustrating.

Unlike the other items, the tax cuts required action because of the pending expiration – both sides agreed on that much. Neither Republicans nor Democrats wanted the Bush tax cuts to lapse entirely since that would mean a substantial tax increase for many millions of Americans. Where the two sides differed, as they had since the start of the Obama presidency, was on what to do about the tax cuts for the wealthiest American households. Obama wanted to let the tax cuts expire for those in the top two percent of families, while the Republicans wanted to extend all the cuts as they were, regardless of income.

Neither side was ready for a permanent compromise, but they settled on a temporary solution that included victories for both the White House and the Republicans. They agreed to extend the tax cuts unchanged for two more years – including for the wealthy – effectively punting the larger question. As part of the package, Obama won a temporary cut in payroll taxes, which would benefit lower-income workers more than the rich, and a thirteen-month extension of jobless benefits for the long-term unemployed, as well as extension of a series of other, smaller tax breaks included in his stimulus program. In addition to preserving all of the Bush tax cuts for the time being, Republicans succeeded in lowering the scheduled tax rate for the largest estates. Neither side came up with spending cuts to offset the tax cuts, so the $858 billion cost of the package would be added to the national debt. That only exacerbated the nation's long-term financial woes, but Obama considered the net effect to be like another short-term stimulus to the economy.

Obama announced the deal by himself, not alongside his Republican counterparts, a sign that neither side wanted to be seen with the other. Compromises in Washington at that point were to be condemned, not celebrated. When Obama emerged from the Oval Office to defend the agreement, he was clearly in a sour mood. He denounced his erstwhile Republican partners as "hostage takers" because they refused to extend the middle-class tax cuts unless the wealthy kept theirs too. And he lashed out at "sanctimonious" critics on the left who were thrashing him for caving in on the tax cuts for the rich.

"This is the public-option debate all over again," he fumed. "Now, if that's the standard by which we are measuring success or core principles, then, let's face it, we will never get anything done. People will have the satisfaction of having a purist position and no victories for the American people. And we will be able to feel good about ourselves and sanctimonious about how pure our intentions are and how tough we are."

*

If Obama accepted a middle-ground resolution on taxes, he opted for all-or-nothing confrontation on his three other lame-duck priorities. In the end, he won two of three – the end of the don't-ask ban and ratification of the nuclear arms treaty with Russia – but lost the third, the immigration overhaul.

The prohibition on gays and lesbians serving openly in the military was first enacted under Bill Clinton as a compromise with the generals and others who objected to his campaign promise to repeal the ban altogether. Under the policy, gay and lesbian troops over the past seventeen years could serve only if they did not disclose their sexual orientation; those who did were court-martialed. Since the policy went into effect, some 17,000 service members had been discharged.

Obama had promised since his election to do away with the rule. But unlike Clinton, who tried to move immediately after taking office only to run into a buzz-saw of opposition, Obama took his time, allowing Robert Gates and Mike Mullen to conduct a lengthy review that would smooth the way. While activists hammered away at Obama for taking so long, accusing him of vacillation and irresolution, Gates and Mullen patiently massaged the uniformed leadership to the point that most – although not all – vocal opposition faded inside the ranks by the time Congress acted. A survey of 400,000 service members found that only a third opposed the change, far less than anticipated, a sign of just how much society had shifted since the 1990s.

Republicans tried to leverage Obama into dropping the proposed rule change in exchange for their consent to his New Start arms control treaty, but the president refused to make such a deal and pressed hard for ratification even as he lobbied for the repeal of the military ban. While the nuclear treaty was relatively modest in scope, it was significant in resuming a mutual inspection regime that had lapsed and preserving the arms control architecture that had governed the two powers for four decades. With Sarah Palin, the former Republican vice-presidential candidate, leading the charge from the outside, conservatives in the Senate put up a vigorous fight against ratification. To secure enough Republican support for the two-thirds vote required by the Constitution, Obama promised to spend $85 billion over the next decade modernizing America's aging nuclear complex, a promise that helped win over twelve Republicans to join his united Democratic caucus in the final 71-to-26 vote.

Obama had less luck with his effort to pass the so-called Dream Act, which would have provided a path to citizenship for younger immigrants who were brought to the United States illegally as children. It was meant to be a small but politically appealing down payment on a broader overhaul of the immigration system, but Republican opponents recognized that it was only a first step to what they considered a more objectionable revision of the law allowing millions of illegal immigrants to stay in the country.

The Dream Act went down about an hour after passage of the legislation lifting the prohibition on gays and lesbians in the military, providing a roller coaster afternoon. "There was an hour of cheering and then an hour of tears," said Cecilia Muñoz, the president's domestic policy adviser. Obama climbed the stairs to Muñoz's office to join the staff members who were whipsawed emotionally and reminded them that their victory on don't ask, don't tell was seventeen years in the making. It was important to remember that there were defeats along the path to change, but it was still possible to get there.

While disappointed at the immigration defeat, Obama was energized by the victories he did achieve – especially coming just weeks after the election drubbing. Of course, this was the last gasp of a Democratic-controlled Congress on the way out of town, not the acquiescence of a new Republican-controlled House. But Obama presented the surprising lame-duck successes as proof of his continued vigor in Washington. "One thing I hope people have seen during this lame duck – I am persistent," Obama said at a valedictory news conference before heading off for his annual Christmas vacation in Hawaii. "If I believe in something strongly, I stay on it."

In private, he was less sanguine. When Valerie Jarrett talked with him about all they had accomplished against the odds during the lame-duck session, he chose to focus on an issue that was still months down the road, the moment when the government would bump up against its borrowing limit unless Republicans in Congress went along with an increase. Already he was forecasting a bruising fight.

"I'm worried about that debt ceiling," he told Jarrett.

"Come on," she said. "Can't we just enjoy the moment?"

"The debt ceiling," he repeated, "is going to be a problem."

By the time Air Force One took off for Hawaii, though, he was in a better mood, relishing the string of victories as he headed toward a much-needed holiday. He sang *Mele Kalikimaka*, the Hawaiian Christmas song. Aides could not remember seeing him that cheery. "I've won and I've lost," he told them, "and I can tell you, winning is a lot better than losing."

*

With the arrival of 2011, Obama faced a new era, and he was assembling a new team to do so. Even before the midterm election, Rahm Emanuel, the hard-charging chief of staff, had stepped down to run for mayor of Chicago. Pete Rouse, the quiet, behind-the-scenes presidential adviser and master political technician, filled in at first, and then the president tapped Bill Daley to take over.

Daley, the brother and son of legendary Chicago mayors who had served as commerce secretary under Bill Clinton, was an outsider to Obama's world, but the president hoped his pro-business, moderate sensibilities would bridge the divide with the newly ascendant Republicans. The choice was telling. Daley's diagnosis of Obama's problem was that he had shifted too far to the liberal side of the spectrum. "They miscalculated on health care," he had told *The New York Times* the year before. "The election of '08 sent a message that after thirty years of center-right governing, we had moved to center left – not left."

Robert Gibbs, the public face of the White House and one of Obama's closest advisers, stepped down as press secretary, replaced by Jay Carney, a former *Time* magazine correspondent who had been working as communications director for Joe Biden. David Axelrod and Jim Messina, the president's top political gurus in the West Wing, left to begin building a re-election campaign based in Chicago. David Plouffe, the manager of the first campaign, arrived in Washington and moved into Axelrod's closet-sized office just down the hall from the Oval Office, fulfilling a deal the two Davids had made at the onset of the presidency to each spend two years on the inside. Other aides were brought in or given promotions, including Nancy-Ann De Parle, Alyssa Mastromonaco, Stephanie Cutter and Rob Nabors.

The economic team underwent a slow-motion shuffle that was largely complete by the beginning of Obama's third year in office. More than any other part of the White House, the economic team had never embraced the No Drama Obama code, and trying to figure out what had gone wrong was like picking through the ruins of a messy divorce. At the center was Larry Summers, a larger-than-life figure who by many accounts was ill suited to run a bureaucratic process. To some of his colleagues, Summers was an eye-rolling intellectual bully, better at finding flaws in their arguments than building a consensus. There were flaps over status, whether he got a White House car or marched onto the floor of the House for the State of the Union address along with cabinet members. There were flaps over who got to attend which meeting. When Austan Goolsbee told Obama during the debate over the car industry bailout that rescuing auto suppliers would signal that they would also save the automakers, Summers cornered him afterward and "exploded," according to Steven Rattner, the leader of Team Auto. "You do not relitigate in front of the president," Summers scolded. "I was not litigating in front of the president," Goolsbee retorted.

Goolsbee was not alone on Summers's list of adversaries. Summers also clashed with Christina Romer and Peter Orszag, the budget director. Orszag, for his part, at one point got into a feud with Ray LaHood, the transportation secretary, after LaHood went around the budget director to appeal a decision to Rahm Emanuel, then told a reporter about it. Paul Volcker, the former Federal Reserve chairman serving in an advisory role, bristled at being ignored by the rest of the economic team. The feuding at times overshadowed the policymaking. "Unfortunately," Orszag later acknowledged, "I think the environment often brought out the worst in people instead of the best in people. And I'd include myself in that." By 2011, Summers, Romer and Orszag were gone.

The arrival of a Republican House was always expected to usher in a fresh period of conflict, but the new Congress had barely begun when it was struck by violence. Representative Gabrielle Giffords, an energetic young Democrat from Arizona who was popular with her colleagues on Capitol Hill, was shot in the head on January 8, 2011, while meeting with constituents outside a supermarket in Tucson. Her assailant was a deranged gunman who believed in mind control. The explosion of gunfire killed six other people, including the chief judge of the United States District Court for Arizona and a nine-year-old girl, and wounded thirteen others. It also touched off an emotional national debate about gun control and the rise of incivility and demonization in modern politics, driven in part by the fact that Sarah Palin before the shooting spree had put Giffords's district in crosshairs on a map of election targets and wrote on Twitter: "Don't Retreat, Instead – Reload!"

Giffords was a favorite of the president and he stayed up until 1:20 a.m. working on a speech to deliver a few days after the rampage. "At a time when our discourse has become so sharply polarized, at a time when we are far too eager to lay the blame for all that ails the world at the feet of those who think differently than we do, it's important for us to pause for a moment and make sure that we are talking with each other in a way that heals, not a way that wounds," Obama said at a memorial service for those who were killed.

But measuring the political temperature on Capitol Hill, Obama made no serious effort to pass new laws restricting access to firearms following the incident. After bemoaning the tragedy, lawmakers on both sides of the aisle quickly returned to the coarse politics of anger that had dominated Washington in recent years. Aided by her husband, Mark Kelly, an astronaut, Giffords recovered, albeit with permanent damage to her ability to speak, and she went on to become a symbol of courage and a voice for new gun laws. But it was a voice that went largely unheard.

*

While Obama pushed off a permanent resolution of the tax fight, he now faced a Republican House that was eager to rein in spending – and the president at the same time. During Obama's first two years in office, the deficit had shot up to its highest levels as a share of the economy since World War II as the Great Recession sapped tax revenues and the government pumped money into the economy to try to restart its engines. The gap between spending and revenues rose to $459 billion in the fiscal year that ended in the fall of 2008, the last before George W. Bush left office, and then skyrocketed to $1.4 trillion in the fiscal year that included his final three and a half months in office and the first eight and a half months of Obama's presidency. It dipped back down to $1.3 trillion in the 2010 fiscal year, but it still represented 8.7 percent of the gross domestic product. As the new Congress arrived in town, the total national debt, meaning the accumulation of decades of deficits, had just passed $14 trillion, or roughly 93 percent of the nation's entire economy.

To get control of the situation, Obama appointed a bipartisan panel led by Erskine Bowles, a former White House chief of staff under Bill Clinton, and Alan Simpson, a Republican former senator from Wyoming. Just before the new Congress took office, the commission came back with a plan of breathtaking ambition – and breathtaking political risk. It proposed to slash $4 trillion in accumulated deficits projected for the next decade through a mix of painful spending cuts and tax increases, eventually balance the budget by 2035 and cut in half the national debt's share of the economy. Many sectors of society would feel the pain. Homeowners would lose their mortgage interest deduction. Workers would face a retirement age of sixty-nine instead of sixty-seven. The military would endure significant cutbacks. In the end, seven of the commission's eighteen members refused to support it, including Representative Paul Ryan, the incoming Republican chairman of the House Budget Committee. And Obama, while praising it in concept, quickly and quietly put it aside, unwilling to embrace its politically explosive provisions.

The newly empowered Republicans opted instead to move forward with a deficit plan that only addressed spending, not taxes. During the fall campaign, Ryan, John Boehner, now the incoming speaker, and other Republicans had promised to cut $100 billion in spending in their first year in power. Because Democrats had failed to pass regular, full-year spending bills before the last Congress expired, the government was operating on temporary authority that would expire in the spring, giving the Republicans leverage to exact some spending discipline right away. But they still only controlled one house of Congress, and the president sat on the other end of Pennsylvania Avenue with a veto pen.

In the weeks that followed, the two sides engaged in a game of budget chicken, running up against a deadline that would force the government to shut down all but essential services unless a new spending bill was approved. As midnight approached on April 8, Obama and Congressional leaders finally compromised on a plan to cut $38 billion in spending over the next six months and keep the government operating until fall. Lawmakers raced to the floor to vote just before 11 p.m., barely an hour before the cutoff.

Boehner hailed it as the "largest real-dollar spending cut in American history." But it was hardly the sweeping, long-term plan Bowles and Simpson had advocated, nor even as much as the

Republicans had promised on the campaign trail. In effect, it was another temporary truce, not the end of the battle.

Indeed, Joe Biden believed Obama made a mistake by giving in. "I thought we should have let them shut the government down, let them have a taste of what it was," he said later. "I think we would have been in a stronger position. I was in the minority on that." Biden said Obama considered it and may have regretted not forcing the confrontation with the Republicans at that point. "I think it would have been better to have them face the music right then and there," Biden said.

Just days later, Obama headed to George Washington University to deliver a high-profile speech setting the terms of the next round of fighting with his own plan to eliminate $4 trillion in deficits over twelve years, eschewing deep cuts in social entitlement programs and relying in part on tax increases for the wealthiest Americans. This was to be his opening bid in what he anticipated would be rough yet necessary negotiations to get to an eventual bipartisan compromise. But he was planning to lay it out with a sharp, in-your-face challenge to Republicans.

As Obama hovered backstage getting ready to go out, his new chief of staff, Bill Daley, spotted an unexpected guest in the audience – Paul Ryan, the Republican chairman whose budget blueprint Obama was about to shred.

"Try to tell the president!" Daley directed an aide.

It was too late. Obama went on stage and flayed Ryan's plan, declaring that its deep tax cuts and deeper spending reductions would harm students, seniors, the disabled and the nation.

"It's not going to happen as long as I'm president," Obama vowed sternly.

Ryan, who thought he had been invited to hear the president speak about a new collaboration on fiscal matters, fumed in the front row, feeling ambushed as he was singled out for attack in front of a hostile audience. As he stalked out, Gene Sperling, who had succeeded Larry Summers as Obama's national economic adviser, chased after him to explain it was not meant as a set up. "I can't believe you poisoned the well like that," Ryan snapped and kept walking. Obama later recognized the screw-up. "We made a mistake," he said.

With the short-term government spending plan now in place, Republicans turned to another deadline to force action on the deficit on their terms just as Obama had warned Valerie Jarrett about the previous winter: the debt ceiling. Unless Congress voted to raise it, the government would soon be unable to borrow money, which could theoretically put the United States into default. For years, presidents and lawmakers had increased the debt ceiling as a matter of course, sometimes arguing about it, but rarely flirting with the idea of not raising it. Yet egged on by their most conservative and aggressive members, Republican leaders threatened not to raise the debt ceiling unless Obama agreed to deeper spending reductions, potentially reneging on the nation's obligations and, according to the International Monetary Fund, delivering a "severe shock" to the global economy.

To say that Obama and Congressional Republicans talked past each other on this and virtually every other issue would be an understatement. The president and opposition leaders were so far apart that they could barely even hold a conversation. While on the telephone with the president, John Boehner would grow weary of the long-winded lecturing, put the receiver down on the desk and light up a cigarette while Obama kept talking. Senator Mitch McConnell, the Republican minority leader, did not put the phone down, but sometimes watched baseball on television while the president went on and on.

Hailing from opposite parties, they might never have been friends. But Obama's fractious and dysfunctional relationships with the leaders of the other side of the aisle proved an acute challenge during his presidency and contributed to a broader polarization of American politics likely to endure for years. To Obama, the Republicans were dedicated to a strategy of deliberate partisan obstruction set by that secret meeting on the night of his inauguration. He had little patience for the argument of Washington's old hands who wanted him to spend more time trying to woo Republicans, as if inviting them to a Super Bowl party at the White House would change their minds.

To be sure, he made a few fitful efforts, having dinner with a series of Republican senators, for example. But then when they would vote against him a week or two later, he would throw up his hands and see that as evidence that it was pointless. Obama did not invest in the sort of long-term relationship building that might have paid off over time. "Why do they need so much attention?" he groused at one point to Joe Biden.

To Leon Panetta, who spent the better part of four decades in Washington, that was Obama's "most conspicuous weakness, a frustrating reluctance to engage his opponents and rally support for his cause." Obama was as smart as anyone in politics, Panetta thought. "He does, however, sometimes lack fire. Too often, in my view, the president relies on the logic of a law professor rather than the passion of a leader." As Obama viewed it, if his position on an issue was the right one, then lawmakers should see that on the merits. If they did not, then he concluded that they must be acting out of unworthy political motivations. That applied to Democrats as much as Republicans. Obama spent little time courting his own party either. Senior Democratic lawmakers privately groused that they spent more time at the White House when George W. Bush was president. Even members of the Congressional Black Caucus, who assumed that they would have more access than ever to the Oval Office, were frustrated that Obama would go as long as a year or two without seeing them as a group. When he did spend time with Democrats from Capitol Hill, they had the distinct impression that he was only checking the box so that he could say that he did. "Obama really doesn't have the joy of the game," Larry Summers observed. "Clinton basically loved negotiating with a bunch of other pols, about anything." But "Obama, he really doesn't like these guys."

To be sure, Republicans were not disposed to compromise with him and the tenor of Washington had changed dramatically since the days when Lyndon Johnson would work out a deal across the aisle with Everett Dirksen, the Senate Republican leader, or Ronald Reagan would have after-hours drinks with Thomas P. "Tip" O'Neill, the Democratic House speaker. Republicans took an instant dislike to Obama. They bristled at what they considered his high-handed intellectual arrogance. In his memoir, McConnell, an old-school Kentucky conservative, called Obama "condescending" and "annoying," adding that two hours together "would have been more productive had I spent them napping." Obama aggravated him. "He's like the kid in your class who exerts a hell of a lot of effort making sure everyone thinks he's the smartest one in the room," McConnell wrote. "He talks down to people, whether in a meeting among colleagues in the White House or addressing the nation."

McConnell famously said in October 2010 that "the single most important thing we want to achieve is for President Obama to be a one-term president." Obama used that line to discredit McConnell, falsely telling audiences that it came at the start of his presidency, suggesting it was proof that the Republican leader was out to get him from the start. Actually, it was said after nearly two years and in the context of a discussion about the upcoming midterm election when it was the goal of both parties to limit the terms of the other side. Moreover, Obama never quoted what McConnell said next. Asked if his comment meant endless confrontation with Obama, McConnell said no, that he would do business with the president "if he's willing to meet us halfway." He added: "I don't want the president to fail; I want him to change." But the selective quotation sealed Obama's view of McConnell as an enemy and was useful ammunition to paint the Senate Republican as a hopeless obstructionist. And to be sure, McConnell did not give the impression of someone eager to meet halfway. He was as fierce a partisan as there was in Washington.

Obama scorned the idea that if he simply got along with McConnell, everything would have been better. "'Why don't you get a drink with Mitch McConnell?' they ask," Obama once joked during a black-tie dinner monologue. "Really? Why don't *you* get a drink with Mitch McConnell?"

Obama was friendlier with Boehner, with whom he did not mind getting a drink. The perpetually tanned son of a bartender from Ohio, Boehner preferred a good merlot, and while he too found Obama patronizing at times, he was instinctively a dealmaker and willing to find that elusive middle ground. Obama and Boehner shared a love of golf and cigarettes (even if the president had in theory quit smoking). Boehner was an establishment, country-club Republican like those Obama once played poker with during his days in the Illinois State Senate. "He reminds me a lot of the guys I used to serve with in Springfield," Obama once told David Axelrod.

But Boehner was constrained by rebellious conservatives in his own caucus who considered compromise a dirty word. By his own account, he had to "sneak into the White House" just to talk with Obama. When Obama invited him to play golf once in June 2011, fellow Republicans lambasted Boehner. "You can't believe the grief I got," he recalled. He turned down subsequent invitations – not because he did not want to spend time with Obama but because he did not want to have to put up with the pummeling that would follow it.

*

After that one famous golf round, Obama and Boehner retired to the nineteenth hole for a few drinks and a casual conversation about the upcoming debt ceiling deadline. In the course of their discussion, the two leaders discovered that each of them yearned for something bigger than simply avoiding disaster, a grand bargain that would solve the country's fiscal problems for years to come and end the repeated games of political chicken that kept threatening the government's stability and credit.

Both men were attracted to the idea of finally resolving twenty years of budget stalemates in a big way and calculated that if they were going to endure the pain that would come with any budget deal, they might as well aim high and come up with something that would be far-reaching. Indeed, they believed, it could almost be easier to pass a more sweeping measure since it would be easier to justify sacrificing some priorities in order to solve the problem for a generation. "There's no point in dying on a small cross," Joe Biden said.

To have any chance of succeeding, they decided they had to keep their negotiations hidden from public view. Confiding in almost no one, Obama and Boehner opened up a secret channel to see if they could come up with a compromise. Among those kept in the dark was Eric Cantor, who had moved up to House majority leader and was now in the middle of public talks on the budget with Biden. When Biden offhandedly mentioned Obama's clandestine conversations with Boehner, Cantor was stunned. Boehner had effectively lied to him, Cantor felt. He was furious.

Obama invited Boehner over to the White House for an unscheduled Sunday evening chat on July 3, just before the Fourth of July holiday. Needing a cigarette, Boehner suggested they sit on the patio outside the Oval Office where he asked for a glass of merlot. It was a hot evening and the two hashed through a possible deficit package that would include both spending cuts and additional tax revenue. At one point, Boehner reflected on the two men sitting there in the steamy heat. "All you need to know about the differences between the president and myself," he said later, "is that I'm sitting there smoking a cigarette, drinking merlot, and I look across the table and here is the president of the United States drinking iced tea and chomping on Nicorette."

The Republicans were demanding that any increase in the debt ceiling be matched by at least as much in budget cuts over ten years. Obama wanted the debt limit increased high enough that it would last until after his re-election campaign in 2012 so he would not have to revisit the issue in his first term. He also insisted that if he was going to take the risk of alienating his liberal base by curbing entitlement programs like Medicare, then he had to have additional tax revenues as part of the agreement, which would force Boehner to challenge the conservatives within his own party.

With Cantor now clued into what was happening, he effectively forced his way into the room and the discussions turned even more difficult. During a fractious meeting at the White House, Cantor suggested that they instead agree on a short-term increase in the debt ceiling to get through the immediate crisis, but Obama refused. "This may bring my presidency down," he said, "but I will not yield on this." He stormed out of the room.

Eventually, Obama and Boehner found themselves with the outlines of a handshake deal. They would agree on roughly $2 trillion in spending cuts first identified by Biden and Cantor in their talks and then add another $800 billion in new revenue through what Boehner called tax reform. By closing loopholes and eliminating special provisions, they could actually lower rates yet still bring in more money than currently raised, bolstered by better compliance and economic growth stimulated by simplifying the code. Boehner thought he could sell that to his conservative caucus, or at least most of it, by arguing that no one's tax rates would actually go up and so it did not count as actually raising taxes.

But then an unexpected development suddenly unraveled the emerging deal. A bipartisan group of senators called the Gang of Six separately announced their own plan to reduce $3.7 trillion in deficits over ten years that would include $1.2 trillion in new tax revenues. That scrambled Obama's calculations. If three Republican senators were willing to support that much in new taxes, then suddenly it looked like there was room for the president to get $400 billion more than he had expected. Without notifying Boehner first, Obama marched down to the White House briefing room and embraced the Gang of Six plan. At the Capitol, the speaker's team watching on television was flummoxed.

When Obama and Boehner later spoke by phone, the president made clear he had to have another $400 billion in taxes. "I can't have the Gang of Six to the left of me," he explained. But Boehner knew that they could not raise that much in tax revenue just through reforming the code and stimulating extra economic activity – that would mean they would have to actually raise tax rates and that, as far as he was concerned, was a non-starter with his conservative caucus. What exactly was said during that phone call between the president and the speaker would later become a point of contention. Obama said he only asked the speaker to consider more taxes; Boehner said the president made it a demand. The president for his part was willing to go back to the original $800 billion in new tax revenue but with commensurately smaller spending cuts. The speaker briefly considered making a counteroffer that would match what Obama was looking for in taxes but when he ran it by Cantor, his majority leader rejected it. Boehner was aggravated that Obama would try to change the terms of the deal that they had all but finalized. "He had to have known that this was going to set my hair on fire," he said later.

On the night of July 21, Obama called Boehner around 10:30 and left a voicemail message asking him to call back.

By the next morning, Obama still had not heard from the speaker. He tried again at 10 a.m. Boehner was still not available.

No one could remember a time when anyone, much less a House speaker, refused to take or return a call from the president of the United States. *What was going on?*

At the Capitol, Boehner had decided that there was no deal to be had with Obama. No way House Republicans would go along with so much in new taxes; Boehner would face an internal revolt. Realistically, even the $800 billion he had agreed to previously would be a heavy lift. So Boehner decided to pursue a backup plan instead and rather than call Obama back right away, he worked to get everything set up. He reached out to Mitch McConnell and Senator Harry Reid, the Senate Democratic leader, to craft a patchwork agreement that would get them through the debt-ceiling deadline without the grand bargain that Obama had been seeking.

Boehner did not talk with the president until 5:30 p.m., some nineteen hours after Obama tried to get hold of him. "We can't go forward with this," Boehner said. "I'm sorry, I think we've run out of time."

Obama was incensed. Boehner was using the president's request for more taxes as an excuse to walk away. "That's not a reason to cut off the conversation," he told the speaker. "I asked you to consider it. And you never got back to me."

They went back and forth for some time as Obama grew angrier and angrier. "He was spewing coals," Boehner recalled later. "He was pissed."

After hanging up, Obama headed to the briefing room and vent-ed in public, something he rarely did. "I couldn't get a phone call returned," he fumed to reporters. "I've been left at the altar now a couple of times." He laid down an ultimatum – he would not sign any short-term debt ceiling increase; any measure that came to him had to extend the issue beyond the next year's election.

Boehner decided he had to go out in public to counter the president's characterization of what had happened. It was Obama who walked away from a tentative deal by insisting on more taxes, Boehner insisted, far more calmly than the president. "The White House moved the goal posts," he said. "Dealing with the White House is like dealing with a bowl of Jell-O."

Finally, the two sides agreed on a makeshift, punt-the-problem-down-the-road compromise. They crafted a measure to raise the debt ceiling by $900 billion and reduce the deficit by roughly the same, mainly through spending cuts. A special joint Congressional committee would then be charged with coming up with a more comprehensive plan to rein in the deficit. But if it could not, another $1.2 trillion in spending cuts would automatically take effect across the board, half in domestic agencies and half in national security, a process called sequester. The theory was that neither side wanted cuts that drastic in their favorite programs and so the threat of an indiscriminate ax coming down on most of what government did would be incentive for both sides to finally put their differences aside and reach a long-term deal. In effect, it was a mutual suicide pact and both sides assumed the other would put down the gun first. "Let's not do this again," Obama told aides as they finalized the deal.

For Obama, the collapse of the grand bargain fundamentally reshaped his attitude toward Washington. "That was a searing experience," said David Plouffe. The outsider who thought that legislating in the nation's capital was like putting together a bill on police cameras in the Illinois state legislature had gotten a master class in negotiations in the major leagues, a process that had only grown more fraught in the era of polarization. The failure of the grand bargain would force a change in his approach. No longer would he sit down with Republicans and expect to come to a reasonable deal. Boehner was a fine man and maybe in a different environment, the two of them could do business together, but as far as Obama was concerned, the speaker was a captive of the most conservative elements of his caucus. So if the inside game would no longer work, it was time to turn to the outside game. Forget negotiations and use the bully pulpit. Policy was not about applying reason; it was about applying power. "You're never going to convince them by sitting around the table and talk about what's good for the country," John Podesta said. "You had to demonstrate that there's political pain if you don't produce an acceptable outcome."

*

The failure of the negotiations took place against the backdrop of an economy that remained deeply troubled. A few days after the breakdown, Gene Sperling arrived in the Oval Office with the latest job report. Each month, Obama and his team waited anxiously to discover how many jobs had been produced or lost during the previous month. It had become perhaps the most important metric of his presidency, even more than his job approval rating. Now Sperling had brought awkward news.

"I don't think I like the look on your face," Obama said as his adviser entered.

"It's zero," Sperling said grimly. "The job number was zero."

"What do you mean 'zero'?" Obama asked, incredulous.

"It's zero."

"You mean exactly zero?'

"Yes."

"You mean if I grab that piece of paper from your hand, I'm going to see a zero?"

"Yes, sir."

"Has this ever happened before?'

"Not to my knowledge."

Another first for the Obama presidency, and not one to be happy about – not a single new job had been created the previous month. Within hours, Republicans in Congress were passing out pins that said, "President Zero." There was something symbolically powerful about the giant zero in the jobs column, maybe even worse than a small decline would have been. Statistically, of course, it was only an estimate – indeed, it would later be revised upward as the numbers-keepers would determine that in fact 112,000 new jobs had been created that month. But in the heat of the moment, it became a metaphor for Obama's failure so far to turn the economy around.

CHAPTER SEVEN

'Justice Has Been Done'

In a cramped, low-ceilinged anteroom off the main Situation Room in the basement of the White House, Obama stared at a screen and waited for news. He was surrounded by his national security team, all as anxious as he was. The room was eerily quiet that Sunday, May 1, 2011. The president looked stone-faced, his eyes intense and narrowed. The vice president fingered his rosary beads. "The minutes passed like days," recalled John Brennan, the White House counterterrorism chief.

From a live hookup across the Potomac River in Langley, Virginia, Obama and his team could hear Leon Panetta, the CIA director, narrating from his agency headquarters what was happening in faraway Pakistan, where it was already Monday morning.

"They've reached the target," he said. Minutes passed.

"We have a visual on Geronimo," he said.

A few minutes later: "Geronimo EKIA."

Enemy Killed in Action. There was silence in the Situation Room. Finally, the president spoke.

"We got him," Obama said, as some people clapped awkwardly.

Geronimo was the code name for Osama bin Laden, author of the most devastating foreign attack on American soil in modern times and the most wanted man in the world. After a decade-long manhunt, CIA operatives had finally tracked him down, and a team of Navy Seals in stealth helicopters slipped into Pakistan on a moonless night in a daring raid to end the chase. America's enemy number one finally met his fate in a sprawling compound at the end of a long dirt road, an American bullet blasting into his skull just above his left eye and at least one more piercing his chest.

"Justice has been done," Obama told the world a few hours later in a hastily arranged televised address from the East Room that Sunday just before midnight.

The news touched off an extraordinary outpouring of emotion as crowds gathered outside the White House, in Times Square and at the ground zero site where the World Trade Center once stood, people waving American flags, cheering, shouting and laughing. As Obama walked down the Colonnade back to the residence part of the White House, he could hear the chanting: "USA, USA!" In New York, crowds burst into "The Star-Spangled Banner." Throughout downtown Washington, drivers honked horns.

That night would prove to be the most unadulterated moment of unity and success in Obama's presidency, the one time Americans of all stripes and ideologies joined together to rejoice. Obama's poll numbers shot up temporarily, his re-election prospects were surely bolstered and at least one triumphant line was etched into his paragraph in the history books. For once, even Obama's most virulent critics gave him credit, if sometimes grudgingly.

The elation, however, soon evolved into a fierce debate about whether George W. Bush's program of harsh interrogations had played a role in ultimately hunting bin Laden down, an argument highlighted with the release of a popular Hollywood movie, *Zero Dark Thirty*. Veteran CIA officials asserted that waterboarding essentially led to bin Laden. An exhaustive report by Senate Democrats disputed that, saying the detainee who provided the most important piece of information did so before he was subjected to the techniques widely deemed torture, not after. Panetta later said it was more complicated, that at the very least such interrogations provided a broader understanding of Al Qaeda and its leadership that was critical. What remained unknowable, he said, was whether such information could have been gained even without what he called the damage to American values.

Either way, the dispatch of bin Laden, as emotionally satisfying as it was, would be a fleeting victory in a season of tumult that rocked the greater Middle East and challenged the Obama administration. A string of popular uprisings that came to be known as the Arab Spring spread from country to country, pitting Obama's commitment to democracy and internationalism against his instincts for cautious pragmatism and restraint. In Egypt, Libya, Bahrain, Yemen and Syria, Obama would adopt different approaches, often on the fly, with none of them yielding the results he had sought, at least in the medium term. Where he initially hoped for the sort of inspiring peaceful revolution that transformed Eastern Europe after the fall of the Berlin Wall – the ultimate reproach to bin Laden's perversion of Islam – eventually Obama would see the events of that period as a case study in all the ways good intentions could go wrong.

No wonder, then, that he permitted himself to savor that spring night when he announced the final reckoning for bin Laden. It was perhaps the biggest gamble of his presidency to that point, a decision haunted by the ghosts of past botched operations like the failed mission to rescue American hostages in Iran in 1980 and the ambushed effort to capture warlords in Somalia that resulted in the downing of a couple of Black Hawk helicopters and a deadly standoff in 1993. Obama was told that if the Pakistan raid went wrong, it could damage him politically just as the debacle in the Iranian desert hurt Jimmy Carter. He knew that killing civilians by mistake would further inflame the Muslim world. And he realized that even a successful operation conducted without telling Pakistan first could provoke a diplomatic crisis with a key ally in the war with terrorists. "There were," as Panetta told *The New York Times* later, "a hell of a lot of risks."

Obama learned that the government's bin Laden hunters might have finally cornered their quarry months earlier when Panetta arrived for a meeting with the president and his national security team that was kept so secret that White House officials did not list the topic in their alerts to each other. Panetta told Obama that day that after years of hearing about a trusted courier for bin Laden, the CIA at last had found the man and tracked him to a compound in Abbottabad, a wealthy enclave barely thirty miles north of the Pakistani capital of Islamabad. It was hardly the spartan cave in the mountains that many had envisioned as bin Laden's hiding place. Instead, it was a three-story house ringed by twelve-foot-high concrete walls topped with barbed wire and guarded by two security fences. Rather than getting as far away from local authorities as he could, bin Laden had chosen a hideout about a mile from Pakistan's military academy. He was, Brennan said, "hiding in plain sight."

No one could be totally sure, however, that bin Laden was really there. The discovery of the compound led to months of surveillance to assemble what analysts called a pattern of life. They found that the house was unusually cut off from the outside world, with no phone lines or Internet access. Those inside were so concerned about security that they burned their trash rather than putting it on the street for collection. Nearly two dozen people were spotted living there, including women and children.

Intelligence officers studied the laundry on the clothes line and even set up a fake vaccination program to try to get a firsthand look at the residence and its occupants. Satellite imagery detected a tall man who regularly emerged for brisk walks around the yard, a man they dubbed The Pacer. "He would go out and he'd walk real fast, like a guy coming out of confinement, you know, in a prison yard," Panetta said. "Kids would walk with him. They'd be all around. It was clear that people there were giving him deference."

Panetta and Vice Admiral William McRaven, commander of

the Pentagon's Joint Special Operations Command, developed three options for Obama to consider: a strike with B-2 bombers that would obliterate the compound, a joint raid with Pakistani intelligence operatives who would be told about the mission only hours ahead of time, or a secret helicopter assault using only American commandos penetrating Pakistani territory from a base in Afghanistan.

Telling the Pakistanis was quickly ruled out. No one trusted them. That bin Laden could go undetected in their country for so long fueled longstanding suspicions that at least some Pakistani authorities were aware of his presence and protecting him. A B-2 strike was rejected too because it would leave a giant crater but no body; if they were going to try to kill bin Laden, they wanted to be sure they got him and avoid conspiracy theories that he had somehow survived. "This sounds like a bad plan," Obama said.

So it came down to the commando raid. McRaven showed up one day in the Situation Room with a complete mock-up of the compound to show how it could be done. Four lawyers were assigned to come up with a legal rationale that would allow the United States to send military forces into the sovereign territory of another nation with which it was not at war, a research project so secret that it was kept even from Attorney General Eric Holder.

But it was an option that worried many who were in the loop, like Joe Biden and Robert Gates. Given that some intelligence analysts were saying the chances of The Pacer actually being bin Laden were fifty-fifty, Biden suggested waiting longer to be sure. Gates, who was preparing to step down soon, cited the bungled Iran rescue mission as a reason for caution. Hillary Clinton offered cautious support for the operation, but Panetta, who was about to replace Gates as secretary of defense, was the only full-throated advocate. "It was a divided room," said Tom Donilon, who had succeeded James Jones as national security adviser.

After a sober discussion that included long stretches of silence, Obama told advisers he would think about it some more and adjourned the meeting. By the next morning, he had made up his mind. He summoned four top aides and, before they could start briefing him, cut them off.

"It's a go," he said.

*

The timing of the raid was awkward politically. Just days before Navy Seals were to take off, Obama had been busy trying to once and for all dispatch the conspiracy theory that he was actually born in Kenya, a canard promoted by the likes of Donald Trump, who had vowed to send his own investigators to look into the controversy and was nursing his own presidential ambitions.

The so-called "birther" movement played off racial attitudes and fears, stoking the notion that Obama was somehow an outsider, not really an American. Never mind that there was no evidence or that the theory rested on the fanciful notion that his parents back in 1961 had the foresight to imagine that their newborn baby might one day run for president and therefore faked a birth certificate and published a birth notice in a Honolulu newspaper just in case someday he might need to prove he was a natural-born citizen eligible to run. Nonetheless, a *New York Times* poll that spring found that nearly 25 percent of Americans – and 45 percent of Republicans – believed that Obama was born in another country.

Obama had grown so annoyed by the false narrative that he had gone rummaging through boxes at his home during a trip back in Chicago looking for an original copy of his birth certificate since the short-form version produced by the state of Hawaii in the past had not sufficed. He was delighted to find a small four-paneled booklet with the name of Kapi'olani Maternity and Gynecological Hospital and a page inside with his name, his mother's name, his date of birth and his baby footprints. "Hey," he told his staff when he returned to the White House, "look what I found out there." But it was a ceremonial handout from the hospital, not a legal birth certificate. Not willing to give up, he had lawyers contact the government in Hawaii to obtain a copy of the long-form version of the document and he was determined to release it. Some aides were flabbergasted when they learned about his plan and hoped to talk him out of it. When Dan Pfeiffer, his communications director, arrived in the Oval Office, Obama did not even let him get a word out. "I bet you don't love my idea," he said. He did not. Pfeiffer and other aides thought it would be demeaning to the presidency to have to address this fringe theory, like holding a news conference to deny that aliens were being sheltered at Area 51.

But Obama was determined to put the matter to rest if he could and released the long-form birth certificate. Marching into the White House briefing room on April 27, he declared that the document should stop the "silliness" distracting the country from more important matters. "We're not going to be able to solve our problems if we get distracted by sideshows and carnival barkers," he said, without naming Trump as chief barker.

Undaunted, Trump claimed victory rather than acknowledge that his hoax had been exposed. "Today, I'm very proud of myself," he said during a visit to New Hampshire. "I've accomplished something that nobody else has been able to accomplish."

Just days later, Obama was scheduled to attend the annual black-tie dinner of the White House Correspondents' Association, where by tradition he would give a comic speech that would give him another chance to take on Trump. Some wondered about launching the raid to get bin Laden on the same night as the dinner, which would require the president and other senior officials to slip away to monitor its progress. "Fuck the White House Correspondents' Dinner," Clinton said.

Obama agreed and decided to proceed as if nothing special was going on. As it happened, bad weather forced the raid to be postponed by a night. Kept in the dark about what was about to happen in Pakistan, the president's political advisers focused on the jokes. But there were clues for those paying attention.

While the president had lunch that Friday with David Axelrod, a national security aide interrupted. "Obviously something was going on," Axelrod said later. "He asked me to step out." As he waited outside the room, Axelrod overheard someone saying that the national security team did not want Obama playing golf the next day because they might need him for a meeting.

The biggest hint, though, may have come during a discussion about the lines for his correspondents' dinner speech. One of the draft jokes had the president poking fun at Tim Pawlenty, the former governor of Minnesota positioning himself for a run for the Republican presidential nomination: "Oh, poor Tim Pawlenty," Obama was to say. "He had such promise, but he will never get anywhere with that unfortunate middle name bin Laden."

The president rejected the line. "Oh, bin Laden, that name is so hackneyed," he told the joke writers. "Let's find a different name."

One of the speechwriters suggested "Hosni" instead, referring to Egypt's embattled president Hosni Mubarak.

"Let's do that," Obama agreed.

"It wasn't until the next night that we realized why he had taken bin Laden out of the joke," Axelrod recalled.

Obama was not a natural wit. Dry and discursive, he did not exactly keep them laughing at news conferences or spontaneously throw out one-liners in interviews. He was not one for waggish banter or a roguish double entendre. But when the moment demanded it, he had pitch-perfect comedic timing and could deliver jokes scripted for him with a wry tone that brought down the house. He had a way of telling a joke from a teleprompter at a formal Washington dinner and then stopping to chuckle at the cleverness of the joke as if he were reading it for the first time.

He was also a good sport and played along with his generation's new brand of comedy, bringing a younger, rawer, edgier sensibility drawn from pop culture. He slow-jammed the news with Jimmy Fallon on *The Tonight Show*, read mean tweets on *Jimmy Kimmel Live!* and filled in for Stephen Colbert on *The Colbert Report*. He drove around the White House compound with Jerry Seinfeld and shot a cheerfully goofy video for *BuzzFeed* with a selfie stick. If some traditionalists thought it was a little unseemly at times, others celebrated it. *Vanity Fair* called him "America's Cool Guy in Chief." *The Washington Post* dubbed him "the first alt-comedy president."

He used humor as a way to vent his frustrations with what he saw as the absurdity of Washington. At one White House Correspondents' Association dinner, he teamed up with Keegan-Michael Key of *Key & Peele*, who served as Luther, Obama's "anger translator." Obama would mouth a typical presidential platitude and Key would "translate" his inner thoughts.

Obama: "Despite our differences, we count on the press to shed light on the most important issues of the day."

Luther: "And we can count on Fox News to terrify old white people with some nonsense. *Sharia law is coming to Cleveland! Run for the damn hills!*"

Unlike some other presidents, Obama did not favor self-deprecation in his humor so much as mockery of others. His most common pokes at himself focused on his graying hair, his supposed Muslim past and his mythical birth in Kenya. Even there, he was really making fun of others who criticized him.

No one presented a bigger and more satisfying target than Donald Trump. Obama's aides reached out to Judd Apatow, the Hollywood comedy producer, for help in the speech and he came up with such a cutting line about the billionaire with the odd hair that some thought Obama would never go along with it. They need not have worried.

Obama spent that Saturday night, April 30, in his tuxedo on the dais at the Washington Hilton Hotel making fun and chatting with journalists as if it were any other night. Indeed, even though he had edited the bin Laden line out of his presentation, the evening's professional entertainer, Seth Meyers, delivered his own joke about the terrorist leader as part of a riff about how no one watched C-Span.

"People think bin Laden is hiding in the Hindu Kush," Meyers quipped, "but did you know that every day from 4 to 5 he hosts a show on C-Span?"

Obama flashed a huge smile. Robert Gates roared with laughter.

During his own speech, Obama took aim at Trump, ridiculing his birther fixation just days after the release of the Hawaii birth certificate. "Now, I know that he's taken some flak lately, but no one is happier, no one is prouder to put this birth certificate matter to rest than The Donald," Obama said. "And that's because he can finally get back to the issues that matter – like, did we fake the moon landing, what really happened in Roswell and where are Biggie and Tupac?"

The decision to go after Trump was as strategic as it was personal. Much as Obama enjoyed holding the developer up to derision, he was also trying to make Trump the symbol of the Republicans, casting the other party as a joke. "Our view was lifting Trump up at the White House Correspondents' Dinner, you know, as kind of the example of the Obama opposition," said David Plouffe. "There was a strategy behind the material and the amount of time we spent on Trump. *Let's really lean into Trump here. That'll be good for us.*" Or so they thought.

Trump, who was in the audience as a guest of *The Washington*

Post, kept a tight, unhappy grimace on his face during Obama's ribbing, clearly simmering at all the laughter at his expense.

"All kidding aside," Obama continued, addressing Trump. "Obviously, we all know about your credentials and breadth of experience."

He noted that on a recent episode of *Celebrity Apprentice*, Trump's reality television show, a men's cooking team had failed to impress the judges. "You fired Gary Busey," Obama recalled. "And these are the kinds of decisions that would keep me up at night."

The audience loved it. But they would be shocked just twenty-four hours later when they learned what decision *really* was keeping Obama up that night.

*

The next day, as the Navy's Seal Team Six gathered their gear at their base in Jalalabad, Afghanistan, the White House canceled tours lest the unusual flurry of meetings on a Sunday be noticed. Only late in the day were the political aides notified. Dan Pfeiffer was at the movies (*Fast and Furious 5*) when he checked his Black-Berry and found a message summoning him to the White House. "As I'm coming in, the cast of *True Blood* is outside the gate trying to figure out why their tour has been canceled," he recalled.

In the Situation Room, national security officials monitored incoming feeds for Operation Neptune Spear, as it had been designated, while someone brought provisions from Costco – turkey pita wraps, cold shrimp, potato chips and soda. Because Tom Donilon was concerned about looking like the White House was micromanaging the action on the ground, the screen in the Situation Room was oddly blank. When Obama discovered that there was an actual link in the "breakout" room next door, he gravitated over there, ultimately followed by most of his top advisers who crowded into the small space, all glued to the screen of a general's laptop with a video feed from the compound. "I need to watch this," Obama said. The White House photographer, Pete Souza, snapped a picture that would later become one of the most enduring images of the Obama presidency. The looks on the faces of all the people staring at the screen seemed to say it all. Most interesting was the president himself, seated behind the general operating the laptop, hunched over, his faced locked in an intense glare that made clear just how much was riding on his shoulders in that very moment.

The Black Hawks carrying twenty-three Seals plus an interpreter and a combat dog named Cairo, decked out in his own body armor, raced across the dark Pakistani night sky and reached the compound at Abbottabad. Suddenly, one of the helicopters stalled and came down hard on the ground. There were no fatalities or serious injuries, but the Seals were unable to get it to take off again, so some of them set about blowing it up to keep sensitive technology from falling into the wrong hands, while the rest of the team raced through the building searching for bin Laden.

When the helicopter went down, "it was kind of a big gulp," recalled Michael Morell, the deputy CIA director.

But Panetta was reassured by Admiral McRaven's cool. "He basically was drinking a Coke and I said, 'Bill, what's going on?'" Panetta recalled. "And he said, 'No problem. We've got the backup helicopter. It's called in.'"

As the Seals stormed into the main building, Obama and his advisers were left in the dark since the scratchy video provided by an overhead drone could not record what was happening inside. As the Seals bounded up the stairs, they encountered a bearded man in a tan shalwar kameez robe who turned out to be bin Laden and they shot him in the face and chest. He was not armed and there would later be some debate about whether he really posed a threat. He could have been hiding a gun or holding a grenade in his hand, but in fact for all his menacing statements over the years, the fifty-four-year-old man went down without a fight. In the end, no one seemed that concerned. As one of the Seals quoted a government lawyer telling the commandos before they left, "If he is naked with his hands up, you're not going to engage him." Otherwise, the lawyer said, he would not tell them how to do their job. There would not be any serious second-guessing.

After the fatal shots, the Seals uploaded photographs of the dead man to two sets of specialists who fed them into facial-recognition programs, which produced a 95 percent confirmation that it was bin Laden. The troops put the corpse into a body bag and loaded it as well as a trove of documents and computer hard drives onto a back-up Chinook helicopter that came in to replace the downed bird and made their escape even as Pakistani authorities were scrambling to respond to mysterious reports of gunfire and explosions. "This was the longest forty minutes of my life," Obama later said.

The commandos made it out safely and brought the body and other recovered materials back to their base in Afghanistan. McRaven unzipped the body bag to find the bloodied remains. He wanted to measure the corpse to compare it to bin Laden's known height of six-foot-four. But for all the meticulous preparation, for all of the training and practice runs, no one had remembered to bring a simple tape measure. So McRaven had one of the commandos, who was six-foot-two, lie down next to the corpse for comparison purposes. The body was a couple inches longer. Then McRaven reported back to Obama on the videoconference.

"Mr. President, I can't be certain without DNA that it's bin Laden, but frankly, it's probably about 99 percent chance that it is bin Laden," McRaven told him. "In fact, I had a young Seal lie down next to him and the remains were a little taller."

There was a pause on the other end. Finally, Obama spoke up. "Bill, let me get this straight," he said, with a tone of astonishment. "We have $60 million for a helicopter and you didn't have $10 for a tape measure?"

In any case, DNA tests comparing samples with relatives found a 99.9 percent match, officials said, far more meaningful than a height comparison. Obama later gave McRaven a tape measure mounted on a plaque as a memento. Bin Laden's body was washed and placed in a white sheet in keeping with Muslim tradition. Since no country was willing to take it and a burial site might become a shrine for jihadists, the Americans flew the corpse to the aircraft carrier USS Carl Vinson, where it was placed in a weighted bag and eased into the sea, never to be seen again.

Back at the White House, there was a brief debate about whether to announce the raid and its results that night or wait until the following day for a fuller report and more confirmation. But journalists in Pakistan were already reporting the downing of the helicopter – although the initial assumption was that it was a Pakistani military chopper – and when Mike Mullen called his counterpart in Islamabad to inform him about the raid, the Pakistani general urged him to put out the news right away. Obama called President Asif Ali Zardari personally and was struck to learn that the Pakistani leader was not upset. Indeed, Zardari called it very good news and wished God's blessings on the American people, even though he would have to take a different stance in public protesting the American intrusion into Pakistani territory.

Obama called George W. Bush, who was having dinner at a Dallas restaurant, to let him know that the hunt that he had initiated nearly ten years earlier had finally come to fruition. As Obama changed into a suit to address the nation, he found Michelle and told her the good news. "We got him," he said. "And no one got hurt." Panetta called his wife, Sylvia, in California. Four months earlier, his friend, Ted Balestreri, the owner of the Sardine Factory, a Monterey restaurant, had dared him to find bin Laden, vowing to open an 1870 bottle of Château Lafite Rothschild, worth $10,000, if he did. "Call Ted," Panetta told his wife, "and tell him he owes me that bottle of wine."

Dan Pfeiffer and David Plouffe headed over to the East Room to prepare for Obama's televised announcement. "There's just two guys slowly moving chairs," Pfeiffer said. "Plouffe and I are like, We better go get people so we can do this ourselves. We may have killed bin Laden, but we don't have a room to speak in."

The wave of emotion around the country especially washed over relatives of the victims of September 11, who had waited nearly ten years for justice. A nation that had spent a decade tormented by its failure to catch the man responsible for nearly 3,000 fiery deaths at long last had a sense of finality. The celebratory cheering outside the White House was so loud that it even woke up Malia Obama through the normally sound-proof ballistic windows of her bedroom.

"It cannot ease our pain or bring back our loved ones," said Gordon Felt, president of Families of Flight 93, a group representing the interests of relatives of the victims. "It does bring a measure of comfort that the mastermind of the September 11th tragedy and the face of global terror can no longer spread his evil."

Like thousands of others, Maureen Hasson, twenty-two, a recent college graduate wearing a fuchsia party dress and flip-flops, raced out into the night and headed to Lafayette Square across from the White House to celebrate. "This is full circle for our generation," she said. "Just look around at the average age here. We were all in middle school when the terrorists struck. We all vividly remember 9/11, and this is the close of that chapter."

*

Other chapters, however, were just opening. At the same time Obama was huddling with intelligence officers studying satellite images and trying to decide whether The Pacer spotted in the mysterious compound in Pakistan was really a terrorist mastermind, the rest of the Middle East was convulsing with change that would test the president in fresh ways and force him to rethink his views about American power and America's role in the world.

In a rural town in Tunisia in December 2010, an unlicensed fruit seller ordered to turn over his wooden cart and slapped by a female police officer protested his humiliation by setting himself on fire. In that instant, a far greater blaze was ignited across the region. Moved by his desperation, Tunisians mobilized protests. Clashes with authorities broke out, killing dozens. Under pressure from the streets, the government fell in January 2011, and President Zine el-Abidine Ben Ali fled to Saudi Arabia after twenty-three years in power, the first time popular demonstrations had forced out an Arab leader.

Inspired by the events in Tunisia, dissenters began agitating around the region, in places like Bahrain, Libya, Syria and most notably Egypt, the historic center of the Arab world. Hundreds, then thousands, then hundreds of thousands of protesters crowded onto Tahrir Square in Cairo demanding that President Hosni Mubarak step down. Mubarak, a powerfully built former air force commander, had ruled Egypt with a firm hand for thirty years, since the assassination of President Anwar Sadat, and had become the epitome of a Middle East autocrat. But he was also a stalwart friend of the United States as well as a reliable guarantor of the peace treaty between Egypt and Israel born out of Jimmy Carter's Camp David summit.

Watching from Washington, Obama felt torn. He had scorned Bush's "freedom agenda" promoting democracy around the world, seeing it as messianic, hypocritical and at times counterproductive. He focused instead on promoting mutual respect and understanding. In his Cairo speech just a few months after taking office, he had tempered his words of support for democratic aspirations by noting that "there is no straight line to realize this promise." When Iranians upset at rigged elections took to the streets that same summer in what was dubbed the Green Revolution, Obama remained mostly quiet, reasoning that American support would only discredit the homegrown opposition.

But he had come to regret the silence, and two years later, as he watched young Egyptians fighting for their freedom in the streets and on Twitter and Facebook, he felt increasingly drawn into their struggle. Joe Biden, Hillary Clinton, Robert Gates and other, more seasoned figures cautioned him against throwing Mubarak overboard. "It all may work out fine in twenty-five years," Clinton said, but in the meantime it would be "quite rocky." Younger, more idealistic advisers like Denis McDonough and Ben Rhodes, however, urged the president to be on the right side of history, as they put it. Obama agreed. If this really was a repeat of the popular uprisings in Eastern Europe, he wanted to be remembered as a champion of freedom.

Clinton asked Obama to give her a chance to work out a solution by sending a special envoy, Frank Wisner, a diplomatic veteran and son of one of the architects of the early Cold War national security structure. But Wisner not only failed to persuade Mubarak to step down, he made matters worse by then telling a conference in Munich, Germany, that the Egyptian leader should stay in order to steer changes through. By that point, he had finished his assignment for the government and was technically speaking as a private citizen, but given his recent mission his comments were taken as a signal of official policy.

Obama only learned about Wisner's comments when an exercised David Cameron, the British prime minister, called to ask what was going on. Obama was livid. Tom Donilon said later that he had never seen the president that upset. Obama called Clinton, who was also at the Munich conference.

"What was Wisner doing speaking at the Munich Security Conference?" he asked. "And why was he saying different things than I have?"

Clinton had no good answer. "He took me to the woodshed," she later wrote.

In Cairo, anger on the street continued to grow. Obama's national security advisers were thirty minutes into a meeting on what to recommend to the president when he suddenly came through the door to join the conversation. The question on the table: Should Obama call on Mubarak to step down?

Amid the discussion, an aide handed a note to Donilon. "Mubarak is on," Donilon announced.

The Situation Room television screens were tuned into Al Jazeera as Mubarak addressed his nation. The Egyptian leader was defiant and imperious. He agreed not to run for another term but would not step down right away. "This is my country," he declared. "I will die on its soil."

The American officials watched in grim silence. Finally, Obama spoke up. "That's not going to cut it," he said.

Obama made a telephone call to Mubarak to tell him he had not gone far enough. The line crackled with tension.

"I know the last thing you want to see is Egypt collapse into chaos," Obama told him. "How can you help manage the change?"

Mubarak did not even wait for Obama's words to be translated. "You don't understand my people," he scolded. "I do understand my people."

"Let's talk tomorrow," Obama said.

"We don't need to talk tomorrow," Mubarak shot back. "You'll see. It'll all be done in a few days."

After they hung up, Obama resolved to publicly push Mubarak to do what he was refusing to do. The president already had a statement drafted declaring that a "transition must begin now."

Biden, Clinton and Gates objected, urging him either to not make a statement or at least to take out the "must begin now" line.

Obama refused. "If 'now' is not in my remarks," he replied, "there's no point in me going out there and talking."

"Now" stayed in. In fact, when Robert Gibbs went out to brief reporters and was asked what "now" meant, he went even harder. "Now started yesterday," he declared.

Ten days later, Mubarak was driven from power. Suddenly, the whole Middle East appeared to be heading in a new direction. It was heady and powerful. How decisive Obama's push was in sealing Mubarak's fate could be debated. Americans tend to give great weight to their own ability to shape events in far-off countries that in many cases are determined by their own internal dynamics and politics. But if Mubarak was to go anyway, Obama at the very least had put himself and the United States on the side of change. What he did not fully anticipate was how much other allies in the region like Saudi Arabia, the United Arab Emirates and Kuwait would see that as a betrayal. If the American president was willing to cut loose a longtime friend as loyal as Mubarak, they concluded, he could not be relied on to back them in moments of crisis.

So when protests broke out days later in the Persian Gulf island state of Bahrain, where the United States Navy based its Fifth Fleet, the Saudis and Emiratis decided to take matters into their own hands. Shiite protesters were standing up to a Sunni monarchy, a situation that did not sit well with the neighborhood's other Sunni rulers. Without telling the Americans, Saudi Arabia sent a column of tanks, artillery and troops across the sixteen-mile King Fahd Causeway into Bahrain to help the government clear out Pearl Square in the capital of Manama by force. The Emiratis also sent troops.

Obama stewed at the intervention and violent suppression of

demonstrations but Saudi Arabia was different from Egypt. Not only did the conservative Saudi royal family play an outsized role in the world economy through its oil fields, it held a much firmer grip over its people. It saw the Shiite uprising next door as a threat that could embolden Iran and encourage Shiites in its own country to follow suit. And in effect, the Saudi sheiks were challenging Obama even as they turned guns and tear gas on peaceful protesters.

This time, Obama looked away. There were limits to how far he was willing to go to nurture change in a volatile region. He later mused on the disparities in his own approach, noting that personal relationships really did drive foreign policy, as Biden often said. "You know," he told aides, reflecting on Egypt, "one of the things that made it easier for me is that I didn't really know Mubarak." He mentioned that George H.W. Bush had called Mubarak at the height of the protests in a show of support. "But it's not just Bush," he said. "The Clintons, Gates, Biden – they've known Mubarak for decades." His thoughts turned to Jordan, where he did have a closer relationship with the ruler. "If it had been King Abdullah," he said, "I don't know if I could have done the same thing."

*

While Obama relied on strong-arm diplomacy in Egypt, he was drawn into using real arms next door in Libya. The same popular wave sweeping through the rest of the region led many in the North Africa pariah state to finally rise up against Colonel Muammar el-Qaddafi, who had ruled with an iron fist for forty-two years. With his wild hair, beady eyes and trademark sunglasses, Qaddafi had become one of the world's most recognizable tyrants, an iconic if iconoclastic figure in the Arab and African worlds who once strode across the international stage but now seemed tired and corrupt.

Once put on the cover of *Newsweek* with the headline, "The Most Dangerous Man in the World?" Qaddafi had been the bête noire of Ronald Reagan, who called him the "mad dog of the Middle East" and retaliated for his terrorist acts by bombing his compound in 1986. Qaddafi was the sponsor of one of the world's most notorious acts of mass murder before September 11 in the 1998 bombing of Pan Am Flight 103 over Lockerbie, Scotland, which killed 270 on board and on the ground. By 2003, he grew nervous about experiencing the fate of Saddam Hussein in Iraq and so voluntarily gave up a fledgling nuclear weapons program to the United States and Britain in exchange for the beginning of a rapprochement with the West. But he had not loosened his hold on power, and now the Arab Spring was threatening an end to his maniacal rule.

The first protests began in the seafront city of Benghazi in February just four days after Hosni Mubarak's ouster. Qaddafi had watched Mubarak's end and had no intention of sharing his fate. Rather than go down peacefully, he ordered his army to move against those rebelling against his rule. In a typically defiant tirade, he went on television to denounce his opponents as "rats" and "cockroaches" and called on his supporters to "attack them in their dens."

Worried about a slaughter, France and Britain pushed the United Nations Security Council to approve a resolution authorizing foreign powers to establish a no-fly zone over Libya. Never enamored of Qaddafi, the Arab League pushed for intervention as well. With American troops still fighting in Afghanistan and in the process of withdrawing from Iraq, though, Obama and his team had little interest in getting involved. Susan Rice, the president's ambassador to the United Nations, called her French counterpart, Gérard Araud, and warned him against Western military interference.

She suggested that she feared that if the Europeans went in themselves, the United States would be sucked in too. "You are not going to drag us into your shitty war," Rice told Araud. "We'll be obliged to follow and support you and we don't want to."

But in fact, within Obama's team, she was pushing for action, recalling her time in Bill Clinton's administration when they had failed to act soon enough to stop a genocide in Rwanda. That had long troubled Rice, who had taken a never-again vow at least to herself. "We have a moral responsibility to act," she said as the danger rose in Libya.

One of her allies was Samantha Power, whose book had chronicled the failures of the Clinton White House to stop mass slaughters. As Ben Rhodes later put it, Rice had "been a minor character in Samantha's book, and not one of the good guys." This was a chance for both of them to get right what they thought had gone wrong in the 1990s. Also in their camp was another veteran of that administration, Hillary Clinton. Unlike in Egypt, where she sided with the established order, Clinton was ready to stand up to Qaddafi after a late-night meeting in a Paris hotel with the Libyan opposition leader Mahmoud Jibril, whom she found "impressive and polished." The three women – Clinton, Rice and Power – would later be dubbed the Valkyries in the newspapers for pushing for military action.

Nonetheless, there was fierce resistance in the Situation Room to American intervention. "Can I finish the two wars I'm already in before you guys go looking for a third one?" Robert Gates asked. As far as he was concerned, Libya posed no threat to American national interests. Joe Biden, Mike Mullen, Bill Daley, John Brennan, Tom Donilon and Denis McDonough agreed with him. His mind on Iraq, Biden asked what would happen not just the day after but the decade after.

In the end, though, Clinton's advice may have proved decisive.

Obama later told Gates privately in the Oval Office that the Libya operation was a "51-49" decision – and Gates was convinced that Clinton was the one who put it over the top. An unhappy Gates again contemplated resigning but decided against it since he was already planning to leave in a few months anyway.

Susan Rice ended up making a second call to Gérard Araud, the French ambassador, that same night. Not only would the United States support intervention, she told the astonished diplomat this time, but it wanted United Nations support for more than just a no-fly zone.

In March, a month after protests began, the United Nations Security Council authorized "all necessary measures" to protect Libyan civilians. Russia's President Dmitri Medvedev, who by that time had forged a constructive working relationship with Obama and had been given considerable leeway in international affairs by Vladimir Putin, agreed not to block the resolution and ordered his ambassador to abstain. Qaddafi responded by arguing that he was really suppressing Islamic terrorism and that the outside world should be on his side. "We in Libya are confronting the terrorist of Al Qaeda," he wrote in a letter to Obama. "In Libya, there are no political and administrative demands, nor are there any disputes." He added sarcastically, "If you decided that terrorism need not be fought, then let's negotiate with bin Laden."

While Obama had agreed to the operation, he insisted on one condition: The Europeans, for once, would have to take the lead. Libya was their problem, just 300 miles from their southern borders and far from the shores of the United States. The Americans would use their overwhelming airpower to stop the feared massacre, but after the first ten days it would be up to London and Paris to take over the operation and figure out what came next. In effect, exhausted from its own international exertions of the past decade, the world's last superpower was subcontracting out the latest crisis. One aide told Ryan Lizza of *The New Yorker* that Obama was "leading from behind," an infelicitous phrase that would be used against him for the rest of his presidency as a metaphor for passivity.

Obama gave the order to open the attack from the office of the president of Brazil, which he borrowed during a visit to make the momentous phone call. Within a month, the airstrikes succeeded in stopping the advance of Qaddafi's forces, saving the civilians of Benghazi. Obama went on national television to declare victory. "When people were being brutalized in Bosnia in the 1990s, it took the international community more than a year to intervene with air power to protect civilians," he boasted, a nod to Samantha Power. "It took us thirty-one days."

Emboldened, Obama in August injected himself into yet another roiling Arab crisis, calling for the resignation of President Bashar al-Assad of Syria, who was beginning a bloody crackdown on protesters. Momentum seemed on the side of change. Just days afterward, Libyan rebels stormed Qaddafi's compound in Tripoli, ending his reign once and for all. Two months later, they found Qaddafi himself in a sewer pipe, dragged him out, beat him to a pulp and sodomized him with a bayonet. He was soon dead. Grisly and unseemly as his demise was, Washington celebrated the elimination of a man who had been a threat for four decades. "We came, we saw, he died!" Clinton exulted privately.

Around the same time, another enemy of America, this one from a newer generation, met a similar fate. Anwar al-Awlaki, the American-born propagandist and recruiter for Al Qaeda who had inspired and helped orchestrate a host of attacks, including the Fort Hood shootings and the attempted Christmas airline bombing, was killed by a CIA drone strike in Yemen. At forty years old, Awlaki was one of the most hunted terrorist figures after Osama bin Laden. The military dubbed him Objective Troy, after a randomly selected small town in Ohio, and American intelligence had been looking for him for months. Few mourned his death, but the missile that delivered retribution in the desert sparked a different kind of debate back in the United States. Unlike bin Laden or other Al Qaeda figures targeted by drones, Awlaki was a United States citizen, born in New Mexico, and for the first time in the war on terror a president had authorized the killing of an American without trial. Also killed in the strike was Samir Khan, another American who was with Awlaki at the time but was not an intended target.

Obama's drone war had aggressively taken out many terrorists in battlefields that were hard to reach without putting American troops at risk, a darkly antiseptic way of bringing death to the country's enemies, and sometimes nearby civilians, with the flick of a joystick sometimes thousands of miles away. "It turns out that I'm really good at killing people," Obama told aides, a line he would repeat over the years.

But in putting Awlaki on the "kill list," Obama had gone where even George W. Bush had not. Despite the traditional constitutional right to due process guaranteed to Americans, Obama's Justice Department lawyers argued that the government in a time of war could seek to kill an American abroad when the target posed "a continued and imminent threat" to the United States. Awlaki, they determined, posed just such a threat. Even though there was no armed conflict in Yemen at the time, administration lawyers further concluded that the United States could still target its enemies there given Al Qaeda's activities in the country. Civil libertarians and other critics decried the decision, saying it gave the government too much power to kill its own citizens – a position that Obama might have taken himself before he became president, when he was criticizing Bush for taking on too much authority in the name of national security. But in Awlaki's case,

Obama accepted the evidence. The government had the account of the would-be Christmas bomber, intercepted communications between Awlaki and Al Qaeda members plotting attacks and Awlaki's public assertions that Muslims had a religious duty to kill Americans. "This is an easy one," Obama told aides.

Still, Obama publicly acknowledged the tricky larger issues and said such actions should be reserved for only the most dire circumstances, comparing Awlaki to a sniper shooting down on a crowd and taken out by a police SWAT team. "I would have detained and prosecuted Awlaki if we captured him before he carried out a plot, but we couldn't," Obama said later. "And as president, I would have been derelict in my duty had I not authorized the strike that took him out."

As weighty as the issues involved were, this was an invigorating period for Obama, the commander in chief. Osama bin Laden, Muammar el-Qaddafi and Anwar al-Awlaki were all dead. The president asserted that Al Qaeda was on the ropes. And now he was about to end the war in Iraq, or at least the American involvement in it. Under the agreement with Iraq that Bush had left behind and that Obama had embraced, American troops were to leave by the end of 2011. The situation on the ground seemed calm enough. Obama and his team were ready to claim victory and go home. Still, both sides had originally imagined they might negotiate a follow-up deal to keep a small American detachment behind as a force for stability, and Obama now had to decide whether and how to do that.

General Lloyd Austin, the commander on the ground, developed proposals for keeping as many as 24,000 troops after 2011, but he ran into instant resistance at the White House. To Obama's aides, it looked like the beginning of a permanent presence akin to the deployment in South Korea, now six decades old, with the military still trying to do everything it was doing before in Iraq, just with fewer troops. The White House said no. Austin and the Pentagon refined the proposal, developing options for leaving behind 19,000 troops, 16,000 troops and 10,000 troops. The general preferred the highest number and deemed the lowest unwise. Tom Donilon asked Robert Gates if he could live with 10,000. Gates said he could. But even that would not last. The plan was later reduced to 5,000 troops.

If Obama seemed ambivalent about troops staying behind, so did Iraq's prime minister, Nuri Kamal al-Maliki. Even while the debate over numbers raged, Washington and Baghdad became mired in a dispute over legal protections for American troops. The Obama administration wanted a liability shield approved by the Iraqi parliament, continuing the same protections the United States had had over the past eight years. But even though Maliki agreed to submit it to parliament, no one thought it would pass. Maliki suggested that the United States rely instead on his own authority as prime minister to approve such a measure, but American lawyers insisted it have the sanction of Iraq's querulous lawmakers.

As they haggled over the matter, Obama's team seemed half-hearted at best. "To my frustration, the White House coordinated the negotiations but never really led them," Leon Panetta said later. At loggerheads, the two sides finally quit the talks altogether. There would be no residual force of any size. The failure to resolve the liability issue in some ways provided the public rationale for an outcome that did not trouble either Obama or Maliki. "We really didn't want to be there, and he really didn't want us there," a top aide to Obama at the time said privately, referring to Maliki. "It was almost a mutual decision, not said directly to each other, but in reality that's what it became. And you had a president who was going to be running for re-election, and getting out of Iraq was going to be a big statement."

In December, Obama sent Joe Biden to officially end the mission in an emotional ceremony at Al Faw Palace in Baghdad. Afterward, Biden called Obama back in Washington.

"Thank you for giving me the chance to end this goddamn war," Biden said.

"Joe," Obama responded, "I'm glad you got to do it."

In a public statement, Obama declared the withdrawal "a moment of success," one he had promised in his original campaign. "We're leaving behind a sovereign, stable and self-reliant Iraq, with a representative government," he said.

But for how long?

CHAPTER EIGHT

'Fought Our Way Back'

By the time Obama took the stage at the Fox Theater in Redwood City, California, that spring evening in 2012, he was in the eighteenth hour of a nineteen-hour day. His tie was still knotted all the way to the top as he launched into his stump speech, attacking his opponent's record and defending his own. "I still believe in you," he told the audience, "and I hope you still believe in me."

That was a proposition Obama was about to test four years after the political winds converged behind his original, improbable journey to the White House. In marathon trips across the nation, he tried to justify the faith supporters had invested in him. He was running against himself as much as the Republicans, or rather, two versions of himself – one, the radical ruining the country that conservatives saw and the other, the savior of the country that he had struggled to live up to.

Obama had pulled the nation back from the edge of the economic precipice, saved the auto industry and imposed new regulations on Wall Street, but unemployment still topped 8 percent, millions of Americans who did have jobs were stuck with low pay and the national debt had skyrocketed. American troops had come home from Iraq, but the war in Afghanistan raged on inconclusively, and the situation in Libya was beginning to unravel amid factions battling each other for power. Obama had taken out Osama bin Laden, signed a nuclear arms treaty with Russia and put two liberal justices on the Supreme Court, but he had failed to close the prison at Guantánamo Bay, overhaul immigration rules, pass climate-change legislation or usher in a new era of bipartisanship. His biggest legislative accomplishment, his health care program, was a double-edged sword. It expanded coverage to millions who were vulnerable but alienated many Americans who resented government interference in their lives, while still leaving some in his liberal base disgruntled that he did not go further.

The protesters waiting outside a campaign fund-raiser in Denver one day in May were probably never supporters to begin with, but some of their signs cut close to the bone for a president who had built his career on inspiration.

Out of Hope, Ready for Change.

Obama's Blvd. of Broken Promises.

Indeed, this was a president who had yet to realize the lofty expectations that had propelled him from obscurity to the Oval Office. This was a proud yet humbled president, a confident yet scarred president, a dreamer mugged by reality, a pragmatist confounded by ideology, a revolutionary to some, a sellout to others. He would "never be a perfect president," he conceded at one campaign stop after another. Long after the messiah jokes had vanished, the oh-so-mortal Barack Hussein Obama was left to make the case that while progress was slow, he was taking America to a better place – and that he would be a better president over the next four years.

Obama started out the 2012 election cycle in uncertain shape. "I know we're probably underdogs," Obama told advisers when they gathered for the first time in the fall of 2011 to discuss the coming race. "But I intend to win this race." Pundits agreed with the underdog part. "Is Obama Toast?" asked the headline on a piece a couple of months later in *The New York Times Magazine* by Nate Silver, the numbers-crunching election forecaster. Given the weakness in the economy and the possible strengths of the emerging Republican field, "the odds tilt slightly toward Obama joining the list of one-termers," Silver wrote, demonstrating the hazards of political prognostication.

To be sure, Obama was not the instinctive campaigner that Bill Clinton or George W. Bush were. He did not throw himself into a rope line with abandon. And while he would do what he deemed required to win a second term, he did not live for glad-handing. "He seemed intellectual enough that some of the requisites of campaigning – perhaps even public life – didn't necessarily sit well with him," observed John Kerry, who gave Obama his first national platform at the 2004 Democratic National Convention. "He could be naturally gregarious, exuding that big, warm, flashy smile, but he didn't seem to exult in the give-and-take or love the process. It became tedious and mechanical faster than it might have for other candidates."

Still, Obama had a number of factors going for him. While his approval rating had slid from its highs after the Osama bin Laden raid, it was still hovering around 50 percent. Obama could summarize his argument for a second term in a pithy bumper sticker slogan that Joe Biden would later use at the Democratic National Convention: "Osama bin Laden is dead and General Motors is alive."

And Obama had two other advantages. The first was a clear path to the nomination for a second term. The only incumbent presidents to be defeated at the polls or driven from the race in the previous eighty years all had primary challenges within their own parties, either reflecting or exacerbating internal divisions that weakened their public standing. Obama had dispensed with the biggest threat of that by putting Hillary Clinton in the Cabinet, not only eliminating her as a would-be challenger but squelching the will-she-or-won't-she speculation that otherwise would have played out for months.

The second advantage was a Republican opposition driven by rural, anti-elite Tea Party populism but represented by a moderate, wealthy New England investor who enacted a precursor to Obama's health care program in his own state. Mitt Romney, the former governor of Massachusetts soon to be nominated by the Republicans, once favored abortion rights and "full equality" for gay and lesbian Americans, but now was trying to lead a far more conservative party in his bid for the White House, a challenge even after his selection of Paul Ryan, a smart, policy-minded favorite of the right, as his running mate.

A tall, dignified patrician with a ramrod posture, cultivated manners and impeccably coiffed hair, Romney, sixty-five, looked like a Hollywood version of a president and had spent his life in and around politics, but was running on his strength as a businessman. Born Willard Mitt Romney to a Mormon family, he was raised in Michigan, graduated from Brigham Young University and later earned a master of business administration degree from Harvard University. He worked on campaigns for both his parents. George Romney, his father, served for six years as governor of Michigan only to have his own presidential bid in 1968 cut short when he said that he had been fooled into supporting the war in Vietnam due to "brainwashing" by the generals. Lenore Romney, his mother, ran unsuccessfully for the Senate in 1970.

Mitt became a management consultant in Boston, worked his way up to chief executive of Bain & Company and later spun off a private equity firm called Bain Capital. He jumped into politics with a failed challenge to Ted Kennedy in 1994, then revived his public fortunes by taking over the struggling Winter Olympics in Salt Lake City in 2002 and turning it around. That propelled him to a victory in the Massachusetts governor's race that fall.

During his four years as the Republican chief executive of a deeply blue state, Romney governed as a moderate, reaching across party lines and even teaming up with his old rival, Kennedy, to push through the state's health care overhaul. But when he set his sights on the White House for the first time in 2008, he veered to the right, coming out against abortion and positioning himself as a conservative in an unsuccessful primary race in which invested $45 million of his own money. After losing the nomination to John McCain, Romney spent the next four years assiduously building support, making himself into the prohibitive favorite for the party nod in 2012 as he outpaced a series of other contenders like former House Speaker Newt Gingrich, former Senator Rick Santorum of Pennsylvania and Governor Rick Perry of Texas. In doing so, Romney had reinvented himself as a "severely conservative" figure, feeding the impression of a flip-flopper trying to rally a party base suspicious of his bona fides.

In the process, Romney adopted a claim popular on the right that Obama was not sufficiently appreciative of American exceptionalism and, instead, went around the globe apologizing for the United States. The indictment of Obama's patriotism stemmed from some of his early speeches attempting to repair what he saw as the damage done by George W. Bush's approach to international affairs. "There have been times where America has shown arrogance and been dismissive, even derisive," Obama told an audience in France a few months after taking office. Two weeks later, he told a Latin American audience that "the United States will be willing to acknowledge past errors where those errors have been made." And a couple of weeks after that, he said in a Washington speech that after the September 11 attacks "we went off course."

The string of regrets came to be called Obama's apology tour. The indictment often ignored other parts of the speeches – for instance, when he pivoted in France to reproach the "insidious" anti-Americanism too often found in Europe that ignores "the good that America so often does in the world" – and it interpreted rejection of his predecessor's policies as a larger rejection of the idea that his home country was a unique beacon in the world. Obama found the suggestion outrageous, maintaining that any black man who had risen to the heights he had knew just how special America really was. To his advisers, the portrayal was part of a larger, racially charged effort to paint Obama as the "other" in keeping with Donald Trump's "birther" lie – he does not love his country, he may be a secret Muslim, he may not even have been born in the United States. But parts of the country were discomforted by the president's tone and Romney even titled his campaign book *No Apology: The Case for American Greatness* to play off the theme.

With his own public standing in question, Obama and his team resolved to define Romney for the public before he could do it himself. The Republican candidate would be presented as a rapacious capitalist whose firm, Bain Capital, snatched up distressed companies and laid off workers to squeeze out profits for itself. With his privileged lifestyle and multiple houses, including one with a car elevator, Romney played into the image of a manicured plutocrat. Advertisements featuring interviews with workers who lost jobs at some of the failed companies that Bain bought were aired long before the fall contest would even formally get under way. It was a cynical strategy that ignored Bain's successes at turning around many firms that otherwise would have gone out of business to the detriment of entire work forces, and at one point the line of attack was renounced even by Bill Clinton and other Democrats close to Wall Street. But at a time of economic anxiety, it would prove devastatingly effective.

By contrast, Obama planned to position himself as a champion of the middle class left behind by the likes of Romney and his corporate barons, denouncing the "breathtaking greed" of those at the top of the economic ladder. Starting with a speech in Osawatomie, Kansas, on December 6, 2011, Obama was trying to co-opt the arguments of the left wing of his party that had staged Occupy Wall Street sit-ins to protest the super-wealthy. He even adopted their formulation by complaining that the top one percent of Americans were benefiting at the expense of the other 99 percent.

"This is a make-or-break moment for the middle class and all those who are fighting to get into the middle class," the president told an auditorium of supporters in Osawatomie, a hardscrabble town of 4,500 chosen because it was the place where Theodore Roosevelt laid out his own progressive platform called the New Nationalism a century earlier – and because it was in the state from which Obama's family on his mother's side hailed. "At stake is whether this will be a country where working people can earn enough to raise a family, build a modest savings, own a home and secure their retirement."

Obama's economic case was marred, however, by the mixed public views of the stimulus plan he signed three weeks after taking office. While it had created or saved jobs and financed a variety of appealing projects, the collapse of a solar energy company that received money from the program and that Obama had visited gave the impression of political self-dealing. The company, Solyndra, received $500 million only to go bankrupt in the fall of 2011, putting 1,100 out of work. Emails that became public showed how politically minded government officials paid attention to the optics of the company's progress, although the White House insisted that the loan was granted on the merits by staff experts at the Energy Department.

Moreover, as the incumbent, Obama was now the owner of the economy, for good or ill, and at times he struggled to find a balance between touting his successes in halting the free fall and recognizing that many people were still suffering. At a news conference in June, he said "the private sector is doing fine." He was comparing it to the public sector, where teachers and firefighters were still being laid off, even though many in the private sector still felt that they were doing anything but fine. A month later, during a campaign stop in Virginia, Obama told an audience, "If you've got a business, you didn't build that." His point was that government played an important role in creating the environment for business to thrive, but it sounded as if he were diminishing the importance of individual initiative and drive.

Obama's attempts at intellectualized arguments only made him seem out of touch about the depth of the economic pain in the country and outright disdainful of American entrepreneurship, much like John McCain when he declared in 2008 that the fundamentals of the economy were sound. And they handed Republicans useful ammunition when they depicted Obama as an enemy of capitalism who had failed to rebuild the economy after the crisis of 2008. Obama knew he had screwed up. After the "private sector" line, he apologized to aides. "I hate being sloppy," he said. "That was sloppy."

*

As he headed toward the fall contest, Obama had one more issue to confront to consolidate his own base. While much of the rest of the country had moved steadily toward favoring a right to marriage for same-sex couples, Obama had been left behind officially in opposition. For years, he had officially supported civil unions, but not marriage, for gays and lesbians. Civil unions had once been seen as a relatively safe position for liberal politicians, but the center had shifted and that was no longer acceptable to activists pressing for full gay rights.

Few around Obama thought he genuinely opposed same-sex marriage. At one point in the 1990s he had even checked a box on a questionnaire from a gay newspaper stating that he favored it, only to later say he was undecided and later still to formally come out against it. But as president, he had pushed through legislation finally allowing gays and lesbians to serve openly in the military, and his Justice Department had refused to defend in court the Defense of Marriage Act, the 1990s law barring federal recognition for same-sex weddings, deeming it unconstitutional. As the years passed and support for same-sex marriage grew, he had tried to fudge his position, saying that his thinking was "evolving." But as more states adopted laws and polls showed growing support, especially among key young voters, Obama found himself at odds with his own backers.

With the election on the horizon, his advisers began exploring ways for the president to reverse himself as gracefully and painlessly as possible. David Plouffe even sought advice from a surprising source – Ken Mehlman, the former Republican National Committee chairman under George W. Bush. Mehlman himself had come out as gay after leaving the party leadership. Plouffe invited Mehlman to have lunch with Obama. Afterward, Mehlman sent an email on how the president should announce his reversal, recommending that he do it with Michelle Obama at his side: "Should come up as a question in a larger interview with both POTUS and FLOTUS together. Interviewer should be a woman. All 3 should be sitting. Soft lighting." By spring, Obama was ready to proceed. In keeping with Mehlman's suggestion, the president and first lady would appear together on *The View*, the daytime talk show hosted by a panel of women.

Any plans for an elegant, carefully scripted reversal, however, were abruptly upended a little more than a week before the scheduled appearance. During the taping of an interview with David Gregory for NBC's *Meet the Press* on May 6, Joe Biden, who like Obama had opposed same-sex marriage until then, was asked if he was comfortable with it now. Caught off guard, the habitually outspoken vice president chose to say what he thought.

"I am absolutely comfortable," Biden said, "with the fact that men marrying men, women marrying women and heterosexual men and women marrying one another are entitled to the same exact rights, all the civil rights, all the civil liberties, and quite frankly I don't see much distinction beyond that."

Aides watching the taping recognized that the vice president had just put his boss in a box. "I think you may have just gotten in front of the president on gay marriage," his communications director, Shailagh Murray, told Biden in the limousine leaving the television studio.

The vice president's staff highlighted portions of a transcript of the interview with yellow pen and sent it to the president's advisers to warn them before it aired. Obama's advisers were furious. "I was really angry about this," recalled David Plouffe. "We were completely shocked." Now it was untenable for the president to maintain his position or wait to announce a new one. Anything he did would look like a reaction to Biden rather than a principled decision by the president. Aides fed anonymous quotes to newspapers chastising Biden, who in turn bristled at the trash-talking. "There was a little apoplexy around here," Biden admitted later to *The New York Times*. But the vice president was unapologetic. "I was going to sit there and not say what I believe at this point in my career? They can have the goddamn job."

Obama and Biden were as incongruous a pair as could be imagined – the cool, diffident, fifty-something African-American community organizer and the voluble, back-slapping Irish-American career politician nearly two decades older. And to be sure, Obama did not initially warm to Biden, put off by the vice president's loquacious, gaffe-prone style. When the speak-first, think-later vice president said in the early weeks of the administration that in fashioning the stimulus program, there was "a 30 percent chance we're going to get it wrong," an irritated president dismissed it publicly. "I don't remember exactly what Joe was referring to – not surprisingly," Obama told reporters. Annoyed and unwilling to be presented as the Uncle Joe of the administration, Biden complained to Obama during a private lunch and the president resolved to avoid diminishing his partner in public.

Biden did not always follow directions and his influence waxed and waned over the years. He was often the go-to negotiator when tensions flared with Capitol Hill and he was given some of the highest profile assignments of Obama's presidency, including overseeing the implementation of the stimulus package and managing the withdrawal of American troops from Iraq. Biden was the in-house skeptic on the use of force, arguing against the troop surge to Afghanistan, military intervention in Libya and the raid that killed Osama bin Laden. That put him on the opposite side of many debates with Robert Gates, who called Biden "wrong on nearly every major foreign policy and national security issue over the past four decades." Obama did not see it that way but as Ben Rhodes put it, "In the Situation Room, Biden could be something of an unguided missile."

In some ways, Biden became the human face of an administration led by a president known for robotic stoicism. Where Obama rarely revealed any inner life, Biden rarely disguised his. Anger, joy, frustration, eagerness – if he felt it, he expressed it. He grew up in a middle-class Catholic family in Scranton, Pennsylvania, and Wilmington, Delaware, drawing modest grades before earning a law degree at Syracuse. He was elected to the Senate from Delaware in 1972, served for thirty-six years and ran for president twice unsuccessfully before accepting Obama's invitation to join his ticket in 2008. He played the seasoned mentor, helping a young and inexperienced president navigate the treacherous politics of the capital.

James Comey, who would serve as FBI director, described the dynamic between the two: "President Obama would have a series of exchanges heading a conversation very clearly and crisply in Direction A. Then, at some point, Biden would jump in with, 'Can I ask something, Mr. President?' Obama would politely agree, but something in his expression suggested he knew full well that for the next five or ten minutes we would all be heading in Direction Z. After listening and patiently waiting, President Obama would then bring the conversation back on course."

Still, Obama grew genuinely fond of his vice president, coming to appreciate Biden's authenticity and embracing his contrary voice during internal debates. "Joe, in that sense, can help stir the pot," Obama told *The New York Times*. And Biden, who at first bristled at the idea of serving as junior partner to a newcomer nineteen years his junior, came to appreciate Obama's strengths and place at the top of their partnership. As the re-election campaign approached, Obama brushed off aides who floated the idea of replacing Biden on the re-election ticket in 2012. Not only would it be politically suspect, the two had forged a real bond.

"You know what has surprised me?" Obama said at one of their weekly lunches. "How we have become such good friends."

"Surprised *you*?" Biden joked in response.

When the vice president's son, Beau, died of a brain tumor at age forty-six, it felt like a blow to Obama, who had come to think of Biden as a member of the family. "Joe," an uncharacteristically emotional president once told his number two during the eulogy, "you are my brother."

At the White House press briefing the day after *Meet the Press* aired, Jay Carney, the press secretary, was pummeled with questions from skeptical reporters about Obama's stance. How could he continue to oppose same-sex marriage when his own vice president supported it?

The next morning, as Obama was about to leave the White House for an event in Albany, New York, several aides intercepted him in the Oval Office and told him he had to change his position promptly. He agreed. "I've got to put Jay out of his misery," he said. The next day, he sat down with ABC's Robin Roberts to complete his "evolution."

"At a certain point," Obama told her, "I've just concluded that for me personally it is important for me to go ahead and affirm that I think same-sex couples should be able to get married."

Obama's shift was not without risk, coming just a day after voters in North Carolina, site of the upcoming Democratic National Convention and a key battleground state in the fall election, approved a ban on same-sex marriage. But polls showed dramatic changes in attitudes nationally. While just 27 percent of Americans supported same-sex marriage in 1996, when Bill Clinton signed the Defense of Marriage Act, fully 50 percent now thought it should be legal.

Among Democrats, support reached 65 percent, making it almost unsustainable for a Democratic president to remain in opposition when nearly two-thirds of his party was on the other side. In this case, Obama was a follower more than a leader. To his benefit, the Republicans, who made opposition to same-sex marriage a key part of their strategy in 2004, were now led by a nominee who once boasted of his support for gay rights and opted not to engage on the issue in a meaningful way this time, a sign of how much had changed in just eight short years.

Obama took the initiative on another issue important to his base just weeks later. With Congress balking at immigration reform, he decided to act on his own, citing his executive authority to allow as many as 800,000 young people brought into the United States illegally as children to stay without fear of deportation, to work legally and obtain driver's licenses and other documents. With the Deferred Action for Childhood Arrivals program, or DACA as it would come to be called, Obama in effect was asserting that he had the power to do what Congress had specifically rejected when it defeated the Dream Act nearly two years earlier. He was arguing that as the executive in charge of enforcing the laws, he had discretion to prioritize limited resources, and this category should not be a high priority. Conservatives decried what they saw as executive overreach; the president was obliged to enforce the laws, not unilaterally rewrite them.

And yet the opposition on the right seemed to some extent tempered. The younger immigrants who benefited were among the most sympathetic of the undocumented population, brought into the country through no action of their own. Called the "dreamers" by their champions, they were often students, workers and even members of the United States military. While liberal advocates applauded Obama's move, they pressed him to help their parents and others too. The president, however, said that was as far as he could go; he did not have the power to go further. At least that was his position for the moment.

*

Heading into the campaign season, much of Obama's record hinged on the health care program that now effectively bore his name. It had been dubbed "Obamacare" by scornful opponents in a bit of pejorative mockery, but the president decided to embrace the name. "You know what?" he told one crowd of supporters. "They're right, I do care."

The question was whether Obamacare would survive until the election. Its fate lay in the hands of Chief Justice John Roberts, the man who had mangled Obama's first inaugural oath and who had become a conservative check on the liberal president. Obama and Roberts in some ways had followed similar paths. They both studied at Harvard Law School, although they did not know each other then; Roberts graduated nearly a decade before Obama arrived. But they both excelled at the nation's most prestigious legal academy, graduating magna cum laude. Cerebral, charming and ambitious, each of them vaulted to the highest offices in the land after just short stints at the next level down. And each was seen initially as a conciliator only to end up leading on the strength of his own majority. Many years after their campus days, Obama and Roberts now emerged as the intellectual gladiators in a great battle over the role of government in American society. In a moment of churning uncertainty and ideological ferment, it was a struggle that defined Obama's presidency – and perhaps surprisingly few other figures outside the White House would ultimately play as critical a role as Roberts did in shaping Obama's legacy.

The two had gotten off to a bad start when Obama, as a senator, opposed Roberts's confirmation, a start only made worse by the bungled inaugural oath. But the real tension came with the 2010 case of *Citizens United v. Federal Election Commission*, in which the Roberts court ruled that corporations have First Amendment rights to spend money in election campaigns. Obama criticized the decision sharply a week later during his State of the Union address with Roberts and other justices seated not far away. Justice Samuel Alito was so bothered by the president's attack that he mouthed the words "not true" at one point during the speech. Roberts later called the partisan atmosphere of the event "very troubling" for justices who were supposed to remain above politics.

Yet when it came to the most important domestic initiative of Obama's presidency, it was Roberts who would come to his rescue. Twenty-six states and other plaintiffs had gone to court challenging the constitutionality of the Affordable Care Act, arguing that the Obama administration and Congress had exceeded their authority to intervene in the private marketplace, particularly by mandating that individuals buy health insurance. In effect, they argued, the government was forcing Americans to buy a commercial product that they might not want, an intrusion on their fundamental liberty. The Obama administration disagreed, pointing to the clause of the Constitution that empowered Congress to regulate interstate commerce.

After three days of oral arguments, Roberts and the rest of the conservative majority on the Supreme Court agreed with the plaintiffs that the government could not force individuals to buy insurance under the commerce clause. But in a move that stunned the legal and political communities, Roberts broke from his allies to side with the four liberal justices in finding that the government could enact such a requirement using its power to tax since the health care program punished those who failed to buy insurance by imposing a tax penalty. The reasoning may have been different, but the bottom line was the program was constitutional. It would go forward. Conservatives howled in protest but Roberts said he would not use the power of the bench to undo an election. "It is not our job," he wrote in the decision handed down on June 28, 2012, "to protect the people from the consequences of their political choices."

Obama was standing outside the Oval Office watching cable television when two networks, CNN and Fox, announced that the Supreme Court had just struck down his health care program. For a few moments, Obama absorbed the news that his signature domestic achievement, the program he thought would help define his place in history, was no more. But just then, Kathryn Ruemmler, his White House counsel, rushed into the room and flashed two thumbs up. The networks were wrong – the court had in fact upheld the program. Obama held his hand over his head and closed his eyes tightly, savoring the moment. Aides in the room applauded and shook his hand. Obama hugged Ruemmler and called Solicitor General Donald Verrilli, who had argued the case before the court, to congratulate him. "It seemed that a weight had been removed from his shoulders," Ben Rhodes said later.

Still, there was a pretty big asterisk. The court also ruled that Washington could not force states to expand Medicaid by threatening them with the loss of existing federal payments. That was a key element of the program to extend coverage to millions of poor Americans who did not otherwise qualify. Now states would choose whether to participate and many Republican governors quickly made clear they would not. Obama nonetheless chose to interpret the split verdict as a victory and declared vindication. Mitt Romney, hoping to mobilize conservatives behind him, vowed to overturn the law if he were elected, never mind the similarities to his own program in Massachusetts.

It was a mark of Obama's presidency that the program remained so controversial two years after its passage. Aides had once predicted that when the fury of the partisan battle surrounding its passage faded, Americans would accept and even welcome the program. But in the weeks leading up to the Supreme Court decision, just 34 percent of Americans told pollsters that they supported it, essentially unchanged from the 32 percent who favored it when it passed in 2010. The president's advisers argued that social programs often were unpopular when first enacted, only to build support once they were put in place and Americans came to rely on them. But history suggested otherwise. Social Security was popular from the start, supported by 73 percent of Americans in early 1937 and by 78 percent a year later. Medicare had the approval of 62 percent in early 1965 and 82 percent by the end of that year.

In the face of relentless conservative opposition, the White House never made a sustained effort to win over an unenthusiastic public. The strategist hired to design public outreach for the program was soon given other projects as well. Attempts to educate voters about the program were sporadic and underfunded. From the time of its passage to the Supreme Court decision, opponents spent $235 million on ads attacking the program, compared with the $69 million spent on those supporting it.

In essence, Obama's team had concluded that the issue was a political loser in the short term and decided to focus energy elsewhere. When the president delivered his State of the Union address in 2012, heading into his re-election campaign, he devoted just two sentences to the program that he had once hoped would be his main argument for a second term – forty-four words out of more than seven thousand. Instead, he and his advisers decided to emphasize jobs. As it turned out, the best thing Obama had going for him when it came to health care was the fact that Mitt Romney had sponsored his own version in Massachusetts and was just as reluctant to talk about it.

*

Romney's campaign against Obama rested more on promise than policy – specifically the unrealized promises of a president who could not live up to the stratospheric expectations he himself had set. While he assailed the incumbent for his approaches to the economy and foreign affairs, Romney mainly focused on the disappointments of the Obama era. And he sought to reclaim his mantle of business virtuoso after months of withering attacks by Democrats on his record in the private sector.

As he accepted the nomination at the Republican National Convention in Tampa, Florida, at the end of August, Romney sought to give permission, in effect, to once-hopeful Obama supporters to give up on him and try someone else without feeling guilty for abandoning the nation's first African-American president. "You know there's something wrong with the kind of job he's done as president when the best feeling you had was the day you voted for him," Romney told the delegates as his wife, Ann, and their five sons watched. "This president can tell us it was someone else's fault," he added. "This president can tell us that the next four years he'll get it right. But this president cannot tell us that you are better off today than when he took office."

He had a case to make. Unemployment that August was stubbornly stuck at 8.1 percent, almost exactly where it was when

Obama took office, although lower than its peak of 10 percent in October 2009. The economy was growing again, but only at a meager 1.3 percent in the second quarter of 2012. The federal deficit was still over $1 trillion a year. Median wages remained slightly lower than they were at the start of Obama's presidency in inflation-adjusted dollars. Some 15 million more people were on food stamps. Fully 87 percent of Americans said the economy would be very important to their vote, more than any other issue and the exact same as in the fall of 2008 at the height of the crisis, and only 37 percent thought the president was doing a good job on creating jobs. Obama could make the argument that he had pulled the country back from the brink, but the economy had yet to reach a point where many Americans were feeling an improvement.

Romney's debut on the biggest platform he would have until the fall debates, however, took an odd turn when he gave the convention stage to Clint Eastwood, the legendary actor who delivered a rambling, unscripted talk and then confused many in the hall and watching at home by using an empty bar stool positioned next to him to have an imaginary conversation with Obama. "What do you want me to tell Mr. Romney?" Eastwood asked the invisible president. "I can't tell him that," Eastwood answered. "He can't do that to himself."

A few days after Romney's nomination, Obama arrived in Charlotte, North Carolina, for the Democratic National Convention that would nominate him for the second time, now facing the challenge of converting his onetime message of hope and change into one of continuity and patience. No longer the outsider, no longer the critic of the status quo, Obama was left in the position of defending the country as it was and explaining how he would keep it moving toward a better place, an infinitely more complicated and less satisfying challenge.

He asked his newfound ally, Bill Clinton, to help him make the case. Clinton was never the inspiring orator that Obama was, but he had a gift for captivating a friendly crowd. Clinton was a talker more than a speaker, gifted less at stirring emotions than drawing out an argument. He connected various subjects and observations and blended them into a whole that somehow made sense to many in his audience. As he pulled together his speech for the convention, he summoned many of his old advisers for a two-day, nonstop crash session transforming his sheaf of handwritten notes on yellow pages into a coherent text. Obama's team sent a couple of their colleagues who were veterans of the Clinton White House to find out what was happening, only to have them disappear into "Clinton's Bermuda Triangle," never to be heard from again. Texts messages asking for a copy of the speech went unanswered.

Finally, Clinton and his widening circle of ad hoc advisers managed to slash the speech from an hour and a half to the twenty-eight minutes allotted him. But while the text fed into the teleprompter came in at just a little more than 3,000 words, the version he ended up delivering topped 5,000 words. In effect, he ad-libbed back in much of the material that had been edited out.

The Republicans were his favorite target. "They want to go back to the same old policies that got us into trouble in the first place," Clinton said. Then he appropriated their hero Ronald Reagan's line: "As another president once said, there they go again." The speech electrified the convention and even some Republicans grudgingly praised it. Obama afterward joked that he needed to appoint Clinton "secretary of 'splaining stuff."

Obama's own speech the next night tried to reconcile his promises with his accomplishments while asking the country for more time. The "Change" signs waved in the audience in 2008 had been replaced with placards saying "Forward." The word "promise," which he used thirty-two times in his acceptance speech four years earlier, came up just seven times. Even the traditional balloon drop was missing because of a last-minute change of venue.

"I won't pretend the path I'm offering is quick or easy; I never have," he told a packed arena of 20,000 party leaders and activists. "You didn't elect me to tell you what you wanted to hear. You elected me to tell you the truth. And the truth is, it will take more than a few years to solve challenges that have build up over decades."

*

If Obama was hoping the rest of the world would cooperate with his bid to win another term, the harsh reality was on display that summer. Europe seemed unable to contain its rolling economic crisis. Flare-ups of violence in Baghdad recalled the worst of the Iraq war. Vladimir Putin had reclaimed the presidency in Russia, forcing Obama's friend Dmitri Medvedev to step down at the end of his four-year term even as the Kremlin cracked down at home and rattled sabers abroad.

The Arab Spring that had started out with so much hope was taking an ominous turn as well. Egypt's popular revolution had elevated the Muslim Brotherhood to power and was now at risk of being reversed by the military. Libya was falling into a miasma of revenge killings as rival militias and Islamists competed for power. And in Syria, where President Bashar al-Assad had casually defied Obama's call for him to step down, a full-blown civil war was raging with government forces shelling civilian neighborhoods while insurgent groups begged for help from Arab states and the West.

Obama wanted no part in their war but over one weekend in August, the White House received alarming intelligence reports. American spy agencies had detected signs that the Assad government was moving part of its huge stockpile of chemical weapons out of storage, and the Syrian military was mixing chemicals, a possible indication that they were being prepared for use. As

Obama's national security team rushed back to the White House for weekend consultations, the president cautioned Assad not to employ the poisonous weapons on his own people, sending secret messages through Russia, Iran and other governments.

Obama went public with his warning the next day when asked about Syria at a news conference. Moving or using large quantities of chemical weapons, he declared, would cross a "red line" and "change my calculus" about American involvement in the conflict.

The advisers who had attended meetings on Syria over the weekend listened with surprise, wondering where the "red line" came from. With such an evocative yet off-the-cuff phrase, the president had defined his policy in a way some advisers soon wished they could take back.

A few weeks later, Obama was back in the Situation Room listening to David Petraeus, who had become CIA director when Leon Panetta took over the Pentagon. Petraeus had developed a plan to arm selected Syrian rebels to take down the government. Petraeus was passionate, arguing about the need to move "now versus later." Hillary Clinton backed him up, as did Panetta. Joe Biden, on the other hand, thought it was a "stupid idea," and Tom Donilon and Denis McDonough were skeptical as well. Susan Rice, once a leading voice for intervention in Libya and now feeling burned, argued strenuously against getting deeper into Syria's civil war, warning that Petraeus's plan would be the first step that would ultimately suck the United States into a quagmire. For Obama, there was still much to think about.

While Syria occupied the front burner in the Situation Room, Libya was "farmed out to the working level," as Dennis Ross, a top Middle East adviser to the president, put it. Now that the Libyan civilians were saved and Muammar el-Qaddafi was gone, Obama and his team were intent on avoiding getting entangled in the sort of nation-building in North Africa that dragged down the Bush administration in Afghanistan and Iraq. The United States would now help Libya with its emergence from tyranny only if three conditions were met: First, it had to be a situation in which America had unique capability that Europe or others did not. Second, Libya had to explicitly ask. And third, Libya would have to pay for the help with its oil revenue. By setting the bar so high, the White House effectively ensured that it would stay on the sidelines. Even when Hillary Clinton proposed sending a hospital ship to treat wounded fighters, the White House rejected the idea.

Christopher Stevens, Clinton's handpicked ambassador to the new Libya, sent warning flares to Washington about a "security vacuum" in Benghazi. In a memo he titled "The Guns of August," after Barbara Tuchman's history of the epic miscalculations that led to World War I, Stevens said Benghazi was moving "from trepidation to euphoria and back as a series of violent incidents has dominated the political landscape."

At age fifty-two, Stevens was a longtime foreign service officer with deep experience in the Arab world and an equally deep commitment to making Libya work. He was willing to take risks that others might not. As dangerous as he knew Benghazi was, Stevens was back there on September 11, 2012. He spent the day in meetings and then retired for the evening to an American diplomatic post. Suddenly, though, the visit turned tragic. Libyan gunmen stormed the compound, firing into the main building and setting it on fire. Over the course of the next few hours, Stevens was killed along with three other Americans: Sean Smith, an information officer with the State Department, and Tyrone Woods and Glen Doherty, two former Navy Seals working as security contractors for the CIA. It was the worst attack on an American diplomatic facility in more than a decade, coming on the anniversary of that traumatic day eleven years earlier.

Back at the White House, confusion reigned about what was going on. The assault in Benghazi happened on the same day that demonstrations got out of control at the American embassy in Egypt, where protesters angry about an anti-Islam video made by a Florida pastor expressed their rage and, in a few cases, scaled the fence. Some in Washington thought the Benghazi attack must also have stemmed from anger at the video. But the State Department's operations center sent an email to the White House, Pentagon, FBI and other agencies reporting that Ansar al-Sharia, a terrorist group, had claimed credit for the Libya assault on Facebook and Twitter. In an email to her daughter, Chelsea, later that night, Clinton made clear she considered the episode a terrorist attack. "Two of our officers were killed in Benghazi by an Al Qaeda-like group," she wrote.

In public, though, the White House and State Department cited the video as if the attack were simply a protest that got out of control. Addressing reporters in the Rose Garden the next day, Obama did use the word terror – "No acts of terror will ever shake the resolve of this great nation" – yet he also focused on the video. "We reject all efforts to denigrate the religious beliefs of others," he said. "But there is absolutely no justification to this type of senseless violence. None."

During an interview later in the day, Obama agreed when Steve Kroft of CBS News noted that he had shied away from using the word terrorism. Kroft asked if he believed it was a terrorist attack.

"Well, it's too early to know exactly how this came about, what group was involved," Obama replied. "But obviously it was an attack on Americans and we are going to be working with the Libyan government to make sure that we bring these folks to justice one way or the other."

By the weekend, the administration was sticking to the narrative of a video-inspired retaliation. After Clinton begged off weekend television appearances, Susan Rice was sent onto five Sunday talk shows. Relying on talking points that had been scrubbed in prickly negotiations between the White House, State Department and CIA, she repeated the suggestion that the assault in Benghazi was a protest taken over by extremists, not a premeditated terrorist operation. It would not be until eight days after the incident that a high-ranking American government official – Matt Olsen, director of the National Counterterrorism Center – would call it a "terrorist attack." Even then, Obama continued to avoid the term over the next few days.

Republicans quickly accused the president of trying to play down what happened in Benghazi because it would undermine his election-year claim to have crippled Al Qaeda. Democrats accused the Republicans of exploiting a tragedy for partisan advantage. What started as a human calamity and foreign policy nightmare quickly became a political football. Legitimate questions about the security of American installations overseas and the larger Obama approach to Libya were lost in the crossfire of political figures more eager to defend or denigrate than to undertake a sober examination of what went wrong and why.

Either way, the situation left Obama on the defensive just weeks before voters were to go to the polls to render their verdict on his presidency. "Instead of Obama being the successful guy that got bin Laden, we're talking about Obama as the second coming of Jimmy Carter," said Michael Rubin, a Middle East scholar and former Bush administration official. "And that's not something the campaign wants to see." The backlash would also dog Hillary Clinton for years to come and cost Rice her chance of succeeding Clinton as secretary of state.

Just a few days after the attack in Benghazi, Obama paid tribute to the slain Americans at a somber ceremony outside Washington at Joint Base Andrews, still better known as Andrews Air Force Base, as their bodies were returned. The president put his arm around Clinton as she fought back tears watching four flag-draped caskets being loaded into four hearses.

*

After he was done, Obama headed to Democratic Party headquarters to practice for his upcoming election debate. The juxtaposition of the two obligations that September day, one deeply profound, the other acutely political, came across as unseemly but underscored the challenges for an incumbent president seeking re-election. While a challenger could schedule time as he or she saw fit, a president had to juggle campaign commitments with the duties of the office. Aides noticed that Obama seemed distracted that day after the Benghazi ceremony as he tried to bone up for his confrontation with Mitt Romney. He never cared much for debates to begin with, much less debate preparations. They were, he said, "a drag."

On his heels as critics attacked him over Benghazi, Obama got a break the day after Susan Rice's television appearances. While in Columbus, Ohio, for a campaign event, David Plouffe joined him in the back of the presidential limousine and showed him a secret videotape made at a Republican fund-raiser at which Romney seemed to disrespect nearly half the country. The videotape, obtained and posted online by the liberal journal *Mother Jones*, showed Romney dismissing tens of millions of voters as freeloaders who live off the government teat and therefore were bound to support Obama. "There are 47 percent of the people who will vote for the president no matter what," Romney said on the videotape, which was surreptitiously made by a waiter. "All right, there are 47 percent who are with him, who are dependent upon government, who believe that they are victims, who believe the government has a responsibility to care for them, who believe they are entitled to health care, to food, to housing, to you-name it." He added that these people "pay no income tax" and he should not worry about reaching out to them. "I'll never convince them that they should take personal responsibility and care for their lives."

Obama and his team knew instantly that this was campaign dynamite that would blow up Romney's campaign, at least for a day or two. Romney was correct that about 47 percent of Americans paid no income taxes, half because they were too poor and half because they benefited from various tax breaks. Many of them, of course, did pay payroll taxes, not to mention local and state taxes and other levies. But the dismissive way Romney assigned all of those people to the other camp, the assumption that they were, in effect, lazy and feeding off the federal trough, played right into the Obama campaign argument that Romney was an out-of-touch aristocrat who would never fight for the middle class.

Plouffe had immediately told campaign advisers not to say anything publicly about the tape. Better to let it take on a life of its own as the news media put Romney on the defensive. When Plouffe showed it to Obama in the limousine, the president had the same reaction. "He understood its significance," Plouffe said, "though his instinct was even stronger than ours, which was, don't do anything with this right away." But they could put it in their pocket for the upcoming showdowns with Romney. "Man," Obama said when he reached David Axelrod by phone late that night, "we'd better not lose to *this* guy! I mean, you can't make this stuff up."

Obama scorned Romney and did not think him worthy, an impression he had a hard time masking in public and did not bother to in private. At one point earlier in the year, as a meeting in the Oval Office was breaking up, Jon Favreau, his speechwriter, told Obama that the conservative commentator Laura Ingraham had been struck by the president's poise at a recent public appearance.

"She said, 'I don't know if Mitt Romney can beat him,'" Favreau told him.

Obama, who was showing his staff to the door, stopped and puffed up. "Well," he answered, "Mitt Romney *can't* beat me."

That certainty was both Obama's strength and weakness. He had been warned that incumbent presidents tended to lose their opening debate during re-election campaigns. Not only do they have competing demands on their time and mental energy, they are often rusty, while their challengers are fresh off a primary season and at their most practiced at the verbal jousting that comes during a debate. After nearly four years in office, a president can grow unaccustomed to being challenged so frontally and can unintentionally come off as arrogant. A challenger is elevated in stature simply by sharing a stage with the incumbent.

Obama seemed to prove that during mock debates with Senator John Kerry playing Romney. "Too much defense throughout," David Plouffe emailed after one session. It did not get better with practice. After the final rehearsal, Axelrod began to give some criticisms when Obama cut him off testily. "Motherfucker's never happy," he snapped in a rare lapse into profanity. He then stormed out. In a decade of working together, Axelrod had never seen him lose his temper this way, certainly not directed at him. Obama's mood improved by the time of the debate, as he shrugged off the worries of his advisers. "I'll be there on game day," he assured them. "I'm a game-day player."

But forewarned is not always forearmed. Obama proved no exception to the incumbent's curse at his first debate in Denver on October 3, with 67 million Americans watching. Appearing opposite his challenger at the University of Denver, the president was flat, long-winded and pedantic. He kept looking down and did not use the attack lines advisers had given him. Obama did not mention Bain Capital, the centerpiece of his campaign case against Romney. He did not even pursue the most potent line of attack he had available – the secret videotape secretly showing Romney dismissing 47 percent of the nation as people who were "dependent upon government." Democrats had pounced on the tape, using it to paint Romney as an out-of-touch elitist. But not Obama, who never mentioned it on stage.

Sitting in the audience, Michelle Obama and Valerie Jarrett knew that Romney was getting the better end of the exchange. "Boy, he's good," Jarrett whispered to Michelle. The first lady later confessed that her husband had "bombed." Watching in a back room, Obama aides groaned their way through the debate as real-time dial focus group findings consistently favored Romney. Some aides shut their laptop computers rather than keep monitoring the devastating commentary among political reporters on Twitter. They did not even wait for the debate to end to convene a damage-control conference call. Top Colorado Democrats left the debate hall practically despondent, convinced that the president's poor performance had put their state back in play for Republicans. Suddenly, for Obama, a race that seemed well in hand appeared up for grabs.

The president himself walked off stage thinking he had done well. "This was a terrific debate," he said in its closing minutes. Only after he began reading early reviews on his iPad did he realize how badly it had gone. He called Axelrod on the way back to his hotel room.

"I guess the consensus is that we didn't have a very good night," Obama said.

"That is the consensus," Axelrod said.

Jim Messina, the campaign manager, was grim. "No one had ever lost a debate as badly as we lost that first debate," he said. "It just had been a slaughter." He was summoned back to Washington to reassure anxious Congressional Democrats who were "losing their minds." After one poll showed that Obama had lost the debate according to 89 percent of the respondents, Messina said, "Who knows who those 11 percent were? They had to be related to Barack Obama or me." After watching a videotape of his performance, Obama understood better and began calling panicky donors and supporters to reassure them. "This is on me," he told them, vowing to do better the next time.

Hillary Clinton tried to cheer Obama up by sending him a photoshopped image of Big Bird strapped to Romney's family car, making fun of Romney's support for cutting government funding for PBS (and therefore for *Sesame Street*) and his much mocked habit of traveling with his pet dog in a cage on top of his car.

"Please take a look at the image below, smile, and then keep that smile near at hand," Clinton told Obama.

"We'll get this done," he replied. "Just hold the world together five more weeks for me."

In confronting the depth of his debate debacle, Obama "faced his own political mortality," as Dan Pfeiffer put it later. In attempting a course correction, Obama concluded that he had been "too polite" in the first debate and dispensed with any fears he harbored of alienating swing voters by coming on too strong. "If I give up a couple of points of likability and come across as snarky," he told advisers, "so be it." Ron Klain, his debate coach, came up with a handy alliterative list of tips for the next debate in a memo:

Advocate (don't explain)
Audience
Animated
Attacks
Answers with principles and values
Allow yourself to take advantage of openings

Even so, in the mock debates that followed Denver, Obama remained flat and testy, not at the top of his game. Aides were nervous. "If we don't fix this," David Plouffe told colleagues, "we could lose the whole fucking election." Plouffe, who normally dismissed "bed-wetters" who worried too much, joined Axelrod, Klain and Jack Lew, who had succeeded Bill Daley as White House chief of staff, in holding an intervention with Obama and pressing him about his performance. No one doubted that he knew the issues, they told him, but professorial lectures were not going to cut it. He had to be quicker, shorter and sharper.

Rarely lacking in confidence, Obama admitted that he was struggling. For one thing, he acknowledged, he had no real agenda that he was selling the country, nothing like when he ran the first time at least. Four years earlier, he was brimming with ambitious plans to remake health care, the environment, energy, the economy and immigration while ending two wars; now, he had either achieved much of what he wanted to do or was offering rehashed versions of the same programs that had not passed. It felt smaller. And besides that, the format just did not suit him. These so-called debates seemed so fake to him, so cheap. A real debate would be an exchange of ideas, not a televised gladiatorial contest. "I am wired in a different way than this event requires," he told the worried aides. "I just don't know if I can do this."

His team encouraged him and told him that he could do it. However unnatural it might feel, all he had to do was perform for ninety minutes. Nothing less than his presidency was at stake.

Then they joined the rest of the team for one last mock debate.

"Fast and hammy! Fast and hammy!" Klain called out when Obama droned on too long.

"Punch him in the face," added Karen Dunn, another adviser on the team, when he was too mild.

Something eventually got through. The next evening, thirteen days after he took presidential decorum to a Xanax extreme, Obama tucked away a dinner of steak and potatoes and went on stage at Hofstra University in Long Island with plenty of red meat for anxious supporters watching his second debate. He waited all of forty-five seconds into the encounter before making clear that he came not just ready for a fight but intent on picking one.

He talked right over Romney, who tried to talk over him back. The president who had waited patiently for his turn the last time around forced his way into Romney's answers this time. At one point, Obama squared off with Romney face to face, almost chest to chest, in the middle of the stage, as if they were roosters in a ring.

"What Governor Romney said just isn't true."

"Not true, Governor Romney, not true."

"What you're saying is just not true."

Obama painted Romney as a tool of big oil who was soft on China, hard on immigrants, politically crass on Libya and two-faced on guns and energy. He deployed many of the attack lines that went unused in Denver, going after Romney's business record, income taxes and the 47 percent remark. When Romney assailed Obama for taking two weeks to admit that Benghazi was a terrorist attack, the president noted that in fact he had called it an "act of terror" the very next day in the Rose Garden – and Candy Crowley of CNN, the debate moderator, even stepped in to pronounce that accurate. Professor Obama was gone. Candidate Obama was back.

A front-page *New York Times* analysis the next morning summed up the event in a concise three-word headline: "Punch, Punch, Punch."

*

From that point on, Obama was back in command of the race. The third debate in Boca Raton, Florida, did nothing to change that, although it featured a moment that the president's team would have cause to regret after the election. With the debate focused on international affairs, Obama decided to go after Romney for saying that Russia was the biggest geopolitical threat facing America, using the line to portray his challenger as out of touch. "The 1980s are now calling to ask for their foreign policy back," Obama chided him, "because the Cold War has been over for twenty years." Within eighteen months, the opening of a new Cold War would make that look misguided at best, naïve at worst.

The end of the campaign, however, was shaped not by any of the issues that had dominated it to that point. The last-minute election surprise turned out to be Hurricane Sandy, which ravaged New York, New Jersey and other parts of the east. Keenly aware of how much the bungled response to Hurricane Katrina had hurt George W. Bush, Obama resolved to make sure the federal government this time measured up to the crisis. "The world is watching and I'm going to be judged by my response," he told advisers on a videoconference in the Situation Room. "You guys have got to get that power back up."

Obama called Governor Chris Christie, a leading Republican who had considered running against the president that year. "He gave me his personal phone number that night and said, 'You call me any time, day or night, if there's something that isn't happening that should be happening,'" Christie recalled later. "He was as good as his word." Obama even flew to New Jersey to appear beside Christie – a bipartisan show of solidarity that made him seem above the trivial politics of the moment. "I never felt good about the race after Sandy," said Stuart Stevens, a senior strategist for Romney.

Wrapping up the campaign, Obama very rarely encountered the nearly half of America that did not support him, those who blamed him for the economic troubles still afflicting the country.

He seemed taken aback at Cleveland's West Side Market when he asked a chicken vendor how business was going.

"Terrible since you got here," the man said.

The vendor meant only that the presidential visit with its extensive entourage had interfered with business that day, but he inadvertently voiced the frustration of many Americans.

Obama woke up on November 6 and went to play basketball with friends, an Election Day tradition. Arne Duncan, his old Chicago friend and education secretary, asked how he was feeling. "I'm good," Obama replied. "I got a wife who loves me and I got two great kids. Whatever happens, I'm going to be fine."

For Obama, the question was whether the critics whose voices had so dominated the national conversation reflected a majority of voters who would go to the polls. For a few hours, it looked like they did. "There was this moment where you think you might actually lose," Dan Pfeiffer said. The first report Obama's team got on Election Day, he said, "showed in some states a very jacked-up Republican turnout relative to what we thought it would be – and youth and African-American and Latino turnout down from what we thought it would be. It was a 'holy crap' moment."

That first report was wrong, as so many had been in recent elections, but as Obama watched the returns come in on television that evening, he was primed for bad news. When MSNBC called the race for him, he remained cautious.

"Let's wait and see when Fox calls it," he told excited aides.

A few minutes later, Fox called it for Obama too. It was time to celebrate.

Obama garnered 51 percent of the vote to Romney's 47 percent, not a landslide but a clear and convincing victory in an evenly divided country. He was the first president since Ronald Reagan to win a majority of the popular vote twice, and he secured a decisive Electoral College majority as well, with 332 votes to 206 for Romney. But he lost two states he had won four years earlier – Indiana and North Carolina – and his share of the overall popular vote was down two percentage points, making him the first president since Andrew Jackson in 1832 to win a second consecutive term with less popular support than his first.

Nonetheless, Obama relished the moment. For the forty-fourth president, there would be four more years, a chance to preserve what he had accomplished and finish what he had not. He would have an opportunity to secure a legacy as a president who made a mark not simply by virtue of his original barrier-breaking election but by transforming America in his image. As Obama relished the victory that night, his aides thought he looked more relaxed than they had seen him years.

"In some ways, this one is sweeter than 2008," Obama observed.

"Two thousand eight was pretty good," Dan Pfeiffer said.

"This one feels better. Folks know you pretty well after four years."

They knew him now. He was no longer the fresh face, no longer the new kid. He was the country's president. The voters had judged him and decided he was worthy. For Obama, it was especially gratifying because just two years earlier he had a near-death political experience when voters handed control of the House to his adversaries. Now, instead of being written off, Obama could write a few more sentences for his paragraph.

CHAPTER NINE

'Governing By Crisis'

Obama was fighting back tears. It was just a month after his re-election and he had been feeling optimistic about the path ahead when aides suddenly brought him gut-wrenching news: A young man armed with a Bushmaster XM-15 semi-automatic rifle had rampaged through an elementary school in Newtown, Connecticut, killing twenty children, all six or seven years old, as well as six adult staff members. Never before in American history had anyone shot and killed so many children in a schoolhouse.

Obama the president prepared to make a statement. But Obama the father of two girls was struggling to hold it together. He asked his staff to find his wife and ask her to come to the Oval Office, the only time in his eight years in the White House that he would summon her during the workday. When she arrived, they hugged without a word. Then he started to tell her the details of the bloodbath but stopped. She could see in his eyes "how broken they'd left him." His speechwriter, Jon Favreau, arrived to help with editing and was stunned to find the usually stoic president racked with emotion. "I had never seen him like that as long as I've known him," Favreau said later. "He was sitting at his desk and he was looking down at the statement and he was making some edits and he was barely looking up at us and his voice was the most somber and the most halted that I had ever heard it." At that moment, Favreau said, "everything kind of weighed on him."

Going through the text of the statement he would read, Obama crossed out a paragraph in which he would reflect on his own daughters in their classrooms and what it would be like if he got that call, what it would take to stop him from running to school as fast as he could and how he would not be able to breathe until he knew they were safe. "I won't be able to get through this," he said as he took his pen through those lines. "It's too raw."

Obama got up and steeled himself to go down to the briefing room to face the cameras. Joe Biden came to the Oval Office to see if the president wanted him to join him but one of Obama's aides waved him off, saying the president was too emotional and would only be more so if Biden were with him. "He was having real trouble," Biden recalled.

Standing at the lectern moments later, Obama could not mask his feelings from reporters either. His face was drawn, his eyes ringed with grief. He noted that the dead were just children, then wiped a tear from his eye. He paused, staring down, trying to regain his composure. Twelve long seconds passed in silence before he spoke again, an eternity in the life of a televised presidential statement. "They had their entire lives ahead of them," he finally said, "birthdays, graduations, weddings, kids of their own."

He paused again, unable to speak for another seven seconds before mourning the adults who were killed as well. He wiped away another tear. "Our hearts are broken today," the president at last continued. "This evening, Michelle and I will do what I know every parent in America will do, which is hug our children a little tighter and we'll tell them that we love them and we'll remind each other how deeply we love one another. But there are families in Connecticut that cannot do that tonight."

Obama would later call that day, Friday, December 14, 2012, the worst of his presidency. He had delivered similar statements after a series of mass shootings over his first term – at Fort Hood, in Tucson and in Aurora, Colorado. Each time, he would mourn the deaths, maybe make a perfunctory call for more gun control and then move on. He knew that the politics of gun rights made legislation difficult if not impossible to pass and he always had other priorities on which to focus his limited energy. This time was different. As he flew to Connecticut a few days later for a memorial service, he sat in his cabin on Air Force One, a jumble of anger and sadness, scratching out what he would say, his aides not at all certain how far he would go. As they would soon discover, to their own surprise, this time his grief would be channeled into a cause.

"No single law, no set of laws, can eliminate evil from the world or prevent every senseless act of violence in our society," Obama told a gathering of 1,700 in the small New England town of Newtown, a crowd that included children clutching stuffed puppies handed out by the Red Cross. "But that can't be an excuse for inaction." He added that "in the coming weeks I'll use whatever power this office holds in an effort aimed at preventing more tragedies like this. Because what choice do we have? We can't accept events like this as routine. Are we really prepared to say that we're powerless in the face of such carnage? That the politics are too hard?"

The massacre at Sandy Hook Elementary School reframed the start of Obama's second term before it even began. While he had plenty of other issues on his priority list, suddenly gun control vaulted to the top. He assigned Joe Biden to assemble a plan and began revising his strategy to use whatever honeymoon he had earned from his re-election. "I will put everything I've got into this," Obama said at one point, "and so will Joe."

The politics of guns had been hazardous for Democrats for a generation. While polls showed that the vast majority of the public supported an array of measures intended to keep firearms out of the hands of criminals and the mentally unstable, the National Rifle Association wielded disproportionate influence by mobilizing its fervent membership behind a no-compromise position. Any gun-control measure, no matter how modest or uncontroversial, represented a threat to the Second Amendment guarantee of the right to bear arms, in the NRA's view, the first step down a slippery slope to jackbooted government agents seizing guns from everyday owners. The organization proved its power in 1994, when it punished Democrats who voted for Bill Clinton's legislation requiring a background check before most gun purchases and banning the sale and manufacture of military-style semi-automatic rifles called assault guns. Republicans captured control of both houses of Congress in midterm elections that year, at least in part because of the gun issue, and the memories had kept many Democrats from rural and suburban districts far away from the issue for years to come. When the assault rifle ban expired after ten years, Congress let it slide away without renewing it.

Before he could get started on his newfound cause, Obama had to first clear out the underbrush remaining from his first four years. Thanks to the collective failure in Washington to find a resolution to the economic issues plaguing the country, a series of tax cuts from both the Bush and Obama eras were due to expire at the same time while the deep, automatic, across-the-board spending cuts known as the sequester were scheduled to be enacted at the end of the year – a massive cumulative hit on the economy that Ben Bernanke, the chairman of the Federal Reserve, had dubbed the "fiscal cliff." Unless Obama and the Republicans came together to put the brakes on, the country might easily tumble over the edge into another recession.

Burned by past negotiations and emboldened after his re-election, Obama this time refused to budge until Republicans allowed the part of George W. Bush's tax cuts that went to the richest Americans to expire. The Republicans were not willing to give in entirely, but in the aftermath of Obama's re-election, they recognized that they had lost the fight, so for the first time they were ready to make a permanent compromise. Instead of raising rates back to their pre-Bush levels for those earning $250,000 a year and above, they went up only for those making at least $400,000. In addition, Obama succeeded in increasing estate and capital gains taxes and renewing his own tax credits for child care, college tuition and renewable energy production. He also managed to extend unemployment benefits for 2 million jobless Americans. Yet the two sides could not agree on spending, so once again they punted the issue down the road by simply extending current levels. Liberals groused that Obama had given away too much, but he felt satisfied that he had finally put the Bush tax cut debate behind him, largely on his terms.

*

Obama formally opened his second term a few days later with an assertive eighteen-minute Inaugural Address delivered from the West Front of the Capitol on January 21, 2013, because January 20 fell on a Sunday. Reaffirmed by a convincing re-election victory, he offered a robust articulation of modern liberalism in America. Dispensing with the post-partisan appeals of four years earlier, a more hardened president instead laid out a forceful vision of advancing gay rights, easing the lives of illegal immigrants, preserving the social welfare safety net and acting to stop climate change. Instead of declaring the end of "petty grievances," as he did the first time he took the oath, he challenged Republicans to step back from their staunch opposition to his agenda.

> *Progress does not compel us to settle centuries-old debates about the role of government for all time – but it does require us to act in our time. For now, decisions are upon us and we cannot afford delay. We cannot mistake absolutism for principle or substitute spectacle for politics or treat name-calling as reasoned debate. We must act.*

Absolutism and spectacle, however, were hardly going away in Obama's Washington. And those who had invested such hopes and dreams in him the last time were a little more subdued this time. For the ceremony, hundreds of thousands of people gathered on a brisk but bright day, a huge crowd by any measure but significantly smaller than the record turnout of four years earlier. If the day felt restrained compared with the historic mood of 2009, it reflected a more restrained moment in the life of the country. The expectations that loomed so large with Obama's arrival in office, even amid economic crisis, had long since faded into a starker sense of the limits of his presidency.

Now fifty-one years old and noticeably grayer, Obama appeared alternately upbeat and reflective. When he re-entered the Capitol at the conclusion of the ceremony, he stopped his entourage to turn back toward the cheering crowds on the National Mall and soak it in.

"I want to take a look, one more time," he said. "I'm not going to see this again."

His daughters, Malia, now fourteen, and Sasha, eleven, were in a playful mood. Malia at one point sneaked up behind her father and cried out, "Boo!" Sasha used a smartphone to take a picture of her parents kissing in the reviewing stand outside the White House, then made them do it again.

Obama once again used Abraham Lincoln's Bible to take his oath, but also added a second Bible once owned by Martin Luther King. He became the first president ever to mention the word "gay" in an Inaugural Address, linking the struggle for gay rights to past movements for women and African-Americans. "Our journey is not complete until our gay brothers and sisters are treated like anyone else under the law," he said.

But scarred by four years of battles, the president felt little need to reach out to the opposition, and some Republicans took his message as inappropriately partisan for an inaugural ceremony that historically tended to emphasize more unifying themes. "I would have liked to see a little more on outreach and working together," said Senator John McCain, his vanquished opponent from 2008. "There was not, as I've seen in other inaugural speeches, 'I want to work with my colleagues.'"

As he recharged his presidency, Obama shuffled his Cabinet and White House staff. Hillary Clinton, Leon Panetta, Timothy Geithner and others departed as the president assembled a second-term team to confront the challenges ahead. For secretary of state, he tapped Senator John Kerry, his patron from the Democratic National Convention in 2004. For secretary of defense, Obama chose former Senator Chuck Hagel, a Republican maverick who had been a sharp critic of George W. Bush. For treasury secretary, Obama appointed Jack Lew, and to replace Lew as chief of staff, he promoted Denis McDonough, the national security aide who had been with him from the beginning.

Obama devoted little of his Inaugural Address to foreign policy because he wanted to focus his energies on domestic affairs, like gun control. But he was hoping to straighten out his international agenda to clear the way. In his initial overseas trip after his re-election, he became the first sitting president to travel to Burma, also called Myanmar, as part of his effort to encourage its emergence from decades of isolation and repression, making a personal pilgrimage to the home of opposition leader Daw Aung San Suu Kyi, who had been held under house arrest for nearly two decades. In his State of the Union address, Obama announced that he would withdraw 34,000 more troops from Afghanistan over the next year, or more than half the remaining force, in hopes of winding down the war by the time he left office. And he paid his first visit as president to Israel to try to ease longstanding friction with its conservative prime minister, Benjamin Netanyahu.

For a brief moment, Obama could begin to think about the mark he would leave on history. He traveled to Dallas in April to join all the other living presidents for the opening of the George W.

Bush Presidential Library and Museum. Obama recalled that the last time all the presidents had assembled in one place was right before he had taken office. He had learned something since then, he said. "No matter how much you think you're ready to assume the office of president," he told the audience, "it's impossible to truly understand the nature of the job until it's yours." The nature of the job was unrelenting, it was brutal and it was taxing.

Even before his election, Obama had told aides that a president could control perhaps 20 percent of what he spent his energies on while the rest was controlled by events. If he understood that intellectually then, he had come to understand it viscerally by now – and there were times that 20 percent looked a little optimistic. His vision of a presidency marked by great strides toward a progressive future had become complicated by an economy that was still struggling and a capital that was still polarized. Even having won re-election, Obama barely commanded the support of a majority of Americans and Republicans showed no willingness to diminish their unyielding opposition to his agenda.

He looked around the stage that day in Dallas and saw his living peers – Jimmy Carter, George H.W. Bush, Bill Clinton and George W. Bush. He had scorned them at times, looked down on them even, but four years after taking the oath for the first time and a few months after taking it for the second, he had come to respect each of them more for their dedication to their country and their determination to make it better, whatever their mistakes.

Even the younger Bush looked better to Obama these days, if only because the forty-third president had treated the forty-fourth president so graciously and declined to join the bandwagon of bile, saying his successor "deserves my silence." Obama appreciated that and had come to see Bush in a different light. "To know the man is to like the man," Obama said. "Because he's comfortable in his own skin. He knows who he is. He doesn't put on any pretenses. He takes his job seriously, but he doesn't take himself too seriously. He is a good man." It was as if to say that whatever their differences, and they were manifold, they were now colleagues in the world's most exclusive club.

By spring, Obama had found his post-inaugural optimism soured by a cloud of partisanship and controversy. Despite his vision of an activist government as a force for good in American society, the first months of his second term seemed to reinforce fears of an overreaching state while calling into question Obama's ability to master his own presidency. His drive to enact new gun-control measures proved to be the first casualty. Painfully aware of the power of the National Rifle Association, Obama put forward a package of relatively modest initiatives. He called on Congress to reinstate Clinton's assault rifle ban and pushed to outlaw armor-piercing bullets and magazines with more than ten rounds, like those used in Newtown and other mass shootings. He also proposed closing a longstanding loophole that allowed buyers to avoid criminal background checks by purchasing weapons from unlicensed sellers at gun shows or through private sales. The vast majority of Americans interviewed by pollsters supported such ideas.

But as the shock of Newtown faded, so did the momentum for change. "Nothing the president is proposing would have stopped the massacre at Sandy Hook," said Senator Marco Rubio, a Republican rising star from Florida. "President Obama is targeting the Second Amendment rights of law-abiding citizens instead of seriously addressing the real underlying causes of such violence." The NRA, which in the past had originally supported background checks, now lobbied furiously against expanding them to gun shows. Instead, the organization argued that more people should own guns to stop crazed killers like the one in Newtown. "The only thing that stops a bad guy with a gun," said

236

Wayne LaPierre, the NRA's executive vice president, "is a good guy with a gun."

By April, Obama's push for gun control, the effort he made the opening bid of his second term, was effectively over. While Senators Pat Toomey, a conservative Republican from Pennsylvania, and Joe Manchin III, a conservative Democrat from West Virginia – both gun owners, both with A ratings from the NRA – put together a bipartisan package of new restrictions, they failed to garner the sixty votes necessary to cut off a filibuster in the Senate. Three other Republicans joined Toomey in supporting it, but four Democrats from states that Obama lost in 2012 refused to go along. Sitting in the Senate gallery, the mother of a woman killed in a 2007 mass shooting at Virginia Tech and a survivor of the shooting in Tucson that injured Gabrielle Giffords shouted in unison, "Shame on you!"

For Obama, it was a devastating blow. He had promised to put "everything I've got" behind the gun-control legislation, and it had not been enough. A second-term president coming off re-election has one chance to use the mandate that comes with victory and Obama had nothing to show for it. "We got an F," Arne Duncan, Obama's friend and education secretary, said ruefully. "We absolutely failed. There's no other way to put it."

Obama's enemies now knew they could beat him, even in a Democratic-controlled Senate and even though his proposals had the strong support of voters. In effect, he repeated Bush's experience when he started his own second term with a proposal to restructure Social Security and allow some payroll taxes to be invested in the stock market, only to watch it die in Congress. "I've heard some say that blocking this step would be a victory," Obama said after the gun-control vote, surrounded in the Rose Garden by angry parents of children killed in Newtown. "And my question is, a victory for who? A victory for what? All that happened today was the preservation of the loophole that lets dangerous criminals buy guns without a background check. That didn't make our kids safe."

A defeated Obama found himself in a season of setbacks and scandal, on the defensive amid revelations and controversies, some of his own making and some generated by his political opponents. The Justice Department disclosed that it had seized telephone records of reporters for The Associated Press as part of a national security leak investigation. It also searched the personal emails of James Rosen, the chief Washington correspondent for Fox News, in a separate leak investigation, going so far as to describe the reporter as "an aider, abettor and/or co-conspirator." The actions undercut Obama's promises of transparency and raised questions about his commitment to freedom of the press. While he could wax eloquently about the virtues of an independent news media, he also conducted more leak investigations than all other presidents before him combined.

On top of that, a mushrooming Congressional investigation into the terrorist attack in Benghazi, Libya, was highlighting the administration's failure to guard its diplomats and its manipulation of talking points. With Hillary Clinton now out of office and contemplating another run for the presidency when Obama's term was over, the inquiry focused on her actions, or lack of actions, during the episode. And then there was the revelation that the Internal Revenue Service had singled out for extra scrutiny conservative nonprofit groups seeking tax-exempt status by searching for the terms "Tea Party" or "patriots" in their titles, a revelation that roiled the president's opponents, fueled questions about abuse of power and cost the agency commissioner his job. Only years later would it emerge that the IRS did the same with liberal groups by focusing on names that included words like "progressive," "occupy" and "green energy," and there was never convincing evidence that Obama or anyone close to him had anything to do with it.

Amid those troubles came a chilling new terrorist attack on American soil, this time a pair of pressure-cooker bombs set off twelve seconds apart at the Boston Marathon on April 13, 2013. Three people were killed and about 240 others seriously injured amid the chaos and confusion, with seventeen people losing one or both legs. During a subsequent manhunt, the bombers, a pair of Chechen brothers named Dzhokhar and Tamerlan Tsarnaev, killed a Massachusetts Institute of Technology police officer and carjacked a sports utility vehicle. They wound up in a blazing firefight that wounded another pair of officers. Tamerlan, twenty-six, died after Dzhokhar, nineteen, ran over him with a car attempting to escape. Dzhokhar was later apprehended and would eventually be convicted and sentenced to death. The brothers were inspired by Anwar al-Awlaki, the cleric killed in the 2011 drone strike.

*

In that spring of his discontent, Obama grew exasperated at his inability to shape events. He felt trapped in a system in which he could not even speak forthrightly. In private, he talked longingly of "going Bulworth," a reference to the offbeat 1998 Warren Beatty movie about a senator who risked all to say what he really thought. While Beatty's character had neither the power nor the platform of a president, the metaphor highlighted Obama's desire to be liberated from what he saw as the political constraints holding him back.

Obama scorned Washington. The politicians were hypocritical and too often motivated by power, not the public good. The lobbyists made money hand over fist slipping special-interest provisions into bills. The news media were shallow and sensational. Too often the loudest voices were rewarded and the sensible ones smothered by a system geared toward conflict rather than compromise.

The opposition seemed interested only in finding advantage in any situation, perfectly willing to distort and even lie to score points. The capital kept pushing him to bend to its ways and he kept refusing. He would rather have dinner with his daughters than with well-heeled donors or some committee chairman who controlled the fate of a favorite bill. He would rather explain his policies in forty-five minute lectures than forty-five second sound bites.

The fact was, of course, that he had been the one to raise expectations that were difficult to live up to. But he resented the constant criticism, especially from his own side, the notion that he was letting people down, that he was ineffective, as if he could just snap his fingers and force Congress to follow his wishes. He particularly hated the comparisons to Lyndon Johnson, the notion that if he were simply more like LBJ, he would get more done. LBJ, he noted to anyone who would listen, had a Congress with overwhelming Democratic majorities, a true point that, however, ignored the fact that Democrats themselves were split in that era between Southern conservatives and Northern liberals.

In Obama's view, he was being held to an impossible standard, a dream ideal of what his liberal base thought a president should be like. He bristled at a column by Maureen Dowd in *The New York Times* that compared him unfavorably to Michael Douglas's title character in *The American President*, written by Aaron Sorkin. At the White House Correspondents' Association dinner in April, Obama turned to Douglas, who happened to be in the audience. "Michael, what's your secret, man?" Obama asked, in a tone that probably sounded more bitter than he intended. "Could it be that you were an actor in an Aaron Sorkin liberal fantasy?"

Obama grew ever more derisive a few days later when a reporter skeptically asked about the prospects for further legislation given his setbacks. "As Mark Twain said," he responded testily, "rumors of my demise may be a little exaggerated at this point."

240

In June came a challenge of a different sort, one that confronted the image he liked to project of someone who was not part of the system. *The Washington Post* and *The Guardian* newspaper began publishing a series of explosive reports about secret American surveillance programs with vaster reach than previously known. The government, they reported, had forced telecommunications firms to hand over telephone records for millions of Americans in the name of hunting terrorists.

The National Security Agency used the records to search the so-called metadata – information such as which phones called which other phones, when they were in contact and how long the calls lasted. Warrants were still required to actually listen in on Americans' phone calls themselves. But the scope of the net was breathtaking and set off a new furor over the sacrifice of civil liberties for national security. More disclosures followed. It turned out that the NSA had been eavesdropping on the phone calls of foreign leaders, including allies like Chancellor Angela Merkel of Germany. Not surprisingly, Merkel was furious.

Soon, the source of the leaks revealed himself publicly, a former NSA contractor named Edward Snowden, who proclaimed himself disturbed by what he saw as the government's unjustified intrusions into privacy. Snowden had fled the United States before going public and after a circuitous route wound up at an airport in Moscow, where Russian authorities decided to give him temporary asylum while crowing about his disclosures. In response, Obama canceled a trip to Moscow for a scheduled summit with Vladimir Putin, the first time a meeting of the top Russian and American leaders had been scrapped out of anger since Francis Gary Powers's U-2 spy plane was shot down over the Soviet Union more than half a century earlier.

The Snowden revelations not only disrupted Obama's relations with Merkel and Putin but tarnished his image as a reformer. As a candidate, Obama had vowed to rein in what he described as a surveillance state run amok. "That means no more illegal wiretapping of American citizens," he declared in 2007.

Like other presidents before him, though, the idealistic candidate wary of government power found that the tricky trade-offs of national security issues looked different to the person receiving intelligence briefings first thing each day detailing threats to American lives. "When you get the package every morning, it puts steel in your spine," said David Plouffe. "There are people out there every day who are plotting."

Still, the public disclosure of the surveillance seemed discordant with Obama's own effort to pivot away from the limitless war on terrorism. Just a couple of weeks earlier, in a much-touted speech at the National Defense University, Obama had forecast the eventual end of the struggle, saying that while America still needed to work to dismantle terrorist groups, "this war, like all wars, must end."

Obama privately viewed Snowden as a self-important narcissist who had not thought through the consequences of his actions, but aides said the president was himself surprised to learn just how far the surveillance had gone. Obama ordered the NSA to stop tapping Merkel and other close allies and appointed a task force to reconsider the programs. "Things seem to have grown at the NSA," Plouffe said, citing specifically the tapping of foreign leaders' telephones. "I think it was disturbing to most people and I think he found it disturbing."

*

Because Congress had not passed the necessary spending bills, the federal government would run out of money to operate on October 1, 2013, and reach its debt ceiling a couple of weeks later, leaving the nation in default. Two years after the failed grand bargain negotiations, Republicans were determined to use the twin deadlines to force concessions from Obama on health care and other issues, but he resolved to stand firm. Unlike the last time, there was no meaningful effort to stop the collision. Both sides seemed willing to take their chances in a high-stakes political game of chicken, gambling that the other side would blink first.

Ever since Bill Clinton emerged victorious from a budget fight in 1995 and 1996, it had been an article of faith for more experienced Republicans that shutting down the government in fiscal disputes was bad politics. But the newer generation of conservatives, elected on the strength of the Tea Party movement in the Obama era, did not see it that way and they were itching for a fight. Their attempts to either repeal or gut Obama's health care program had become a mission and they were willing to take any risk. Obama was never going to sign a bill that meant doing away with his signature domestic achievement, even at the cost of letting much of the government close temporarily. And so the deadline came and went with no spending bill to keep the doors open.

At 12:01 a.m. on October 1, an uneasy calm descended in the halls of the Capitol as the money officially ran out. By morning's light, tourists were barred from entering the building and government offices across Washington and the country remained locked. While essential services continued, the military service academies suspended intercollegiate sports competitions, the Food and Drug Administration halted routine establishment inspections, the Consumer Product Safety Commission stopped recalling products that did not present an imminent threat and the National Zoo's online "Panda Cam" showing images of the latest panda bear cub was turned off. National attractions from the Statue of Liberty in New York to Alcatraz prison in San Francisco Bay were closed. Angry veterans from World War II and Vietnam pushed past barricades at a closed memorial in Washington. Some 800,000 federal workers were told to stay home.

Appropriately enough, perhaps, the start of the shutdown coincided with the first real day of Obama's health care program. Obama brought to the Rose Garden several uninsured Americans who would benefit from expanded coverage to illustrate the consequences and showcase his defiance of his Republican critics. "As long as I am president, I will not give in to reckless demands by some in the Republican Party to deny affordable health insurance to millions of hard-working Americans," he said. Gesturing toward his guests, he said, "I want Republicans in Congress to know – these are the Americans you'd hurt if you were allowed to dismantle this law."

For sixteen days, the two sides remained at loggerheads while Republicans watched their poll numbers sink and their options narrow. On the eve of the debt-ceiling deadline, they finally gave in. A partially shuttered government was one thing, but a national default was too much. Senate Republicans, never as enthusiastic about flirting with fiscal disaster as their hard-line House counterparts, cut a deal with Democrats to reopen the government and increase the debt ceiling. Eighty-seven House Republicans broke ranks to support the agreement and end the impasse.

"We fought the good fight," John Boehner said afterward. "We just didn't win."

Conservatives were not convinced their leaders really had their hearts in it. "Unfortunately," said Senator Ted Cruz, a firebrand Republican from Texas and champion of the Tea Party movement, "the Washington establishment is failing to listen to the American people."

Obama, for his part, bemoaned the scorched-earth confrontation that led to the deal. "We've got to get out of the habit of governing by crisis," he said.

But crisis seemed to be a permanent feature of his presidency. If the Republicans were partly responsible at times, Obama had his own team to look at for the next one. A few days before his new health care system was supposed to debut, Obama previewed it for the public. "This is real simple," he said in a speech in Maryland. "It's a web site where you can compare and purchase affordable health insurance plans side by side the same way you shop for a plane ticket on Kayak, same way you shop for a TV on Amazon. You just go on and you start looking and here are all the options."

Real simple. Except it wasn't. On October 1, the same day that much of the government shut down, the health care web site went live. Unlike Amazon's web page, though, it was a disaster. Millions of Americans tried going to the site on its first day and many came away unable to navigate it. The site would not allow many to create accounts, shop for plans or fully enroll. While Obama and sympathetic celebrities like Lady Gaga tweeted to followers to #GetCovered, many could not.

"An unknown error has occurred," they saw on their screens.

What Obama and his team hoped was a temporary problem soon extended into days and then weeks. The president chewed out aides in private, demanding to know how this could go so wrong. But his White House had no one to blame but itself, since it had assigned political officials with no background in major software systems to manage the creation of a web site for a nationwide insurance marketplace.

Evoking Bush's troop surge to turn around the Iraq war and his own in Afghanistan, Obama launched a "tech surge" to bring what the administration called "the best and the brightest from both inside and outside government" to fix the web site. The problems, however, defied quick resolution and provided endless fodder for late-night television comedians.

"Today, there were more problems with the web site," Jay Leno joked on *The Tonight Show* on NBC. "It seems when you type in your age, it's confusing because it's not clear if they want the age you are right now or the age you'll be when you finally log in."

Stephen Colbert, on the Comedy Channel, attempted to sign up for Obamacare on camera. When he pressed the button, the screen said, "The webpage cannot be found." Colbert, in his faux conservative persona, cheered. "Whoo! Obamacare's a train wreck! Whoo!"

As it happened, truth was imitating comedy with stunning precision. After weeks of efforts to fix the problem, Kathleen Sebelius, Obama's secretary of health and human services, visited a Miami medical center to talk with local residents trying to sign up for coverage, only to watch haplessly as the web site failed while television news cameras recorded the moment for maximum public embarrassment.

"Sorry, our system is down," the screen told the husband and wife who were attempting to enroll in front of her.

"Uh oh," Sebelius said.

Just as bad, insurance companies were kicking many customers off their old plans even though Obama had promised they would not. It was one of the most explicit and categorical assurances he had offered when the health care law was being written back in 2009: "No matter how we reform health care," he had said, "we will keep this promise to the American people: If you like your doctor you will be able to keep your doctor, period. If you like your health-care plan, you'll be able to keep your health-care plan, period. No one will take it away, no matter what."

But in fact, whenever an insurance company changed an existing plan, it was no longer grandfathered under the law and therefore had to be upgraded to meet the higher standards of the Obama program. That meant many Americans were being sent cancellation notices and told they had to replace their plans with other, more comprehensive versions that conformed to the new law – and that invariably cost more money. Glenn Kessler, the fact-checker for *The Washington Post*, gave the president four Pinocchios for a false statement. PolitiFact, another journalistic effort to truth-squad politicians, judged the "you can keep it" promise to be the "Lie of the Year." Obama apologized and tried to temporarily extend existing health plans for many of those affected. But the damage was done. In the years to come, it would be cited as Exhibit A anytime critics wanted to make the case that Obama lied about the reach of his health care plan in order to sell it to an unwitting public.

The botched kickoff of the health care web site proved a short-term blow to the system, since it depended greatly on drawing in younger, healthier workers whose premiums in the aggregate would subsidize medical services for less healthy, older customers. The troubles enrolling alienated many of those younger workers. They also proved a balm for Republicans emerging from the government shutdown. Instead of enduring the backlash from a public turned off by their tactics, they could change the subject by focusing attention on Obama's failed web site. And the president, instead of converting his victory over the Republicans in the budget standoff into fresh momentum for other initiatives, found himself on the ropes as many of his own supporters wondered whether he and his team were up to the task.

"No one is madder than me," Obama declared at one point. With plenty of reason.

CHAPTER TEN

'Red Line'

They circled the oval pathway on the South Lawn once, twice, three times and kept going. As Obama paced outside the White House that late-summer evening, he wrestled out loud with Denis McDonough over one of the most profound decisions any commander in chief makes: Whether to go to war. For forty-five minutes, he walked and talked, weighing the consequences of action and inaction, before coming to his conclusion. He and McDonough then headed back into the Oval Office to reveal his decision to the rest of his team.

For Obama, that day at the end of August 2013 would prove a turning point in his approach to the world – and its approach to him. After publicly drawing a "red line" warning Syria not to use chemical weapons against its own people, he now confronted compelling evidence that the government of President Bashar al-Assad had done just that. American and European intelligence agencies had confirmed that a sarin gas attack killed an estimated 1,400 men, women and children in Ghouta outside the Syrian capital of Damascus ten days earlier and Western analysts concluded that all signs pointed to the government.

Still, the legacy of the blown intelligence that led to the Iraq war hung over the case. When James Clapper, the director of national intelligence, reported to Obama in the Oval Office on the evidence that Assad had ordered the strike, he made a point of saying it was not yet a "slam dunk" and even used air quotes to make the point. "Slam dunk" was the phrase that George Tenet, then the CIA director, had famously used to tell George W. Bush that they could easily make the case to the public that

Iraq had weapons of mass destruction. Obama was annoyed. "Jim," he said, "no one asked you if it was a slam dunk."

The Syrian civil war had raged for two and a half years by that point, with ruinous results. While popular uprisings in other Arab countries had either resulted in quick and relatively nonviolent change or were quickly suppressed, the anti-government movement in Syria had evolved from peaceful protests into a full-blown armed rebellion exploited by outside Islamist extremists and met with brutal and unrelenting violence by Assad's forces. Tens of thousands of people on both sides of the war had been killed by that point and many times more than that had been injured or displaced from their homes. Obama's call on Assad to step down had been ignored with impunity. Now the question was whether his "red line" would be as well.

Obama had steadfastly resisted pressure to get involved in Syria's civil war. After nearly five years in office, he had learned unforgiving lessons about the limits of America's ability to influence the course of events abroad through the use of military force. His surge of troops to Afghanistan had not yielded a clear-cut victory and he was now busy pulling forces out. He had resisted pressure to keep a residual force in Iraq. And even his prolific use of drone strikes to take out key terrorists on his "kill list" was proving less satisfying and the president had promised to begin reining in their use by shifting more of them from the CIA to the Pentagon.

Most searing was the war in Libya, which may have been the most significant foreign policy hinge point in Obama's presidency. His intervention had averted a threatened massacre and toppled Muammar el-Qaddafi but otherwise left behind a broken state and a stew of factionalism and radicalism that led to the attack that killed an American ambassador and three other Americans in Benghazi. What was left of Qaddafi's arsenals ended up arming terrorist and criminal groups around the region and fueled the bloodletting in Syria. The civil war in Libya had produced two rival governments, thousands of casualties, a newfound outpost for terrorists and a flood of refugees attempting to make it across the Mediterranean to Europe on often rickety boats.

The chaotic outcome weighed on Obama every time the question of intervention came up afterward. Until Libya, Obama had been open to advisers urging him to exercise American power abroad; after Libya, he was far more skeptical. "It's the day after Qaddafi is gone, when everybody is feeling good and everybody is holding up posters saying, 'Thank you, America,'" he recalled during a conversation with Thomas Friedman of *The New York Times.* "At that moment, there has to be a much more aggressive effort to rebuild societies that didn't have any civic traditions. So that's a lesson that I now apply every time I ask the question, 'Should we intervene militarily? Do we have an answer for the day after?'"

Obama became a master of asking the follow-up questions – what then? There was never really a satisfying answer. He saw the pitfalls of every proposal for action and ultimately opted not to act rather than take chances of another disaster like Iraq or Libya. When it came to Syria, Obama had rejected advice from around the table in the Situation Room to become more involved. He dismissed the idea of setting up a no-fly zone over parts of Syria to protect civilians from Assad's air force after General Martin Dempsey, who took over from Mike Mullen as chairman of the Joint Chiefs of Staff, presented a slide show reporting that it would require 70,000 ground troops to dismantle the antiaircraft system and create a safe space for civilians, the kind of maximalist estimate the Pentagon gives when it does not really want to get involved. And while the CIA was arming select rebels, the president had rebuffed a plan advanced in his first term by Hillary Clinton, Leon Panetta and David Petraeus for a broader training program by the United States military to create a Syrian rebel force capable of taking out Assad.

To Obama, the chance that American weaponry could end up in the wrong hands on a battlefield that increasingly attracted sympathizers of Al Qaeda outweighed any possible benefit of the program. Even if they did not, he reasoned, they would not actually accomplish the goal of toppling the far better armed government. Greater American involvement, he concluded, would simply lead to greater chaos. As he told Friedman, "This idea that we could provide some light arms or even more sophisticated arms to what was essentially an opposition made up of former doctors, farmers, pharmacists and so forth, and that they were going to be able to battle not only a well-armed state but also a well-armed state backed by Russia, backed by Iran, a battle-hardened Hezbollah, that was never in the cards."

So when Obama heard about the Ghouta attack, he felt he was in a bind. Three days after the massacre, he gathered his national security team in the Situation Room and told them that he was devastated by the images of women and children convulsing from the effects of the sarin gas. He asked for military options to be ready by the afternoon.

"I set a red line," he said. "It looks like he crossed it. If that's the case, we need to respond forcefully."

Most of the aides in the room nodded forcefully, but Denis McDonough remained mute and clearly skeptical.

"You don't agree, Denis?" Obama asked.

"I don't," he said.

"I figured you would say that," Obama said. "But why?"

"Our position all along has been not to get involved," McDonough said. "We shouldn't get involved."

"Denis, Assad just carried out a chemical weapons attack," Obama said. "I was pretty clear about what that would mean."

In the days that followed, Chancellor Angela Merkel of Germany argued for more time for a United Nations inspection team to submit a report and bring it to the Security Council, but Obama resisted, knowing that it would take weeks and that the already thin support for a strike might diminish further. Obama seemed to be clearly moving toward a decision to attack Assad's government in retaliation. Any attack would last just a day or two with missiles and bombs, not troops, a "pinprick strike" designed to make a point, not to genuinely shift the dynamics of the war. American destroyers armed with Tomahawk missiles sailed into position in the eastern Mediterranean Sea. Secretary of State John Kerry, who had been privately urging a more robust approach to Syria, led the public charge, declaring that "history would judge us all extraordinarily harshly if we turned a blind eye to a dictator's wanton use of weapons of mass destruction against all warnings."

All the same, Obama's own ambivalence was plain to see. Where Kerry was fiery, Obama was restrained. While Kerry described a moral imperative to act, Obama was stressing the "limited, tailored" nature of what he had in mind. "We don't have good options, great options, for the region," the president told Gwen Ifill and Judy Woodruff from PBS. His uncertainty reflected public attitudes. Even though he was only talking about a quick airstrike, much like those ordered by previous presidents without much public opposition, many Americans reacted this time as if he were contemplating a new Iraq-style land war.

Six in ten Americans opposed a strike on Syria and a similar proportion said the United States should not take a leading role in trying to solve foreign conflicts; fully 72 percent did not want the United States intervening to turn dictatorships into democracies, the highest such opposition in a decade of polling on the question. There was little international appetite for a strike outside the Middle East either. Obama had no hope of support from the United Nations with Russia holding a veto and even Britain, America's closest ally, backed out of any military operation after its Parliament voted against authorizing action.

Suddenly, Obama looked – and felt – all alone. During a National Security Council meeting on the afternoon of August 30, Kathryn Ruemmler, the White House counsel, speaking over a video link, reminded Obama that as a senator he had called for presidents going to Congress before military operations. "I'm well aware of what my position is," Obama snapped. But it planted a thought. A few hours later, he took that walk with McDonough on the South Lawn.

Stewing about the right course, Obama thought Britain's Prime Minister David Cameron had mishandled the matter in London. But if Cameron had submitted the question to lawmakers, Obama said, maybe he should too. After all, Americans were no less war-weary than the British. And authorizing a strike all on his own, Obama reasoned, would flout his own statements about moving away from a permanent war footing and unilateral executive action. He found a sympathetic ear in McDonough, who had been one of the leading voices against the troop surge to Afghanistan in 2009 and other military entanglements since then.

*

Heading back into the Oval Office shortly before seven o'clock that Friday night Obama gathered some of his other top aides, including Susan Rice, who had taken over from Tom Donilon as the president's national security adviser; her deputies, Antony Blinken and Ben Rhodes; the deputy chief of staff, Rob Nabors; Dan Pfeiffer, now a senior adviser, and others. Notably absent were John Kerry and Defense Secretary Chuck Hagel.

"I have a pretty big idea I want to test with you guys," Obama told them as he tried to couch his change of heart.

As he explained his decision to go to Congress, he recalled

something he had said during his first presidential campaign: "'It is too easy for a president to go to war.' That quote from me in 2007 – I agree with that guy. That's who I am. And sometimes the least obvious thing to do is the right thing."

If he was testing the idea, though, it did not earn high grades. Obama's aides were aghast at the notion of letting Congress decide whether to launch the strike. During all the discussions over the past week, that option had not come up except in passing, and it reeked of desperation. Among other things, presidents had long reserved the power to initiate quick, limited military actions without requiring Congressional approval, and Obama would be setting a precedent that could tie not only his hands but those of his successors. Moreover, international opposition might only grow while he waited for Capitol Hill to consider the idea. What was worse, the advisers told him, he very likely could lose the vote, a debilitating defeat that would weaken him on foreign policy for the rest of his presidency. "Congress is never going to give you this authority," Rice told him. Moreover, she added, "It gives away too much of your power as commander in chief."

For two hours, the president and his team debated the merits and drawbacks of his idea, but he was not moved by the opposition of his advisers. He had come to a resolution and he felt comfortable with his decision. Only then, after he had made up his mind, did Obama call Kerry and Hagel to tell them, essentially cutting his top diplomat and top military adviser out of any real role in the deliberations.

The next morning, Saturday, August 31, the White House summoned reporters and cameras to the Rose Garden for an unusual weekend announcement. Nearly everyone in Washington assumed he was about to announce that the expected airstrike was under way. Television news channels aired wall-to-wall coverage waiting for the president's statement as journalists and analysts speculated on the impact of a military operation.

Instead, Obama shocked the world by saying he would defer to Congress. "I'm prepared to give that order," the president said. "But having made my decision as commander in chief based on what I am convinced is our national security interests, I'm also mindful that I'm the president of the world's oldest constitutional democracy."

The reaction was instant and scathing. As Obama's aides predicted, lawmakers still feeling the hangover of Iraq and the nonexistent weapons of mass destruction were not at all enthusiastic about getting the United States into another ugly war in the Middle East. "They may have heard the word 'Syria,' but all they saw was Iraq," Kerry observed. On this issue, at least, Obama had no reliable base of support on Capitol Hill from either side of the aisle. Liberals were instinctively anti-war and conservatives were instinctively anti-Obama. "Obama hasn't got a chance to win this vote if he can't win the majority of his own party, and I doubt he can," Representative Tom Cole, a Republican from Oklahoma, pointed out within hours of the president's announcement. "He is a war president without a war party."

While the Constitution gave Congress the power to declare war, lawmakers had not formally done so since World War II, essentially ceding that authority to the president. In modern times, presidents have used military force with and without Congressional approval. George H.W. Bush and George W. Bush both sought and won authorization votes from Congress before going to war with Iraq, while Ronald Reagan and Bill Clinton took action in Grenada, Libya, Bosnia, Afghanistan, Sudan, Iraq and Kosovo without securing explicit permission ahead of time from Capitol Hill. As a candidate, Obama had said a president had no power to launch a military attack except to stop "an actual or imminent threat to the nation." But he acted unilaterally in Libya in 2011 without any clear, immediate threat to the United States.

The real difference here was the perilous politics. If Obama was going to take the chance, he wanted Congress to take it with him – McDonough called it "wearing the jacket." Biden, Kerry and Hagel, all Senate veterans, thought lawmakers would back a Syria strike on the theory that Congress traditionally supported a commander in chief in times of conflict. Susan Rice, however, was right. If Obama genuinely thought it would get support on Capitol Hill, he badly misjudged the political environment. And failing to secure the authorizing votes he now sought would leave him in an untenable position. If he went ahead with a strike anyway, he would surely provoke a powerful backlash – and, his aides worried, even possibly an impeachment effort for ignoring Congress and public will. If he backed off his threat because Congress would not go along, he would look weak in the eyes of the world and, aides argued, would basically be deprived of any credible threat of military action for the rest of his presidency, no matter what the circumstances.

Why would Iran, for example, worry anymore that the United States might use force to stop it from obtaining a nuclear weapon when Obama would not use force to punish Syria for actually using chemical weapons? Even if war with Iran was a horrific possibility, making Iran fear that America might resort to it certainly had some value as deterrent. But even some aides suspected Obama knew perfectly well that Congress would never go along and that he was looking for a way out that he could blame on lawmakers.

Amid the furor that followed his Rose Garden speech, Obama flew to St. Petersburg, Russia, for the annual summit meeting of the Group of 20 nations, called the G-20, hosted by Vladimir Putin. Strongly opposed to any attack on Syria, an old client state of Russia's, Putin had used the threat of a veto at the United Nations to block any Security Council action. During a long, late-night discussion about Syria in St. Petersburg, the two presidents effectively competed for the support of the other leaders, each man arguing his position and soliciting peers as if they were voters. "I don't agree with his arguments," Putin said later, "and he doesn't agree with mine."

At the end, Putin boasted that most of the big powers present joined him in opposing an American military strike on Syria, including China, India, Germany, Italy and Brazil. The only ones that backed it, such as France and Saudi Arabia, were already on Obama's side before he arrived. In other words, he won no converts. As he raced home on Air Force One, Obama pivoted quickly back to the domestic debate. From the air, he phoned lawmakers from both parties in hopes of winning them over. He also ordered aides in Washington to fan out with speeches, briefings, conference calls and television appearances, and he announced that he would deliver a prime-time televised address to the nation from the White House to lay out his case to the American people.

But before he left St. Petersburg, there was an intriguing moment. Just as the summit was breaking up, Putin approached Obama and began chatting casually. Breaking the ice of their dispute over Edward Snowden, Obama suggested the two leaders sit down and they pulled chairs into a corner of the room. As they talked, Putin brought up an idea. What if Syria voluntarily surrendered its stockpiles of poison gas to the international community? Would that be an acceptable alternative to military action? Obama was cautious but interested and suggested they have their top diplomats explore it further.

A couple of days later, while in London, Kerry seemed to open the door to such an idea publicly when he was asked by Margaret Brennan of CBS News if there was anything Syria's Assad could do to avert a strike.

"Sure," Kerry said. "He could turn over every single bit of his chemical weapons to the international community in the next week, turn it over, all of it, without delay and allow a full and total accounting before that." Then, realizing that he had opened the door a little too widely in public, Kerry quickly added: "But he isn't about to do it and it can't be done, obviously."

Aides later downplayed his comments as a throwaway line, a hypothetical discussion prompted by a reporter's question. But as Kerry flew home, he got word that his Russian counterpart, Sergey Lavrov, wanted to talk. When Kerry reached him, Lavrov cited the secretary of state's comments and said Russia would make a public proposal that Syria give up its weapons and allow in international monitors.

For Obama, it seemed like a lifeline and he clutched it as a way out of his no-win scenario. When he went on television for his prime-time address, instead of pressing Congress to vote for war, Obama announced that he would try Russia's plan first – hitting the pause button on his airstrikes for the second time in two weeks. Rarely had a commander in chief changed his mind on the fly quite so publicly.

In the end, Obama's fits-and-starts handling of the matter arguably accomplished some good in terms of substance but failed miserably in terms of politics and perception. Over the coming months, Syria did give up its chemical weapons, or at least most of them, which Obama argued was a far better result than just blowing up a few buildings in Damascus and leaving the munitions in Assad's hands. After leaving office, Obama insisted that aborting the airstrike on Syria was the decision that "required the most political courage" of his presidency.

But years later, Syria either reconstituted some of its toxins or pulled them out of hiding, once again using them on civilians and reinforcing the incomplete nature of Obama's solution. Just as damaging, in its own way, his painfully public vacillation was taken by many in the region as a sign of irresolution, especially by America's Arab allies. It would be cited as evidence that he had grown so allergic to military entanglement in the Middle East that he would not back up his own "red line" threats. Even many in Obama's own circle considered it "a blow to American credibility," as Leon Panetta put it.

"There's absolutely no question he's very uncomfortable being commander in chief," said Senator Bob Corker, a Republican from Tennessee who was working with the White House to rally support for a strike until it was called off. "It's like he wants to slip the noose. It's like watching a person who's caged, who's in a trap and trying to figure a way out."

*

If Obama was trying to find a way out, there would be no easy escape. No matter how much he tried to focus on other priorities, he kept finding himself drawn back to crisis after crisis in the Middle East. At the same time he was struggling with what to do about Syria, he was struggling with what to do about Egypt. The traditional anchor of the Arab world, Egypt had yet to find its way in the two years since mass demonstrations pushed out Hosni Mubarak with Obama's support. Democratic elections after Mubarak's ouster installed Mohamed Morsi, leader of the Muslim Brotherhood, as the new president and for a time Obama thought he had found a partner he could work with. When fighting erupted in Gaza in late 2012, Obama teamed up with Morsi to quell the violence.

But Morsi failed to broaden his base of support at home beyond Islamists and Obama became increasingly worried that the Egyptian's approach was destabilizing his country. Morsi had a habit of demonizing his critics and accusing them of treasonous conspiracies, an approach that, combined with a dire economic situation, generated widespread opposition. Once again, Cairo's Tahrir Square was filled with tens of thousands of demonstrators and this time they were pressing Morsi to step down. The military and intelligence services, a bulwark of Mubarak's Egypt, had always despised the Muslim Brotherhood and now they saw that Morsi had made the group more vulnerable than at any time in its eight decades underground. In July, the military moved in, arresting Morsi and rounding up scores of his allies.

Obama reacted with typical caution, making no public comments, opting instead for measured written statements. Since 1979, Egypt had been the top recipient of American foreign aid behind only Israel, slated to receive $1.5 billion in the next year. But under law, Obama was required to cut off assistance in the case of a military coup. That led to all sorts of definitional gymnastics in Washington over whether Morsi's ouster qualified. Egypt's new authorities argued that it was not technically a military coup, but a popular uprising, and that the military only stepped in to preserve order. To almost everyone who did not have a stake in the matter, it seemed a fairly obvious dictionary version of a military coup, given that the generals locked up the democratically elected president and sent soldiers into the streets.

In the Situation Room, the State Department's top lawyer, Mary McLeod, said it was a clear-cut example of a coup. While other advisers to the president were looking for ways out of following the law as written, she gave no ground. But Obama himself surprised aides by saying that they could not call it what everyone understood it was, backed by John Kerry, Chuck Hagel and most other advisers. Still, it was not like Obama to directly defy the law. Eventually, Obama and his team decided to resolve the dispute by not resolving it – they would not formally judge whether the transfer of power was a coup or not. If they did not characterize it one way or the other, they reasoned, the aid cutoff would not be triggered. It was a semantic game to skirt the law, they knew, but one they concluded was in the nation's best interest to maintain an alliance that had been critical to the United States for generations.

In Cairo, the generals made a cold-eyed calculation that Obama would not suspend assistance – and that even if he did, they could replace the lost money from Saudi Arabia or other Gulf states that bitterly opposed the Muslim Brotherhood and were happy to see the military back in power in Egypt. Unconstrained by the Americans, Egyptian forces opened a ferocious assault on protesters in the streets, killing sixty Morsi supporters at a sit-in a few days after his ouster, eighty more at a subsequent demonstration and eventually more than 1,000 others. As with Syria, Obama now faced another lose-lose situation: Risk a partnership that had been the bedrock of Middle East peace for thirty-five years or stand by while longtime allies held onto power by mowing down opponents. From one side, the Israelis, Saudis and other Arabs lobbied Obama to go easy on the generals in the interest of thwarting what they saw as the larger and more insidious Islamist threat. From the other, an unusual mix of American conservatives and liberals urged him to stand more forcefully against the sort of autocracy that had been a staple of Egyptian life for decades.

Ultimately, Obama decided the relationship with Egypt's military was more important than a stand on democracy. He suspended just part of the aid, about $260 million, and temporarily withheld the delivery of several big-ticket weapons systems, including Apache attack helicopters, Harpoon missiles, M1-A1 tank parts and F-16 warplanes. "The administration is trying to have it both ways," complained Senator Patrick Leahy, a Vermont Democrat and chairman of the subcommittee that oversaw aid to Egypt. "By doing that, the message is muddled."

*

On New Year's Day, just hours after Americans welcomed the arrival of 2014 with fireworks and festivities, Obama and his advisers tuned in their televisions to find a different, darker sort of celebration. Convoys of up to 100 trucks flying the black flag of Al Qaeda and armed with mounted heavy machine guns and antiaircraft guns stormed into the western Iraqi cities of Falluja and Ramadi. The Islamic extremists who had ruled there during the grim and bloody days of the previous decade cheered. They were back.

Two years after the last American troops pulled out of Iraq, the enemy once driven from the field had reconstituted itself, this time vowing to create a caliphate, or an Islamic state, stretching across national borders. Operating from neighboring Syria, where they took advantage of the chaos of the civil war, the Sunni Muslim militants were now calling themselves the Islamic State, or ISIS, ISIL or Daesh in some renditions. Unlike the original Al Qaeda, they aspired to hold territory. Indeed, they were intent on redrawing the map of the Middle East.

The sight of black flags flying once again in that part of Iraq sent a chill through the American military, which fought some of its fiercest battles there in the war that followed the invasion of 2003. Many veterans bristled at the thought of all that blood being spilled only to see the extremists take over again. But as disturbing as he found the latest developments, Obama was determined not to let the United States be dragged back into a war that he had opposed from the start. Obama was convinced that the United States was too quick to pull the military lever whenever it confronted a foreign crisis. He would not repeat what he considered George W. Bush's mistake. In Obama's mind, not every extremist with a gun posed an existential threat to the United States – and if they did not, then America should restrain itself rather than get sucked into another vortex of sectarian rivalry and ethnic violence. "Just because we have the best hammer," he observed at one point, "does not mean that every problem is a nail."

If he was avoiding Bush's mistake, however, his own mistake was to underestimate the Islamic State. "The analogy we use around here sometimes, and I think is accurate, is if a JV team puts on Lakers uniforms that doesn't make them Kobe Bryant," Obama told *The New Yorker's* David Remnick. The Islamic State, in other words, was junior varsity, not a threat, not a concern to the United States. Obama drew a distinction between Al Qaeda and "jihadists who are engaged in various local power struggles and disputes, often sectarian."

"But that JV team just took over Falluja," Remnick pointed out.

"I understand," Obama said. But terrorism is a global phenomenon and he argued that Americans should not "think that any horrible actions that take place around the world that are motivated in part by an extremist Islamic ideology is a direct threat to us or something that we have to wade into."

In the two years since pulling out of Iraq, Washington had engaged in an awkward dance with Baghdad over how involved the Americans would be now that their military mission was officially over. As security in Iraq worsened, American officials tried to reinsert themselves by proposing a joint intelligence center and offering other support, only to be brushed off by Prime Minister Nuri Kamal al-Maliki, who was eager to demonstrate his independence from the United States. But when violence began spilling over the border from Syria, Maliki changed his mind and sought American help, only to find that the Obama administration was now the reluctant partner.

In the months leading up to the takeover of Falluja, suicide bombings in Iraq spiked to fifty a month, up from just five a month when the Americans left. The Americans were so removed from the brewing crisis that they were flying just one surveillance flight over Iraq each month at the time. Obama's administration sent a handful of Special Operations troops to advise Iraqis on targeting, but efforts to provide Apache helicopters and F-16 fighter jets stalled in Congress, where lawmakers were wary of empowering Maliki, a Shiite who had ruled with an increasingly sectarian hand since the American withdrawal, provoking Sunni resentment.

After Falluja fell, Obama resisted a military response and focused instead on pressing Maliki to hold genuinely free and fair elections in April in hopes of undercutting the popular resentment that was fueling the jihadist movement. But in the White House, the assumption was that Falluja and Ramadi were anomalies, longtime hotbeds of Sunni extremist sentiment that could essentially be walled off and contained, eventually even rolled back.

That was an assumption others warned against. Intelligence agencies had been raising alarms about the Islamic State for months, only to grow discouraged that the White House seemed not to be taking it seriously enough. Lieutenant General Michael T. Flynn, director of the Defense Intelligence Agency, even took his concerns public in his annual threat assessment to Congress. "ISIL," he told lawmakers six weeks after the jihadists muscled their way into western Iraq, "probably will attempt to take territory in Iraq and Syria in 2014, as demonstrated recently in Ramadi and Falluja."

Obama was not convinced. He wanted to end wars, not start them, and he gave a major speech at the United States Military Academy commencement ceremony at West Point intended to forswear future adventurism. "I am haunted by those deaths," he said of casualties resulting from operations he had ordered. From now on, when the United States was not directly threatened, he said, "the threshold for military action must be higher."

If Falluja were all that would confront Obama in 2014, that would still make it a challenging enough year. But 2014 would soon prove to be Obama's *annus horribilis*. By February, he not only had a growing crisis in Iraq and Syria but a new Cold War developing in Eastern Europe.

For months, the former Soviet republic of Ukraine had been at the center of a geopolitical tug of war between its former masters in Moscow and a beckoning new Europe. President Viktor Yanukovych negotiated a trade agreement with the European Union only to reverse himself and renounce it after Russia offered him a $15 billion loan. Pro-western demonstrators flooded the streets of Kiev, the capital, leading to a violent clash that killed about 100 protesters in the city's Maidan Square. A furious backlash over the deaths pushed Yanukovych to flee and the opposition took control.

But Vladimir Putin was not about to accept the turn of fortunes. In a move that shocked the world, he sent masked Russian troops disguised in unmarked green uniforms – "little green men," as they became known – to the Ukrainian peninsula of Crimea, where many ethnic Russians lived and Moscow maintained a military base under a contract with Ukraine. Crimea had been a flashpoint between Russia and Ukraine ever since the end of the Cold War. Historically a part of Russia, Crimea had been transferred by the Kremlin to control of the Ukrainian Soviet Republic in 1954 as a sop to the junior partner in the Soviet Union. When the union fell apart in 1991 and Ukraine became its own country, it kept Crimea, much to the consternation of nationalists in Moscow. With the ouster of Yanukovych, Putin decided the time had come to take it back. Within days of the arrival of the little green men, the Russians staged a referendum in Crimea about whether to break away from Ukraine; given the presence of

Russian troops and the sizable Russian-speaking population, the vote perhaps unsurprisingly favored Moscow. Putin then annexed the peninsula, the first time a European power had forcibly seized the territory of another since the end of World War II.

Suddenly, a relatively contained crisis in a second-tier Eastern European country turned into the most combustible confrontation between East and West since the Cold War. Not satisfied with just Crimea, Russia escalated the clash by fomenting a separatist uprising in eastern Ukraine, threatening to rip the country in half. A few weeks earlier, Obama had had only limited interest in whether Ukraine was anchored in Europe or remained under the influence of Moscow – he even referred to it as *the* Ukraine, unknowingly using an outdated formulation left over from the Soviet era that Ukrainians considered insulting. But once Russia used force to redraw the boundaries of Europe established nearly a quarter-century earlier, the president felt obliged to respond.

The turn of events represented the final collapse of Obama's efforts to restore relations with Moscow. Putin's decision to resume the presidency in 2012 was fueled in part by his pique over Dmitri Medvedev's failure to stand up to the west over Libya, and effectively ended the reset. Putin publicly accused Hillary Clinton of inciting protests against his return to power. He presided over a harassment campaign against Obama's ambassador to Moscow, Michael McFaul, even before offering shelter to Edward Snowden. While they collaborated on destroying Syria's chemical weapons, Obama and Putin operated on radically different wavelengths. Putin, Obama said at one point, had a "kind of slouch" that made him look "like that bored schoolboy in the back of the classroom."

The bored schoolboy was now challenging the American president with a war of aggression in Europe. Obama crafted a response intended to quarantine Russia and turn it into an international pariah. In conjunction with Europe, he forced the ouster of Russia from the Group of Eight major powers also called the G-8, cut off a variety of civilian and military cooperation programs and imposed a series of escalating travel and financial sanctions. But Europe had far deeper economic ties to Russia and was far more skittish about confronting Moscow and there were limits to how far Obama was willing to go as well.

To preserve solidarity, Obama limited the sanctions and other actions to no more than European leaders would agree to. And wary of being drawn into an armed clash with a nuclear superpower, Obama similarly resisted calls to ship arms to the Ukrainians, much less offer more overt military aid. "We're not going to send in the Eighty-Second Airborne, Joe," he told Biden. "They have to understand that."

Russia for its part showed no such restraint and armed its separatist allies in eastern Ukraine. On July 17, an antiaircraft battery it provided the insurgents was used to shoot down Malaysia Airlines Flight 17, a civilian jet passing overhead, killing all 298 passengers and crew members on board, including eighty children.

"Russia is once again isolating itself from the international community, setting back decades of genuine progress," Obama said soon afterward as he ratcheted up sanctions again. "It didn't have to come to this. It does not have to be this way. This is a choice that Russia – and President Putin in particular – has made."

CHAPTER ELEVEN

'Don't Do Stupid . . .'

One day in June 2014, Obama decided to go for a cup of tea, but instead of ordering it from the Navy stewards who cater to the president's every desire or even wandering down to the White House Mess, he resolved to actually *go* for a cup of tea. He gathered up Denis McDonough and, trailed by a retinue of nervous Secret Service agents, marched out the doors of the White House, through the gates and into the street on a hot and humid day, heading toward a nearby Starbucks.

Presidents do not just go to the coffee shop on a whim. Every movement a president makes is carefully choreographed and meticulously planned in advance. And the Secret Service never allows a president to just walk down the street if it can help it. Even a trip from the White House to St. John's Church across from Lafayette Square, where nearly every president has worshipped at least once, typically involves a ride in the armored limousine known as the Beast for what would otherwise be a couple-minute stroll across the park. The church is so close that the lead car in the motorcade typically arrives before the last car in the motorcade has even left the White House grounds.

But Obama was feeling trapped and anxious to break out of the bubble, if only for a few minutes. Counting the campaign, he had been under Secret Service protection for six years, his life controlled by others to a suffocating degree. For Obama, one of the biggest tradeoffs of becoming president was the inability to simply walk down the street anonymously, wander into a book store and browse the shelves or sit in a park for a few moments. He was hardly suffering, he knew, living in the grand mansion he occupied with access to the sprawling Camp David or the spacious houses he rented in Hawaii and Martha's Vineyard each year. But in the second year of his second term, he was increasingly restless and frustrated, so stymied on both the domestic and international fronts that he seemed to some aides to be losing interest in the job.

So an unplanned, unannounced and unsanctioned jaunt to Starbucks was his small protest. "The bear is loose!" he declared with as much glee as the self-controlled Obama ever expressed.

It took a few minutes for startled White House pool reporters, who were supposed to travel with the president anywhere he went, to realize what had happened and scramble out the door to catch up with him. Once they did, he seemed a bit miffed that they had found him.

"C'mon, guys, give me some space," he pleaded.

Someone asked what he had ordered. Instead of answering, he turned to Pat Cunnane, a junior White House aide known as a wrangler because he was in charge of managing the press pool. "Let's test your wrangling skills," Obama directed.

Cunnane dutifully began yelling at the reporters. "Back up! Back up! Let's go, pool!" Trying to shuffle the reporters away from Obama to give him some room, he shouted the universal White House code meant to end a press encounter with the president. "Thank you, pool!"

For Obama, the whole year was spent trying to free the bear, but without much success. Just as he suffered one setback after another overseas, he found his legislative agenda stalled at home. His gun-control proposals were dead and nothing else he had proposed after his second inaugural had gone far in Congress either. And so he essentially gave up on legislating altogether. He opened 2014 by traveling to Capitol Hill to declare independence from Congress in his State of the Union address and vowed to tackle economic disparity with a series of limited initiatives on jobs, wages and retirement that he could advance without legislative approval. In effect, he was saying, the bear was loose when it came to policy as well.

He promised "a year of action" as he sought to rejuvenate a presidency mired in low approval ratings. "I am eager to work with all of you," he told lawmakers from the rostrum in the House chamber. "But America does not stand still – and neither will I. So wherever and whenever I can take steps without legislation to expand opportunity for more American families, that's what I'm going to do." Still, as he vowed to act "with or without Congress," his defiant approach was more assertive than any of the individual policies he advanced.

His staff called it the "pen and phone" strategy – he would use his pen to sign executive orders and his phone to lean on important figures like governors, business executives and labor leaders to accomplish what a Congress riven by partisanship would not or could not. It was an alliterative smoke screen to obscure Obama's retreat from the field. But weakened as he was, Obama was determined to make the most of what he could do in the magisterial space of the Oval Office. In the months to come, he signed a series of executive orders to raise the minimum wage from $7.25 to $10.10 an hour and set other employment standards for employees of federal contractors. Since he could not unilaterally order such changes for the private sector as a whole, he would use the federal government's leverage as a paying customer to force at least some private employers to adopt the changes he favored. Because of Washington's vast reach, that move alone could affect up to 29 million workers. And to an important degree, he succeeded in setting the terms of the national conversation, so that even though Congress refused to go along with a minimum wage hike, many states, localities and even companies like Wal-Mart,

Costco, Gap, Ikea and Disney raised pay floors on their own.

Many of Obama's executive actions, to be sure, were penny-ante stuff, more symbolic than significant. He grandly announced the issuance of small-bore grants for various goals even though they represented barely an asterisk in the overall federal budget. He politely asked business leaders to hire longtime unemployed workers since he could neither force them to nor entice them to with incentives. He set out to reorganize federal job training, a longtime bipartisan goal that had eluded nearly every recent president, leaving their successors to declare that the programs were still ineffective and in need of reform.

But other unilateral moves had wider reach, especially labor regulations that made millions more workers eligible for overtime pay and sought to extend basic workplace protections to the so-called gig economy of independent contractors like those working for Uber. Rhetorically, at least, these efforts stemmed from Obama's 2011 speech in Osawatomie, Kansas, which Dan Pfeiffer called "perhaps the most substantively important speech of the Obama presidency." Obama's condemnation of income inequality, Pfeiffer said, created "a set of marching orders to the entire government." By his last year in office, Obama had put in place more than 500 regulations with significant impact, making him perhaps the most aggressive wielder of executive power in modern times, to the point that Republicans accused him of imperial overreach.

One of the areas where he had the broadest power to act on his own was in fighting climate change. Having given up on legislation after the Democratic Congress in his first two years in office failed to pass a bill creating a cap-and-trade system, Obama now turned to the Environmental Protection Agency to use its sweeping authority to achieve the same goal. In June, the administration announced a proposed rule that would set state-by-state limits on carbon emissions and let each state decide how to meet those targets. The overall goal was to slash pollution from existing power plants by 32 percent from 2005 levels by 2030. The far-reaching rule would effectively reshape the nation's energy industry without a vote of Congress, likely forcing hundreds of coal-fired plants to close their doors. The power plant rule came on top of new regulations requiring new cars and light trucks to be so fuel-efficient that they would get fifty-five miles per gallon by 2025, reducing the consumption of oil and emissions at the same time. While some of his executive actions pushed the boundaries of presidential power, Obama seemed to be on stronger legal ground with his climate push because the Supreme Court had already ruled that, under the Clean Air Act, the EPA had to regulate carbon emissions. But with tens of billions of dollars at stake, industry opponents still mounted a legal challenge.

The other major initiative Obama decided to pursue on his own was immigration reform. That had been the one area after his re-election where he had harbored hopes of reaching a bipartisan compromise with Republicans, given that opposition party leaders wanted to stop alienating Hispanic voters, who were becoming a larger force in the electorate. A group of senators from both parties formed what they called the Gang of Eight to broker an agreement that passed, 68 to 32, in 2013 only to die in the House. A year later, John Boehner and other Republican leaders resolved to fashion a plan that would finally settle the matter and take it off the table for the next election.

Obama was happy to work with Boehner. After all, the president was under enormous pressure from Hispanic leaders and advocates of liberalized immigration, who had grown impatient and restless. By that point, Obama had deported more than 2 million people, effectively delivering on the part of his promise to enforce the law, but he had failed to deliver on the part where he would overhaul the rules to offer forgiveness to many of those already in the country. In March 2014, Janet Murguia, president of the National Council of La Raza, denounced Obama in a speech as the "deporter-in-chief," a line that deeply irked the president. During a subsequent meeting with activists, he scolded her, saying that if advocates for reform fought among themselves, they would only take the onus off Republicans.

But as much as the business-oriented, poll-reading Republican hierarchy wanted a deal, the ascendant Tea Party wing of the party did not. They saw any easing of the rules as an illegitimate amnesty. Immigrants who were in the country illegally had broken the law and were taking jobs at a time when there were still millions of American citizens out of work. The Republican rebels made clear they would punish party leaders who made an agreement with Obama.

They proved their power in June, when a little-known conservative college professor came out of nowhere to upset Representative Eric Cantor, the Republican majority leader, in a primary in his Virginia home district. Cantor had been the conservative champion in the Republican leadership, the voice of the base often curbing Boehner's deal-making instincts. When Cantor lost, there were no tears shed in the White House. His relationship with Obama had been prickly from the start, when Cantor joined Republicans plotting to undercut his presidency on the night of his inauguration and Obama put down the upstart congressman during a later meeting by pointedly reminding him who won the election. Obama considered Cantor a partisan obstructionist and his main bête noire in the House. Cantor viewed Obama as an aloof liberal intent on shoving his agenda down the throat of Congress.

But over the past year or so, Cantor had moved to find ways to resolve the fiscal fights over taxes and the government shutdown. And even though he opposed Obama's immigration plan, he had signaled willingness to consider more limited measures like legalizing the children of adults who came to the country illegally. For that, he was judged insufficiently stalwart in standing up to Obama by his home district Republican voters.

"It is incredible to me that Eric Cantor moved from the singular, highest-profile, most-important political figure on Capitol Hill stopping the president's agenda to the guy who was the chief compromiser with the president," said John Murray, a Cantor strategist. "The disconnect there is insane. It's so out of whack with reality."

Or perhaps reflective of the new reality.

*

Obama began to think about how else he could use his pen and phone. In the modern world, of course, a phone was no longer just a phone and Obama was not just calling people. The goal was to reach out to the public in a way that no other president had done before. His predecessors had dreamed of finding ways to communicate directly with the public without the filter of the news media – FDR with his fireside chats, Ronald Reagan with his weekly radio addresses and so on – but Obama was a technological pioneer in all sorts of ways. He was the first president to set up a Facebook page, the first to write messages on Twitter, the first to answer questions on Reddit and Google+, the first to post an essay on Medium and the first to have accounts with Instagram, Snapchat, Vine, Tumblr and Flickr. With the help of the first White House videographer, his team aired essentially its own television program on the White House web site every Friday called *West Wing Week*.

Obama had a staff of twenty to manage those accounts, but by any measure, he was the first social media president. He was also a bit of a gear head. He was the first commander in chief to receive his daily intelligence briefing on an iPad and he used it at night to scan the Internet for news stories of interest. During a trip to Alaska to highlight climate change, he was given a GoPro camera and a selfie stick to take his own photographs and video of disappearing glaciers, images that were shared online. "Ever competitive, Obama was very proud of his ability to get a twoosh, which is a tweet that is exactly 140 characters on the first try," Dan Pfeiffer wrote later. "This was a little too *Rain Man*-esque for my tastes, but he loved it."

Obama eschewed traditional East Room news conferences in favor of unconventional outlets. Although he gave many one-on-one interviews to carefully selected mainstream journalists, often on predetermined topics, he all but ignored the White House reporters who covered him most regularly and were most attuned to the sometimes subtle policy changes and truth-shading that a president tries to get away with. Obama took questions from the pool of journalists that followed him day in and day out barely a third as often as George W. Bush did and less than a fifth as often as Bill Clinton. Even Reagan, famous for circumventing the media, took questions from White House pool reporters far more often than Obama did.

But he gave interviews to all sorts of new-generation media figures. He traded deadpan insults with Zach Galifianakis on the quirky show *Between Two Ferns*. He sat down with a YouTube host named GloZell Green, who was famous for wearing bright green lipstick and once on camera soaked in a bathtub filled with milk and Fruit Loops. He chatted with a young man named Adande Thorne, a self-described "time traveler" and "professional cuddler" who used the screen name sWooZie and asked Obama for his favorite *Star Wars* character ("I've got to go with Han Solo," Obama answered. "He's a little bit of a rebel.")

If some of that came across as a little bit unpresidential, it also seemed necessary to Obama and his staff in an era when even 500 channels were no longer enough for many Americans and no single method allowed the White House to reach large segments of the voting public. "Ultimately, what all of this is about," said Pfeiffer, who helped devise the strategy, "is finding ways to communicate with people in a time when media has become so disaggregated that simply communicating through the traditional means is woefully insufficient."

It was a way especially of connecting to his base among younger Americans and an opportunity to get across a serious policy point or two that would otherwise go unnoticed. Obama had never seen Galifianakis's show when Valerie Jarrett pitched the idea of going on it but Malia had watched every episode. He went on the show to urge uninsured young people to sign up for coverage under his health care program and the federal web site saw a 40 percent increase in traffic afterward.

*

The challenges of 2014 kept coming, one after the other in a cascade that left Obama and his advisers wondering at times whether they could ever get out from under them. Obama's proactive initiatives were more or less lost in the inexorable wave of crises. For a time, a year earlier, Obama had seemed to be growing tired of the job. Now he faced questions about whether he was even up to the job.

Spring brought fresh revelations about the deeply dysfunctional Department of Veterans Affairs, an agency long plagued by mismanagement and funding problems even as its mission grew more critical to so many American troops coming home from overseas battlegrounds with deep physical and psychological injuries. Americans were shocked by reports that Veterans Affairs officials manipulated data to hide long delays for patients seeing physicians. The furor underscored a more fundamental danger for

Obama as he once again found himself on the defensive over issues of basic management of the federal government. For a president who came to office hoping to restore public faith in government as a force for good in society, the mess at Veterans Affairs, coming after the botched rollout of the health care web site and the politicized decisions at the Internal Revenue Service, called into question Obama's mastery of the Washington bureaucracy over which he presided.

In the halls of the West Wing, there was more palpable concern over the veterans' situation than there ever was about other scandals that afflicted the administration, like the Benghazi talking points or the IRS misconduct. If those controversies riled Republicans, poor treatment of veterans had the potential to offend a broader portion of the public across party lines, as evidenced by the outcry from Democratic members of Congress demanding the resignation of Eric Shinseki, the secretary of veterans affairs.

For once, Obama went along with those who wanted heads to roll. Like Bush before him, Obama had long resisted the idea of dismissing loyal advisers in the face of criticism just because that was how Washington worked. He had adamantly refused to push out Kathleen Sebelius, the secretary of health and human services, after the health care debacle and similarly resisted tossing other top officials overboard when things went wrong. Indeed, Obama had never before pushed out one of his own appointees with as high a profile as Shinseki in the thick of a crisis amid the braying of the media and the political class. But now he wasted little time showing Shinseki the door.

A ritual sacking in Washington typically released the pressure of a controversy and pushed it off the front pages. In this case, however, what diverted attention from the veterans' mistreatment was yet another uproar that erupted the day after Shinseki was told to clean out his office. On orders from Obama, American troops met with Taliban fighters to conduct a swap, picking up Sergeant Bowe Bergdahl, the only American prisoner of war from the conflict in Afghanistan, on May 31 in exchange for the release of five detainees from Guantánamo Bay, Cuba. A video of the exchange later released by the Taliban showed a Black Hawk helicopter touching down in an arid field and American special forces troops emerging. They briefly shook hands with Taliban gunmen, then took Bergdahl to the helicopter, whose rotors never stopped spinning. Dressed all in white with a checkered scarf over his shoulders, the twenty-eight-year-old Bergdahl looked dazed, his eyes blinking. The American troops patted him down to make sure he was not laced with hidden weapons, then put him on the helicopter and lifted off. The encounter lasted just seconds.

The relief over his release, however, barely lasted much longer. Obama appeared in the Rose Garden alongside Bergdahl's ecstatic parents to hail his freedom. But as the details emerged, Obama was quickly accused of negotiating with terrorists despite longstanding policy and castigated for letting five dangerous men back onto the battlefield. In making the trade, Obama ignored a law passed by Congress requiring thirty days' notice before any Guantánamo detainee was freed. And much of the sympathy for Bergdahl after five years of captivity dissipated with reports that he been captured after walking away from his unit, raising questions about whether the United States should trade enemy fighters for a deserter.

Obama defended the decision, saying that the urgency of the situation made it impractical to give notice to Congress and that the five Guantánamo detainees were turned over to the Persian Gulf state of Qatar, which promised to keep them under control and bar them from traveling for a year. "The United States has always had a pretty sacred rule," Obama told reporters during a visit to Warsaw, "and that is: we don't leave our men or women in uniform behind." Whether Bergdahl deserted or not, the president added, did not change that. "Regardless of circumstances, whatever those circumstances may turn out to be, we still get an American prisoner back. Period. Full stop. We don't condition that."

*

One day during a weeklong tour of Asia in April, Obama wandered to the back of Air Force One to talk with the reporters traveling with him. He had been mulling the pressures he was under to intervene more forcefully in Syria and Ukraine and resented the second-guessing. Accompanied by Ben Rhodes, Obama wanted to get something off his chest. He was particularly miffed at two *New York Times* articles that questioned his foreign policy. "Ben and I have been talking about giving a speech that lays out my foreign policy," he told the reporters, including Mark Landler of *The Times*, author of one of the offending articles. "I can sum up my foreign policy in one phrase," Obama added, and then paused for effect. "Don't do stupid shit."

It was not the most elegant expression of a foreign policy doctrine that a president had ever come up with, but it did effectively sum up his evolving thinking. He had come into office on the back of his opposition to the Iraq war while open to the idea that the United States could still assert itself on the world stage if circumstances warranted. And yet with each experience, he seemed to grow more jaundiced about America's ability to actually shape events the way it would like. He went along with the military's request for a massive buildup of troops in Afghanistan, but at the end of the day it did not seem to fundamentally change the equation on the ground for the long run. He went along with Hillary Clinton and the other Valkyries who pressed him to intervene in Libya, but it wound up disintegrating into a quagmire of tribal violence, corruption and dysfunction.

When America got in trouble, he told the reporters on the plane, it was when it did too much, not too little – like in Iraq or Vietnam. The United States should get involved only in places where its core national interests were at stake. Otherwise, it could find itself in a place like Syria where, as awful as the civil war was, it did not directly threaten the United States, nor was there any real sense that an American intervention could actually make things better. If anything, the experiences in Iraq and Afghanistan had shown that intervention could even make things worse.

Warming to his subject, Obama kept talking even as the jumbo jet ducked below the clouds and landed at his next destination. He braced himself against the side of the plane as it touched down, still lecturing the reporters on his views of the world.

"Now what's my foreign policy philosophy?" he asked before leaving, like a teacher repeating the lesson to a class of slow learners.

"Don't do stupid shit," the reporters replied in sing-song unison.

The conversation had been off the record and, complying with the ground rules, none of the reporters wrote about it in the immediate aftermath. During a news conference a couple days later, though, a reporter tried to draw Obama out in a public setting, asking him if he would describe his doctrine. Obama gave a lengthy answer about the limits of American ability to shape events in places like Syria and Ukraine, favoring "targeted, clear actions" that can make a difference and avoiding feel-good but dangerous options in the name of looking strong.

"And that may not always be sexy," he said. "That may not always attract a lot of attention and it doesn't make for good argument on Sunday morning shows. But it avoids errors. You hit singles, you hit doubles; every once in a while we may be able to hit a home run. But we steadily advance the interests of the American people and our partnership with folks around the world."

It took him nearly 1,000 words to describe a doctrine that he needed just four to outline on the plane, but the minimalist ambition of "singles" and "doubles" was enough to catch attention back home. And word of the president's airborne monologue and his more concise foreign policy doctrine quickly spread too until it eventually showed up in print, albeit usually cleaned up to something more family-friendly like "don't do stupid stuff."

*

The president's fidelity to this mantra would soon be tested again. Within weeks of the flight on Air Force One, thousands of fighters from the Islamic State swept through the northern part of Iraq, seized the major city of Mosul and drove into Tikrit, the ancestral home of Saddam Hussein. Suddenly, the Sunni extremists were not contained in the Sunni extremist part of the country – they were on the march through regions where they had less natural popular support and were even bearing down on the capital of Baghdad. Now Obama would be required to decide whether Iraq counted on his list of American national interests and, if so, what he could do that would not count as stupid shit.

Just as Bush had before him, Obama found that any faith he had in the Iraqi security services was badly misplaced. For all of their American training and American-style uniforms, Iraqi troops simply melted away in the face of an aggressive, even fanatical, enemy. Without help, it was unclear how Iraq would resist. And so Obama reluctantly agreed to send 300 Special Operations troops back to Baghdad, not to engage in combat but to try to help the Iraqis organize their own forces more effectively. It was a small deployment, but a profound turn for Obama.

The Islamic State now controlled a wide swath of the Middle East, stretching from the eastern half of Syria all the way through the western Iraqi desert toward the approaches to Baghdad, a territory larger than the nation of Jordan. In this new caliphate they were carving out for themselves, the jihadists imposed a harsh form of Islam and threatened those who did not meet their religious standards. Obama was open to taking more direct action and even authorized a secret commando operation into Syria in July to try to rescue Americans being held hostage, only to be deflated when the troops failed to find them where they were thought to be. "Dry hole," came the dispiriting news over the radio.

The militants won more stunning victories against the Kurds, America's most loyal and reliable allies in Iraq, and they drove thousands of Yazidis, another religious minority, to Mount Sinjar and threatened to wipe them out. There was also fear that the Islamic State would capture the strategic Haditha Dam on the Euphrates River and open its floodgates, releasing a wall of water that would overwhelm nearby towns and villages.

In early August, Obama took a fateful step. He ordered the Pentagon to launch a series of airstrikes to aid the Kurds and save the Yazidis. In sending warplanes back into the skies of Iraq, Obama found himself exactly where he did not want to be. The president who had vowed to end the war in Iraq was starting another one – or arguably jumping back into the old one, which was never actually finished. He comforted himself by focusing on the fact that he was not deploying a large ground force the way George W. Bush did. He would not get America enmeshed in nation building again. He would keep the mission limited and manageable. Yet his presence in the State Dining Room the night he announced the new mission testified to the bleak reality that the tide of events in that ancient land had defied his predictions and aspirations. Just three months earlier, he had told cadets at West Point that he was raising the bar for military action. Now he was crossing over the bar all over again.

As he addressed the nation, he sounded almost as if he was trying to reassure himself as much as the American public:

I know that many of you are rightly concerned about any Ameri-can military action in Iraq, even limited strikes like these. I un-derstand that. I ran for this office in part to end our war in Iraq and welcome our troops home, and that's what we've done. As commander in chief, I will not allow the United States to be dragged into fighting another war in Iraq.

★

Among the reasons Obama was reluctant to agree to the airstrikes was fear of bolstering Maliki as prime minister. Obama, aides said, did not want the United States to be "Maliki's air force." To the Americans, Maliki was the source of much of the problem. The Shiite prime minister had turned increasingly authoritar-ian since the departure of American troops at the end of 2011–indeed, within days of the withdrawal, he arrested a Sunni vice president, foreshadowing a more sectarian approach. In cracking down on Sunnis, Maliki fed resentment of his Shiite-led govern-ment and seeded the ground for the arrival of the Islamic State.

Now Obama was ready to cut the cord. At the urging of the Americans, Iraq's president in August tapped another member of Maliki's party, Haider al-Abadi, to take over as prime minister. Maliki hesitated for a few days, stirring fears that he would use force to retain power, then finally stepped aside. Obama and Joe Biden each called to congratulate Abadi and came away hopeful that the new Iraqi leader would take a more inclusive approach, undercutting Sunni support for the Islamic State.

Iraq, though, was only part of the problem. It would mean little if the United States took on the Islamic State on one side of the border and did nothing about it on the other side in Syria. The jihadists did not respect lines on the map. And they showed in grim fashion that they would use their territory to produce ter-ror in far-off America. In quick succession, they released videos showing terrorists beheading two American journalists, James

Foley and Steven Sotloff, as they were forced to wear Guantánamo-style orange jumpsuits and kneel on the ground to await their grisly fate.

The videos shocked Americans and produced calls for revenge. Obama seemed genuinely troubled and declared himself "heartbroken," but sent the opposite message by heading to the golf course in Martha's Vineyard, where he was on vacation immediately after denouncing the Islamic State's actions to news media cameras. Obama was determined not to let terrorists dictate the president's schedule, but even Democrats thought the quick juxtaposition of grief and golf came across as unseemly.

As Obama considered how to respond, he grappled with the lines that the Islamic State ignored. In Iraq, he had the invitation of the Baghdad government to operate inside its territory and he had the cooperation of the Iraqi army to fight the enemy. But he had no such alignment with the government of Syria and no such allies on the ground in that war-torn country. Obama finally agreed to try to create from scratch a ground force in Syria by training and equipping a rebel army, much as Hillary Clinton and David Petraeus had recommended years before. And in a dramatic intervention, Obama ordered American airstrikes on Islamic State forces inside Syria, reasoning that he had the right to act in the nation's self-defense. This time, he made no move to ask Congress for a vote first, rationalizing that the authorization to use force against terrorists passed during George W. Bush's presidency would apply.

In announcing his decision to extend the bombing campaign into Syria, Obama tried to strike a balance, again presenting himself as the anti-Bush even as he ordered a military action that Bush himself had not. Obama talked almost as much about what he would not do – "We will not get dragged into another ground war in Iraq" – as what he *would* do to counter the Islamic State.

But he also advanced an argument that in some ways mirrored Bush's much-debated strategy of pre-emption – that is, acting to forestall a potential threat rather than waiting for it to gather. Obama acknowledged that the Islamic State did not pose a direct threat to the United States at that time, but he contended that "if left unchecked" it could.

Obama's measured approach reflected a country weary of war in the Middle East and wary of another one. While commanders in chief typically enjoy a surge in public support when they take the nation into conflict overseas, Americans did not rally behind Obama this time around. A fresh battery of polls indicated that most Americans did want him to go after the Islamic State, yet disapproved of his leadership. In other words, they supported the policy but not the president.

*

Just how much they did not support him became clear in November, when voters repudiated Obama by handing Republicans control of the Senate and adding to their majority in the House. Only two years after Obama's re-election, the midterm results underscored how far he had fallen in the public estimation. Nearly six out of ten voters interviewed by pollsters as they exited balloting stations expressed negative feelings about his administration. For every two voters who said they cast ballots to back Obama, three said they were voting to express their opposition to him.

While winning two historic elections himself, Obama in the course of his presidency had presided over the disintegration of his party on Capitol Hill and around the country. In six years, Democrats had lost a net thirteen seats in the Senate and sixty-eight in the House, the most dramatic reversal for an incumbent president's party in more than a half-century. Democrats had also lost multiple governorships and over the course of his presidency would lose nearly 1,000 state legislative seats. The 2014 midterm election climaxed a year in which almost everything seemed to go wrong for Obama, and the Republican victory appeared to foreshadow a challenging final two years in office for the president with minimal chance for significant legislation.

The one person in the White House who did not seem all that upset was Obama. "We got beat," he admitted publicly afterward. But he consciously avoided using any kind of memorable, headline-friendly word like "shellacking," the term he used after the 2010 midterm elections. Moreover, he sounded anything but defeated. He dismissed the notion that the election was a referendum on his leadership. The electoral map was stacked against him, he argued, making Democrats underdogs from the start.

His staff told him that no president since the 1950s had as many vacant Senate seats up for grabs in states previously lost by the president. "This is probably the worst possible group of states for Democrats since Dwight Eisenhower," Obama told an interviewer on Election Day. And privately he groused that his own party had kept him off the campaign trail, with many of its most embattled candidates refusing to let him come to their states or districts, meaning he never really got the chance to make his case. In the last days of the campaign, he was brought into just five states to campaign, compared with the ten visited by Bush in similar circumstances in 2006.

In a way, although he would not say this out loud with the cameras on, Obama felt liberated by the defeat of the Democrats. Now, at least, he no longer had to defer to Senator Harry Reid of Nevada, the cantankerous Democratic leader in the upper chamber who often made the president's life difficult. Now Obama did not have to subordinate his own priorities to those of a vulnerable Congressional caucus obsessed about the next election. Now he could essentially bypass his own petulant party allies to deal directly with Republican leaders in areas where they might come to agreement and publicly take them on in areas where they could not.

In the days following the election, Obama seemed almost revitalized and determined to advance his agenda using the power he already had – and the power that he was about to claim. He wasted little time exercising it. He started by weighing in on a long-running debate over "net neutrality," urging his appointees on the Federal Communications Commission to regulate the Internet as a public utility like electricity and telephone service. He told the FCC, with three Democratic appointees to two Republicans, that it should adopt strict rules requiring providers to treat all Internet traffic equally and bar them from favoring high-paying advertisers at the expense of, say, a teenager's blog. In so doing, he was seeking to influence an area that touched the lives of many millions of Americans through the executive branch, again without involving Congress.

Obama quickly turned to another high-stakes issue during a post-election trip to China, where he announced a deal with the Beijing government to fight climate change. Until then, China had been an outlier, churning out ever-increasing volumes of carbon emissions as its economy expanded dramatically but refusing to go along with international efforts to curb greenhouse gases. In the agreement Obama reached with President Xi Jinping, China would for the first time adopt targets for reductions of carbon emissions, vowing to stop its emissions from growing by 2030, paralleling the efforts Obama was already launching at home through the Environmental Protection Agency. For Obama, the pact was a powerful breakthrough that he hoped would prod other nations to join a global climate change agreement that he was trying to negotiate before leaving office.

After returning home, Obama cleared away some other outstanding business by forcing out Defense Secretary Chuck Hagel.

Now at war again in Iraq and for the first time in Syria, Obama decided he needed someone at the Pentagon more in tune with his way of thinking. Hagel, a former Republican senator, had been a head-scratching choice from the beginning since he did not have a close relationship with Obama and was so estranged from his fellow Republicans that his appointment did not buy any bipartisan good will. During his confirmation hearing, Hagel seemed uncertain about several national security issues and even Obama's own policies. Republicans accused him of being soft on Iran and insufficiently supportive of Israel, assertions he denied.

To White House officials, Hagel had proved to be a strikingly passive figure, sitting in the Situation Room without speaking up, leaving it to General Martin Dempsey, the Joint Chiefs chairman, to articulate the military's positions on various issues. For his part, Hagel bristled at what he considered White House micromanagement and butted heads with Susan Rice. Left out of the decision not to strike Syria for crossing Obama's "red line" on chemical weapons, Hagel sent the White House a memo complaining that it had no strategy for Syria. And Hagel clashed with White House aides over their desire to move more aggressively on transferring detainees from Guantánamo Bay to other countries, which he considered a security risk. "I'd get the hell beat out of me all the time on this at the White House," he told *Foreign Policy* magazine after his resignation. He left bitter about the way he was treated, complaining that White House aides were trying "to destroy me." Replacing him would be the deputy defense secretary, Ash Carter, a physicist and technocrat who was close to Obama's team.

With that unpleasantness out of the way, Obama finally moved ahead in another area that had bedeviled him for six years. No longer willing to wait for Congress to find a way forward on immigration, Obama decided to take matters into his own hands by building on his "dreamers" program allowing younger illegal immigrants to stay. In a prime-time address from the East Room of the White House on November 20, he announced a directive that would essentially shield up to 5 million of the 11 million illegal immigrants from deportation and allow many of them to work in the country legally, although his new policy would not provide them a path to citizenship.

Opponents howled at what Representative Kevin McCarthy, who took over from Eric Cantor as House Republican majority leader, called a "brazen power grab." The idea that a president could simply choose not to enforce the duly enacted law of the land struck many as outrageous and even unconstitutional. It was a critical question defining the scope and limits of a president's authority. Among those who once said the president did not have such sweeping power was none other than Barack Obama, who for years had told activists urging him to simply order a halt to deportations that he could not do so. Now, however, he had secured a new legal opinion from his Justice Department and abruptly claimed that he did have the power after all.

In his televised address, Obama all but dared his critics to challenge his new interpretation. "The actions I'm taking are not only lawful, they're the kinds of actions taken by every single Republican president and every Democratic president for the past half-century," he said. "To those members of Congress who question my authority to make our immigration system work better, or question the wisdom of me acting where Congress has failed, I have one answer: Pass a bill."

Nearly three dozen Republican governors took him up on the dare, not by passing a bill but by going to court to challenge Obama's order as an abuse of power. In effect, they were asking a judge to determine which was correct – Obama's original estimate of his authority or his new one. Other Republicans complained that Obama was defying the verdict of voters rendered just two weeks earlier. "By ignoring the will of the American people, President Obama has cemented his legacy of lawlessness and squandered what little credibility he had left," said John Boehner.

To Obama, though, the lesson of the election was different. It was this: Time is short. Time to act. The year of his discontent was over.

CHAPTER TWELVE
'Could Have Been Me'

Obama was sitting on Marine One as the iconic white-topped helicopter lifted off from the South Lawn of the White House. He was thinking about race in America. Here he was, the first black man to live in the executive mansion built in part by slaves, the first to command the tools of the presidency like the aircraft ferrying him to his next destination, a living symbol of progress in a country long divided along lines of color. But he was heading off to South Carolina to deliver the eulogy for a black pastor and eight of his parishioners gunned down in church on June 17, 2015, by a twenty-one-year-old white supremacist, the kind of mindless act of hate that seemed to belie the hope his election had inspired.

"When I get to the second part of referring to *Amazing Grace*," he ventured out loud as he thought about his speech during the flight, "I think I might sing."

Sing? That was not something presidents typically did, not in public anyway, especially not in the age of YouTube when every moment lives on forever. Michelle Obama and Valerie Jarrett seemed skeptical.

"Why on earth would that fit in?" the first lady asked.

The president demurred. Maybe he would not do it. He was not sure. "We'll see how it feels at the time," he said.

It must have felt okay. In the pulpit of the stately Emanuel African Methodist Episcopal Church in Charleston later that day, Obama came to the end of a forty-minute eulogy delivered in revivalist cadences, then paused, looked down, then up, then down again, almost as if deciding whether to go through with it. Finally, after twenty long seconds, he began singing, to the surprise of nearly everyone in the room – slowly, alone and unaccompanied by any instruments or chorus.

> *Amazing Grace, how sweet the sound*
> *That saved a wretch like me.*
> *I once was lost, but now am found*
> *T'was blind but now I see*

The bishops in purple robes sitting behind him smiled with delight as they realized what he was doing and rose to their feet to join him. The president's baritone voice went flat at one point, not quite hitting the right note, but his performance as a whole stirred people inside the church and around the country. Something about that moment captured the roiling emotions of a nation struggling to make sense of racial violence in what was supposed to be an era that had moved past that. For all of the heady assumptions about the larger meaning of his election, Obama's presidency revealed just how far the nation had yet to go when it came to bridging the enduring divisions that once led it into civil war. A series of deadly encounters between police officers and young black men, riots in the streets of cities big and small and the massacre of African-American churchgoers praying to God put race back on the table in Obama's later years in office.

Many presidents have governed during times of racial tension, but Obama was the first to glance in a mirror and find a face that looked like those on the other side of history's ledger. While his first term was consumed by the economy, war and health care, his second kept coming back to the societal scars that were not healed by his ascension. He had been determined to be judged as a president who happened to be black, not as a black president, and yet the color of his skin still defined him as no other president. "Obama is plagued by inescapable blackness," wrote Michael Eric Dyson, a Georgetown University professor and author of the book, *The Black Presidency*, a critical examination of the first African-American chief executive's handling of race relations. Obama's "palpable discomfort with race has made him a sometimes unreliable and distant narrator of black life." Yet as he headed into the final half of his presidency, Obama stopped trying to escape his blackness and seemed to find his voice again as he lamented the fate of the Emanuel Nine and young men like Trayvon Martin, Michael Brown and Freddie Gray.

Obama was not able to resolve those tensions during his eight years, nor could he be expected to, but many debated whether his presidency helped or hurt. At times, it felt like Obama's ascent to power had given new life to old hatreds rather than buried them. "For many people, it feels worse because we have seen such a reaction to this presidency that has been really alarming and, without question, from many quarters has been based in part on his race," said Sherrilyn Ifill, president of the NAACP Legal Defense and Educational Fund.

To many of his supporters, it was self-evident that the ferocity of opposition to Obama was fueled by racism, that his detractors simply could not stomach the sight of an African-American in power. The unrelenting antagonism by Republicans in Congress had to be a function of race, they concluded, to the point that it became an article of faith in some circles: *They would never do that to a white president.*

That was a conviction shared by some of those close to Obama – and, while he did not always say so out loud, by the president himself. Ben Rhodes later recalled a series of questions asked in private that revealed Obama's true feelings, however masked he kept them in public.

What would it take for protests in black communities to stop?

"Cops need to stop shooting unarmed black folks," Obama answered.

Why did he think he had failed to bring the country together?

"Because my being president appears to have literally driven some white people insane."

Was some of the opposition he faced about race?

"Yes! Of course! Next question."

Others argued that such a conclusion said more about the racial lens of Obama and his supporters than that of the other side, that America's corrosive politics had resulted in virulent and ugly opposition to white presidents like George W. Bush and Bill Clinton too. To be sure, Obama had faced stubborn assertions that he was not born in the United States, but Clinton was accused by some of involvement in the supposed murder of his aide Vincent Foster, who actually committed suicide, and Bush was accused by others of complicity in the September 11 terrorist attacks. At one point, moviemakers released a film depicting Bush's assassination. To the extent that racial tensions had been exacerbated during Obama's presidency, some of his critics maintained that Obama himself was at least partly to blame by embracing the politics of grievance and undercutting police officers with snap judgments in disputed cases. "President Obama, when he was elected, could have been a unifying leader," said Senator Ted Cruz of Texas, who was preparing a campaign for the Republican presidential nomination in hopes of succeeding Obama. "He has made decisions that I think have inflamed racial tensions."

One thing that was not debatable was that the vision of a post-racial society remained elusive by the end of Obama's presidency. He presided over a country where blacks were still twice as likely to be unemployed as whites, where gaps in income and wealth between races were widening rather than closing, where blacks were five times likelier to be in prison and young black men nine times as likely to be killed in a homicide as their white counterparts and where blacks got sick more, died younger and owned less. Frustrated activists felt compelled to organize behind a slogan that might have seemed unnecessary with an African-American in the White House – Black Lives Matter. "His candidacy suggested we had reached a new moment in America," Ifill said, "and I think some people overestimated the meaning of that moment."

Obama maintained that his economic and health care policies, while not specifically designed to help minorities, had nonetheless disproportionately benefited African-Americans and other disadvantaged groups. Indeed, 1.7 million more blacks had health insurance coverage by 2015 than before Obama's program, a proportionately greater change than among whites. And Valerie Jarrett maintained that Obama's mere presence in office made a huge difference in setting expectations for a whole new generation of young Americans who came of age not knowing any other presidents. "By breaking through that barrier," she said, "there are children growing up today who think it's perfectly normal to have an African-American president because that's all they have ever known."

In a country long riven by race, that was no small matter.

*

Obama had spent years reflecting on race in America and his own identity as the son of a black father from Kenya he met just once and a white mother from Kansas who took him to live overseas but eventually sent him back to Hawaii to live with his white grandparents. His early memoir, *Dreams from My Father*, written as the first African-American to serve as president of the *Harvard Law Review*, explored his own struggles to straddle lines between white and black and to define what it meant to be an American. With the bracing candor and self-absorption of youth, Obama wrote about race in an unvarnished way that no one planning a political career would ever have done.

When it came time to launch his own political career, Obama hoped to build on rather than join the civil rights movement that had made it possible. If Martin Luther King Jr., Jesse Jackson and Al Sharpton represented the Moses generation, Obama aspired to lead the Joshua generation, the next wave of African-American leaders who would transform the system from the inside rather than flog it from the outside. "While other black politicians did not mind barking at the big dogs of American politics," wrote Michael Eric Dyson, "Obama wanted to run with them before eventually leading the pack." Obama's own biracial identity made it almost natural for him to blur the color lines in ways that would appeal to African-Americans without alienating white people. "I can't sound like Martin," he told campaign advisers at one point. "I can't sound like Jesse."

Indeed, Jesse Jackson bristled at Obama's effrontery in claiming the leadership of black America, but the next generation in his own family embraced the change. Jesse Jackson Jr., the reverend's son, who served in Congress, served as co-chairman of Obama's campaign and pushed back whenever his father groused too publicly about the upstart candidate. Santita Jackson, the reverend's daughter, was a childhood friend of Michelle's, maid of honor at their wedding and godmother to Malia Obama.

It took time for the older generation of African-American leaders to come to terms with Obama; many like John Lewis were in Hillary Clinton's camp for the 2008 primary battle, loyal to her husband, who was once called the first black president, and convinced that the challenger had not paid his dues, walked in their shoes or proved that he was black enough. Only after Obama proved his crossover appeal by winning the first-in-the-nation caucuses in predominantly white Iowa did many African-Americans begin to see him as a plausible president.

In his more reflective moments, Obama figured his race had

helped his political career as much if not more than hurt it. He understood perfectly well that a certain percentage of white Americans still found the idea of a black man in the White House intolerable but almost surely a greater share was drawn to him by the historic nature of his candidacy or hoped to finally purge any share of white society's larger guilt. His unparalleled appeal to African-Americans after Iowa likewise gave him a base of support no other president could so readily claim and at times shielded him from criticism that his predecessors would have endured.

"In the same way that some of the people who don't like me probably don't like me because of race, there are some people who probably like me because of race and put up with me in ways that they wouldn't if I weren't African-American – the folks in African-American neighborhoods who identify with me even if they disagree with my policies," he told Dyson. "And my hope would be that when you wash out those aspects of it, that people are judging me on what I do as opposed to who I am." He wished, in other words, to be judged on the content of his character.

Obama arrived at the White House understanding how he had gotten there. He placed a bust of Martin Luther King in the Oval Office and hung on the wall a framed copy of the program from the March on Washington of 1963. On his custom-designed office rug, he included one of King's favorite quotations (often credited to the civil rights leader but actually just adopted and popularized by him): *"The arc of the moral universe is long, but it bends toward justice."*

But now he was a politician, not an activist. And absorbed as he was by the greatest economic crisis in decades and two overseas wars, he had entered office reluctant to talk about race. When Attorney General Eric Holder said shortly after the start of the administration that the United States was "a nation of cowards" for not having a more honest discussion of race, Obama quietly reined him in, making clear he did not want such a conversation. "It's fair to say that if I had been advising my attorney general, we would have used different language," he told *The New York Times*. "I'm not somebody who believes that constantly talking about race somehow solves racial tension," he added. When he did talk about race, he often delivered tough-love messages to black audiences about the need to take more responsibility for their children and their lives. "There's no longer any room for excuses," he told graduates at a historically black college. It was a theme that grated on some African-American commentators who thought he effectively laid racism at the feet of its victims rather than ever holding white society to account. The writer Ta-Nehisi Coates dubbed Obama the "scold of 'black America,'" adding that African-Americans "deserve more than a sermon."

On the rare occasions that Obama did step directly into racial controversy in his early years in office, he found himself singed. When Professor Henry Louis "Skip" Gates Jr., the eminent Harvard University historian and an acquaintance of the president, was arrested in his own home in Cambridge, Massachusetts, even after the white police officer confirmed that he was not an intruder, Obama said the police had "acted stupidly." It seemed like such a self-evident conclusion. He was surprised by the resulting uproar among those who complained about him inserting himself into a local dispute and second-guessing a law enforcement officer. To try to smooth over the flap, Obama invited both Gates and the officer to the White House to join him and Joe Biden for a beer on the South Lawn, in what was quickly dubbed "the beer summit" by the media.

The experience served as a searing reminder to Obama that no matter how measured or considered or common-sensical his comments on race, no matter how much he tried to be the racial arbiter explaining both sides to each other, he was invariably heard in different ways in different quarters of the country. Just as his lectures to the black community were taken as one-sided reprimands, any criticisms of racial profiling or police brutality were interpreted by at least some whites as unfairly tarnishing all law enforcement. Stung by the Gates episode, Obama sought to avoid the fraught politics of race as much as he could, at least until he had safely won re-election to a second term.

He made a brief exception when Trayvon Martin, a seventeen-year-old African-American, was shot to death by a white man in Florida in 2012. "If I had a son, he'd look like Trayvon," Obama pointed out. But some African-American figures bristled at his overall reluctance to talk about race and accused him of betraying his special historical responsibility. Cornel West, the firebrand Princeton University professor, called Obama "a black mascot of Wall Street oligarchs" and a "Rockefeller Republican in blackface." Tavis Smiley, the radio host, accused Obama of being "timid" on issues that had really mattered to King. "If you're not going to address racism, if you're not going to address poverty, if you're not going to address militarism, if you're going to dance around all three of them, then you're not doing justice to Dr. King," Smiley said. Other African-American commentators published articles under headlines like "Still Waiting for Our First Black President" and "A President for Everyone, Except Black People." Obama resented the pressure and the assumption that he should be focusing disproportionately on Americans who looked like him. "I'm not the president of black America," he said. "I'm the president of the United States of America."

Finally, after his re-election, freed of worries about political consequences, Obama began talking about race more often. In the days after securing a second term, he told aides that he wanted to overhaul criminal justice policies that disproportionately affected young African-American men. He also said he wanted to focus more on income inequality, and he used his second Inaugural Address to pledge to fight restrictions on voting rights. In part, his increased public focus on race was a function of the calendar – a series of fifty-year anniversaries from the civil rights era prompted him to reflect on the progress, or lack thereof, over his lifetime. He addressed commemorations of the March on Washington, the passage of the Civil Rights Act and the police beatings in Selma, Alabama. But his changing focus also owed to disturbing events across the country.

The acquittal of Trayvon Martin's killer in July 2013 prompted Obama to address the case in a more expansive and personal way than he had before. "Trayvon Martin could have been me thirty-five years ago," he told reporters in the White House briefing room. He talked about his own experiences of being followed while shopping in a department store or hearing car door locks when he crossed the street. "It's inescapable for people to bring those experiences to bear," he said.

Then came Ferguson, Missouri, where in the summer of 2014 a white police officer shot to death Michael Brown, an unarmed eighteen-year-old African-American who was reported to have his hands up when the bullets ripped into him. The episode touched off angry protests and riots and led to a federal investigation showing that authorities in that part of Missouri disproportionately targeted black residents.

Obama was on vacation on Martha's Vineyard, where he huddled with Eric Holder. A photograph of the two released by the White House unintentionally captured the contrasting approaches of the two men, the most powerful African-American officials in the country. Holder was the one leaning forward, both in the photograph and on the issues underlying the crisis in Ferguson. Obama, sitting back in his chair with two fingers pressed to his temple as he listened intently, was the one seemingly holding back, contemplative, even brooding, as if seeking to understand how events could get so out of hand and unsure how deeply to involve himself.

Unlike Obama, Holder grew up in the civil rights era and felt its legacy acutely. His sister-in-law integrated the University of Alabama. Obama, a decade younger, was removed from that experience by time, geography and family background as a result of his upbringing in white households an ocean away in Hawaii and Indonesia. Some black activists concluded that he could not feel intuitively what they did. "There is no blood flowing through the veins with empathy," said Michael Eric Dyson.

A grand jury eventually declined to indict the Ferguson police officer, who argued that he had felt threatened during an altercation amid evidence that contradicted the report that Michael Brown's hands were actually up. Convinced of another cover-up by the white establishment, protesters returned to the streets not just in Ferguson but around the country.

Then came Staten Island, where another grand jury declined to indict a police officer in the death of Eric Garner, an African-American who called out, "I can't breathe," as he was being restrained by a chokehold.

Then came Baltimore, where Freddie Gray, a twenty-five-year-old African-American, died while in police custody. Some of the Baltimore protesters turned violent, looting stores, setting fires and throwing rocks and cinder blocks at police officers. Obama, trying to settle the streets, went on television to appeal for calm and deplore the cycle of poverty and hopelessness. At the same time, he condemned the "criminals and thugs" who were taking advantage of the situation, a line that aggravated some of the activists.

Then came Charleston. In June 2015, a young white racist named Dylann Storm Roof walked into Emanuel African Methodist Episcopal Church and sat down with a group of African-

Americans who were praying before suddenly pulling out a gun and opening fire. Bug-eyed with a bowl haircut, a broken family and a history of drug use, the twenty-one-year-old Roof had descended into hate and extremism in the months leading up to the slaughter, spewing racist views and posting a photograph of himself on Facebook wearing a black jacket with flags of apartheid-era South Africa and white-ruled Rhodesia. Among those he killed was the Reverend Clementa Pinckney, who was both the church pastor and a state senator – and someone both Obama and Joe Biden had met during past campaign trips to South Carolina.

Before 6,000 mourners at T.D. Arena in Charleston, Obama eulogized Pinckney with the rhythm and tone of a pastor himself. "Maybe we now realize the way racial bias can infect us even when we don't realize it," Obama said behind Pinckney's coffin, draped in a blanket of red roses. "So that we're guarding against not just racial slurs, but we're also guarding against the subtle impulse to call Johnny back for a job interview, but not Jamal. So that we search our hearts when we consider laws to make it harder for some of our fellow citizens to vote." By treating every child as important regardless of skin color and by opening up opportunities for all Americans, Obama said, "we express God's grace."

A few days later, Obama called Denis McDonough, Ben Rhodes and his deputy chief of staff Anita Decker Breckenridge to the Oval Office. Instead of walking over to the chair he usually occupied during meetings, he remained seated behind his desk, holding a letter that had been sent to him. He read it out loud:

Dear Mr. President,

I used to not like you because of the color of your skin. My whole life I have hated people because of the color of their skin. I have thought about things since those nine people were killed and I realize I was wrong. I want to thank you for everything you are trying to do to help people.

Obama put the letter down. "Grace," he said. Then he got up and walked over to his chair. "It's a shame that those nine people had to die for that to happen."

*

Obama's sermon in Charleston – one of the preachers referred to him as the "Reverend President" – harkened back to his speech on race during his 2008 presidential campaign, when he was forced to repudiate his own pastor, Reverend Jeremiah Wright, whose inflammatory, hate-filled "God damn America" rhetoric belied Obama's message of racial harmony and threatened his nascent candidacy. But as his second term progressed, Obama increasingly resolved to lean forward as Eric Holder had in order to take the initiative on issues related to race.

Most prominent was his drive to overhaul a criminal justice system tilted against African-Americans. A month after his eulogy in South Carolina, Obama addressed the annual convention of the NAACP in Philadelphia and called for a sweeping bipartisan effort to fix what he called "a broken system." He endorsed legislation to reduce mandatory minimum sentences "or get rid of them entirely," argued for treatment or other alternatives for many drug offenders, proposed better living conditions for prisoners, ordered a review of solitary confinement and advocated making it easier for offenders to get jobs and regain their right to vote.

Few if any presidents had extolled the rights of prisoners or called for lighter sentences, even for nonviolent criminals. But Obama tackled the issue at a time of remarkable convergence of the political left and the political right backing change. Democrats and Republicans who agreed on little else found themselves together in concluding that the tough-on-crime policies of the past had gone too far. Liberals and progressives saw the issue as a matter of social justice and racial fairness while fiscal conservatives and libertarians viewed excessive imprisonment as a drain on public resources and a sign of overreaching government, and religious conservatives focused on the opportunity for redemption. The drive for change had generated odd-bedfellow alliances between groups on the left like the Center for American Progress and American Civil Liberties Union and leaders on the right like the billionaire brothers David and Charles Koch, known for bankrolling Republican candidates and causes. In Congress, Republicans like Senator Rand Paul of Kentucky were teaming up with Democrats like Senator Cory Booker of New Jersey to introduce bipartisan legislation.

More than 2.2 million Americans were behind bars, and a study found that the state and federal prison population in 2009, when Obama took office, was seven times what it was in 1973. Although the United States made up less than 5 percent of the world's population at the time, it had more than 20 percent of its prison population. The issue was especially pronounced among younger African-American men. One in twelve black men from age twenty-five to fifty-four was locked up, compared with one in sixty non-black men in that age group.

Obama became another black man in prison, albeit just for a day, in July 2015, when he flew to Oklahoma to visit Federal Correctional Institution El Reno, about thirty miles west of Oklahoma City. In touring the facility, Obama went where no sitting president ever had before, both literally and perhaps even figuratively, hoping to build support for the bipartisan overhaul of the justice system.

As he stared into Cell 123, a cramped space of nine feet by ten feet with three bunks, a toilet with no seat, night table with books, small sink and metal cabinets, Obama could not help think of what might have been. After all, as a young man, he had smoked marijuana and tried cocaine. But he did not end up with a prison term lasting decades, like some of the men who had occupied Cell 123 or its equivalents.

As it turned out, Obama noted, there was a fine line between president and prisoner. "There but for the grace of God," Obama said somberly after the tour. "And that, I think, is something that we all have to think about."

*

With his presidency heading through its final years and toward history's judgment, Obama was more willing to be seen in terms of his race and heritage. Just days after Oklahoma, Obama jetted off to Africa for a journey to the land of his father. Obama had not visited Kenya since taking office, unwilling to provoke the political circus that might have ensued, given the birther conspiracy theory promoted by Donald Trump that he was actually born there and, therefore, ineligible to be president. "If you're asking me, 'Was there a political discussion as to whether it would be disadvantageous to show up in Kenya when Donald Trump was questioning his citizenship,' I don't recall ever having that discussion," said David Axelrod. "But maybe no one needed to have that discussion." It was obvious.

During his entire first term, Obama spent just about twenty-four hours in sub-Saharan Africa, and even then on the other side of the continent from his father's home. Some critics said that the first president with African roots was doing less for Africa than the white president he had succeeded. With re-election behind him, Obama now showed fresh interest in Africa, making a longer trip to Senegal, South Africa and Tanzania, launching a Power Africa initiative to spread electricity through the continent, hosting a summit meeting in Washington for African leaders and pushing a renewal of an African trade preference program through Congress. Now at last, he was heading to Kenya.

Obama seemed moved to be back in his family homeland, but the trip that July was surreal and strangely impersonal at the same time. The first time he had visited Kenya, as a young man, he was by his own account seeking to fill "a great emptiness" he felt inside and figure out how he fit in. He rode in from the airport in his half-sister's beat-up car with a muffler that fell off during the drive. Now he returned with an entourage of hundreds, an armored car with a working muffler and no question about his place in the world. "Obviously, this is personal for me," he said after arriving. "My father came from these parts and I have family and relatives here." His half-sister, Auma Obama, told an excited crowd at a stadium that he was one of them. "He's not just our *familia*," she said. "He gets us. He gets us."

Obama resented the security net that prevented him from visiting his father's village or even just strolling around the capital, Nairobi, as he did when he visited years before. The streets had been swept of people, and the city had an eerie, empty feeling. With Obama unable to come to them, dozens of cousins and stepaunts and other members of his extended family, some of whom he had never met, were brought for dinner with him at his well-appointed and heavily guarded hotel in Nairobi. As journalists were allowed in to snap a few quick pictures, they could see the president looking to his right and looking to his left, clearly not really recognizing all of the people who claimed kinship seated around him.

"Part of the challenge that I've had during the course of my presidency is that, given the demands of the job and the bubble, I can't come here and just go upcountry and visit for a week and meet everybody," Obama said. "I'm more restricted, ironically, as president of the United States than I will be as a private citizen."

But with his unique status as the first American president descended from Africa, Obama used the visit to Kenya and nearby Ethiopia to send a message to a continent ruled by potentates clinging to power. It was time to stop rewriting constitutions and rigging elections. "Nobody should be president for life," he said in a speech at the African Union in Addis Ababa.

If he was willing to present himself as a son of Africa, Obama was likewise more prepared to embrace the role of civil rights leader at home. While he stayed away from such settings in his first years, Obama spoke from the same Lincoln Memorial that Martin Luther King did and from the same bridge in Selma near where John Lewis was beaten. "Because they marched," he said, "city councils changed and state legislatures changed and Congress changed and, yes, eventually the White House changed."

Obama was too young to remember those events himself, but some who watched him mark their anniversaries were old enough to have seen the changes and marveled at the presence of a black president standing where King had.

"If you say that's not the function of the dream, I don't know what is," Bill Carr, a black licensed clinical social worker from Montclair, New Jersey, said as he watched Obama speak at the fiftieth anniversary of the March on Washington.

"Who would have guessed fifty years ago that in less than fifty years we would re-elect – re-elect! – a black president?" asked Bill Tate, a white retired engineer who wore a button from the original march. "No one can deny that we've made some progress."

But racism was not defeated just because Obama sat in the White House. "We don't need the Ferguson report to know that's not true," he said at the foot of the Edmund Pettus Bridge in Selma with 40,000 mostly black people watching. "We just need to open our eyes and our ears and our hearts to know that this nation's racial history still casts its long shadow upon us. We know the march is not yet over; we know the race is not yet won. We know reaching that blessed destination where we are judged by the content of our character requires admitting as much."

★

After bemoaning the limits of progress of one civil rights movement in his *Amazing Grace* eulogy in Charleston, Obama arrived back in Washington to celebrate the advances of another. On the same day as the funeral for the nine slain black worshipers, the Supreme Court ruled that same-sex marriage was a constitutional right in all fifty states, a decision that resonated for many Americans the way the landmark civil rights rulings of the 1950s did. The president had the White House bathed in the rainbow colors of the gay rights movement that night to celebrate. While a slow convert to the cause, Obama had come to believe that his presidency would be remembered as a signal moment in the advance of gay rights and he wanted to be associated with that. He would even advocate for the rights of transgendered Americans, a group that had never been the focus of sympathetic presidential attention before.

But race remained the radioactive rod of the Obama presidency, one that burned no matter who touched it. As Obama sought to highlight the concerns of African-Americans who felt victimized, some law enforcement veterans worried that the fear of being accused of racism had caused many officers, consciously or unconsciously, to hold back, a trend dubbed the "Ferguson effect." James Comey, the FBI director, finally spoke out, saying that the criticism of the police might have inhibited officers so much that it was leading to a spike in violent crime. "I don't know whether that explains it entirely," he said in a public talk in Chicago, "but I do have a strong sense that some part of the explanation is a chill wind that has blown through American law enforcement over the last year."

Soon after his comments, Comey was summoned to the White House to meet with Obama. When he walked into the Oval Office, he was surprised not to see anyone else there. He had never met with Obama one on one and now he feared he was there to be chewed out.

Instead, Obama invited him to sit down and explain his thinking. "What are you seeing and what's worrying you?" the president asked.

Comey replied that more than forty of the nation's sixty largest cities were seeing more killings of young black men, all at the same time. He said that he hoped that by raising the question he could help change behaviors if police really were holding back.

Obama listened carefully and then offered some perspective for the FBI chief. He pointed out that some of the phrases that Comey had used went over badly in the black community – "weed and seed," meant by police to pull out the bad guys from a neighborhood, sounded to African-Americans that their young men were being deemed "weeds." Obama talked about the impact on a community of so many young black men caught up in the criminal justice system and how they experience law enforcement and the courts so differently.

Comey for his part described how police officers saw it, how they did not like to be portrayed as agents of "mass incarceration," a phrase that was used by reformers but sounded to law enforcement professionals as if they were being accused of rounding up people indiscriminately for a concentration camp.

In the end, Comey said, it was a remarkably healthy conversation in which both men saw at least a little bit of where the other was coming from. "Our discussion was the total opposite of the Washington listen: each of us actually took the time to really understand a different way of looking at something and with a mind open to being convinced," Comey said.

As his time in office grew short, however, Obama found himself stymied in his efforts to bring larger reform. Even with bipartisan support, legislation to revamp the criminal justice system stalled on Capitol Hill. So Obama once more turned to his executive power. He ordered new restrictions on the use of solitary confinement in federal prisons and banned federal agencies in many circumstances from asking about an applicant's criminal record until later in the hiring process in order to give freed prisoners a better chance of finding work. The federal sentencing commission reduced terms for many nonviolent drug crimes and decided to make the reduction retroactive, leading the Justice Department to release about 6,000 inmates.

Obama also made aggressive use of his clemency power, commuting the sentences of 1,715 prisoners, nearly all in his last two years in office. Altogether, he commuted more sentences than his thirteen most recent predecessors combined. Still, he was stingy with full pardons, granting fewer than all but two presidents in more than a century of record-keeping, and his commutations benefited only a fraction of the 30,000 inmates who applied for them.

Understanding that his presidency would not be the end of the matter, Obama prepared to continue the struggle for reconciliation over the long term. He founded an organization called My Brother's Keeper to help young Latino and African-American men. In many ways, he was focused on younger versions of himself, like a teenager named Malachi, whom he met during a My Brother's Keeper event in New York. "Malachi and I shared the fact that our dad wasn't around, and that sometimes we wondered why he wasn't around and what had happened," Obama told reporters afterward.

Obama set up the program to continue after he left office, and planned to make it a pillar of his activities after the White House. "This will remain a mission for me and for Michelle," he said, "not just for the rest of my presidency but for the rest of my life. And the reason is simple. We see ourselves in these young men."

But however well-intentioned, a program was not enough to stop the battle in the streets that only seemed to be heating up as his time in office grew short. As powerful as a president was, Obama headed into the final stage of his tenure painfully aware that his election had not settled anything.

After eight years of Obama, America was not ready to declare a cease-fire in the perpetual war over race. If anything, it seemed to be escalating again.

CHAPTER THIRTEEN
'Never Fear to Negotiate'

A week before Christmas 2014, Obama marched into the Cabinet Room of the White House to make a stunning announcement televised around the world. Nearly fifty-four years after the United States broke off ties with Fidel Castro's Cuba, Obama declared that he was ordering the restoration of diplomatic relations and the reopening of an embassy in Havana in a dramatic act intended to sweep aside one of the last vestiges of the Cold War. "These fifty years have shown that isolation has not worked," he said. "It's time for a new approach."

Obama rarely displayed much emotion in public, but anyone who had followed him over the years could detect a hint of a grin on his face and a tone of vindication in his voice. The surprise decision capped eighteen months of secret talks prodded in part by Pope Francis and concluded by a telephone call between Obama and President Raúl Castro, Fidel's brother and successor. The historic deal broke an enduring stalemate between two countries divided by just ninety miles of water but oceans of mistrust and hostility dating from the days of Theodore Roosevelt's charge up San Juan Hill and the nuclear brinkmanship of the Cuban missile crisis.

The opening to Cuba was part of a broader effort by the president to transform America's relations with the world and reach out to its enemies. When he first ran for president, Obama had promised to talk with leaders of renegade states like Cuba, Iran, Syria, North Korea and Venezuela without precondition in his first year in office. While Hillary Clinton ridiculed his promise during the campaign as "irresponsible and frankly naïve" and

John McCain said it betrayed his "inexperience and reckless judgment," Obama pointed repeatedly to John Kennedy's Inaugural Address when he said, "Let us never negotiate out of fear but let us never fear to negotiate." At his own inauguration, Obama addressed the nation's most intransigent adversaries by promising to "extend a hand if you are willing to unclench your fist."

It did not happen in his first year nor without preconditions – nor did it happen across the board. But deep into his second term, Obama was ready to follow through on the thrust of his promise with two of the five rogue states mentioned in his original campaign, Cuba and Iran. As with his diplomatic overture to Havana, Obama decided it was time to talk with Tehran, now more than three decades after the Islamic revolution and the subsequent 444-day hostage crisis that gripped the world, doomed Jimmy Carter's presidency and touched off a relentless ideological struggle for influence in the region. As with Cuba, Obama authorized secret talks that, in this case, eventually led to an agreement curbing Iran's nuclear program in exchange for the lifting of international sanctions.

Obama explained his thinking about such diplomatic initiatives to Thomas Friedman of *The New York Times*, arguing that it was better to see if talking would work. "We are powerful enough to be able to test these propositions without putting ourselves at risk," he said when the two sat down for a one-on-one conversation in the Oval Office. Cuba was not a country "that threatens our core security interests" and even if Iran was more dangerous, the mullahs understood that they could not hope to match the power of the United States. "You asked about an Obama Doctrine," he told Friedman. "The doctrine is: We will engage, but we preserve all our capabilities."

Not everyone was impressed. For all the self-congratulations, Republicans and even some Democrats viewed Obama's outreach to Cuba and Iran as dangerously misguided. Cuba had done nothing to ease its iron grip over its own people and reopening relations would simply reward the hemisphere's most brutal dictatorship. Iran had a record of cheating when it came to building a nuclear capability and would simply use the estimated $100 billion it would recoup after sanctions were lifted to finance further terrorism and instability in the Middle East.

Moreover, the Iran deal widened a rift between Obama and the leadership of Israel, never close to begin with. While five other international powers – Britain, France, Germany, Russia and China – signed off on the Iran deal, America's closest friend in the region definitively did not. Indeed, Prime Minister Benjamin Netanyahu became the world's leading opponent of the agreement, dismissing Tehran's promises to abide by new restrictions and calling the deal an existential threat to his small country that would only trigger an arms race with Arab states wary of Iranian aspirations to regional hegemony. He went so far as to accept an invitation from John Boehner to address a joint meeting of Congress to attack the president's diplomacy with Iran without even telling the White House first, a major breach of protocol; indeed, Israel's ambassador met with John Kerry the day before the speech was announced without giving him a heads up.

It was a spectacle with few if any modern precedents and one that outraged Obama. "This deal won't be a farewell to arms – it would be a farewell to arms control," Netanyahu declared on March 3, 2015, from the rostrum of the majestic chamber of the House of Representatives, where Republicans greeted him with standing ovations even as dozens of Democrats, including Joe Biden and Nancy Pelosi, the House minority leader, stayed away. "And the Middle East would soon be crisscrossed by nuclear tripwires. A region where small skirmishes can trigger big wars would turn into a nuclear tinderbox." Kerry later complained that it was "a speech that hit below the belt."

Pugnacious and determined, Netanyahu had never gotten along with Obama. In Obama's view, Netanyahu was enthralled with a hard-line philosophy and unwilling to make necessary concessions to finally end the decades-long struggle with the Palestinians. Netanyahu, for his part, considered Obama hopelessly naïve about one of the world's most volatile neighborhoods and insufficiently aware of just how threatened Israel really was. Even before it ruptured over the Iran agreement, their tortured relationship had been a story of crossed signals, misunderstandings and slights, perceived and real.

It got off to a bad start when Obama insisted shortly after taking office that Israel freeze construction of new settlements in the West Bank so that negotiations could be held with the Palestinians, a demand that rankled Netanyahu and his right-of-center coalition. The settlements were a major source of contention between Israel and the Palestinians, which had been vying for control of the land west of the Jordan River for decades. Palestinians viewed the West Bank as the home of their future state, while Israelis kept building new housing in territory they considered part of their ancestral home. Obama believed the Israelis were in effect creating facts on the ground, making it harder for Palestinians to claim the West Bank for their future state. Netanyahu argued that the real problem was not settlements but Palestinian terrorism.

It did not help matters when Obama went to Cairo for his speech to the Muslim world without also visiting Jerusalem while in the region, as was customary for American presidents. When Obama sent Biden to visit Netanyahu instead, the Israeli government embarrassed the vice president by announcing new settlement construction while he was on the ground, a move that was taken in Washington as an affront. Obama and Netanyahu clashed again when Israel, worried that Tehran was on the precipice of a nuclear breakthrough, prepared to attack Iran early in 2012 before ultimately being talked out of it.

As far as Obama was concerned, George W. Bush's policy of close ties with Israel's government was misguided and had hardly made a difference in forcing it to come to terms with the Palestinians. When leaders of Jewish-American groups came to see Obama during his first year in office, they said the lesson of history was that there should never be daylight between America and Israel because their mutual enemies would exploit it. Obama was not convinced, pointing to his predecessor. "Eight years, no daylight," he said. "Eight years, no progress."

By his second term, Obama decided to lay out his own principles for Middle East peace consisting of four parts: A Palestinian state would be created with borders drawn along the lines before the 1967 war with mutual land swaps to accommodate at least some Israeli settlements in the West Bank. Israel would be formally recognized as a Jewish state. Jerusalem would be the capital of both states. Palestinian refugees who left or were driven out after the Israeli state was created in 1948 would not be granted a right of return, but they could be resettled in the West Bank. In the end, advisers convinced Obama to compromise by only making public the first two points, but even that was enough to infuriate Netanyahu, who felt sandbagged. When they met shortly afterward in the Oval Office, Obama sat with his jaw clenched and his eyes narrowed as Netanyahu lectured him in front of television cameras on the realities of the Middle East.

"This is as annoyed as I've been as president," Obama told Ben Rhodes afterward. "Dealing with Bibi is like dealing with the Republicans."

Rhodes sympathized, noting that he once belonged to the American Israel Public Affairs Committee, or AIPAC. The friction with Israel was frustrating for him on a personal level.

"Me too," Obama said. "I came out of the Jewish community in Chicago. I'm basically a liberal Jew."

When Obama later talked with Thomas Friedman about the Iran deal, the president sounded more emotional than the columnist had ever heard him as he discussed his distress over being portrayed as anti-Israel. Obama had devoted enormous taxpayer resources to Israeli defense needs, protected it from hostile resolutions at the United Nations and, in his view, worked hard to neutralize a major threat by curbing Iran's nuclear program. Indeed, he had authorized a covert campaign he inherited from George W. Bush called Olympic Games that inserted a killer worm developed in conjunction with Israeli scientists to sabotage Iranian centrifuges, a worm later dubbed "Stuxnet" by hackers. But Netanyahu had gotten under his skin. "You're fed up with him," Obama was overheard on another occasion telling his French counterpart with manifest frustration, "but I have to deal with him even more often than you."

For Obama, the gambits with Cuba and Iran represented a conflict of visions between his faith in diplomacy as the most rational way to resolve differences among international actors and his critics' deep skepticism over the wisdom of negotiating with adversaries they could not trust. It was something of a season for diplomacy – in addition to the Cuba opening and the Iran nuclear deal, Obama was putting the finishing touches on a sweeping Asian-Pacific trade pact that would encompass 40 percent of the world's economy and was pushing for a global climate change accord that would commit even outliers like China and India to restraining toxic emissions.

"Part of our goal here has been to show that diplomacy can work," Obama told Friedman in a second interview after the Iran agreement was sealed in July 2015. "It doesn't work perfectly. It doesn't give us everything that we want." But, he added, "what we can do is shape events in ways where it's more likely that problems get solved, rather than less likely, and that's the opportunity we have now."

*

The United States broke off diplomatic relations with Cuba in January 1961, seven months before Obama was born, and over the subsequent years made fitful efforts to topple Fidel Castro's regime, most disastrously in the Bay of Pigs operation. Ten presidents either failed or refused to bridge the gap, and the relationship remained frozen in time long after the fall of the Berlin Wall and collapse of the Soviet Union.

Obama was determined to succeed where his predecessors had not, convinced that America's half-century trade and commercial embargo on Cuba had failed to undermine the Castro government while worsening Washington's standing in Latin America. In his early months in office, Obama eased limits on people visiting relatives in Cuba and sending money to them, expanded cultural and academic exchanges and resumed talks on migration, drug-trafficking and postal services. But the early thaw ended in late 2009 when the Havana government arrested Alan Gross, an American contractor distributing mobile telephones, laptops and other communications equipment in Cuba on behalf of the United States government.

After his re-election, Obama told aides he wanted to do "something big on Cuba" in his second term, and assigned Ben Rhodes to establish a confidential channel. For eighteen months, Rhodes, accompanied by Ricardo Zuniga, a career diplomat who had served in Havana, snuck out of Washington periodically to fly to Canada to meet secretly with Cuban counterparts, inventing cover stories to shroud their travels even from relatives. In doing so, Obama cut out the State Department but reasoned that the only way to convince the Cubans that this was a serious initiative was to send someone known to be in his inner circle. The

Cubans evidently got the message because their delegation was led by Alejandro Castro, the son of Raúl and nephew of Fidel.

To clear the way for broader changes, Obama knew he had to win Gross's freedom. Raúl Castro's government insisted on a swap for the Cuban Five, spies who had been locked up in American prisons for years and become folk heroes back home. But Obama was reluctant to agree to an explicit trade because it would imply that Gross really was a spy, as Cuba claimed.

As the talks progressed and the two sides began to develop a relationship, they found ways to test the sincerity of the other side. When Edward Snowden, the NSA leaker, was flying around the world looking for a refuge from the United States, he appeared headed at one point to Cuba. Rhodes made clear to Alejandro Castro that accepting him would unravel everything they had accomplished and make it impossible for Obama to take a politically risky chance on changing the relationship. "If you take in Snowden," Rhodes said, "that political space will be gone." Cuba ultimately rebuffed Snowden, which Obama and his team took as a signal of Havana's seriousness.

Searching for a way to resolve the dispute over Gross, Obama's advisers came up with an alternative that would allow them to deny making a direct swap – Havana would release a Cuban imprisoned for spying for the United States in exchange for the three members of the Cuban Five who had not yet finished their federal prison terms. Gross would be released at the same time in a theoretically separate humanitarian gesture. Cuba would also release more than fifty political prisoners, while the United States would allow more travel, banking and commercial ties, although Obama could not lift the trade embargo entirely without Congress.

The breakthrough was aided by a surprise outside figure. Pope Francis sent secret letters to both Obama and Raúl Castro urging them to follow through on a deal and once the two sides negotiated the details, delegations visited the Vatican to present the package to the pope's advisers, all but cementing the agreement. "At that point, you're on the hook to the pope," Rhodes later said.

The day before the planned announcement, the White House set up a telephone call between Obama and Raúl Castro, the first direct substantive contact between leaders of the two countries in more than fifty years. As Obama and his aides sat in the Oval Office waiting for the call to be put through, the president was feeling heady about the history of the occasion.

"As Joe Biden would say, this is a big fucking deal," he told Rhodes and Susan Rice.

When Castro came on the line, he too seemed energized by the moment. "Señor Presidente!" he declared.

For the next half-hour, though, the isolated Cuban leader delivered a rambling lecture about all the ways the United States had tried to kneecap his government over the decades, a quintessentially long-winded Castro rant. Obama listened patiently. Eventually, Rhodes passed him a note letting him know that he could cut this off.

Obama shook his head and covered the receiver. "It's been a long time since they've talked to a U.S. president," he said. "He's got a lot to say."

The next day, December 17, 2014, Gross walked out of a Cuban prison, boarded an American military plane and flew to Washington, happily devouring a corned beef sandwich on rye bread with mustard during the flight. Obama announced the opening of diplomatic relations in a televised address from the Roosevelt Room of the White House, after aides made sure to move a painting of Theodore Roosevelt charging up San Juan Hill.

While the release of Gross was widely welcomed, not everyone was happy with warmer relations. "This entire policy shift announced today is based on an illusion, on a lie, the lie and the illusion that more commerce and access to money and goods will translate to political freedom for the Cuban people," said Senator Marco Rubio, a Florida Republican and son of Cuban immigrants who was then readying a campaign for the presidency.

Undeterred, Obama would go on to meet with Castro on the sidelines of a regional summit several months later and the American flag was raised over a new embassy in Havana not long after that. An enthusiastic Obama now set his sights on traveling to Cuba himself in his final year for what he hoped would be a trip for the history books.

Months later, Obama would celebrate his alignment with Pope Francis by hosting the holy father for his first visit to the United States. Standing together on a sunny day in September 2015 on the South Lawn of the White House, Obama welcomed Francis with an elaborate arrival ceremony complete with fife-and-drum corps – but skipped the traditional twenty-one-gun salute that might have seemed discordant for a man of peace. The president and the pontiff could hardly have come from more starkly disparate backgrounds, and yet commonalities now united the fifty-four-year-old community organizer from Chicago and the seventy-eight-year-old priest from Argentina, both of whom saw themselves as champions of the powerless.

Unlike his two immediate predecessors, Francis had embraced the social justice side of the Catholic message, putting him in sync with the liberal American president on many issues – so much so that critics derided him as "Obama's Pope." Obama certainly must have been satisfied when the pope used the visit to effectively bolster the president's side of America's fractious debates over climate change, immigration and economic inequality. "You shake our conscience from slumber," Obama told him.

Yet Obama was not the only fan. John Boehner, a devout Catholic, had been hoping to host a pope for twenty years and was literally moved to tears when Francis addressed crowds on the West Lawn of the Capitol from a balcony. Boehner considered this moment the culmination of a long career in Washington. When he went home that night, he decided that it was the right moment to move on. The next morning, he announced that he would step down as speaker.

The spiritual influence aside, Boehner's decision also resulted from a cold calculation that he had lost his caucus. After years of trying to steer the Republican majority toward what he considered sensible policies and even occasional compromise with Obama, he could no longer control the Freedom Caucus conservative wing of the party. And he was tired of the fight.

He would soon be replaced by Paul Ryan, the young chairman of the House Ways and Means Committee and 2012 vice presidential candidate, one of the few Republicans Obama respected because of his intellect and policy heft. But Boehner's departure was bad news for the president. It meant that any hope of legislative compromise for his remaining sixteen months in office had vanished.

The day Boehner announced his decision, Obama called him.

"Boehner, man, I'm going to miss you," he said.

"Yes, you are, Mr. President," Boehner replied. "Yes, you are."

★

Like the Cuba opening, Obama's accord with Iran also had its roots in a telephone call. Picking up where George W. Bush had left off, Obama came to office intent on tightening sanctions against the Islamic government to force it to give up its nuclear program. After choking off international financing and drying up its oil exports, Obama hoped to get Iran to the negotiating table, and a newly elected, seemingly less extreme Iranian government appeared open to talking.

When President Hassan Rouhani came to New York for the

opening of the annual United Nations General Assembly session in September 2013, the White House explored the chances for a breakthrough. Jake Sullivan, who was Joe Biden's national security adviser, spent a day with an Iranian intermediary secretly negotiating a meeting between Obama and Rouhani, right down to where and how long they would get together and what they would talk about.

The next morning, the Iranian called Sullivan: the meeting was off. A picture of the two shaking hands was a step too far for an Iranian president, even one styling himself as a reformer. But then, at the end of the week, as Rouhani was getting ready to depart, the Iranian called Sullivan back. What about a telephone call? Sullivan agreed and took the cellular number to reach the Iranian president.

So as Rouhani rode in his car on the way to the airport to leave New York and return to Tehran, the phone rang and the White House connected him to Obama. The fifteen-minute conversation was the first between American and Iranian leaders since the hostage crisis of 1979-81.

Even before Rouhani's election, the Obama administration had been in contact with the Tehran government through a back channel first opened by John Kerry, then still a senator, through the Middle East country of Oman, a friend to both nations. Much like the Cuba outreach, Obama authorized Sullivan and William Burns, a senior State Department official, to kick off clandestine negotiations in 2012 to explore the possibility of an agreement that would transform the relationship. Rouhani's subsequent election energized the talks, which were taken over in Obama's second term by Wendy Sherman, the under secretary of state for political affairs.

The secret-channel talks proceeded even as the United States and five other world powers were engaged in public negotiations with Iran that were called either the P5+1 (for the Permanent Five members of the United Nations Security Council, plus Germany) or the E3+3 (for the three European powers plus the others). Obama kept the secret channel hidden even from Britain and France, not to mention Israel, which learned about it through its own spying and felt betrayed. The key to breaking the longstanding impasse was Obama's decision to accept a small amount of uranium enrichment by Iran as part of any agreement, not enough to build a weapon but enough to allow Tehran to save face.

Eventually the cloaked channel went public and the other world powers were brought into the talks. Kerry, now secretary of state, took the lead, determined to make a nuclear agreement with Iran the centerpiece of his diplomatic legacy. Kerry was not in the president's inner circle. While Obama was cautious and dubious, Kerry was energetic and optimistic. While Obama described his approach to foreign policy as "don't do stupid shit," Kerry regularly declared that he would rather get "caught trying" than hold back. White House aides joked that Kerry was like the astronaut in the movie *Gravity*, somersaulting through space, untethered from the White House. He clashed with Susan Rice. "Susan, this is a goddamn good deal," he shouted at her over the phone one day. At another point, even Obama felt compelled to rein him in. "John, don't go overselling it to me, brother," Obama told him in a meeting. But the president gave him license to see what he could bring back.

The negotiations were extremely complicated, involving seven nations and multiple political factions within each one, plus the details of nuclear science that required experts like Energy Secretary Ernest Moniz, a physicist, to be brought in. Sherman described it as "the world's most complex and consequential Rubik's cube." The talks took their toll, both physically and psychically. At one point, Sherman tripped and broke her finger while on Capitol Hill to testify about the talks, but went ahead with her House hearing anyway. At another point, she smashed into a glass door rushing to answer a phone call from Kerry, breaking her nose. Kerry, too, was a casualty, fracturing his leg in three places when he slammed his bicycle into a curb during a ride meant to let off steam. He insisted on returning to the negotiations soon after surgery despite what his chief of staff Jonathan Finer called "a high level of pain" throughout the remaining talks.

Kerry left little doubt how much he wanted an agreement – too much so, in the view of critics and even some friends. In any negotiation, the person who can walk away from the talks has the upper hand. At one point, as Kerry and Moniz were nearing the end stage of the process, Obama sought to restrain him, telling him that it would be better to give up than to have a bad deal. "John, I've already got my legacy," Obama told him, referring to health care and other achievements. "I don't need this." But Kerry did and as the talks finally neared completion, he devoted eighteen straight days in Vienna, the longest any American secretary of state had ever spent in one place overseas while in office.

The Iran negotiation underscored how much Obama relied on a tight circle of advisers – and even more so on his own judgment. During a secure video conference call with his negotiating team to settle on the final terms that would be acceptable for a deal with Iran, Obama methodically outlined his bottom lines on various issues one after the other. Advisers nodded in agreement. Obama encountered no real resistance, no dissent that would give him pause, no objection from anyone telling him he was giving away too much.

In part, the consensus owed to how long the talks had lasted, narrowing the remaining issues by that point. But it also underscored how policy was made in the final stretch of Obama's administration. An untested president who entertained fierce disputes when he arrived in office now had enough experience to know his own mind and needed, or invited, less debate. The so-called team of rivals he assembled at first had been replaced by a team of facilitators who channeled his ideas and executed his policies. "It's not our job to question him," said one adviser. "It's our job to figure out what he wants and get it done." Not everyone thought that was healthy. "The president suffers when he doesn't have that kind of robust debate," Robert Gates said as he watched from the outside.

Under the deal that Kerry sealed in July 2015, Iran agreed to shutter its heavy-water reactor, ship nearly all of its nuclear fuel out of the country and dismantle two-thirds of its centrifuges. With intrusive international inspections, the Americans argued that the rollback should make it impossible for Iran, if it decided to cheat, to actually develop a bomb in less than a year, a long enough "breakout" time for the world to react. In exchange, American and international sanctions were to be lifted, freeing up long-frozen funds for a cash-starved government.

The agreement included a series of "sunset clauses" in which certain provisions would expire starting in ten years, a concession to the Iranians that became seen as a major flaw of the agreement. As the deal was crafted, Iran could begin producing nuclear fuel again as soon as 2030, although even then only at minimal levels suitable for civilian purposes.

For good measure, Obama's aides also secretly negotiated the resolution of a longstanding dispute over military equipment that the United States sold Iran before the Islamic revolution of 1979 and then never delivered. The administration agreed to return $400 million in Iranian payments along with $1.3 billion in accrued interest, sending the first installment in giant pallets of cash, a detail that would later provoke a firestorm once disclosed by *The Wall Street Journal* just because of the image of piles and piles of bills being sent to a leading sponsor of terrorism.

At the same time, Obama's team won the release of four Iranian-Americans held by Tehran on spurious charges in exchange for seven Iranian or Iranian-Americans imprisoned in the United States for violating the sanctions. The White House insisted that the release of the prisoners was unrelated to the money being sent to Tehran, but to many critics it smacked of ransom. And even that deal almost collapsed at the last minute as Iranian authorities at the Tehran airport tried to stop the wife and mother of one of the Americans, Jason Rezaian, *The Washington Post's* bureau chief who had spent 545 days in captivity, from leaving with him. An American official said it "was like a scene out of *Argo*," the Ben Affleck movie about the Carter-era hostage crisis.

For many Iranians, the deal offered a bright moment of hope that their country would finally rejoin the community of nations and escape the shackles of sanctions that had helped cripple their economy. "I am desperate to feed my three sons," Ali, a fifty-three-year-old cleaner, told a *New York Times* reporter in Tehran. "This deal should bring investment for jobs so they can start working for a living."

But for many Israelis, it seemed a backstab. Benjamin Netanyahu called it "a historic mistake." The deal, he and other critics charged, would only postpone Iran's quest for a nuclear bomb, not end it permanently, even assuming that inspectors could detect any cheating. Obama was allowing a country that regularly threatened Israel's very existence out of the diplomatic and economic isolation that the world had effectively imposed. Netanyahu made common cause with Congressional Republicans in hopes of blocking the agreement.

Critics complained that the agreement did nothing to constrain Iran's missile program, nor did it address its hegemonic efforts to dominate the region by sponsoring terrorist groups like Hezbollah in Lebanon, Hamas in Gaza or the Houthis in Yemen. Obama and his team argued that the agreement was never intended to deal with every issue involving Iran, any more than arms-control treaties with the Soviet Union resolved disputes over its adventurism in various parts of the world. If Iran was going to be a menace in the region, Obama reasoned, better it be a menace without nuclear weapons.

The Israelis were not the only ones unhappy about the deal, however. America's Arab allies, most notably the Sunni-led Saudi Arabia, had been waging a virtual proxy war against the Shiite-led Iran for years, and they now worried that the nuclear agreement would free up once-sanctioned resources for Tehran to flex its muscles even more around the region. Obama tried to reassure nervous Arabs with arms sales and a summit meeting at Camp David. But he dismissed their request for a mutual defense treaty along the lines of the one with Japan, and so King Salman of Saudi Arabia and most of the other Persian Gulf heads of state skipped the Camp David meeting, sending lower-level officials instead. The bid to repair relations with the Arab states led Obama to finally abandon his Arab Spring aspirations altogether when he restored the fraction of military aid to Egypt suspended after the military coup, even though the new leadership had not restored democracy as he had demanded.

In the end, Congress was unable to stop the Iran nuclear deal, although several prominent Democratic lawmakers opposed it and Republican presidential candidates vowed to scrap it if they were to capture the White House. To win the vote on Capitol Hill, the Obama team set up a war room, only they called it the Antiwar Room.

*

Just three months after sealing the Iran deal, Obama finalized the Asian economic pact known as the Trans-Pacific Partnership, bringing together twelve nations, including Japan, Canada, Mexico, Malaysia and Australia, to create the largest free-trade zone in history. The agreement would phase out thousands of tariffs and other barriers to international trade, like Japanese regulations to keep out some American-made autos and trucks. It would establish uniform rules on corporations' intellectual property. And it would open the Internet even in communist Vietnam.

Rather than a revolt from Republicans, Obama this time faced one from his fellow Democrats, who argued that the deal would ship even more American jobs overseas and enrich companies at the expense of workers. Led by Senator Elizabeth Warren of Massachusetts, architect of the Consumer Financial Protection Bureau created by the Dodd-Frank law and a hero of the anti-corporate left, Democrats tried to strangle the agreement in the cradle by blocking legislation giving him authority to negotiate the deal on a fast-track basis in the first place. Obama had to beat that back by teaming up with John Boehner, Paul Ryan and other Republicans to get Congress to sign off on the negotiating authority he needed. Now he looked ahead to another fight in his final year in office to get the actual agreement approved by Congress. But once again, he argued, diplomacy had paid off.

Obama had little time to savor his victories. In November 2015, terrorists from the Islamic State fanned out across Paris and killed 130 people in a series of bombings and shootings that panicked the French capital and horrified the world. A little more than two weeks later, a husband and wife inspired by the Islamic State shot up a holiday party in San Bernardino, California, killing fourteen people. The carnage made clear that the Islamic State was no longer just a threat in the Middle East but in fact a fresh danger to America and Europe.

Obama had been waging war against the group for more than a year with mixed results at best. A military program he authorized to train Syrian rebels to fight the Islamic State collapsed after it yielded only four or five trained fighters on the battlefield. The situation then grew exponentially more complicated when

Russia suddenly intervened militarily to save Bashar al-Assad's faltering government, launching its own airstrikes, many of them targeting allies of the United States.

Obama did not help himself by telling George Stephanopoulos of ABC News just a week before that Paris attack that the United States had effectively halted the spread of the Islamic State. "We have contained them," he said. He meant that American military action had stanched the group's territorial gains in Iraq and Syria, but in light of the mayhem in France and California, the terrorists seemed anything but contained and the president seemed out of touch. His response after the attacks also tended toward the intellectual rather than channeling the visceral fear and outrage felt by many Americans; indeed, he saved his real passion for arguing with Republicans, who opposed admitting Syrian refugees to the United States for fear that some might be Islamic State operatives or sympathizers.

Obama was personally irritated by what he saw as the jingoistic response to the attacks, particularly by Republican candidates in the emerging campaign to succeed him, and he resolved not to be railroaded into taking unwise military action. While even Hillary Clinton and other Democrats were calling for a no-fly zone, Obama rejected what he called "half-baked ideas" that amounted to "a bunch of mumbo-jumbo." Asked if those ideas included Clinton's, he demurred, saying she was not half-baked but then essentially dismissed her statements as mere campaign rhetoric that should not be taken seriously. "There's a difference between running for president and being president," he said.

In a private, off-the-record meeting later with opinion writers and columnists, Obama acknowledged that he had been slow to respond to the understandable public anxiety and fear generated by the attacks. Perhaps one reason, he told the columnists, was that he did not watch much cable television – as much a jab at the media for sensationalizing terrorist attacks as an admission that he was not attuned to public sentiment. But he made clear he would not send large numbers of ground troops to the Middle East unless there was a terrorist attack that was so destructive that it disrupted the normal functioning of the United States.

The focus on the Islamic State detracted from one of Obama's most cherished policy goals even as it came to fruition. As he imposed regulations on power plants and tailpipe emissions at home, he was finally pulling together a global accord that would commit virtually all of the world's nations to take similar action to fight climate change, including China and India.

To build support for the agreement, Obama flew north to become the first sitting president to visit Arctic Alaska, where he highlighted the impact of changing climate patterns on glaciers and wildlife. He journeyed to what seemed like the ends of the earth as he traveled across gravel and dirt roads to a town of 900 where caribou and moose antlers adorned wooden houses on pilings, and pickup trucks and all-terrain vehicles were the transportation of choice. Obama joined Bear Grylls for an episode of his popular survivalist reality show, with the president helping make tea from catkins, eating a salmon pre-chewed by a bear and discussing why people would drink their own urine.

If that were not enough to set the stage for the global agreement, Obama waited until just before the final conference to announce that he was blocking construction of the Keystone pipeline that had become a cause célèbre for environmental activists.

John Kerry sealed the climate change deal after a last-minute scramble that nearly killed it – someone surreptitiously substituted the word "shall" for "should" in the text, which would have changed a moral obligation into a legal one had the Americans not objected and forced it back to the original language. Obama signed the pact in Paris just weeks after the Islamic State attacks rattled the French capital, neatly encapsulating the twin sides of his foreign policy.

On the one hand, he was putting together international agreements with lofty goals like curbing nuclear proliferation, spreading free trade and stemming climate change, agreements that, flaws and all, were designed to have lasting impact long after Obama left office.

But for all his success at the bargaining table, he found himself still fighting the same war on terror he inherited from his predecessor and still trying to figure out how to defeat the same forces of darkness that were consuming one region and threatening the rest of the world.

The Obama Doctrine was still a work in progress.

CHAPTER FOURTEEN

'A Personal Insult'

On a soggy winter afternoon in February 2016, Obama traveled up the highway from Washington to a mosque in Baltimore. While George W. Bush had made a point of visiting a mosque after the September 11 attacks to demonstrate that the newly declared war on terrorism was not a war on Muslims, Obama waited until his eighth and final year in office to finally cross the threshold of an Islamic center of religion in the United States.

The reasons for his reluctance were obvious. Even as his motorcade arrived at the Islamic Society of Baltimore, three out of ten Americans believed Obama himself was actually Muslim, even though he was not. Appearing in a mosque was not likely to correct those misperceptions. But Obama finally discarded any concerns because he was angry. The leading Republican running for president was none other than Donald Trump, the same man who had made such a spectacle of supposedly investigating whether Obama was actually born in the United States and hinting that the president was secretly Muslim. Now on the campaign stump, Trump was targeting Muslims as a group, vowing to temporarily ban them from entering the country ostensibly to prevent terrorism.

"We have to understand an attack on one faith is an attack on all our faiths," Obama told the audience that day, barely containing his indignation. "And when any religious group is targeted, we all have a responsibility to speak up. And we have to reject a politics that seeks to manipulate prejudice or bias and targets people because of religion." Trump's name never passed Obama's lips, but it did not have to. Everyone understood exactly whom he was talking about. And in case they did not, he threw in an extra jab. "Thomas Jefferson's opponents tried to stir things up by suggesting he was a Muslim – so I was not the first, " Obama said. "No, it's true. It's true. Look it up. I'm in good company."

Like others, Obama had not taken Trump seriously at first. Trump was a sideshow, a clown, an attention-addicted narcissist. His presidential campaign, Obama and his top advisers thought, was an exercise in vanity. It was not serious. "It's apparently open mike day in the Republican campaign for president," David Axelrod wrote mockingly on Twitter after Trump entered the race in the summer of 2015 with a politically divisive attack on Mexicans. David Plouffe scoffed at the notion that Trump might succeed. He predicted that there was a 100 percent chance Trump would lose a race for the presidency. In an interview before the Republican primaries, Obama called Trump "a great publicity-seeker," but brushed off his chances. "I don't think he'll end up being president of the United States," he said. Trump's loss to Senator Ted Cruz in the Iowa caucuses a few days before Obama's mosque visit seemed to validate the early dismissals.

But Obama found it hard to resist responding to some of Trump's more incendiary statements. During his visit to Africa shortly after Trump announced his candidacy, Obama denounced the candidate's blithe insult of Senator John McCain's record as a prisoner of war. ("I like people who weren't captured.") In a radio interview during his holiday in Hawaii, Obama accused Trump of exploiting the resentment of working-class men for his own political gain. In his final State of the Union address, he warned against trying "to scapegoat fellow citizens who don't look like us or pray like us or vote like we do."

Obama's voice usually dripped with disdain whenever he talked about Trump, leaving abundantly clear that he had no respect for the celebrity candidate. Obama may have disagreed with McCain and Mitt Romney during their contests, but they were both decent men, legitimate contenders and even plausible presidents. By contrast, Obama simply could not imagine a man whose most famous act was to flamboyantly fire contestants on a television show sitting behind the Resolute Desk in the Oval Office.

Trump, after all, was everything Obama was not. Bombastic and boastful, caustic, and crude, Trump reveled in ostentatious shows of wealth and playground style put-downs. A former co-owner of the Miss Universe Organization, he openly ogled beautiful women, denigrated those he did not consider attractive and discarded two wives who had been models before marrying a third, Melania Knauss, a model from Slovenia who once posed nude on Trump's plane for a *GQ* photo spread on sex at 30,000 feet.

But rather than disqualifying Trump, his very outrageousness seemed to be key to his appeal. When he slighted a former prisoner of war like McCain or mocked a reporter with disabilities or called on supporters to "knock the crap" out of protesters, Trump struck broad sections of the country as a straight talker who was willing to throw off the shackles of political correctness and take on the oh-so-smug elites of the ruling political-media class. If he could make a fortune for himself, maybe he could fix a country where so many felt left behind. Maybe he really could make America great again, as the slogan on his signature red baseball caps promised.

At the heart of Trump's campaign was a racial divide that had opened even wider during the tenure of the country's first African-American president. Trump drew support especially among white men without college educations, many of whom were struggling in an era of globalization and vanishing manufacturing jobs. While some were overtly racist and Trump did little to disavow the backing of white supremacist leaders, many voters attracted to him were simply feeling disenfranchised and lashing out at a system in which it seemed everyone else had special protections or attention. Real or not, it was a powerful perception.

Paradoxically perhaps, racial comity in the United States had deteriorated under a black president. While 66 percent of Americans surveyed by *The New York Times* and CBS News declared race relations in America to be good in April 2009, just three months after Obama took office, only 26 percent thought so in July 2016. Indeed, 59 percent of Americans that summer said race relations were getting worse.

Beyond race, the country was just in a foul mood. After years of stimulus and other policies, Obama's economy was finally growing and unemployment was dropping, but most Americans still told pollsters that the nation was on the wrong course. The wealthiest rocketed ahead after the Great Recession, but the rest of Americans barely kept even. And the atmosphere in Washington was as toxic as ever, if not more so. When it came to fixing America's politics, Obama acknowledged he had failed.

"Democracy breaks down when the average person feels their voice doesn't matter, that the system is rigged in favor of the rich or the powerful or some special interest," he said in his final State of the Union address in January 2016. "Too many Americans feel that way right now. It's one of the few regrets of my presidency – that the rancor and suspicion between the parties has gotten worse instead of better. I have no doubt a president with the gifts of Lincoln or Roosevelt might have better bridged the divide." But Obama was neither Lincoln nor Roosevelt.

*

If Obama needed further proof of the breakdown between the parties, it came just weeks later when Justice Antonin Scalia died unexpectedly at age seventy-nine during a hunting trip to Texas. Scalia, the conservative intellectual powerhouse of the Supreme Court, had been a larger-than-life presence on the bench and its longest serving current member. Acerbic, funny and brilliant, he was a hero to the right, the scourge of the left and the primary champion of the school of thought known as "originalism" that held that the text of the Constitution should be evaluated as it was understood at the time of its drafting. His sudden departure meant Obama now had a chance to shift the ideological balance for years to come.

Over the course of his presidency, the court had given Obama fits and given him reprieves. Although Chief Justice John Roberts had saved the Affordable Care Act, the president's signature domestic achievement, the conservative majority had slapped down what they characterized as Obama's executive overreach on several occasions. The court ruled that he had exceeded his power to make recess appointments and overstepped his authority by trying to force family businesses to pay for insurance coverage of contraceptives despite their religious beliefs. The court also overturned part of the Voting Rights Act over Obama's objections. Over all, Obama enjoyed less success before the court than any president in more than a century and possibly since Zachary Taylor in the mid-1800s; his administration won just 50.5 percent of the cases it was a party to, compared with 63 percent under Bill Clinton, 60 percent under George W. Bush and 75 percent under Ronald Reagan.

Obama would attribute that to a partisan court. His critics would attribute that to Obama's abuse of power. Either way, it made for an antagonistic eight years. "It's fair to say he's had a more contentious relationship with the court than any president I can remember, at least since Nixon," said Curt Levey, executive director of the FreedomWorks Foundation, a conservative advocacy group. Which was why Scalia's death was so important to Obama. While he had already installed two liberals on the court in Sonia Sotomayor and Elena Kagan, they had each replaced like-minded justices, leaving the philosophical division roughly the same. Replacing Scalia with a left-leaning justice would be a seismic shift in the closely divided judicial chambers.

Except that Senate Republicans were determined not to let him. They understood that confirming an Obama appointee to fill the seat would be a disaster for conservative jurisprudence on a host of issues like abortion, gay rights, gun rights, religious freedom and government regulation. They were already disappointed that Roberts had upheld Obama's health care program. So they looked at the calendar and gambled that they could hold out for a year. Within hours of Scalia's death, Mitch McConnell announced that the Senate would not consider *any* Obama nominee, no matter whom he named, and would wait for the next president instead.

Obama was flabbergasted. While there were long vacancies during confirmation battles in the nineteenth century, only once in the past 150 years had a seat on the Supreme Court been kept open for a full year and never had the Senate flatly refused to consider any nominee from a president. Obama went ahead and nominated Merrick Garland, the mild-mannered, well-liked and deeply respected chief judge of the United States Court of Appeals for the District of Columbia Circuit, widely considered the second most important bench in America after the Supreme Court.

Considered a relatively moderate liberal with many friends among Republicans and conservative judges, Garland was, in effect, Obama's break-glass-in-case-of-emergency choice, a nominee Republicans would normally embrace as the best they could get from a Democratic president. But with several members of McConnell's caucus running for president and competing to show how tough they could be standing up to Obama, the Republican leader opted to shut down the process altogether.

The impasse would have lasting impact. In June, the understaffed Supreme Court deadlocked, four to four, in a case challenging Obama's executive action allowing up to 5 million immigrants to remain even though they were in the country illegally. Because a lower court had rejected Obama's action, the tie vote by the justices left that ruling in place, meaning that the program had to be canceled. The high court offered no explanation but rendered its verdict in just nine words: "The judgment is affirmed by an equally divided court." Rarely have nine words affected so many lives. Obama's efforts to revamp the immigration system were now over and millions of immigrants would have to await the result of the election to determine their future.

Had Garland filled the empty seat, he likely would have provided the fifth vote to overturn the decision and uphold Obama's action shielding the immigrants. McConnell's gambit had worked.

*

Frustrated on the home front, Obama boarded Air Force One and had the pilots head south to make history overseas. In March, he became the first American president to visit Cuba since Calvin Coolidge some eighty-eight years earlier, a landmark trip meant to cement the diplomatic opening he had negotiated. Accompanied by Michelle and their two daughters, he strolled the streets of Old Havana, albeit drenched by a sudden rain, as Cubans called out, "Obama!"

Under sunnier skies, he attended a baseball game and joined the crowd in doing the wave, even as a clearly embarrassed Sasha stayed seated with her arm over her face. He held a formal meeting with Raúl Castro, the first between leaders of the two countries in half a century, although Obama had the presence of mind to let his arm go limp when the Cuban leader tried to raise their hands together in a gesture of triumph, an image that would have provoked a storm of criticism back in the United States. "It seemed an apt metaphor for our approach – engaging without embracing," Ben Rhodes wrote later.

Heady as it was, Obama's visit did not mean Cuba had changed. Before the president arrived, the Havana authorities cracked down on dissidents to prevent them from drawing attention to the continuing repression of the state. During a joint news conference by the two presidents, Castro brusquely dismissed questions about the lack of freedom in his country.

"What political prisoners?" he snapped at a reporter, demanding a list. He went on to argue that the United States should not lecture Cuba since it had its own human rights problems, including the prison it maintained at Guantánamo Bay. "It's not correct to ask me about political prisoners."

Obama would meet with Cuban dissidents during the trip, but he nonetheless replied with a deference that only confirmed to critics at home that he was going soft on Havana in the interest of pursuing a chimera of new relations. "Cuba's destiny will not be decided by the United States or any other nation," he said mildly.

Nor did Obama even object to Castro's criticisms of American policy. "I actually welcome President Castro commenting on some of the areas where he feels that we're falling short," Obama said, "because I think we should not be immune or afraid of criticism or discussion as well." While an attempt to show that democratic leaders should be open to contrary views, Obama's comment fueled the conservative case that he often seemed intent on apologizing for America rather than appreciating its exceptionalism.

He encountered the same issue two months later when he became the first American president to visit Hiroshima, where in August 1945 the United States dropped the first nuclear bomb ever used in war. "Seventy-one year ago, on a bright cloudless morning, death fell from the sky and the world was changed," Obama told a crowd of Japanese at Hiroshima Peace Memorial Park and many more watching on national television. He did not apologize for Harry Truman's orders to drop the bombs that killed 200,000 at Hiroshima and Nagasaki, a morally fraught decision credited with helping to bring World War II to a swifter end. He did, however, meet with a few of the survivors. One ninety-one-year-old man gripped Obama's hand and would not let go for a long time until he had said what he wanted to tell the American president out of earshot of witnesses. A seventy-nine-year-old who spent years researching aspects of the bombing shared an embrace with the president.

The violence of the past was one thing. The violence of the present was another. As much as Obama could confront painful episodes in history with eloquence, he struggled to grapple with the bloodshed of his own time. Throughout that last year in office, outbreaks of wanton killings plagued the country and its president. In June, Omar Mateen, an American-born son of Afghan immigrants, opened fire in the middle of a gay nightclub in Orlando, Florida, after pledging fealty to the Islamic State, killing nearly fifty people and injuring dozens more in the deadliest terrorist attack in the United States since the World Trade Center and Pentagon were hit. Mateen had crossed the radar screen of the FBI before without triggering alarm. He was investigated in 2013 after telling work colleagues that he had family ties to Al Qaeda and wanted to die a martyr. But the FBI ultimately closed the case.

A few weeks after his attack, a spate of shootings reopened the country's fresh racial wounds. In separate incidents in July, police officers shot and killed black men in Baton Rouge, Louisiana, and Falcon Heights, Minnesota. The shooting of Philando Castile during a traffic stop in Minnesota was streamed live on Facebook by his girlfriend, who along with her young daughter was in the car at the time. Obama learned of the incidents while heading to Warsaw for a NATO summit. He holed up in his cabin on Air Force One composing a Facebook post expressing distress at the tragic events, but he told aides it was not enough. So when the plane landed, Obama went before cameras to personally issue a statement, immediately linking the shootings to race. "When incidents like this occur," he said, "there's a big chunk of our citizenry that feels as if, because of the color of their skin, they are not being treated the same and that hurts and that should trouble all of us."

Obama then headed to bed for a few hours before his diplomatic meetings. But as he slept, his country back home took an even darker turn. At a demonstration in Dallas protesting police shootings elsewhere – a protest guarded by the city's own officers – a heavily armed African-American military veteran opened fire at white men in uniform. The sniper killed five police officers, further convulsing a nation already torn between black and blue. Obama, who just hours earlier had lamented police mistreatment of African-Americans, now made a new statement denouncing the killing of the officers. "Let me be clear," he said. "There is no possible justification for these kinds of attacks or any violence against law enforcement."

Some in the law enforcement community thought it was too little too late, laying blame for the incident at the president's feet. William Johnson, the executive director of the National Association of Police Organizations, said that the Obama administration had appeased violent criminals in ways that "led directly to the climate that has made Dallas possible." It was a provocative accusation, one that the White House rejected. But Obama could hardly help wondering how the country had traveled from the highs of Chicago's Grant Park, where he proclaimed victory in the 2008 presidential election, to the lows of Baton Rouge, Falcon Heights and Dallas not even eight years later.

*

As the campaign to succeed him accelerated, Obama staked his legacy on electing the very person he had worked so hard to keep out of the White House. While once he portrayed Hillary Clinton as the embodiment of everything that was wrong with Washington, he now saw her as the only real chance of preserving the accomplishments of his administration. Politics, of course, is the province of strange bedfellows and Obama was hardly the first president to end up embracing a rival – Ronald Reagan campaigned to elect his 1980 rival, George H.W. Bush, to succeed him in 1988, just as George W. Bush backed John McCain, his vanquished 2000 primary opponent, eight years later. But the evolution of the relationship between Obama and Clinton went beyond mere political expediency. Somehow, Obama and Clinton had actually forged a friendship.

Somehow they got past that discomfort and forgot all those attack ads and campaign quotes, or at least forgave them. For the first term of Obama's presidency, they teamed up in the White House Situation Room to guide the nation through one international crisis after another. She was the hawk on many of the big issues. She advocated a robust troop surge in Afghanistan, lobbied for intervention in Libya, supported the commando raid that killed Osama bin Laden and pressed for arming and training rebels fighting the Syrian government. She was the point person for the ill-fated reset with Russia and the more fitful pivot to Asia. Obama took her advice much of the time but the end results were mixed at best. The war in Libya, her most prominent initiative, saved thousands of civilians and toppled Muammar el-Qaddafi, but left the country in chaos.

Yet when she left office in early 2013, the two were surprised at how well they had gotten along. In a rare joint appearance on *60 Minutes* on CBS, they traded laughs and finished each other's thoughts, agreeing that five years earlier their collaboration would have seemed "improbable," as Clinton put it.

"I consider Hillary a strong friend," Obama offered.

"Very warm, close," Clinton responded.

About a month after she left the administration, the president and Michelle invited Hillary and Bill Clinton for a private dinner and the two couples talked late into the night. Obama ruminated about moving to New York after leaving office, as the Clintons had. That summer, Obama invited Hillary Clinton back for a jambalaya lunch on the terrace outside the Oval Office. "I think he was just a tiny bit jealous of my new-found freedom," Clinton recalled later, "which was a good reminder of how all-consuming the job is."

Obama's public embrace of Clinton was seen as a quasi-official blessing for her anticipated campaign to win the White House. When Joe Biden began contemplating a late entry into the race in 2015, Obama gently helped steer him out of it, urging his vice president to see his pollster in an evident effort to convince him that the race was not winnable. While Obama did not directly tell him not to run, Biden got the message. "The president was not encouraging," he later wrote in a memoir

Clinton started the campaign eager to distance herself from Obama, who at the time was sagging in the polls. She chided the president for his minimalist foreign policy doctrine. "Great nations need organizing principles," she said. "'Don't do stupid stuff' is not an organizing principle." She disavowed the Trans-Pacific Partnership trade deal he negotiated, even though she was the one who got it started while she was in office. She publicly split with his policy of restraint in Syria and Ukraine. Officially, of course, they both denied any rift. A few days after she said that Obama's refusal to arm the Syrian rebels had left a void for the Islamic State to fill, the two encountered each other at a birth-day party in Martha's Vineyard for a mutual friend, Ann Jordan, Vernon Jordan's wife. They hugged and pretended all was well. But they then headed to different parts of the room and were not spotted interacting again for the rest of the evening.

This was a traditional tack-to-the-center general election strategy of a candidate who presumed that the nomination was hers for the asking. To her surprise, the party's affirmation would not be so easily secured. Clinton confronted an astonishingly vigorous challenge on the left from Senator Bernie Sanders, a septuagenarian socialist from Vermont with wild gray hair and a deep Brooklyn accent who had somehow become the champion of the activist younger generation. Trying to fend him off, Clinton reversed course and wrapped herself around the president, portraying herself as the inheritor of Obama's legacy to reassure liberals who were turned off by her interventionist foreign policy, close ties to Wall Street and been-around-forever staleness.

Clinton also faced another hurdle, one of her own making. Her decision as secretary of state to set up a personal email server in her New York home and other servers rather than use the State Department's secure system to send messages had exposed her to questions about her judgment and a months-long FBI investigation that shadowed her campaign. Clinton said she used the private service out of convenience so she would only need to carry one phone rather than separate ones for work and private email. After the State Department requested them, she turned over 30,000 messages for preservation under government rules. But she deleted another 30,000 that she deemed personal, a decision that would raise further questions about whether she was trying to hide anything. Obama did not help by weighing in on the matter publicly, telling interviewers that while Clinton "made a mistake," it had not harmed national security. Such public intervention by a president in a law enforcement matter was considered inappropriate. James Comey, the FBI director, worried that Obama "had jeopardized" the credibility of the Justice Department that reported to the president by seeming to put his finger on the scale.

After months of investigation, the FBI determined that 110 of the 30,000 that Clinton turned over contained classified information, including "a very small number" that bore markings indicating they were secret, despite her claims that none of the emails were classified at the time she sent or received them. But on July 5, just weeks before the Democratic National Convention that would confirm her as the first woman nominated for president by a major political party, Comey announced that he found no cause to file criminal charges even as he sharply criticized her behavior as "extremely careless."

Comey's public statement was extraordinary in several regards. For one, the FBI typically turns over its findings to the Justice Department, which decides whether to prosecute. But here Comey took it upon himself to make the determination rather than leaving it to Attorney General Loretta Lynch, convinced that any decision she would make would be seen as compromised because she was appointed by Obama and had met with Bill Clinton when their planes happened to be parked on the same tarmac in Phoenix. For another, as a general matter, the FBI did not publicly disclose decisions not to prosecute. And lastly, law enforcement agents were not supposed to publicly criticize subjects of investigation who were not charged.

The FBI director's action shook up the presidential race, both relieving Clinton's team and outraging it at the same time. But at least it would put the matter behind her. Or so she thought.

*

While remaining publicly neutral, Obama called Clinton from time to time to offer advice or encouragement. "Don't try to be hip; you're a grandma," he told her teasingly during one call. "Just be yourself and keep doing what you're doing."

By the time she finally dispatched the stubbornly strong Bernie Sanders and Obama arrived on stage at the Democratic National Convention in Philadelphia in late July to promote her candidacy, the evolution was complete and she had effectively become the candidate for Obama's third term. He hugged her with genuine affection and gave a full-throated endorsement. "No matter how daunting the odds, no matter how much people try to knock her down, she never, ever quits," Obama said of his rival-turned-partner in his last convention speech as president. "That is the Hillary I know. That's the Hillary I've come to admire. And that's why I can say with confidence, there has never been a man or a woman – not me, not Bill, nobody – more qualified than Hillary Clinton to serve as president of the United States of America."

As a matter of politics, there was little wonder why Clinton would embrace Obama, literally as well as figuratively. While not sky high, his poll numbers were healthier than they had been in a while. On the day before his convention speech, Gallup put his approval rating at 51 percent and his disapproval rating at 45 percent. More importantly for Clinton, liberals who were disappointed with Obama at times during his presidency had come home to him when it mattered, and she needed to maximize turnout among his voters to win. Especially crucial were African-Americans, the stalwart base of the Democratic Party, who came out in overwhelming numbers in 2008 and 2012 but might not have as much motivation in 2016 without Obama on the ballot.

Obama was enjoying a resurgence of sorts in those days, in part because of the contrast with the two candidates seeking to succeed him. Donald Trump had rebounded from his Iowa defeat and outpaced sixteen other Republican contenders to capture the GOP nomination for president, but much of the country was appalled by his insult-filled, racially charged primary campaign. Many others were disenchanted with Clinton, who failed to excite Democrats and alienated at least some independents she needed.

David Brooks, the center-right columnist for *The New York Times*, captured this sentiment early in 2016 with a column entitled, "I Miss Barack Obama." He wrote: "No, Obama has not been temperamentally perfect. Too often he's been disdainful, aloof, resentful and insular. But there is a tone of ugliness creeping across the world, as democracies retreat, as tribalism mounts, as suspiciousness and authoritarianism take center stage. Obama radiates an ethos of integrity, humanity, good manners and elegance that I'm beginning to miss, and that I suspect we will all miss a bit regardless of who replaces him."

Obama started the fall campaign confident that Clinton would beat Trump. She led in the polls, she led in fund-raising, she led in experience. Despite her battle with Bernie Sanders, she seemed to have united the party leadership behind her while Trump was busy battling with Republicans like House Speaker Paul Ryan and Governor John Kasich of Ohio as they renounced some of his more controversial statements or even announced they could not support him. By one count, Clinton received the endorsement of 240 newspapers, while Trump was supported by just 19. Even staunchly conservative newspapers like *The Arizona Republic*, *Dallas Morning News*, *San Diego Union-Tribune* and *Cincinnati Enquirer*, some of which had not backed a Democrat for president in more than a century, urged their readers to reject Trump and elect Clinton. So did magazines like *Foreign Policy* and *The Atlantic*, which rarely, if ever, endorsed candidates.

For Obama, it was hard to picture a President Trump. How could the country elect a man who insulted Mexicans, Muslims, women, people with disabilities and veterans, who refused to release his tax forms, who was being sued for fraud over a school he called Trump University, who got into a running feud with the Muslim father of a American soldier slain in Iraq and who handed down policy pronouncements in acerbic 140-character Twitter messages?

Obama took it personally. "This is not me going through the motions here," he said at a campaign rally in Philadelphia in September. "I really, really, really want to elect Hillary Clinton." A few days later, speaking at a dinner of the Congressional Black Caucus Foundation, he elaborated. "My name may not be on the ballot, but our progress is on the ballot," he said. "Tolerance is on the ballot. Democracy is on the ballot. Justice is on the ballot." Obama told the crowd that black voters owed it to him to cast ballots for Clinton. "After we have achieved historic turnout in 2008 and 2012, especially in the African-American community, I will consider it a personal insult, an insult to my legacy, if this community lets down its guard and fails to activate itself in this election," he said. "You want to give me a good sendoff? Go vote."

Just how personal it was for Obama became clear that same week, when Trump finally reversed himself after years of promoting the false conspiracy theory that the president was not a natural-born American. "President Barack Obama was born in the United States – period," Trump said in terse remarks at the end of an unrelated campaign stop in Washington. "Now we all want to get back to making America strong and great again." Yet even as he retreated from the longstanding effort to question Obama's citizenship, Trump propagated another falsehood, claiming that it was Clinton's campaign that first stirred the so-called birther movement during the 2008 primaries.

At the black caucus dinner the following night, Obama joked that he had "an extra spring in my step" now that the mystery of his birthplace had been solved. "I mean, ISIL, North Korea, poverty, climate change – none of those things weighed on my mind like the validity of my birth certificate," he said, tongue planted firmly in cheek. "And to think, that with just 124 days to go, under the wire, we got that resolved."

With each passing day, the president grew less inhibited. When Trump taunted him with a tweet, he took the bait. "President

Obama will go down as perhaps the worst president in the history of the United States!" Trump wrote.

Appearing on *Jimmy Kimmel Live!* Obama read the tweet aloud and then responded by mocking Trump as a certain loser. "At least I'll go down as a president," he said, dropping his smart phone as a take-that punctuation.

He hoped he was right. The stakes for Obama could hardly be higher and at some points during the campaign he envisioned a bleak future for his legacy should Trump prevail. "All the progress we've made over these last eight years goes out the window if we don't win this election," he told one crowd.

His contempt for Trump deepened in the final days of the campaign. In Florida, he said Trump only met working people when they were "cleaning his room." In North Carolina, he called Trump a "con artist and a know-nothing" who was "temperamentally unfit to be commander in chief." In Ohio, he mocked the idea that America could pick Trump. "Come on," he said. "This guy?" With just hours to go before Election Day, Obama pointed out that Trump's staff had, briefly, wrested away control of his Twitter account to keep him from sending out impolitic messages. "If your closest advisers don't trust you to tweet," Obama said, "how can you trust him with the nuclear codes?"

It would be a question answered soon enough.

CHAPTER FIFTEEN
'Backed the Wrong Horse'

In the final weeks of the campaign, Obama traveled to Hangzhou, China, for a summit meeting of the G-20 nations. During a break in the proceedings, he pulled aside Vladimir Putin.

We know what you're up to, he told him. *Cut it out or there will be serious consequences.*

Out of earshot of everyone except their translators, Obama told the Kremlin master that American intelligence agencies had determined that Russia was trying to manipulate the upcoming elections in the United States. Moscow was behind the hacking of Democratic email accounts and was probing for weaknesses in the voting systems in dozens of states.

Putin, not surprisingly, admitted nothing and challenged Obama to prove it. Obama left it at that. He had all the proof he needed and he had delivered the message he wanted to deliver. In case Putin missed it, Obama alluded to it in his subsequent news conference when he told reporters that "we've had problems with cyber intrusions from Russia in the past." In a barely veiled threat, he added, "Frankly, we've got more capacity than anybody, both offensively and defensively."

Even as Donald Trump and Hillary Clinton waged their increasingly combative campaign in public, a separate campaign was being waged behind the scenes, one playing out between old Cold War rivals on a different kind of battlefield. Since at least the summer of 2015, Russian hackers had been rummaging around Democratic computers and stealing large volumes of data as part of what American intelligence agencies later determined was a systemic operation to disrupt the coming elections in the United

States. At first, the Russians simply used the stolen information to feed secrets to their propaganda outlets, RT and Sputnik, and to their online trolls. Russian agents were working literally around the clock in shifts posting and manipulating stories online aimed at damaging the United States government in general and Hillary Clinton in particular, promoting conspiracy theories regarding her health or the Benghazi attack.

By the end of 2015, as Trump was emerging as the front-runner in the Republican nomination fight, the goal seemed to shift from general attacks on Clinton to promoting the real estate tycoon. According to American intelligence agencies, Putin and the Russian leadership decided in the spring of 2016 to escalate their cyberattack even at the risk of being caught. On February 6, a memo to the Russian hackers declared that their new target was the American elections and instructed them to "use any opportunity to criticize Hillary and the rest (except Sanders and Trump – we support them)." On March 15, the same day Trump won five primaries on his path to the Republican nomination, a Russian military officer working for a secret outfit called Unit 26165 began probing Democratic National Committee computers. Around the same time, the unit sent a spearphishing email to John Podesta, the former Obama adviser who had become Clinton's campaign chairman. After having an aide check first with a computer technician who said it looked like a legitimate message, Podesta clicked on a link, entered his log-in information and inadvertently gave the Russians access to some 50,000 emails.

In June, Donald Trump Jr., Jared Kushner, the president's son-in-law, and Paul Manafort, his campaign chairman, met with visiting Russians after being promised "information that would incriminate Hillary" as "part of Russia and its government's support for Mr. Trump." The Russians used the meeting to lobby for the removal of sanctions that Obama had imposed on Moscow, and the Trump team insisted they got nothing out of it. But within days, a hacker calling himself Guccifer 2.0 posted a few of the stolen DNC emails online and warned that he had many more. Guccifer was the creation of Russia's Main Intelligence Directorate of the General Staff, the military intelligence agency more commonly known by its old initials GRU, and it passed its entire archive of DNC emails to Wikileaks, the anti-secrecy group that made a mission of unearthing American government documents.

On July 22, the day after Trump accepted the Republican nomination and just days before the Democratic convention, WikiLeaks posted online 19,252 stolen DNC emails in what American officials saw as a major escalation by Moscow and a brazen effort to intervene in the election. While Russian agencies were known to spy on political, governmental and business institutions in the United States, they did not typically release the material they stole. Now it seemed that they were willing, perhaps even eager, to be known in order to play a direct role in American democracy. "That's when the hairs really went up on the back of our necks," said Victoria Nuland, the assistant secretary of state who oversaw relations with Russia.

Both Russia and America had sought to influence elections overseas before, of course. The Soviet Union in 1960 offered help to two Democratic presidential aspirants, Adlai Stevenson and Hubert Humphrey, both of whom turned down any assistance. Leonid Brezhnev personally told Gerald Ford that "we for our part will do everything we can" to help him win the 1976 election, an overture that the American president simply laughed off. The Kremlin dug up dirt on Ronald Reagan in hopes of undercutting his bid for re-election in 1984. For its part, the United States had quietly intervened in elections throughout the world to push for pro-American governments. A study by Dov Levin, a researcher at Carnegie Mellon University, found that the United

States meddled in eighty-one elections overseas from 1946 to 2000, while Russia intruded on at least thirty-six during that time period and probably more. But never before had Moscow constructed such an elaborate and well-orchestrated campaign of electoral sabotage within the United States on behalf of a candidate who seemed so eager to make friends with Russia.

The stolen Democratic emails and documents that were posted online amounted to a trove of internal communications suggesting that the party leadership was effectively backing Clinton in her nomination fight with Bernie Sanders rather than playing the neutral broker it was obligated to be. Julian Assange, the founder of WikiLeaks who once hosted a show on Russia's RT propaganda channel, denied that the emails had been provided by the Russians, but American intelligence agencies were certain that they were. Liberal Democrats were incensed by the perceived manipulation of the nomination contest revealed by the emails, and the resulting controversy forced Representative Debbie Wasserman Schultz of Florida, the Democratic National Committee chairwoman, to resign just as delegates were gathering in Philadelphia for the convention that was to formalize Clinton's nomination, widening the rift within the party at the very moment it was trying to pull itself together for the fall campaign.

Less visible but perhaps even more insidious was a concerted social media campaign by the Russians to inflame America's already existing political divisions. Fraudulent Facebook, Twitter and Instagram accounts, disguised as American-generated, promoted conspiracy theories, vilified immigrants and Muslims and sought to depress minority turnout by promoting allegations that Democrats engaged in voter fraud. A fake Russian-created group dubbed Heart of Texas used Facebook to call on people to show up at a protest outside an Islamic center in Houston, then another called United Muslims of America asked people to show up at the same time and place to "Save Islamic Knowledge." On the designated day, a handful of white supremacists, some armed with guns, confronted a larger group of counter-protesters, separated only by Houston police.

The social media campaign was also designed to generate anger at Clinton and the Democrats while rallying support for Trump. It was not terribly subtle. "Hillary is a Satan, and her crimes and lies have proved just how evil she is," read one posting by a group called Army of Jesus that was in fact a Russian cut-out. "I created all these pictures and posts and the Americans believed that it was created by their people," one of the Russians involved in the operation wrote in an email to her family that was intercepted by the American government. Altogether, a Russian troll factory located in a leased four-story building at 55 Savushkina Street in St. Petersburg and operating under the banal name of the Internet Research Agency created 2,700 fake Facebook accounts with 80,000 posts reaching an audience of 126 million Americans, nearly as many as the 139 million Americans who would vote in the fall election. They posted thousands of tweets a day, as many as 18,634 in a single twenty-four hour period in October. They knew "exactly what buttons to press," said Darren Linvill, a professor at Clemson University who studied 3 million Internet Research Agency tweets.

By this point, the FBI had already quietly opened an investigation called Crossfire Hurricane looking into whether anyone from Trump's campaign was working in tandem with the Russians to influence the election. Trump had been remarkably complimentary about Putin over the years, praising him for "doing a great job in rebuilding the image of Russia and also rebuilding Russia period," calling him stronger than Obama and even saying that he hoped that the strongman of the Kremlin would become his "new best friend." Trump told an interviewer that he could accept Russia's annexation of Crimea and he expressed no criticism of Putin's interventions in Ukraine, Syria or elsewhere. To take over his campaign, he tapped Manafort, a longtime Republican operative widely known his work for a Russian oligarch close to Putin and for the pro-Russian leadership in Ukraine that was toppled in 2014. At the Trump campaign's insistence, the party platform at the Republican convention was rewritten to take out support for providing arms to Ukraine to fight pro-Russian separatist forces.

The coziness with Putin's Russia would have been odd for any American politician but especially for a Republican, fueling suspicions that there must be something behind it. Trump, who had long sought to do business in Russia during his real estate days, did nothing to quell those doubts when he publicly appealed to Moscow to hack into Clinton's emails. "Russia, if you're listening, I hope you're able to find the 30,000 emails that are missing," he said at a news conference in July, a comment he later explained away as a sarcastic aside. Only much later was it discovered that Russian hackers, perhaps taking it more seriously, attempted to penetrate Clinton's personal office computer servers for the first time that very same night. James Clapper, the director of national intelligence, said later that at the time he knew of no "hard evidence" of collusion between Trump's campaign and the Russian government but "my dashboard warning lights were all lit."

*

In early August, John Brennan called Denis McDonough to say he needed to see the president urgently. Brennan, who had taken over as CIA director, sent over a sealed package of classified documents later that afternoon and then arrived in the Oval Office the next day to personally deliver some alarming news. The agency had two sources informing it that Vladimir Putin had personally authorized the operation to intervene in the campaign with the explicit goal of hurting Hillary Clinton, he told the president. Putin, in effect, had mounted one of the most aggressive clandestine efforts of the post-Cold War era aimed at sabotaging American democracy and, worse, possibly shifting the outcome of an election.

The information was so sensitive that only McDonough, Susan Rice and her deputy, Avril Haines, were included in the briefing and nothing was mentioned in the tightly controlled President's Daily Brief, the intelligence report he received every morning on his secure iPad. Even Joe Biden was not told until later. Obama authorized a small task force to figure out what to do, led by Lisa Monaco, who had taken over Brennan's old job of homeland security adviser. She convened secret meetings in the Situation Room to review the evidence and develop options, inviting just four other officials: Brennan; Clapper; Loretta Lynch, the attorney general; and James Comey, the FBI director. Eventually, Biden and a few others were brought in too. The meetings were kept hidden from virtually all others by turning off the cameras in the Situation Room and using the same clandestine protocols employed during the run-up to the raid in Pakistan that killed Osama bin Laden.

As Obama and his advisers huddled over the matter, they were concerned mostly about the possibility that Russia would attempt to attack voting systems on Election Day. Balloting in America is handled in patchwork fashion, each county and state managing its own voting with often varied technological systems. Officials in Washington doubted that Russia could systematically intrude on all of them, but they could do enough damage to seriously disrupt the election. "Our first goal was to make sure that the integrity of the election was not undermined," said Monaco. Jeh Johnson, the secretary of homeland security, convened a conference call with state officials in mid-August, only to run into a wall of resistance, especially from Republicans who were dubious about the evidence and the Obama team's motives.

Within the administration, officials debated whether to retaliate against Russia, either by imposing sanctions or perhaps even by launching a cyber counterattack of their own that would make clear how much damage America could do if Moscow did not call off its interference. "There were a number of us inside arguing that we should make it cost for them," said Victoria Nuland. But Obama, following his cautious don't-do-stupid-shit instincts, rejected any forceful response for fear that it would only prompt Russia to escalate by making a concerted effort to disrupt state voting machines on Election Day. As he did in other circumstances, Obama concluded that the instinct for action would make the situation worse, not better.

If he would not act, some advisers urged him to at least issue a public warning letting the American people know what Russia was up to in hopes of negating the operation's impact. But Trump had already been publicly complaining that the election would be "rigged" by Democrats, so Obama was wary of doing anything to provide him ammunition – especially if Clinton seemed likely to win anyway. "He didn't want to be seen as using the Office of the President to influence the outcome," Clapper said.

So the president had advisers reach out to Republican leaders in Congress to see if they would join him in a statement warning against Russian interference, a joint message that would transcend partisanship. Mitch McConnell was dubious, suspecting the whole thing was just an attempt by Obama to help Clinton. He refused to go along, leading to a shouting match with Brennan, who could not believe the Senate majority leader would, in his view, choose party over the national interest. Obama then invited Congressional leaders to the White House on the pretext of talking about the budget and his trip to Asia but in reality to appeal to them to make a bipartisan warning on Russia. Paul Ryan seemed open but again McConnell refused, coming across as "dismissive, disparaging, disinterested," in the words of one participant. Only much later did the Republicans agree even to sign a relatively generic letter to the president of the National Association of State Election Directors urging them to watch out for cyber-intrusions – without mentioning anything about Russia specifically, much less warning that Vladimir Putin was out to get Clinton.

Without Republicans agreeing to join, Obama abandoned the idea of a public statement for fear of Trump's reaction. "If I speak out more, he'll just say it's rigged," Obama told aides. Comey thought a statement should be issued anyway and volunteered in September to issue one himself in what he called a "voice of inoculation" message meant to immunize the public against the meddling. Obama worried that doing so would actually accomplish what the Russians were trying to do by sowing uncertainty and confusion in the American system. "We were very conscious that we not do their work for them by creating a partisan discussion about this," said Monaco. Comey drafted a possible newspaper column under his name making such a warning to show the president and his national security team what it might look like, but deliberations dragged on without a decision for weeks. Comey suspected that the Obama team assumed that Clinton was all but certain to win and therefore was reluctant to do anything that might jeopardize that. In one meeting attended by Comey, Obama all but predicted a Clinton victory that would upend Putin's malign design. "He backed the wrong horse," Obama said.

Democratic leaders in Congress also pressed Obama to speak out, only to be frustrated by his resistance. "There was a real reticence in the administration to talk about this publicly," said Representative Adam Schiff of California, the top Democrat on the House Intelligence Committee. So he and Senator Dianne Feinstein, another California Democrat and vice chair of the Senate Intelligence Committee, decided to put out a statement of their own. "I thought that the danger of escalation was frankly greater if we did nothing, said nothing, than if we called out Russia on what it was doing," Schiff said. In the statement, released on September 22, they said that "we have concluded that the Russian intelligence agencies are making a serious and concerted effort to influence the U.S. election." The goal, they added, was "to sow doubt about the security of our election" and possibly even to "influence the outcomes." With no Republicans signing on, however, the statement was seen in partisan terms and passed with little notice.

Inside the administration, Jeh Johnson and James Clapper kept pressing for a statement of their own. Obama finally relented, but even then he decided not to put his own name on it, lest it seem like an effort to help Clinton. Instead, he left it to be signed by Johnson and Clapper. Oddly, Comey by this point had changed his mind, deciding not to add his own name because there had now been enough media coverage of the Russian involvement and it was too close to the election for the FBI to weigh in – a rationale that would seem even more curious given later events. In any case, the 386-word statement put out by Johnson and Clapper was carefully drafted to make it seem as neutral yet stark as possible:

> The U.S. Intelligence Community (USIC) is confident that the Russian Government directed the recent compromises of emails from US persons and institutions, including from US political organizations. The recent disclosures of alleged hacked emails on sites like DCLeaks.com and WikiLeaks and by the Guccifer 2.0 online persona are consistent with the methods and motivations of Russian-directed efforts. These thefts and disclosures are intended to interfere with the US election process.

What the statement did not say was that the intelligence agencies had come to the conclusion that the Russian operation was directed specifically to damage Clinton and to help Trump. Early drafts of the statement also named Vladimir Putin as the mastermind behind the operation, *The Washington Post* later reported, but that was taken out too out for fear that it might give away the intelligence methods. Instead, it simply said more blandly, "We believe, based on the scope and sensitivity of these efforts, that only Russia's senior-most officials could have authorized these activities." Voters would have to read between the lines.

Still, even sanitized, it was a fairly striking statement by the American government, accusing Moscow of directly orchestrating the intrusion into Democratic computers and trying to penetrate state election systems. Johnson and Clapper released the statement at 3:30 p.m. on Friday, October 7, a time of day that seemed likely to maximize attention by coming out shortly before the evening news and the daily deadlines of the major newspapers. Johnson and Clapper sat back and waited for the reaction.

But just a half-hour later, at 4:05 p.m., another story surfaced that would dwarf their accusation against the Kremlin. *The Washington Post* posted online a video of Trump talking with Billy Bush of *Access Hollywood* in 2005 and making crude remarks about women. On the tape, Trump described hitting on a married woman. "I did try and fuck her," he said. "I moved on her like a bitch. But I couldn't get there." Because he was a celebrity, he said, he could get away with groping women. "When you're a star, they let you do it. You can do anything. Grab 'em by the pussy. You can do anything."

The tape electrified the campaign and media worlds. Trump defied pleas by his daughter, Ivanka Trump, and advisers like Chris Christie, the governor of New Jersey, to make a full-fledged apology. Instead, he dismissed the tape as nothing more than "locker-room banter" and asserted that "Bill Clinton has said far worse to me on the golf course." In grudging fashion, he added, "I apologize if anyone was offended." Only hours later, when Republicans were abandoning his campaign, did Trump offer an unreserved apology, issuing a video after midnight. "Anyone who knows me knows these words don't reflect who I am," he said. "I said it, I was wrong, and I apologize."

But that was not the end of the swirl of mega-stories that afternoon. At 4:32 p.m., just a half-hour after the *Access Hollywood* story went online, WikiLeaks began posting thousands of the emails stolen from John Podesta, once again exposing internal deliberations, arguments, strategy and palace intrigue in the Democratic camp. But more important than any of the specifics was once again associating Clinton's campaign with emails. Never mind that it was an issue different from the secretary's email server that had caused so much trouble, it just reminded voters of her troubles and distracted from other messages. Even more significantly, the *Access Hollywood* tape and the Podesta emails overshadowed the announcement on Russian interference.

The *Access Hollywood* tape was followed by allegations by a number of women that Trump did more than just engage in locker-room banter – he forcibly kissed and groped them. All of this was too much for Michelle Obama, who normally had little interest in campaigns but had already come out strongly for Clinton and given impassioned speeches urging the country not to turn to Trump. With the tape and the latest accusations, she grew especially distraught. "I have to tell you that I can't stop thinking about this," she told an audience in New Hampshire in perhaps the most emotional speech of her public life. "It has shaken me to my core in a way that I couldn't have predicted."

Further distracting public attention from the Russia connection was a last-minute announcement by James Comey that the FBI had discovered another set of emails from Hillary Clinton "that appear to be pertinent to the investigation" and that the bureau was examining them to see if there might be any evidence that would change his decision to close the case. The emails were found on the laptop of Anthony Weiner, a former Democratic congressman from New York married to Huma Abedin, one of Clinton's closest aides. The disclosure on October 28 erupted in the final days of the campaign like a roadside bomb, reviving the most damaging liability of Clinton's candidacy and throwing her off her message. In the days that followed, the FBI determined that most of the emails on the laptop were actually personal or duplicates of those previously examined, and Comey announced two days before the election that "we have not changed our conclusions" that Clinton should face no charges. But the political damage had been done.

John Kerry made an effort to punish Russia for its intervention. He sent an "action memo" to the White House outlining a series of economic sanctions and other retaliatory measures that could be announced as soon as the election was over. That represented something of a shift for him since earlier he had been uncertain about provoking Moscow at the same time he was negotiating for their help in Syria. But with that effort going nowhere, Kerry was advocating a more assertive approach. Either way, the White House rebuffed the move.

On October 31, the administration sent a message to Moscow using the "red phone," the secure channel intended to be employed during a crisis to avoid nuclear war. The phone was not an actual phone, but an encrypted email line. Obama's message to Putin warned that any intervention in the nation's voting systems on Election Day would be unacceptable. Pointedly, the message noted that "international law, including the law for armed conflict, applies to action in cyberspace." In other words, intrusion into America's voting systems could be considered an act of war.

The warning issued, Obama turned to some last-minute campaigning. Despite Moscow's intrigue, he felt confident that the election was heading to its inevitable conclusion.

*

Obama woke up on Election Day convinced, like most of the country, that he would not be handing the nuclear football over to Donald Trump. The reality television star, he thought, was a joke. No way Americans would turn to him. Hillary Clinton, Obama knew, was hardly a perfect candidate nor had she run a perfect campaign, but she was a serious and seasoned professional who had served at the highest levels of government and provided mature leadership. Just as important, she would continue his policies and cement his biggest achievements. His legacy, he felt, was in safe hands.

With no formal role on Election Day for the first time in years, Obama decided to watch the movie *Dr. Strange* in the White House theater with Michelle and Valerie Jarrett while waiting for results to come in. At one point, his phone buzzed with updates from his staff. "Huh," he said. "Results in Florida are looking kind of strange." Feeling stress already, Michelle opted not to wait for more results and instead went to bed. She may have had the right idea. For Democrats, the stress levels climbed higher and higher as the results were announced.

Her husband flipped on the television in the residence around 10 p.m. There was no surprise when Trump prevailed through the South and the West, traditionally Republican states. But then he won Florida, a key battleground state that the Democrats had been counting on. Then he captured the normally Democratic bulwarks of Pennsylvania, Wisconsin and Michigan, states that had been the foundation of the party's electoral strategy for years.

By the end of the evening, the unthinkable had happened. While Clinton won the popular tally by a whopping 3 million votes, she had lost enough key states to hand Trump a victory in the Electoral College. Fewer than 80,000 ballots in three states made the difference. Obama was as stunned as anyone. He had traveled the country for months and thought he knew the American people. They were, by and large, smart and good-hearted and moving in the right direction. They were not always as progressive as he would like but they had common sense. They simply could not have decided to replace him with a buffoonish showman whose calling cards had been repeated bankruptcies, serial marriages and racist dog whistles.

Yet the results were the results. No matter how unfathomable they were, there appeared no room for dispute. And so it fell to Obama to ease his own candidate into accepting the defeat. Around 1 a.m., he sent a message to Clinton saying that if she was going to lose, she should concede quickly and gracefully. After Pennsylvania was called for Trump about a half-hour later, the die seemed cast.

Around 2 a.m., Obama called Cody Keenan, his chief speechwriter, who had been watching the returns at home with his wife, Kristen, and Ben Rhodes and Dan Pfeiffer. "We're going to have to rework tomorrow's remarks a little bit," Obama said in typical understatement. Keenan, who had been drinking to celebrate what he and most everyone else assumed would be another Democratic administration, sobered up and got to work finding words that would help the president make sense of it all.

About a half-hour later, Clinton gave up and called Trump to concede. Then she called Obama.

"I'm sorry for letting you down," she told him, her throat tightening with emotion.

Obama offered what comfort he could, telling her that she ran a strong campaign, that she had done a lot for the country and that he was proud of her. There was, he said, life after losing.

While Clinton had lost, so had he. The country that had twice elected Barack Hussein Obama as its president had now chosen as his successor a man who had questioned the very circumstances of his birth. Obama may not have been on the ballot, but it was hard not to see the vote as a "personal insult," as he had called it on the campaign trail. "This stings," he said. "This hurts."

The morning after the election, the president and his team were still trying to absorb the magnitude of what had happened. Sitting in the Oval Office, they mulled the prospect of President Donald Trump occupying that most powerful few square feet in the world. But the zen Obama, the never-too-hot, never-too-cold president, tried to keep perspective. Painful as it was, he told his staff, it was not the end of the world. "There are more stars in the sky than sand on the earth," he wrote in a text message to Rhodes.

It was hard to convince the short-timers in the West Wing. Many in the building were crying that day, shaking their heads in shocked disbelief. The place felt like a funeral. As he talked with aides, Obama served as consoler in chief. When he sent for Keenan, an aide told him that the speechwriter was meeting with the communications team to comfort teary young staff members. Obama summoned them all to the Oval Office.

The country had still moved forward on their watch, despite this obvious setback, he reassured them. Change does not follow a straight line, he said. It tends to zig and zag. He and others remembered David Axelrod's prescient observation that as a retiring two-term president heads out the door, the country tends to choose a remedy, not a replica – someone who seems the opposite of the outgoing leader. There could hardly be someone more opposite of Obama.

The second-guessing and hand-wringing were unavoidable. "Never been as wrong on anything on [sic] my life," David Plouffe, who had stuck by his prediction that Clinton had a 100 percent chance of winning, wrote on Twitter. He was hardly the only one. Nearly every political and media outlet that engaged in game-show style predictions found itself humiliated. Only slightly less bullish than Plouffe, *The Huffington Post* thought Clinton had a 98 percent chance of winning. Nate Silver's web site FiveThirtyEight.com, which specialized in political prognostication, was more conservative but still put the likelihood of a Clinton victory at 71 percent. *The New York Times's* Upshot split the difference by pegging her chances at 85 percent – and many of the newspaper's online readers found themselves whipsawed when a graphic dial meter showing its presidential prediction suddenly flipped on election night to give Trump similarly lopsided odds.

No matter how much Obama tried to find the silver lining, Trump's victory imperiled many of the outgoing president's achievements. Suddenly, everything he had worked to accomplish over eight years was on the line. Instead of handing the baton to a like-minded successor who would build on his New Foundation, he was facing a hostile takeover by a bellicose, conspiracy-minded president-elect intent on demolishing the Obama legacy. Trump had made clear that he would try to dismantle the Obamacare health program. Trump had also vowed to scrap Obama's international climate change agreement and the Trans-Pacific Partnership trade pact, renegotiate or pull out of his Iran nuclear deal, repeal the Dodd-Frank regulations on Wall Street and reverse orders sparing illegal immigrants from deportation.

Even though Obama had just days earlier warned that all of his progress would be "out the window" if Trump won, he and his team now argued that that was not true. "Maybe 15 percent of that gets rolled back, 20 percent," he told David Remnick of *The New Yorker*, "but there's still a lot of stuff that sticks." Trump, they argued, would find it harder to shift course than he expected. Taking health care away from millions of Americans would prove problematic. And many of Obama's successes – pulling the country out of the Great Recession, saving the auto industry, killing Osama bin Laden and promoting clean energy – could not be overturned. In private, however, Obama recognized that he was handing over power to someone determined to tear down all he had built. "I feel like Michael Corleone," he told aides, alluding to *The Godfather* mafia movies. "I almost got out."

Remembering the gracious way George W. Bush handled his own transition eight years earlier, Obama resolved to follow that example and reached out to Trump. They sat together in the Oval Office a couple of days after the election, which despite years of long-distance jousting was actually the first time the two had ever met. Over the course of ninety minutes, Obama did his best to steer Trump toward seeing the world the way he had. He warned the incoming president that North Korea and its rogue nuclear program would be his biggest headache. And the two tried to put the rancor of the campaign behind them. For a moment, at least, it seemed as if they might have succeeded.

Obama told reporters afterward that it was an "excellent conversation" and said he was "encouraged" by Trump's interest in working together.

Trump expressed "great respect" for Obama and called him a "very, very good man."

After Trump left the building, though, Obama summoned some of his closest aides to the Oval Office and seemed mystified by the encounter. At various points throughout the meeting, he told them, Trump kept steering the conversation back to the size of his campaign rallies – he could draw huge crowds and so could Obama but Hillary Clinton could not, Trump said.

"I'm trying to place him in American history," Obama told his aides. While Trump seemed pleasant enough in person, he did not seem invested in any particular policy.

"He peddles bullshit," Ben Rhodes replied. "That character has always been part of the American story. You can see it right back to some of the characters in *Huckleberry Finn*."

"Maybe," Obama said, "that's the best we can hope for."

In the weeks after the election, Obama went through multiple emotional stages. At times, he took the long view; at others, he flashed anger. He called Trump a "cartoon" figure who cared more about crowd size than policy. And he expressed rare self-doubt, wondering whether he had misjudged his own influence on American history. "Maybe this is what people want," he mused one day. "I've got the economy set up well for him. No facts. No consequences. They can just have a cartoon."

All of which conveniently exonerated himself for any role in what happened. Obama preferred to think that Trump's election was a function of a racial and economic backlash, an unpleasant but natural and temporary receding of historical tides, rather than a consequence of any of his actions or failures in office. The problem was not that he expanded government too much or that he appeared intent on taking from some to benefit others or that he seemed feckless on the international stage or that he pushed an economic or social agenda too far or that he could not connect with the disaffection sweeping some parts of the country. The problem was that voters did not fully understand or appreciate all he had done for them. Not everyone agreed. Stanley Greenberg, a prominent Democratic pollster who helped elect Bill Clinton, largely blamed Obama for turning working-class voters away from Democrats by dismissing rather than channeling the popular anger after the financial crash of 2008 and "heralding economic progress and the bailout of the irresponsible elites, while ordinary people's incomes crashed and they continued to struggle financially."

To Obama and his team, however, the real blame lay squarely with Clinton. She was the one who could not translate his strong

369

record and healthy economy into a winning message. Never mind that Trump essentially ran the same playbook against Clinton that Obama did eight years earlier, portraying her as a corrupt exemplar of the status quo. She brought many of her troubles on herself. No one forced her to underestimate the danger in the Midwest states of Wisconsin and Michigan. No one forced her to set up a private email server that would come back to haunt her. No one forced her to take hundreds of thousands of dollars from Goldman Sachs and other pillars of Wall Street for speeches. No one forced her to run a scripted, soulless campaign that tested eighty-five slogans before coming up with "Stronger Together."

While Clinton and her supporters blamed James Comey for her loss, Obama did not fault the FBI director. In fact, after a meeting at the White House in late November, Obama pulled Comey aside for a private chat.

"I just want to tell you something," Obama told him, according to Comey's memoir. "I picked you to be FBI director because of your integrity and your ability. I want you to know that nothing – nothing – has happened in the last year to change my view."

Comey felt a wave of emotion and nearly came to tears. In the days since the election, he had been the target of so much anger from so many Democrats that to hear the president reject that view proved a powerful moment of relief. He recognized that Obama was not endorsing his actions but appreciated the testament to his ethical core.

"That means a lot to me, Mr. President," Comey told Obama. "I have hated the last year. The last thing we want is to be involved in an election. I'm just trying to do the right thing."

"I know, I know," Obama said.

Even so, Obama continued to stew over the results. He was trying to process them, to make sense of them, to fit them into his own often self-created narrative. While in Peru for an international summit a couple of weeks after the election, Obama seemed in a sullen mood as he pondered the meaning of the outcome during a motorcade ride.

"What if we were wrong?" he asked aides riding with him in the armored presidential limousine along the streets of Lima. He had read a column in *The New York Times* asserting that liberals had forgotten how important identity was to people and had promoted an empty cosmopolitan globalism that made many feel left behind. "Maybe we pushed too far," he said. "Maybe people just want to fall back into their tribe."

His aides reassured him that he still would have won had he been able to run for another term and that the next generation had more in common with him than with Trump.

Obama did not seem convinced. "Sometimes," he said, "I wonder whether I was ten or twenty years too early."

*

As traumatized as the Obama White House was in the aftermath of the election, the outgoing president still had two more months in power, and with the voting over it was time to decide what to do about Russia's intervention. Even Moscow seemed stunned by the result. The State Duma, the lower house of parliament, literally burst into applause on the news of Trump's victory. "They'd succeeded beyond their wildest imagination," said James Clapper, "and were completely unprepared for their own success."

In late November, Susan Rice asked her staff to draft a menu of possible retaliatory measures that the president could take before leaving office and, in a meeting of his national security team on December 5, Obama ordered the CIA, FBI and National Security Agency to pull together their intelligence into a single, integrated report that he could pass along to Trump and Congress.

A few days later, *The Washington Post* reported that the country's intelligence agencies had concluded that the Russian government had acted covertly to harm Hillary Clinton's chances and promote Donald Trump. The agencies were not able to say that it had changed the outcome, but the story got under Trump's skin and he lashed out at the intelligence agencies that were soon to report to him. "These are the same people that said Saddam Hussein had weapons of mass destruction," he huffed.

Obama finally took action against Russia on December 29, ordering the expulsion of thirty-five Russian officials identified as spies and the seizure of two Russian diplomatic properties. Trump's incoming national security adviser, Michael Flynn, the retired lieutenant general who had been forced out as head of the Defense Intelligence Agency by the Obama administration, told Russia's ambassador, Sergey Kislyak, that the sanctions would be revisited once the new president took office, effectively encouraging Moscow not to respond with the traditional tit-for-tat expulsions common in this sort of diplomatic row. Putin accordingly announced that he would refrain from striking back. Trump then publicly praised the Russian leader for his restraint. "Great move on delay (by V. Putin) – I always knew he was very smart!" he wrote on Twitter.

The intelligence report on Russian interference was released to the public on January 6, 2017, concluding that "Putin and the Russian government aspired to help President-elect Trump's election chances when possible by discrediting Secretary Clinton." When it was all put together, the collective evidence was "staggering," James Clapper said later. Clapper, James Comey and John Brennan briefed Trump on the findings of the report on the same day and then, by prearrangement among the three, Comey separately pulled the president-elect aside to tell him one on one that the FBI had received a dossier during the campaign prepared by a former British intelligence agent working for the Democrats containing sensational compromising information that the Russian government supposedly had about Trump, including incidents in Moscow involving prostitutes. The dossier had not been verified, but Comey told Trump that copies were in circulation in Washington, including among news outlets, and he thought the incoming president should know. Trump did not appreciate the heads up and took it as a way of the FBI telling him they had something on him. When news organizations reported on it a few days later, Trump blamed the intelligence agencies in incendiary terms. "Are we living in Nazi Germany?"

For Obama, that was the end of the Russia affair. But even some of his top advisers left office frustrated that they had not done more to stop the Russians or at least to publicly call them out. Some aides consoled themselves by noting that the Russians did not actually try to disrupt the voting itself on Election Day by hacking into elections systems and they credited Obama's red phone warning with deterring Putin. But that was small comfort given the results. "I feel like we sort of choked," one senior Obama official told *The Washington Post*.

Among those who thought Obama made a mistake by keeping quiet through the fall was Hillary Clinton. "I do wonder sometimes about what would have happened if President Obama had made a televised address to the nation in the fall of 2016 warning that our democracy was under attack," she later wrote. "Maybe more Americans would have woken up to the threat in time."

If history had a way of zigging and zagging, so did the transition. When the United Nations Security Council took up a resolution condemning Israeli settlements in the West Bank and East Jerusalem and Obama would not commit to vetoing it, Prime Minister Benjamin Netanyahu reached out to Trump for help. Trump publicly called on Obama to block the resolution, but the president ignored him and had the United States abstain instead, allowing it to pass. Furious, Netanyahu accused Obama of conspiring against

Israel by secretly orchestrating the resolution, an allegation the White House denied. But Trump used the moment to highlight how he would be different from Obama. "Stay strong Israel," Trump wrote on Twitter. "January 20th is fast approaching!"

Although Obama offered help to the incoming team, that did not stop him from using his final weeks to try to prevent his successor from reversing parts of his legacy. He used his presidential power to ban oil drilling off the Atlantic coast and set aside wide swaths of land as national monuments. He also issued more commutations to nonviolent federal prisoners, transferred more detainees out of the prison at Guantánamo Bay, Cuba, and eliminated a long-suspended national registry program once used to track Muslim men to keep Trump from restarting it.

Obama could not resist tweaking Trump on the way out the door. During an interview with David Axelrod for his new CNN program, *The Axe Files*, Obama even boasted that had he not been barred from seeking a third term by the Twenty-Second Amendment of the Constitution, he could have beaten Trump with a more inclusive message that appealed to the middle class.

"I'm confident that if I had run again and articulated it, I think I could have mobilized a majority of the American people to rally behind it," he said.

Trump fired back hours later on Twitter: "President Obama said that he thinks he would have won against me. He should say that but I say NO WAY! – jobs leaving, ISIS, OCare, etc." That, of course, would have been a contest for the ages. But it was not to be.

Much as he followed Bush's example in managing the transition, Obama was tempted to adopt his predecessor's approach to life after office. Bush had said that Obama "deserves my silence," a deference that the president always appreciated. But as his days in the White House dwindled, Obama felt that a vow of silence might not be tenable. Trump was so offensive to even basic norms that Obama could imagine circumstances that would compel him to speak out.

At his farewell news conference three days before leaving office, Obama said he could be drawn back into the fray if the stakes were high enough. "There's a difference between the normal functioning of politics and certain issues or certain moments where I think our core values may be at stake," he said. Among them would be "systematic discrimination," voting rights violations, "efforts to silence dissent or the press" or the rounding up of young illegal immigrants who have been in the country long enough to be "for all practical purposes" Americans.

The next time Obama and Trump met was Inauguration Day. The incoming president and his wife arrived at the White House in the morning for the traditional tea with the outgoing presidential couple. They chatted amiably on the North Portico and then went inside. After a while, Obama emerged from the White House for the last time as president to escort his successor in the motorcade to the Capitol for the ceremony.

Once the oath was taken and the speech was given and the transfer of power was complete, the Obamas headed to the other side of the Capitol and boarded a white-topped Marine helicopter, which took one final loop over the White House before flying the forty-fourth president and his wife to Joint Base Andrews in the Maryland suburbs for a last farewell before leaving Washington on the presidential jet.

Addressing a crowd of several thousand former aides, advisers and supporters gathered at the air base, Obama said they had reason to be proud of what they had accomplished. But history's paragraph, he said, was yet to be finished.

"This is not a period," he said, "this is a comma in the continuing story of building America."

'Forever President'

Barack Obama was on stage in Miami, his coat and tie off, his sleeves rolled up, his indignation on full display. The hall full of Democrats cheered as he excoriated his successor as a liar and a fraud and a demagogue. His case against the new president was not merely that they disagreed on policy, but that the new president did not even share the fundamental values of the country. President Trump, his predecessor told the campaign rally on the last weekend before the 2018 midterm election, was a danger to the Constitution and the rule of law and to American democracy itself.

Two years after leaving office, Obama returned to the public arena to do what no other former president had done in three-quarters of a century. Not since Herbert Hoover castigated Franklin Roosevelt's New Deal program as "despotism" at the Republican National Convention of 1936 and angled for a chance to run against FDR again in 1940 had a onetime occupant of the White House mounted a systematic campaign against the man who took his place. Obama had come to believe that he had no choice but to dispense with the modern tradition of remaining silent. The stakes were too high. Not only was everything he built during his own eight years in office now at risk but so, he was saying, was everything all of the presidents had built the previous two centuries.

In Miami and at other stops during the midterm election campaign, Obama assailed Trump as a "threat to our democracy" who practiced the "politics of fear and resentment." He excoriated the incumbent president for "lying" and "fear-mongering" and pulling a "political stunt" by sending troops to the border to guard against a caravan of asylum-seeking migrants being portrayed as an invasion. He accused Trump of cozying up to Russia, emboldening white supremacists and trying to weaponize the justice system for his own political purposes. "It did not start with Donald Trump," Obama told an audience of college students in Illinois as he kicked off his fall campaign swing. "He is a symptom, not the cause. He's just capitalizing on resentments that politicians have been fanning for years, a fear and anger that's rooted in our past, but it's also born out of the enormous upheavals that have taken place in your brief lifetimes."

Obama had always intended to follow George W. Bush's example of sliding gracefully off the public stage, refraining from doing anything that would complicate his successor's life – and if it had been Hillary Clinton taking over, or even Jeb Bush or Marco Rubio, he likely would have done just that. He had plenty of other things to do, after all. Other than Bill Clinton, Obama at age fifty-five was the youngest former president since William Howard Taft, with decades of useful time presumably ahead of him and a passel of ideas for how to use his post-presidency other than turning into the leader of the opposition.

With his daughter Sasha still in high school, he and Michelle rented a house in the upscale Kalorama section of Washington where they could stay until her graduation in 2019 – as it happened, choosing a place just around the corner from the house that Trump's daughter and son-in-law, Ivanka Trump and Jared Kushner, would soon rent. In the process, Obama became the first president to remain in the nation's capital after leaving office since Woodrow Wilson, who ended up in the same neighborhood but was physically infirm and no longer able to play a major role on the political stage. Obama, still vital and vigorous, would live just two miles away from the elegant mansion he had occupied for eight years. While he had arrived in Washington vowing not to become a creature of the capital – "renting, not buying," he liked to say – he did eventually buy the house in Kalorama.

At first, he tried to live up to the Bush standard. For most of his first two years after the White House, Obama generally limited himself to issuing occasional written statements taking issue with some action by the new president or delivering mostly oblique criticisms in speeches that did not identify him by name. When Senator John McCain died in the summer of 2018, Obama and Bush both gave eulogies that were taken as implicit critiques of Trump, who was not invited and not welcome at the memorial service at Washington National Cathedral. But with leaderless Democrats desperate for someone of stature to take on the bombastic, bullying president, Obama finally jumped back into the fray with both feet. And it seemed personal. Finally he could vent the exasperation he had been nursing in private.

When he finally did begin discussing Trump in public, his voice had a way of rising an octave in astonishment, almost as if he could still not believe who had taken his place in the White House. At one point in Milwaukee, Obama openly called his successor a liar. America, he said, had long seen politicians who spun or shaded the truth. "But what we have not seen before, in our recent public life at least, is politicians just blatantly, repeatedly, baldly, shamelessly lying," he said. "The president said he'd pass a middle-class tax cut before the next election," Obama went on. "Congress isn't even in session! He just makes it up! He says, 'I'm going to protect your pre-existing conditions' while his Justice Department is in court right now trying to strike down those protections. That is not spin, that's not exaggeration, that's not trying to put a positive glow on things. That's lying!" If Obama was violating the norms of the modern presidency by attacking another member of the White House fraternity, he was arguing that Trump effectively drove him to it.

Trump had spent much of his early presidency taking a wrecking ball to his predecessor's legacy, trying to tear it down brick by brick. On his first day in office, Trump signed an executive order meant to begin taking apart Obama's Affordable Care Act. While he failed to pass a measure repealing Obamacare entirely, thwarted only by the middle-of-the-night thumbs-down vote of John McCain, Trump did manage to gut parts of it through subsequent legislation and administrative action. He likewise wasted little time pulling out of Obama's Trans-Pacific Partnership, the Paris climate accord and the Iran nuclear agreement. He reversed the rejection of the Keystone XL pipeline and began unraveling Obama's increased fuel-efficiency standards and limits on power plant emissions. He took aim at Obama's regulations on Wall Street, his diplomatic overture to Cuba and his order allowing younger illegal immigrants to stay and work. Moreover, every chance he got, the new president publicly denounced Obama, at one point even falsely accusing the former president of bugging Trump Tower during the 2016 presidential campaign, an allegation refuted by Trump's own Justice Department.

Trump, of course, was hardly the first president to scorn his predecessor's tenure or to take the country in a new direction. But few if any modern presidents invested quite so much energy in deconstructing the programs they inherited. Dwight Eisenhower did not overturn Franklin Roosevelt's New Deal nor did Richard Nixon reverse Lyndon Johnson's Great Society. Ronald Reagan promised to eliminate the departments of energy and education created by Jimmy Carter but ultimately did not. George W. Bush kept Bill Clinton's health care program for lower-income children, his revamped welfare system and his AmeriCorps service organization. Obama eventually rescinded the portion of Bush's tax cuts that went to the wealthiest Americans but he kept the vast bulk of the tax cuts as well as his predecessor's Medicare prescription medicine plan, his AIDS-fighting program and most of his counterterrorism apparatus. Trump took a different attitude. If his predecessor did it, not only was it wrong, it must be destroyed. And that was the way his supporters wanted it. They did not send him to Washington to become a member of the club, but to tear the club down.

Many of Obama's accomplishments were beyond Trump's reach. Obama dispatched Osama bin Laden, Anwar al-Awlaki and hundreds of other terrorists with his relentless campaign of drone strikes, commando raids and other actions, breaking the core Al Qaeda organization and averting any further catastrophic attack on American soil on the scale of September 11. He put two women on the Supreme Court and helped break down barriers for gay and lesbian Americans. He rescued a failing auto industry and accelerated a clean-energy boom that he had inherited. The stock markets more than doubled during his presidency. And with the help of the Federal Reserve, he turned around a nation teetering on the edge of depression, ultimately presiding over the longest streak of job creation on record even if the recovery was also historically shallow. More than 11 million new jobs were created on Obama's watch, shy of the 23 million under Bill Clinton or 16 million under Ronald Reagan, but still impressive given the hemorrhage of jobs he inherited.

Obama likewise owned his failures regardless of Trump's actions. History's judgment of his handling of the civil war in Syria or the messy aftermath of the intervention in Libya or the rise of the Islamic State in Iraq after the withdrawal of American troops will not depend on his successor. He remains responsible for doubling the national debt even if Trump then proceeded to pour on even more red ink. He proved unequal to the task of overhauling the nation's immigration laws or its criminal justice system despite the potential for bipartisan support. Despite his ambitions to build a New Foundation, the vast majority of the benefits of his economic recovery still went to the richest of the rich. If anything, America's decision to replace Obama with someone as radically different as Trump may be taken as evidence of Obama's inability to build sustained public support for his agenda or to mitigate the polarization of the country.

Yet for all of his animus toward his predecessor, Trump had Obama to thank for the economy he inherited. The recovery that began in Obama's first term was still under way as Trump came to office, even if it had slowed somewhat near the end of his tenure. Trump liked to claim he built "the greatest economy that we've had in our history" but, as with so many things that he said, it was not true. Unemployment did indeed drop to 3.7 percent under Trump, the lowest in a half-century, and joblessness among African-Americans and Hispanic Americans fell to their lowest levels ever. But that resulted from the accumulation of job growth that began under Obama and continued under Trump. The economy added 4.9 million new jobs during Trump's first two years versus 5.1 million during Obama's last two years. Overall growth has accelerated under Trump, the total economy expanding by 10 percent compared with 6.4 percent during Obama's final two years, juiced by the $1.5 trillion tax cut that Trump passed, although that was financed by increased deficits just as Obama's stimulus package had been.

But Trump could do what Obama could not – he could sell it. Trump's repeated boasting about how great the economy was had convinced many in the country – consumer confidence shot up as did poll numbers showing optimism in the economy while businesses began investing money they had hoarded during the previous few years. Obama was always reluctant to oversell the strength of the economy, wary of being called out by critics and journalists who would point out that many were still suffering and that income growth remained largely stalled for the middle class.

Undaunted by details, Trump bulldozed right over any caveats and promoted the economy with the gusto of a master marketer in a way that Obama never did. Projecting confidence is an important element of presidential leadership and Obama at times seemed to project his own doubts. To the many Americans who supported him, Trump was cleaning up Obama's messes by boosting the economy, cutting taxes and regulations, devoting more money to the military and defeating the Islamic State in the Middle East.

If Trump was bad for Obama's policies, he was nonetheless good for Obama's public standing. By the time Trump took over, the disappointment many on the left once felt toward Obama had to a large extent faded as liberals came to recognize all he had done or tried to do on their shared priorities. Many moderates and even some conservatives who did not like his tax-the-rich, big-government domestic agenda or what they considered his naïve, passive and even dithering approach to foreign policy had nonetheless come to appreciate Obama's fundamental decency and decorum in contrast to what would follow.

Whatever their complaints about Obama, and there were many, he contrasted favorably with a successor who paid hush money to women to keep quiet about alleged sexual affairs, dodged millions of dollars in taxes, profited off business with foreign clienteles while living in the White House, equated white supremacists with those who protested them, fired an FBI director who was investigating him, accepted the word of Russia's president over that of America's intelligence agencies and made thousands of documented false or misleading statements each year as president.

Obama left office with 59 percent of Americans approving of the job he had done, his highest rating since the first months of his presidency nearly eight years before. Of the ten most recent presidents who lived to leave office, only Dwight Eisenhower matched Obama's final number and only Ronald Reagan and Bill Clinton surpassed it. Within a year, 66 percent of Americans viewed Obama positively, more than twenty percentage points above Trump's approval rating. And while Obama did not want to be judged entirely on his success in breaking the racial barrier, he nonetheless changed the paradigm on what was possible. Race was a more overt and vexing issue in the Trump era, but the Congress that emerged from the 2018 midterm elections included more people of color than ever before and as 2020 beckoned, several black candidates were among the most-talked-about Democrats lining up for a potential presidential campaign.

As the next presidential election got under way, Obama weighed in on the debate within his own party about how to take on his successor. Many Democrats, particularly on the left, argued for a more combative approach; Joe Biden said he would have "beat the hell" out of Trump in high school for mistreating women while Eric Holder said Michelle Obama was wrong when she said, "when they go low, we go high," declaring that instead, "when they go low, we kick them."

Barack Obama warned against trying to out-Trump Trump. "There are well-meaning folks passionate about social justice who think things have gotten so bad, the lines have been so starkly drawn, that we have to fight fire with fire, we have to do the same things to the Republicans that they do to us, adopt their tactics, say whatever works, make up stuff about the other side," he said. "I don't agree with that. It's not because I'm soft. It's not because I'm interested in promoting an empty bipartisanship." He said that "yelling at each other" would only further erode civic institutions and not appeal to voters. "We won't win people over," he said, "by calling them names or dismissing entire chunks of the country as racist or sexist or homophobic."

However it was run, it would have to be a campaign for someone other than Obama. That he had felt compelled to step in and confront Trump during the midterm election underscored the vacuum of leadership and coherent message at the top of the Democratic Party, whose titular chiefs were in their seventies and whose next-generation figures had yet to establish themselves as commanding or unifying presences. At that campaign rally in Miami, Andrew Gillum, the Democratic candidate for governor, referred to Obama as the party's "forever president," a phrase that had become popular amoing some of his admirers, but that was a recipe for failure. The party had to move on, to find new voices and perhaps a new identity.

Obama was trying to move on as well. There was much to do. He devoted his time to establishing a presidential library, building a foundation and expanding his My Brother's Keeper initiative helping young Latino and African-American boys. He sat down to write a memoir and he teamed up with Eric Holder on a voting rights project. He wanted to advance his ideas on health care and immigration. He did not miss the office, perhaps, but he was not ready to give up the work.

For Obama, history was still calling.

ACKNOWLEDGMENTS

If a picture is worth a thousand words, then the first version of this book was priceless. An album drawn mainly from *New York Times* photographers, the original edition of *Obama: The Call of History* told the story of eight tumultuous years through compelling, revealing and often unforgettable images. The photographers of *The Times* are unrivaled in their talent for capturing moments in history and it was fun to play a small part in helping to showcase their work.

This updated and greatly expanded edition builds out the modest text from that book into a full-scale history of the Obama presidency, the first of its kind since he left office. It could not have been produced without the inspiration and dedication especially of Alex Ward, Nicholas Callaway and Manuela Roosevelt, who have believed in this project from the start. All three have been unflagging champions of this book whose wisdom and patience at every step of the way were truly invaluable. Also indispensable was David Stout, who brought his sharp eye and good judgment to reviewing every page, every paragraph and every word to make sure the book was the best it could be. Emily Cochrane scoured the manuscript for errors and nothing gets past her fact-checking radar. She's a rising star in Washington journalism; keep an eye on her.

The original photo book could never have happened without Doug Mills and Stephen Crowley, who are responsible for some of the most iconic pictures of the Obama era. It was also the product of so many other first-rate people at *The Times* and Callaway, including Toshiya Masuda, Ivan Wong, Danielle Sweet, Vin Alabiso, Phyllis Collazo, Maggie Berkvist, William P. O'Donnell, Susan Beachy, Guilbert Gates and Jane Farnol. Thanks too to Lee

Riffaterre who provided wise legal counsel and Danielle Rhoades-Ha who helped with promotion. We are indebted to Andrew Wylie and Jeffrey Posternak of The Wylie Agency for their expert assistance.

All of us at *The Times* are privileged to work for A.G. Sulzberger and before him Arthur Sulzberger Jr., stewards of a storied tradition of journalistic excellence that they have preserved and strengthened despite all the challenges of our time, aided in recent years especially by Mark Thompson. Our coverage of the Obama presidency was produced under the stalwart leadership of Bill Keller and Jill Abramson in New York; David Leonhardt, Carolyn Ryan and Elisabeth Bumiller in Washington; and Dean Baquet in both places. Gerald Marzorati, Megan Liberman, Chris Suellentrop, Hugo Lindgren and Joel Lovell edited pieces for *The New York Times Magazine* that shaped parts of this book. Special thanks to Bill Hamilton and Richard Stevenson, who are profoundly great editors, mentors and friends and did as much as anyone during the Obama years to guide our White House team.

At *The Times*, I have been blessed to team up with the most talented White House reporters in the business, especially my friend of a quarter-century, the incomparable Michael D. Shear, as well as, at various points, the fabulous Jackie Calmes, Helene Cooper, Julie Hirschfeld Davis, Maggie Haberman, Gardiner Harris, Annie Karni, Mark Landler, Katie Rogers, Sheryl Gay Stolberg, Michael Tackett, Glenn Thrush and Jeff Zeleny. On top of the daily coverage, journalists at *The Times* have already produced a library of insightful books about President Obama, his family, his team, his policies and his era, authored by Michael R. Gordon, Jodi Kantor, Mark Landler, Mark Leibovich, James Risen, David E. Sanger, Charlie Savage, Eric Schmitt, Janny Scott, Scott Shane, Thom Shanker and Rachel Swarns. Thomas Friedman probably spoke with President Obama more than any of us and his interactions with the president inform a lot of this book. Maureen Dowd's penetrating analysis of Obama and his Washington was invaluable, as was David Brooks's thoughtful commentary.

Every one of us in the Washington bureau has benefited from the assistance of researcher Kitty Bennett and a team of patient, smart and wise editors that includes Jill Agostino, Mikayla Bouchard, Amy Fiscus, Margaret Ho, Lara Jakes, Justine Makeli, Andy Parsons, Thom Shanker, Deborah Solomon, Jaime Swanson, Jonathan Weisman and Nathan Willis. Jennifer Steinhauer and Ari Bevacqua have in different ways moved mountains to bring our bureau into the multi-platform world. Eileen Sullivan has kept us ahead of the game on more mornings than we could count. And my nearby seatmates have been endlessly patient, including Binyamin Appelbaum, Coral Davenport, Lisa Lerer, Adam Liptak, Robert Pear, Jeremy Peters and Alan Rappeport.

I got my start at the White House in 1996 while at *The Washington Post* and will forever be grateful to Karen DeYoung for taking a chance on an unqualified rookie and to Donald Graham for everything he did to make *The Post* a pillar of American journalism. I'm in awe of the current generation of editors and White House reporters at *The Post* who make it so hard to compete. Rafe Sagalyn has been a friend and advocate for two decades now. All the folks at MSNBC and *Washington Week* have been fabulous to work with, none more than Gwen Ifill, who left us way, way too early.

Many thanks especially to our friends for their unstinting support and forbearance including, John Smith and Jan Eckendorf; Heidi Crebo-Rediker and Charlotte and Doug Rediker; Martina Vandenberg and Max, Marshall and Alan Cooperman; Nicole Rabner and Andie Kanarek; Somerset, Heather and Elliott Grant; Indira Lakshmanan and Rohan, Devan and Dermot Tatlow; Susan Ascher and Audrey and Paul Kalb; Sabrina Tavernise and

Rory MacFarquhar; Cristina Dominguez and Lena, Max and Michael Grunwald; Miriam, Katy and Gary Bass; Evan Osnos and Sarabeth Berman; Jane Mayer and Kate Hamilton; Leslie Crutchfield and Caleigh, Quinn and Finn Macintyre; Susan Baer and Mike Abramowitz; Betsyellen Yeager and Glenn Frankel; Jen Bradley and Matthew and Leon Wieseltier; Max, Leo, Julie and Rajiv Chandrasekaran; Paul Quinn-Judge; Natalie Nougayrede and Nicholas Roche; Marilu and Bruce Sanford; Valerie Mann and Katie, Allie and Tim Webster; Juliet Eilperin and Andrew Light; Marc, Anna, Ray and Maria Bonaquist; Lori Aratani and Sophie and Spencer Hsu; Kathleen McBride and Carlos Lozada; Anne Kornblut and Jon Cohen; and Melissa Schwartz and Ben, Emily and David Muenzer.

Finally, I am grateful to my family for their love, in particular Ted and Martha Baker; Linda and Keith Sinrod; Lynn and Steve Glasser; Karin Baker and Kait Nolan; Laura, Jeff, Diana and Jennifer Glasser; Emily Allen; Will and Ben Glasser Allen; Alex, Oliver and Matthieu Fulchiron; Tiffany Hudson; Inge Gross, Sylvia and Dan Baker, Susan and Stephen Fisher and their children and grandchildren. Rosamaria Brizuela has been a member of our family for more than a dozen years. And Ellie Glasser brings us all great happiness.

Susan Glasser, the most extraordinary journalist in America and the best partner anyone could have, was a boundless source of love and inspiration. Theo Baker has become an incisive student of Washington but more importantly the joy of his parents' lives.

BIBLIOGRAPHY

Abrams, Brian. *Obama: An Oral History 2009-2017*. New York: Little A, 2018.

Alter, Jonathan. *The Promise: President Obama, Year One*. New York: Simon & Schuster, 2010.

—— *The Center Holds:* New York: Simon & Schuster, 2013.

Axelrod, David. *Believer: My Forty Years in Politics*. New York: Penguin Press, 2015.

Becker, Jo. *Forcing the Spring: Insight the Fight for Marriage Equality*. New York: Penguin Press, 2014.

Bergen, Peter. *Manhunt: The Ten-Year Search for Bin Laden From 9/11 to Abbotota-bad*. New York: Crown, 2012.

Biden, Joe. *Promise Me, Dad: A Year of Hope, Hardship, and Purpose*. New York: Flatiron Books, 2017.

Bowden, Mark. *The Finish: The Killing of Osama bin Laden*. New York: Atlantic Monthly Press, 2012.

Chandrasekaran, Rajiv. *Little America: The War Within the War for Afghanistan*. New York: Knopf, 2012.

Clapper, James R. *Facts and Fears: Hard Truths From a Life in Intelligence*. New York: Viking, 2018. With Trey Brown.

Clinton, Hillary Rodham. *Hard Choices: A Memoir*. New York: Simon & Schuster, 2014.

—— *What Happened*. New York: Simon & Schuster, 2017.

Cunnane, Pat. *West Winging It: An Unpresidential Memoir*. New York: Gallery Books, 2018.

Comey, James. *A Higher Loyalty: Truth, Lies, and Leadership*. New York: Flatiron Books, 2018.

Draper, Robert. *Do Not Ask What Good We Do: Inside the U.S. House of Representatives*. New York: Free Press, 2012.

Dyson, Michael Eric. *The Black Presidency: Barack Obama and the Politics of Race in America*. New York: Houghton Mifflin Harcourt, 2016.

Garrow, David J. *Rising Star: The Making of Barack Obama*. New York: William Morrow, 2017.

Gates, Robert M. *Duty: Memoirs of a Secretary at War*. New York: Knopf, 2014.

Geithner, Timothy F. *Stress Test: Reflections on Financial Crises*. New York: Crown, 2014.

Gordon, Michael R. and Bernard E. Trainor. *The Endgame: The Inside Story of the Struggle for Iraq, from George W. Bush to Barack Obama*. New York: Pantheon, 2012.

Grunwald, Michael. *The New New Deal: The Hidden Story of Change in the Obama Era*. New York: Simon & Schuster, 2012.

Halperin, Mark and John Heilemann. *Double Down: Game Change 2012*. New York: Penguin Press, 2013.

Heilemann, John and Mark Halperin. *Game Change: Obama and the Clintons, McCain and Palin, and the Race of a Lifetime*. New York: Harper Collins, 2010.

Ifill, Gwen. *The Breakthrough: Politics and Race in the Age of Obama*. New York: Doubleday, 2009.

Kantor, Jodi. *The Obamas*. New York: Little Brown, 2012.

Kerry, John. *Every Day Is Extra*. New York: Simon & Schuster, 2018.

Kirkpatrick, David D. *Into The Hands of the Soldiers: Freedom and Chaos in Egypt and the Middle East*. New York: Viking, 2018.

Leibovich, Mark. *This Town: Two Parties and a Funeral – Plus Plenty of Valet Parking! – in America's Gilded Capital*. New York: Penguin Press, 2013.

Litt, David. *Thanks, Obama: My Hopey Changey White House Years (A Speechwriter's Memoir)*. New York: Harper Collins, 2017.

Landler, Mark. *Alter Egos: Hillary Clinton, Barack Obama, and the Twilight Struggle Over American Power*. New York: Random House, 2015.

Love, Reggie. *Power Forward: My Presidential Education*. New York: Simon & Schuster, 2015.

Mann, James. *The Obamans: The Struggle Inside the White House to Redefine American Power*. New York: Viking, 2012.

Maraniss, David. *Barack Obama: The Story*. New York: Simon & Schuster, 2012.

Mastromonaco, Alyssa. *Who Thought This Was a Good Idea? And Other Questions You Should Have Answers to When You Work in the White House*. New York: Twelve, 2017.

McChrystal, Stanley. *My Share of the Task: A Memoir*. New York: Portfolio/Penguin, 2013.

McConnell, Mitch. *The Long Game: A Memoir*. New York: Sentinel, 2016.

McFaul, Michael. *From Cold War to Hot Peace: An American Ambassador in Putin's Russia*. New York: Houghton Mifflin Harcourt, 2018.

Miller, Greg. *The Apprentice: Trump, Russia and the Subversion of American Democracy*. New York: Custom House, 2018.

Nasr, Vali. *The Dispensable Nation: American Foreign Policy in Retreat*. New York: Doubleday, 2013.

Obama, Barack. *Dreams from My Father: A Story of Race and Inheritance*. New York: Crown, 2007.

———— *The Audacity of Hope: Thoughts on Reclaiming the American Dream*. New York: Crown, 2006.

Obama, Michelle. *Becoming*. New York: Crown, 2018.

390

Owen, Mark. *No Easy Day: The Firsthand Account of the Mission That Killed Osama bin Laden.* New York: Dutton Books, 2012. With Kevin Maurer.

Panetta, Leon. *Worthy Fights.* New York: Penguin Press, 2014. With Jim Newton.

Pfeiffer, Dan. *Yes We (Still) Can: Politics in the Age of Obama, Twitter, and Trump.* New York: Twelve, 2018.

Plouffe, David. *The Audacity to Win: The Inside Story and Lessons of Barack Obama's Historic Victory.* New York: Viking, 2009.

Raghavan, Gautam. *West Wingers: Stories from the Dream Chasers, Change Makers, and Hope Creators Inside the Obama White House.* New York: Penguin Books, 2018.

Rattner, Steven. *Overhaul: An Insider's Account of the Obama Administration's Emergency Rescue of the Auto Industry.* New York: Houghton Mifflin Harcourt, 2010.

Remnick, David. *The Bridge: The Life and Rise of Barack Obama.* New York: Knopf, 2010.

Rhodes, Ben. *The World As It Is: A Memoir of the Obama White House.* New York: Random House, 2018.

Risen, James. *Pay Any Price: Greed, Power, and Endless War.* New York: Houghton Mifflin, 2014.

Sanger, David E. *Confront and Conceal: Obama's Secret Wars and Surprising Use of American Power.* New York: Crown, 2012.

Saslow, Eli. *Ten Letters: The Stories Americans Tell Their President.* New York: Doubleday, 2011.

Savage, Charlie. *Power Wars: Inside Obama's Post-9/11 Presidency.* New York: Little Brown, 2015.

Scheiber, Noam. *The Escape Artists: How Obama's Team Fumbled the Recovery.* New York: Simon & Schuster, 2012.

Schmitt, Eric and Thom Shanker. *Counter Strike: The Untold Story of America's Secret Campaign Against Al Qaeda.* New York: Times Books, 2011.

Scott, Janny. *A Singular Woman: The Untold Story of Barack Obama's Mother.* New York: Riverhead Books, 2011.

Shane, Scott. *Objective Troy: A Terrorist, a President, and the Rise of the Drone.* New York: Tim Duggan, 2015.

Sherman, Wendy. *Not For The Faint of Heart: Lessons in Courage, Power & Persistence.* New York: PublicAffairs, 2018.

Slevin, Peter. *Michelle Obama: A Life.* New York: Knopf, 2015.

Suskind. Ron. *Confidence Men: Wall Street, Washington and the Education of a President.* New York: Harper, 2011.

Swarns, Rachel L. *American Tapestry: The Story of the Black, White, and Multiracial Ancestors of Michelle Obama.* New York: Amistad, 2012.

Wolfe, Richard. *Renegade: The Making of a President*. New York: Crown, 2009.

—— *Revival: The Struggle for Survival Inside the Obama White House*. New York: Crown, 2010.

Woodward, Bob. *Obama's Wars*. New York: Simon & Schuster, 2010.

—— *The Price of Politics*. New York: Simon & Schuster, 2012.

NOTES

PROLOGUE: 'Riding the Wave'

Page 13 **"I have had an ongoing debate"** Two Obama advisers, author interviews.

Page 15 **66 percent of Americans** Ryan Struyk, "George W. Bush's Favorable Rating Has Pulled a Complete 180," CNN, January 22, 2018. https://www.cnn.com/2018/01/22/politics/george-w-bush-favorable-poll/index.html

Page 16 **the last time a majority** In a survey taken from January 2 to 5, 2004, 55 percent of Americans said they were "satisfied with the way things are going in the United States at this time." No majority has felt that way since then. "Satisfaction With the United States," Gallup. https://news.gallup.com/poll/1669/general-mood-country.aspx

Page 19 **only 11 percent of Americans** The satisfaction rate reached 11 percent in two Gallup surveys in 2011, one taken from August 11 to 14 and the next taken from September 8 to 11. "Satisfaction With the United States," Gallup. https://news.gallup.com/poll/1669/general-mood-country.aspx

Page 17 **"Sometimes I think the only"** Dan Pfeiffer, then the White House communications director. Peter Baker, "Comparisons in Chief," *The New York Times,* May 14, 2011. https://www.nytimes.com/2011/05/15/weekinreview/15president.html

Page 17 **"look like all the presidents"** Jonathan Weisman and Juliet Eilperin, "Race Moves to Center Stage," *The Washington Post,* August 1, 2008. http://www.washingtonpost.com/wp-dyn/content/article/2008/08/01/AR2008080102970.html?hpid=topnews

Page 17 **"I am like a Rorschach test"** Michael Powell, "Obama, the Self-Described 'Rorschach Test,' Liberal But Inscrutable," *The New York Times,* June 4, 2008. https://www.nytimes.com/2008/06/04/world/americas/04iht-obama.1.13459637.html

Page 18 **"All right, fire away"** Peter Baker, "The Education of a President," *The New York Times Magazine,* October 12, 2010. https://www.nytimes.com/2010/10/17/magazine/17obama-t.html

Page 19 **"Hard things are hard"** As Obama once recalled, a senior adviser said during a meeting on a particularly thorny issue that "hard things are hard" and the president laughingly said that was profound. The plaque was made as a wry reference to that insight. Obama described this during a speech on July 20, 2016. https://archive.org/details/archiveteam_videobot_twitter_com_755863391084969985

Page 19 **"White," he would say** Michael D. Shear, "Obama After Dark: The Precious Hours Alone," *The New York Times,* July 2, 2016. https://www.nytimes.com/2016/07/03/us/politics/obama-after-dark-the-precious-hours-alone.html

Page 20 **exactly seven almonds** Ibid.

Page 20 **Obama felt compelled to deny** In an interview with Savannah Guthrie on the *Today* show, Obama said that after the original story ran, "All my friends were calling me up and saying this seems a little anal, this is a little weird, and I had to explain to them, no, this was a joke." Scott Stump, "No, President Obama Doesn't

Eat Exactly 7 Almonds Every Night," NBC News, July 28, 2016 https://www.today.com/news/no-president-obama-doesn-t-eat-exactly-7-almonds-every-t101245

Page 20 **"when the rise of the oceans"** Barack Obama's Remarks in St. Paul, June 3, 2008. https://www.nytimes.com/2008/06/03/us/politics/03text-obama.html

Page 20 **"I'm leader of the free world"** Robert Gates, *Duty*, p. 443.

Page 20 **"you are essentially a relay"** David Remnick, "Going the Distance: On and Off the Road with Barack Obama," *The New Yorker*, January 7, 2014. https://www.newyorker.com/magazine/2014/01/27/going-the-distance-david-remnick

CHAPTER ONE: 'This Winter of Our Hardship'

Page 21 **"Is it too late to ask for"** Brian Abrams, *Obama: An Oral History: 2009-2017*, p. 51.

Page 22 **"That was a formative event"** Peter Baker, "The White House Looks For Work," *The New York Times Magazine*, Jan. 19, 2011. https://www.nytimes.com/2011/01/23/magazine/23Economy-t.html

Page 22 **"This was not your father's"** Ibid.

Page 23 **by more than 36 percent** The Dow Jones Industrial Average fell from 12,650 at the start of 2008 to 8,000 at the end of the year for a drop of 36.8 percent. https://finance.yahoo.com/quote/^DJI/history?period1=1199163600&period2=1230872400&interval=1mo&filter=history&frequency=1mo The S&P 500 fell from 1,379 to 826 for a 40 percent drop. https://finance.yahoo.com/quote/^GSPC/history?period1=1199163600&period2=1230872400&interval=1mo&filter=history&frequency=1mo

Page 53 **fell by 55 percent** West Texas crude oil prices fell from $109.73 per barrel in January 2008 to $49.85 per barrel in January 2009. https://www.macrotrends.net/1369/crude-oil-price-history-chart

Page 24 **"Mr. President-elect, this is"** Michael Grunwald, *The New New Deal*, p. 114.

Page 25 **"You never want a serious"** Rahm Emanuel, speaking at a Wall Street Journal conference, November 2008. https://www.youtube.com/watch?v=1yeA_kHHLow

Page 25 **"Your accomplishment is"** Timothy Geithner, *Stress Test*, pp. 258-59.

Page 26 **"I want to pull the Band-Aid"** Baker, "White House Looks For Work."

Page 26 **"How cold do you think"** Reggie Love, *Power Forward*, p. 147.

Page 26 **"For people that look like me"** Peter Baker, "Obama's First Term: A Romantic Oral History," *The New York Times Magazine*, Jan. 16, 2013. https://www.nytimes.com/2013/01/20/magazine/obamas-first-term-oral-history.html

Page 27 **"this winter of our hardship"** Barack Obama, Inaugural Address, January 20, 2009. Online by Gerhard Peters and John T. Woolley, The American Presidency Project. http://www.presidency.ucsb.edu/ws/index.php?pid=44

Page 27 **"Now there are some who"** Ibid.

Page 27 **"I think I could probably"** David Ploufffe, *The Audacity to Win*, p. 8.

Page 27 **"I think I'm a better"** Ryan Lizza, "Battle Plans: How Obama Won," *The New Yorker*, November 17, 2008. Obama said this to Patrick Gaspard, who went on to become his White House political director and later ambassador to South Africa. https://www.newyorker.com/magazine/2008/11/17/battle-plans

Page 28 **"Eccentric in many ways"** Barack Obama, Interview with David Axelrod on CNN's "The Axe Files," December 26, 2016. Online by Gerhard Peters and John T. Woolley, The American Presidency Project. https://www.presidency.ucsb.edu/node/331720

Page 29 **"There's not a liberal America"** Barack Obama, Keynote Address, Democratic National Convention, July 27, 2004. Online by Gerhard Peters and John T. Woolley, The American Presidency Project. http://www.presidency.ucsb.edu/ws/index.php?pid=76988

Page 30 **"a solitude-loving individualist"** Michelle Obama, *Becoming*, p. 171.

Page 30 **"The only way we'll succeed"** Robert Draper, *Do Not Ask What Good We Do*, p. xviii.

Page 31 **"that I will execute the office"** Jeff Zeleny, "I Really Do Swear, Faithfully: Obama and Roberts Try Again," *The New York Times*, January 21, 2009. https://www.nytimes.com/2009/01/22/us/politics/22oath.html

Page 31 **"my fault"** Ibid.

Page 32 **"Are you ready to take"** Ibid.

Page 33 **failed to pay $128,000** Robert Pear, "Daschle Pays 3 Years of Tax on Use of Car," *The New York Times*, January 30, 2009. https://www.nytimes.com/2009/01/31/us/politics/31daschle.html

Page 33 **"screwed up"** "Obama: 'I Screwed Up' in Daschle Withdrawal," NBC News, February 3, 2009. http://www.nbcnews.com/id/28994296/ns/politics-white_house/t/obama-i-screwed-daschle-withdrawal/#.W8gduC-ZOgQ

Page 33 **owed $34,000 in back taxes** Jackie Calmes, "Geithner Questioned on Tax Returns," *The New York Times*, January 13, 2009. https://www.nytimes.com/2009/01/14/us/politics/14geithner.html

Page 34 **"The number of people"** Peter Baker, "The Education of a President," *The New York Times Magazine*, October 12, 2010. https://www.nytimes.com/2010/10/17/magazine/17obama-t.html

Page 34 **"irresolvable conflicts"** Jeff Zeleny, "Gregg Ends Bid for Commerce Job," *The New York Times*, February 12, 2009. https://www.nytimes.com/2009/02/13/us/politics/13gregg.html

Page 34 **"Where the fuck is our"** Abrams, *Obama*, p. 59.

Page 35 **"kicking and screaming"** Rachel L. Swarns, "An In-Law Is Finding Washington To Her Liking," *The New York Times*, May 3, 2009. https://www.nytimes.com/2009/05/04/us/politics/04robinson.html

Page 35 **"we live above the store"** Peter Baker, "Personal Tack by Obama in an Effort to Aid Parents," *The New York Times*, June 23, 2014. https://www.nytimes.com/2014/06/24/us/budgets-schools-dissent-parenting-is-hard-work.html

Page 35 **bleeding 700,000 jobs** The economy lost more than 700,000 jobs each month from November 2008 to April 2009. Bureau of Labor Statistics. https://data.bls.gov/timeseries/CES0000000001?output_view=net_1mth

Page 36 **would rise to 9 percent** Christina Romer and Jared Bernstein, "The Job Impact of the American Recovery and Reinvestment Plan," January 9, 2009. https://www.economy.com/mark-zandi/documents/The_Job_Impact_of_the_American_Recovery_and_Reinvestment_Plan.pdf

Page 37 **"Elections have consequences"** Peter Baker, "Obama's Odds With Congress: Bad to Worse," *The New York Times*, June 12, 2014. https://www.nytimes. com/2014/06/13/us/obamas-odds-with-congress-bad-to-worse.html

Page 37 **"We just have a difference"** Jackie Calmes and David M. Herszenhorn, "Obama Pressing For a Quick Jolt to the Economy," *The New York Times*, January 23, 2009. https://www.nytimes.com/2009/01/24/us/politics/24stimulus.html

Page 37 **"This shit's not on the level"** David Axelrod, *Believer*, p. 354.

Page 38 **1,073-page bill as "Porkulus"** Grunwald, *New New Deal*, p. 8.

Page 39 **The House passed** The plan passed, 246 to 183, with every yes vote coming from Democrats and seven Democrats joining 176 Republicans in voting no. House Clerk. http://clerk.house.gov/evs/2009/roll070.xml

Page 39 **The Senate concurred** The Senate approved it, 60 to 38, with three Republicans, Senators Olympia Snowe and Susan Collins of Maine and Arlen Specter of Pennsylvania, joining fifty-seven Democrats voting for it. United States Senate. https://www.senate.gov/legislative/LIS/roll_call_lists/roll_call_vote_cfm.cfm?congress=111&session=1&vote=00064

Page 39 **twice as big as the expense** Grunwald, *New New Deal*, p. 10.

CHAPTER TWO: 'The Hardest Option'

Page 40 **"Why can't the American car"** Quoted by Brian Deese. Brian Abrams, *Obama: An Oral History 2009-2017*, p. 56.

Page 40 **worst monthly sales** Jim Rutenberg, Peter Baker and Bill Vlasic, "Early Resolve: Obama Stand in Auto Crisis," *The New York Times*, April 28, 2009. https://www.nytimes.com/2009/04/29/us/politics/29decide.html

Page 41 **"failure to adapt to changing"** Ibid.

Page 41 **fell from 16.2 million in 2007** Thomas H. Klier and James Rubenstein, "Detroit Back from the Brink? Auto Industry Crisis and Restructuring, 2008-11," *Economic Perspectives*, Federal Reserve Bank of Chicago, 2012 pp. 35-36.

Page 42 **"I know that"** Rutenberg, Baker and Vlasic, "Early Resolve."

Page 42 **"Where's Goolsbee?"** Steven Rattner, *Overhaul*, p. 129.

Page 42 **plummeting from $70 a share** Neil King Jr. and John D. Stoll, "Government Forces Out Wagoner at GM," *The Wall Street Journal*, March 30, 2009. https://www.wsj.com/articles/SB123836090755767077

Page 43 **"What is this, a *West Wing*"** Rutenberg, Baker and Vlasic, "Early Resolve."

Page 43 **unemployment of 18 percent** Rattner, *Overhaul*, p. 132.

Page 43 **"You're always explaining"** Jonathan Alter, *The Promise*, p. 179.

Page 44 **"All the advisers were divided"** Peter Baker, "Obama's First Term: A Romantic Oral History," *The New York Times Magazine*, Jan. 16, 2013. https://www.nytimes.com/2013/01/20/magazine/obamas-first-term-oral-history.html

Page 44 **"Whatever you do, sir"** Quoted by Gene Sperling. Abrams, *Obama*, pp. 105-06.

Page 45 **pay back the vast majority** The Treasury Department estimated in January 2015 that the automakers paid back all but $9.3 billion of the $80 billion loaned under Presidents Bush and Obama, or 88 percent. https://www.treasury.gov/initiatives/financial-stability/TARP-Programs/automotive-programs/pages/default.aspx

Page 45 **"Look, I wish I had the luxury"** Transcript, "Obama's Interview Aboard Air Force One," *The New York Times*, March 7, 2009. https://www.nytimes.com/2009/03/08/us/politics/08obama-text.html

Page 46 **"It was hard for me to believe"** Ibid.

Page 47 **"Luis, I'm going to assign"** Abrams, *Obama*, p. 102.

Page 48 **"I would hope that a wise"** Charlie Savage, "A Judge's View of Judging Is on the Record," *The New York Times*, May 14, 2009. https://www.nytimes.com/2009/05/15/us/15judge.html

Page 48 **"court of appeals is where"** Ibid.

Page 49 **confirmed Sotomayor, 68 to 31** Nine Republicans joined every Democrat present in voting to confirm, while thirty-one Republicans voted no. United States Senate. August 6, 2009. https://www.congress.gov/nomination/111th-congress/506

Page 49 **"We just put the first Latina"** Baker, "Obama's First Term."

Page 49 **"He was frustrated because"** Ibid.

Page 50 **More than 45 million** Ian Urbina, "A Decline in Uninsured Is Reported for 2007," *The New York Times*, August 26, 2008. https://www.nytimes.com/2008/08/27/washington/27census.html

Page 50 **"I understand the risks"** David Axelrod, *Believer*, p. 372.

Page 52 **"If we're able to stop Obama"** Alter, *Promise*, p. 263.

Page 52 **"They suspect that this is"** Axelrod, *Believer*, p. 377.

Page 53 **"I've got one television station"** "Text: Obama Interview with John Harwood," *The New York Times*, June 16, 2009. At the time, Harwood also wrote for *The Times*. https://www.nytimes.com/2009/06/16/us/politics/16harwood.text.html

Page 54 **"has a deep-seated hatred"** Michael Calderone, "Fox's Beck: Obama is 'a Racist,'" *Politico*, July 28, 2009. https://www.politico.com/blogs/michaelcalderone/0709/Foxs_Beck_Obama_is_a_racist.html

Page 54 **"Obammunism is Communism"** Michael Tomasky, "Something New on the Mall," *The New York Review of Books*, October 22, 2009. https://www.nybooks.com/articles/2009/10/22/something-new-on-the-mall/

Page 54 **"young and pissed and looking"** Dan Pfeiffer, *Yes We (Still) Can*, p. 154.

Page 54 **"We're going to treat them"** Brian Stelter, "Fox's Volley With Obama Intensifying," *The New York Times*, October 2009. https://www.nytimes.com/2009/10/12/business/media/12fox.html

Page 54 **"not really a news station"** David Axelrod, *This Week with George Stephanopoulos*, ABC News, October 18, 2009. https://abcnews.go.com/ThisWeek/Politics/transcript-axelrod/story?id=8846323

Page 54 **"not a news organization"** Mike Allen, "Fox 'Not Really News,' Says Axelrod," *Politico*, October 18, 2009. https://www.politico.com/story/2009/10/fox-not-really-news-says-axelrod-028417

Page 55 **"I am putting some dead fish"** Paul Bedard, "Emails Show Obama Effort to Blackball Fox," *U.S. News & World Report*, July 14, 2011. https://www.usnews.com/news/blogs/washington-whispers/2011/07/14/e-mails-show-obama-effort-to-blackball-fox

Page 55 **"this fight was a mistake"** Pfeiffer, *Yes We (Still) Can*, p. 157.

Page 55 **"And while I will not see"** Edward M. Kennedy, letter to Barack Obama, May 12, 2009. Obama White House archive. https://obamawhitehouse.archives.gov/health-care-in-america

Page 56 **"That means a lot of this"** Baker, "Obama's First Term."

Page 56 **"So can we do this?"** Senior White House official, author interview.

Page 56 **"You lie!"** Carl Hulse, "In Lawmaker's Outburst, a Rare Breach of Protocol," *The New York Times*, September 9, 2009. https://www.nytimes.com/2009/09/10/us/politics/10wilson.html

Page 56 **220 to 215, just two votes** Just one Republican, Representative Joseph Cao of Louisiana, voted yes, while thirty-nine Democrats voted no. Final Vote Results for Roll Call 887, Affordable Care for America Act, November 7, 2009. House Clerk. http://clerk.house.gov/evs/2009/roll887.xml

Page 57 **"There's a constant tension"** Peter Baker, "The Limits of Rahmism," *The New York Times Magazine*, March 8, 2010. https://www.nytimes.com/2010/03/14/magazine/14emanuel-t.html

Page 58 **"We were this close"** David Plouffe, *The Audacity to Win*, p. 388.

Page 58 **"Their bumper sticker has"** Alter, *Promise*, p. 420.

Page 59 **return to the "core elements"** Karen Travers, "Exclusive: President Obama Says Voter Anger, Frustration Key to Republican Victory in Massachusetts Senate," ABC News, January 10, 2010. https://abcnews.go.com/Nightline/Politics/abc-news-george-stephanopoulos-exclusive-interview-president-obama/story?id=9611223

Page 59 **"I don't quit"** Barack Obama: Address Before a Joint Session of the Congress on the State of the Union, January 27, 2010. Online by Gerhard Peters and John T. Woolley, The American Presidency Project. http://www.presidency.ucsb.edu/ws/index.php?pid=87433

Page 60 **"Hand-to-hand combat"** Baker, "Limits of Rahmism."

Page 60 **"A heat-seeking missile"** Ibid.

Page 60 **"Undersecretary for Go Fuck"** Ryan Lizza, "The Gatekeeper," *The New Yorker*, March 2, 2009. https://www.newyorker.com/magazine/2009/03/02/the-gatekeeper

Page 60 **"He's a Malcolm X Democrat"** Baker, "Limits of Rahmism."

Page 60 **questioning Emanuel's team** Ed Luce, "America: A Fearsome Foursome," *The Financial Times*, February 3, 2010. https://www.ft.com/content/b6b4700a-10fb-11df-9a9e-00144feab49a

Page 60 **slam by the blogger Steve** Steve Clemons, "Core Chicago Team Sinking Obama Presidency," *The Huffington Post*, April 9, 2010. (*The Huffington Post* changed its name to *HuffPost* in 2017.) https://www.huffingtonpost.com/steve-clemons/core-chicago-team-sinking_b_452664.html

Page 60 **"Replace Rahm"** Leslie H. Gelb, "Replace Rahm," *The Daily Beast*, February 2, 2010. https://www.thedailybeast.com/replace-rahm

Page 61 **the real problem was not** Dana Milbank, "Why Obama Needs Rahm at the Top," *The Washington Post*, February 21, 2010. http://www.washingtonpost.com/wp-dyn/content/article/2010/02/19/AR2010021904298.html

Page 61 **"You're not resigning"** Axelrod, *Believer*, p. 386.

Page 61 **"The American people are"** Robert Pear and David M. Herszenhorn, "Obama Hails Vote on Health Care as Answering 'the Call of History,'" *The New York Times,* March 21, 2010. https://www.nytimes.com/2010/03/22/health/policy/22health.html

Page 61 **"fiscal Frankenstein"** Ibid.

Page 61 **"one of the most offensive"** Ibid.

Page 62 **"This is what change looks"** Barack Obama, Remarks on House of Representatives *Passage of Health Care Reform Legislation, March 21, 2010. Online by Gerhard* Peters and John T. Woolley, The American Presidency Project. http://www.presidency.ucsb.edu/ws/index.php?pid=87654

Page 62 **This is better then Election Day** Baker, "Obama's First Term."

Page 62 **"they're going to kick our asses"** Mark Halperin and John Heilemann, *Double Down,* p. 13.

Page 62 **"this is a big fucking deal"** John Dickerson, "WTF Did Biden Just Say: A Brief History of Bad Language in Washington," *Slate,* March 23, 2010. https://slate.com/news-and-politics/2010/03/wtf-did-biden-just-say-a-brief-history-of-bad-language-in-washington.html

Page 63 **issue about $165 million** Edmund L. Andrews and Peter Baker, "A.I.G. Planning Huge Bonuses After $170 Billion Bailout," *The New York Times,* March 14, 2009. https://www.nytimes.com/2009/03/15/business/15AIG.html

Page 64 **"Well, it took us a couple of days"** Peter Baker and Adam Nagourney, "In a Volatile Time, Obama Strikes a New Tone," *The New York Times,* March 24, 2009. https://www.nytimes.com/2009/03/25/us/politics/25obama.html

Page 64 **"malefactors of great wealth"** Address of President Roosevelt on the Occasion of the Laying of the Corner Stone of the Pilgrim Memorial Monument, Provincetown, Mass., August 20, 1907. Government Printing Office. https://archive.org/stream/addressofpreside00roo/addressofpreside00roo_djvu.txt

Page 64 **"unanimous in their hate for me"** Franklin Roosevelt's Address Announcing the Second New Deal, October 31, 1936. Franklin D. Roosevelt Presidential Library and Museum. http://docs.fdrlibrary.marist.edu/od2ndst.html

Page 65 **"fat cat bankers"** Obama said this during an interview with Steve Kroft for *60 Minutes* on CBS. Brian Montopoli, "Obama Versus the 'Fat Cats,'" CBS News, December 13, 2009. https://www.cbsnews.com/news/obama-versus-the-fat-cats/

Page 66 **"conservatorship approach"** Timothy Geithner, *Stress Test,* p. 319.

Page 66 **"rapid resolution exit"** Ibid.

Page 66 **"You can't say we're dove"** Ibid., p. 320.

Page 67 **"I'm going to get a haircut"** Axelrod, *Believer,* pp. 358.

Page 67 **"all hell broke loose"** Ibid.

Page 67 **"What are you talking about"** Geithner, *Stress Test,* p. 322.

Page 67 **"Well, that's no good"** Axelrod, *Believer,* pp. 358-59.

Page 67 **"Be careful how you make"** Eamon Javers, "Inside Obama's Bank CEOs Meeting," *Politico,* April 3, 2009. https://www.politico.com/story/2009/04/inside-obamas-bank-ceos-meeting-020871

Page 67 **nine were in such good shape** Board of Governors of Federal Reserve System,

"The Supervisory Capital Assessment Program: Overview of Results," May 7, 2009. https://www.federalreserve.gov/newsevents/files/bcreg20090507a1.pdf

Page 69 **"Because of this law"** Helene Cooper, "Obama Signs Overhaul of Financial System," *The New York Times,* July 21, 2010. https://www.nytimes.com/2010/07/22/business/22regulate.html

CHAPTER THREE: 'Bring Our Troops Home'

Page 70 **"I don't want to be going"** Peter Baker, "How Obama Came to Plan for 'Surge' in Afghanistan," *The New York Times,* December 5, 2009. https://www.nytimes.com/2009/12/06/world/asia/06reconstruct.html

Page 71 **"problems that need managing"** Peter Baker, "For Obama, Steep Learning Curve as Chief in War," *The New York Times,* August 28, 2010. https://www.nytimes.com/2010/08/29/world/29commander.html

Page 71 **"He's got a very full plate"** Ibid.

Page 72 **"He's really the first generation"** Ibid.

Page 72 **"Come on, guys, you don't"** Ibid.

Page 72 **Republican gray-haired "geezer"** Robert Gates, *Duty,* p. 287.

Page 74 **"We will complete this"** Barack Obama, Remarks on Military Operations in Iraq at Camp Lejeune, North Carolina, February 27, 2009. Online by Gerhard Peters and John T. Woolley, *The American Presidency Project.* http://www.presidency.ucsb.edu/ws/index.php?pid=85807

Page 75 **"I came closer to resigning"** Gates, *Duty,* p. 363.

Page 76 **"I can only conclude one"** David Axelrod, *Believer,* p. 394.

Page 76 **"between a college professor"** Baker, "How Obama Came to Plan for 'Surge' in Afghanistan."

Page 77 **"I've got more deeply in the"** Ibid.

Page 78 **One assistant secretary of state** Jonathan Alter, *The Promise,* p. 232.

Page 78 **"like two teenagers on an"** Hillary Clinton, *Hard Choices,* p. 3.

Page 78 **"I heard on the radio"** Peter Baker and Steve Eder, "New Trove of Hillary Clinton's Emails Highlights Workaday Tasks at the State Department," *The New York Times,* June 20, 2015. https://www.nytimes.com/2015/07/01/us/politics/new-trove-of-hillary-clintons-emails-highlight-workaday-tasks-at-the-state-department.html

Page 78 **"This is the second time"** Ibid.

Page 79 **"Richard, I've said no"** Clinton, *Hard Choices,* p. 139.

Page 79 **"The ego has landed"** Manuel Roig-Franzia, "Richard Holbrooke Memorial Events in Washington a Testament to Diplomat's Reach," *The Washington Post,* January 14, 2011. https://www.washingtonpost.com/lifestyle/style/richard-holbrooke-memorial-events-in-washington-a-testament-to-diplomats-reach/2011/01/14/ABYWHWR_story.html?utm_term=.7f730ae8554c

Page 79 **Colin Powell and John Podesta** Peter Baker, "Emails Show Hillary Clinton Trying to Find Her Place," *The New York Times,* July 1, 2015. https://www.nytimes.com/2015/07/02/us/politics/emails-show-hillary-clinton-trying-to-find-her-place.html

Page 79 **"Secret Service spotted Richard"** Mike Allen, "Obama's Top 10 Quips From Dinner," *Politico*, June 20, 2009. https://www.politico.com/story/2009/06/obamas-top-10-quips-from-dinner-023966

Page 79 **"the most egotistical bastard"** Woodward, *Obama's War*, p. 72.

Page 79 **"Not since Clark Clifford"** Mark Landler, *Alter Egos*, pp. 75-76.

Page 80 **"the water bugs" or "the Politburo"** Woodward, *Obama's War*, p. 138.

Page 80 **would be a "disaster"** Ibid., p. 343.

Page 80 **"a complete spin doctor"** Ibid., p. 158.

Page 80 **"Why is this whole thing"** Ben Rhodes, *The World As It Is*, pp. 76-77.

Page 82 **"a crime syndicate"** Baker, "How Obama Came to Plan for 'Surge' in Afghanistan."

Page 82 **"is not an adequate strategic"** Karl Eikenberry, "COIN Strategy: Civilian Concerns," November 9, 2009. https://www.nytimes.com/interactive/projects/documents/eikenberry-s-memos-on-the-strategy-in-afghanistan#p=1

Page 82 **"There are ten ways this can"** David Sanger, *Confront and Conceal*, p. 31.

Page 82 **"The Petraeus surge was much"** Rhodes, *World As It Is*, pp. 76-77

Page 83 **"Max Leverage"** Baker, "How Obama Came to Plan for 'Surge' in Afghanistan."

Page 83 **"I'm not asking you to change"** Ibid.

Page 84 **"They're so young"** Rhodes, *World As It Is*, p. 80.

Page 84 **"If I did not think that the"** Barack Obama, "Remarks at the United States Military Academy at West Point, New York," December 1, 2009. Online by Gerhard Peters and John T. Woolley, The American Presidency Project. http://www.presidency.ucsb.edu/ws/index.php?pid=86948

Page 85 **the strategy "can't work"** Woodward, *Obama's Wars*, p. 333.

Page 85 **review did not "add up"** Ibid., p. 338.

Page 85 **"I have to say that"** Ibid., p. 336.

Page 86 **"As someone who stands here"** Barack Obama, Remarks on Accepting the Nobel Peace Prize in Oslo, December 10, 2009. Online by Gerhard Peters and John T. Woolley, The American Presidency Project. http://www.presidency.ucsb.edu/ws/index.php?pid=86978

Page 87 **"extraordinary efforts to"** Barack H. Obama – Facts. NobelPrize.org. Nobel Media AB 2018. https://www.nobelprize.org/prizes/peace/2009/obama/facts/

Page 87 **"To be honest"** Barack Obama, Remarks on Winning the Nobel Peace Prize, October 9, 2009. Online by Gerhard Peters and John T. Woolley, The American Presidency Project. http://www.presidency.ucsb.edu/ws/index.php?pid=86740

Page 87 **"The real question Americans"** Steven Erlanger and Sheryl Gay Stolberg, "Surprise Nobel for Obama Stirs Praise and Doubts," *The New York Times*, October 9, 2009. https://www.nytimes.com/2009/10/10/world/10nobel.html

Page 87 **"item of interest"** Ibid.

Page 87 **"Gibbs, what the hell"** Axelrod, *Believer*, p. 401.

Page 88 **"I'd like to believe that winning"** Adam Nagourney, "For Presidency in Search of Success, Nobel Add a Twist," *The New York Times*, October 9, 2009. https://www.nytimes.com/2009/10/10/us/politics/10assess.html

Page 89 **"He was deliberate to a fault"** Joe Biden, *Promise Me, Dad*, p. 71.

Page 90 **"My position was this is not"** Baker, "For Obama, Steep Learning Curve as Chief in War."

Page 90 **"That was a degree of"** Robert Gates, author interview.

Page 90 **"I'm really disgusted with this"** Gates, *Duty*, p. 384.

Page 90 **"May 2010 is looking a lot"** Ibid.

Page 91 **"Stanley McChrystal, Obama's"** Michael Hastings, "The Runaway General," *Rolling Stone*, June 22, 2010. https://www.rollingstone.com/politics/politics-news/the-runaway-general-the-profile-that-brought-down-mcchrystal-192609/

Page 91 **"What the fuck were you"** Gates, *Duty*, p. 487.

Page 91 **"Joe is over the top"** Ibid., 487-88.

Page 92 **"I believe if we lose McChrystal"** Ibid.

Page 92 **"short, professional meeting"** Stanley McChrystal, *My Share of the Task*, p. 388.

Page 92 **"I welcome debate"** Barack Obama, Remarks on the Resignation of General Stanley A. McChrystal as Commander of the NATO International Security Assistance Force in Afghanistan, June 23, 2010. Online by Gerhard Peters and John T. Woolley, *The American Presidency Project*. http://www.presidency.ucsb.edu/ws/index.php?pid=88088

Page 93 **"The primary concern"** Vali Nasr, *The Dispensable Nation*, p. 2.

Page 93 **a long piece in *The New Yorker*** George Packer, "The Last Mission: Richard Holbrooke's Plan to Avoid the Mistakes of Vietnam in Afghanistan," *The New Yorker*, September 28, 2009. https://www.newyorker.com/magazine/2009/09/28/the-last-mission

Page 93 **"he needs to tell me himself"** Clinton, *Hard Choices*, p. 141.

Page 93 **"over the objection of your"** Rajiv Chandarsekaran, *Little America*, p. 240.

Page 94 **"Ending the war in Afghanistan"** Jonathan Alter and Christopher Dickey, *The Daily Beast*, January 14, 2011. https://www.thedailybeast.com/inside-holbrookes-war-with-the-white-house See also Rajiv Chandrasekaran and Karen DeYoung, "Holbrooke Mentioned Afghan War Before Surgery," *The Washington Post*, December 14, 2010. http://www.washingtonpost.com/wp-dyn/content/story/2010/12/13/ST2010121305455.html?sid=ST2010121305455&tid=a_inl_manual

Page 94 **"I never did understand"** Transcript of CNN coverage of memorial service, January 14, 2011. http://www.cnn.com/TRANSCRIPTS/1101/14/cnr.08.html

Page 95 **"I'm sick of people writing"** Landler, *Alter Egos*, p. 98.

CHAPTER FOUR: 'Time to Turn the Page'

Page 97 **"isolated extremist"** Peter Baker, "Obama's War Over Terror," *The New York Times Magazine*, January 4, 2010. https://www.nytimes.com/2010/01/17/magazine/17Terror-t.html

Page 97 **"the system worked"** Peter Baker, "A Phrase Sets Off Sniping After a Crisis," *The New York Times*, December 29, 2009. https://www.nytimes.com/2009/12/30/us/politics/30baker.html

Page 97 **"Let me make this very"** Baker, "Obama's War Over Terror."

Page 97 **"What's the deal?"** Ibid.

Page 97 **"systemic failure"** Barack Obama, Remarks in Kaneohe, December 29, 2009. Online by Gerhard Peters and John T. Woolley, The American Presidency Project. http://www.presidency.ucsb.edu/ws/index.php?pid=69600

Page 97 **"The fact that this guy came"** Peter Baker, "Obama's Path From Critic to Overseer of Spying," *The New York Times*, January 15, 2014. https://www.nytimes.com/2014/01/16/us/obamas-path-from-critic-to-defender-of-spying.html

Page 98 **the "mood music"** Baker, "Obama's War Over Terror."

Page 98 **"You've got almost two extremes"** Ibid.

Page 99 **"Up and down the streets"** Barack Obama, *The Audacity of Hope*, p. 291.

Page 99 **"It is time to turn the page"** Barack Obama, Remarks in Washington, DC: "The War We Need to Win," August 1, 2007. Online by Gerhard Peters and John T. Woolley, The American Presidency Project. http://www.presidency.ucsb.edu/ws/index.php?pid=77040

Page 100 **"welcome-to-the-NBA"** Baker, "Obama's Path From Critic to Overseer of Spying."

Page 101 **"The language we use matters"** Barack Obama, Interview with Hisham Melhem of Al Arabiya, January 27, 2009. Online by Gerhard Peters and John T. Woolley, The American Presidency Project. http://www.presidency.ucsb.edu/ws/index.php?pid=85891

Page 101 **"man-caused disasters"** David Johnston, "Homeland Security Nominee Vows to Safeguard the Country, but Offers Few Specifics," *The New York Times*, January 15, 2009. https://www.nytimes.com/2009/01/16/us/16napolitano.html

Page 103 **"The CIA gets what it needs"** Baker, "Obama's War Over Terror."

Page 103 **"I would distinguish between"** Ibid.

Page 103 **"Look, you're the only"** Ibid.

Page 104 **"Hunt one head and hunt it"** Jodi Kantor, *The Obamas*, p. 108.

Page 104 **"The administration came in"** Baker, "Obama's War Over Terror."

Page 105 **"In the fight against terrorism"** Peter Baker, "Obama Faces Pitfalls on Detainees," *The New York Times*, May 21, 2009. https://www.nytimes.com/2009/05/22/us/22assess.html

Page 106 **"against the Islamic Empire"** Manny Fernandez, "Fort Hood Gunman Told Panel That Death Would Make Him a Martyr," *The New York Times*, August 12, 2010. https://www.nytimes.com/2013/08/13/us/fort-hood-gunman-told-panel-that-death-would-make-him-a-martyr.html

Page 106 **"It may be hard to comprehend"** Barack Obama, Remarks at a Memorial Service at Fort Hood, Texas, November 10, 2009. Online by Gerhard Peters and John T. Woolley, The American Presidency Project. http://www.presidency.ucsb.edu/ws/index.php?pid=86870

Page 107 **"martyrdom operation"** A.G. Sulzberger and William K. Rashbaum, "Guilty Plea Made in Plot to Bomb New York Subway," *The New York Times*, February 22, 2010. https://www.nytimes.com/2010/02/23/nyregion/23terror.html

Page 108 **"Our nation is at war"** Barack Obama, The President's Weekly Address,

January 2, 2010. Online by Gerhard Peters and John T. Woolley, The American Presidency Project. http://www.presidency.ucsb.edu/ws/index.php?pid=87368

Page 110 **"one foot in the old ways"** Jennifer Loven, "Putin Has 'One Foot in Old Ways,' Obama Says," Associated Press, July 2, 2009.

Page 110 **"When Putin ranted about the"** Michael McFaul, *From Cold War to Hot Peace*, p. 133.

Page 111 **"We won't let you do that"** Mark Landler, "Lost in Translation: A U.S. Gift to Russia," *The New York Times*, March 6, 2009. https://www.nytimes.com/2009/03/07/world/europe/07diplo.html

Page 111 **"I saw him genuinely angry"** McFaul, *From Cold War to Hot Peace*, p. 150.

Page 112 **"Today is an important"** Peter Baker and Dan Bilefsky, "Russia and U.S. Sign Nuclear Arms Reduction Pact," *The New York Times*, April 8, 2010. https://www.nytimes.com/2010/04/09/world/europe/09prexy.html

Page 112 **called it a "win-win"** Ibid.

Page 113 **"Did you plug the hole yet?"** Barack Obama, The President's News Conference, May 27, 2010. Online by Gerhard Peters and John T. Woolley, The American Presidency Project. http://www.presidency.ucsb.edu/ws/index.php?pid=87963

Page 114 **"He just looks like he is not"** Peter Baker, "Responding to Spill, Obama Mixes Regret With Resolve," *The New York Times*, May 27, 2010. https://www.nytimes.com/2010/05/28/us/28obama.html

Page 114 **"I know how to run big projects"** David Axelrod, *Believer*, p. 419.

Page 114 **"was wrong" to assume** Obama, The President's News Conference.

Page 115 **"guide us through the storm"** Barack Obama, Press Release: Address to the Nation on the BP Oil Spill - As Prepared for Delivery, June 15, 2010. Online by Gerhard Peters and John T. Woolley, The American Presidency Project. http://www.presidency.ucsb.edu/ws/index.php?pid=90002

CHAPTER FIVE: 'Sleepless Nights'

Page 116 **"I didn't get picked?"** Jodi Kantor, *The Obamas*, p. 245.

Page 116 **"this instinct of being a killer"** Jonathan Alter, *The Promise*, p. 305.

Page 117 **"the only guy who ever hit"** Stan Grossfeld, "Man Who Roughed Up Obama Finally Speaks," *The Boston Globe*, May 6, 2013. https://www.bostonglobe.com/sports/2013/05/05/reynaldo-decerega-barack-obama-and-the-elbow/UYx-4MnNgrbis5OwiZQqGZO/story.html

Page 117 **set out to write about** Mark Leibovich, "Man's World at White House? No Harm, No Foul, Aides Say," *The New York Times*, October 24, 2009. https://www.nytimes.com/2009/10/25/us/politics/25vibe.html

Page 118 **"Dear Jackass" or "Dear Socialist"** Eli Saslow, *Ten Letters*, p. 4.

Page 118 **"I will tell you, my staff"** Ibid.

Page 119 **"I want them to understand"** Kantor, *Obamas*, p. 228.

Page 119 **"I'm going home"** Rachel L. Swarns, "An In-Law Is Finding Washington To Her Liking," *The New York Times*, May 3, 2009. https://www.nytimes.com/2009/05/04/us/politics/04robinson.html

Page 120 **"like a wind that threatened"** Michelle Obama, *Becoming*, p. 105.

Page 120 **"You only think about yourself"** Barack Obama, *The Audacity of Hope*, p. 340.

Page 120 **"It was if at the center"** Michelle Obama, *Becoming*, pp. 205-06.

Page 120 **"Each one had put a little dent"** Ibid., p. 223.

Page 120 **"angry and tearful"** Ibid., p. 226.

Page 121 **"I would be sleeping on"** Barack Obama, Remarks on Signing the Healthy, Hunger-Free Kids Act of 2010. Online by Gerhard Peters and John T. Woolley, The American Presidency Project https://www.presidency.ucsb.edu/node/289139

Page 121 **"because I'm scared of my wife"** Morgan Little, "Obama Jokes He No Longer Smokes 'Because I'm Scared of My Wife," *Los Angeles Times*, September 14, 2013. http://www.latimes.com/nation/politics/politicsnow/la-pn-obama-smoking-wife-20130924-story.html

Page 122 **"finger-wagging embodiment"** Michelle Obama, *Becoming*, p. 337.

Page 122 **"Who are you dating?"** Reggie Love, *Power Forward*, p. 174.

Page 122 **"I don't want to be Hillary"** Kantor, *Obamas*, p. 114

Page 122 **"pleasant but powerless"** Ibid., p. 82.

Page 123 **"If we can't do this being"** Alter, *Promise*, p. 274

Page 123 **"For the first time in my"** Ariel Alexovich, "Blogtalk: Michelle Obama Under Fire," *The New York Times*, February 19, 2008. https://thecaucus.blogs.nytimes.com/2008/02/19/blogtalk-michelle-obama-under-fire/

Page 123 **Michelle was descended from** Rachel L. Swarns and Jodi Kantor, "In First Lady's Roots, a Complex Path From Slavery," *The New York Times*, October 7, 2009. https://www.nytimes.com/2009/10/08/us/politics/08genealogy.html Swarns later followed up with a powerfully researched book about the first lady's roots called *American Tapestry: The Story of the Black, White, and Multicultural Ancestors of Michelle Obama.*

Page 123 **"once charmingly referred"** Peter Baker, "Michelle Obama Talks About Race and Success, and Makes It Personal," *The New York Times*, June 10, 2015. https://www.nytimes.com/2015/06/11/us/michelle-obama-king-college-prep-and-tuskegee-graduation-speeches.html

Page 124 **"modern-day Marie Antoinette"** Andrea Tantaros, "Material Girl Michelle Obama Is a Modern-Day Marie Antoinette On a Glitzy Spanish Vacation," *New York Daily News*, August 5, 2010. http://www.nydailynews.com/opinion/material-girl-michelle-obama-modern-day-marie-antoinette-glitzy-spanish-vacation-article-1.200134

Page 125 **"the optics are just bad"** Michelle Obama, *Becoming*, p. 336.

Page 125 **"It's hell"** Michael D. Shear, "Heavens, No, the First Lady Didn't Say That," *The New York Times*, September 16, 2010. https://thecaucus.blogs.nytimes.com/2010/09/16/heavens-no-the-first-lady-didnt-say-that/

Page 125 **"Don't go there, Robert"** Kantor, *Obamas*, pp. 252-54

Page 125 **"VJ thinks" or "VJ says"** Jo Becker, "The Other Power in the West Wing," *The New York Times*, September 1, 2012. https://www.nytimes.com/2012/09/02/us/politics/valerie-jarrett-is-the-other-power-in-the-west-wing.html

Page 125 **"the night stalker"** Ibid.

Page 125 **"We gossip all the time"** Valerie Jarrett, author interview.

Page 126 **"practically a sister"** Douglas Belkin, "For Obama, Advice Straight Up," *The Wall Street Journal*, May 12, 2008. https://www.wsj.com/articles/SB121055336572783989

Page 126 **"I don't make any major"** Ibid.

Page 126 **"Why on earth would you want"** Valentina Zarya, "How a Dinner Invitation From Michelle Obama Changed Valerie Jarrett's Life," *Fortune*, May 5, 2016. http:// fortune.com/2016/05/05/valerie-jarrett-michelle-obama/

Page 127 **"We know that everything we"** Baker, "Michelle Obama Talks about Race and Success, and Makes It Personal."

Page 128 **"insults and slights"** Ibid.

Page 128 **"reminded of how vulnerable"** Michelle Obama, *Becoming*, p. 354.

Page 129 **"I want them to be normal"** Jodi Kantor, "On a Day That's Anything but Normal, Obama Girls Appear Just That," *The New York Times*, January 21, 2013. https://www.nytimes.com/2013/01/22/us/politics/on-a-day-thats-anything-but-normal-obama-girls-appear-just-that.html

Page 129 **"First African-American president"** Alter, *Promise*, p. 106.

Page 129 **"That was a pretty good speech"** Ibid., p. 108.

Page 130 **"Sasha and Malia are huge fans"** Barack Obama, Remarks at the White House Correspondents' Association Dinner, May 1, 2010. Online by Gerhard Peters and John T. Woolley, The American Presidency Project. http://www.presidency.ucsb.edu/ws/index.php?pid=87828

Page 130 **"try showing a little class"** Julie Hirschfeld Davis, "G.O.P. Aide Quits After Ridiculing Obama's Daughters, Sasha and Malia," *The New York Times*, December 1, 2014. https://www.nytimes.com/2014/12/02/us/gop-aide-quits-after-ridiculing-obamas-daughters.html

Page 130 **"We have one who generally"** Julie Hirschfeld Davis, "In Late Night Appearance, Michelle Obama Dishes on Daughters," *The New York Times*, May 1, 2015. https://www.nytimes.com/politics/first-draft/2015/05/01/in-late-night-appearance-michelle-obama-dishes-on-daughters/

Page 132 **"somehow it'll be tagged as"** Lisa Hirsch, "President Obama on Friendship with George Clooney," *ET*, August 19, 2012. https://www.etonline.com/news/124315_President_Obama_on_Friendship_with_George_Clooney

Page 132 **"Matt Damon said he was"** Barack Obama, Remarks at the White House Correspondents' Association Dinner, April 30, 2011. Online by Gerhard Peters and John T. Woolley, The American Presidency Project. http://www.presidency.ucsb.edu/ws/index.php?pid=90314

Page 132 **"If he wants a job curating"** Gardiner Harris, "President Obama's Emotional Spotify Playlist Is a Hit," *The New York Times*, August 14, 2016. https://www.nytimes.com/2016/08/15/us/politics/president-obama-spotify-playlist.html

Page 133 **"I used to play basketball"** Barack Obama, Interview With Marc Maron for the WTF With Marc Maron Podcast in Highland Park, California, June 19, 2015. Online by Gerhard Peters and John T. Woolley, The American Presidency Project. http://www.presidency.ucsb.edu/ws/index.php?pid=123478

Page 134 **"Can you believe that"** Donald J. Trump, Twitter message, October 13, 2014. https://twitter.com/realdonaldtrump/status/521813597799067648?lang=en

Page 134 **"He's a hack, man"** Jason Horowitz, "From the Bleachers, Jordan Jaws Obama's Swing," *The New York Times*, October 30, 2014. https://www.nytimes.com/politics/first-draft/2014/10/30/?entry=4036&module=inline&mabReward=rel bias%3Aw%2C#123;%221%22%3A%22RI%3A9%22&%23125;

Page 134 **"Had an eighty last week"** Michael S. Schmidt, "Obama Is the Nation's Private Golfer in Chief," *The New York Times*, January 3, 2015. https://www.nytimes.com/2015/01/04/us/politics/obama-the-nations-private-golfer-in-chief.html

Chapter Six: 'A Shellacking'

Page 135 **"Brutal," Obama wrote** David Axelrod, *Believer*, p. 427.

Page 135 **"I'm not recommending for every"** Barack Obama, The President's News Conference, November 3, 2010. Online by Gerhard Peters and John T. Woolley, The American Presidency Project. http://www.presidency.ucsb.edu/ws/index.php?pid=88668

Page 136 **It was his "responsibility"** Ibid.

Page 136 **"We didn't realize how deep"** Peter Baker, "Obama's First Term: A Romantic Oral History," *The New York Times Magazine*, Jan. 16, 2013. https://www.nytimes.com/2013/01/20/magazine/obamas-first-term-oral-history.html

Page 136 **"'Arrogance' isn't the right word"** Peter Baker, "Education of a President," *The New York Times Magazine*, October 12, 2010. https://www.nytimes.com/2010/10/17/magazine/17obama-t.html

Page 136 **"You felt like you were finally"** Baker, "Obama's First Term."

Page 137 **actually hit 10 percent in October** Bureau of Labor Statistics. https://data.bls.gov/timeseries/LNS14000000

Page 137 **slid to 43 percent in August** His approval rating reached that level in two back-to-back polls in August, taken August 16-22 and August 23-29. Gallup Poll. https://news.gallup.com/poll/116479/barack-obama-presidential-job-approval.aspx

Page 137 **"History never precisely repeats"** Baker, "Education of a President."

Page 138 **"tactical lessons"** Ibid.

Page 138 **"the inevitable theater of"** Ibid.

Page 139 **"Given how much stuff was"** Ibid.

Page 139 **Even the artist who made the** Shepard Fairey, the artist, Aamer Madhani, *National Journal*, September 2010. http://hotlineoncall.nationaljournal.com/archives/2010/09/shepard_fairey.php

Page 140 **"They're not always happy"** Barack Obama, Remarks at Laborfest in Milwaukee, Wisconsin, September 6, 2010. Online by Gerhard Peters and John T. Woolley, The American Presidency Project. http://www.presidency.ucsb.edu/ws/index.php?pid=88418

Page 140 **"Democrats just congenitally"** Barack Obama, Remarks at a Democratic National Committee Reception in Greenwich, Connecticut, September 16, 2010. Online by Gerhard Peters and John T. Woolley, The American Presidency Project. http://www.presidency.ucsb.edu/ws/index.php?pid=88460

Page 140 **"I make no apologies for having"** Baker, "Education of a President."

Page 141 **"I like him – in doses"** Mark Halperin and John Heilemann, *Double Down*, p. 61.

Page 142 **"There's a lot to learn from what"** Peter Baker, "If Bill Clinton Were President," *The New York Times*, December 10, 2010. https://www.nytimes.com/2010/12/12/weekinreview/12baker.html

Page 143 **unemployment was at 5.6 percent** Bureau of Labor Statistics. https://data.bls.gov/pdq/SurveyOutputServlet

Page 143 **"The next day he came into"** Baker, "Obama's First Term."

Page 145 **"hostage takers"** Barack Obama, The President's News Conference, December 7, 2010. Online by Gerhard Peters and John T. Woolley, The American Presidency Project. http://www.presidency.ucsb.edu/ws/index.php?pid=88781

Page 145 **"This is the public-option"** Ibid.

Page 145 **some 17,000 service** Sheryl Gay Stolberg, "Obama Signs Away 'Don't Ask, Don't Tell,'" *The New York Times*, December 22, 2010. https://www.nytimes.com/2010/12/23/us/politics/23military.html

Page 146 **A survey of 400,000 service** Report of the Comprehensive Review of the Issues Associated with a Repeal of "Don't Ask, Don't Tell," Department of Defense, November 30, 2010. https://www.washingtonpost.com/wp-srv/special/politics/dont-ask-dont-tell/DADTReport_FINAL.pdf

Page 146 **the final 71-to-26 vote** Three Republican senators did not vote. Senate Clerk's Office. https://www.senate.gov/legislative/LIS/roll_call_lists/roll_call_vote_cfm.cfm?congress=111&session=2&vote=00298

Page 147 **"There was an hour of cheering"** Peter Baker, "Obama's First Term: A Romantic Oral History," *The New York Times Magazine*, Jan. 16, 2013. https://www.nytimes.com/2013/01/20/magazine/obamas-first-term-oral-history.html

Page 147 **"One thing I hope people have"** Barack Obama, The President's News Conference, December 22, 2010. Online by Gerhard Peters and John T. Woolley, The American Presidency Project. http://www.presidency.ucsb.edu/ws/index.php?pid=88852

Page 147 **"I'm worried about that debt"** Baker, "Obama's First Term."

Page 148 **"I've won and I've lost"** Jodi Kantor, *The Obamas*, p. 285.

Page 148 **"They miscalculated on health"** Peter Baker, "The Limits of Rahmism," *The New York Times Magazine*, March 8, 2010. https://www.nytimes.com/2010/03/14/magazine/14emanuel-t.html

Page 149 **"You do not relitigate"** Steven Rattner, *Overhaul*, p. 124.

Page 150 **"I think the environment often"** Peter Baker, "The White House Looks For Work," *The New York Times Magazine*, January 11, 2011. https://www.nytimes.com/2011/01/23/magazine/23Economy-t.html

Page 150 **"Don't Retreat, Instead – Reload!"** Sarah Palin, Twitter message, March 23, 2010. https://twitter.com/sarahpalinusa/status/10935548053?lang=en

Page 150 **"At a time when our discourse"** Barack Obama, Remarks at a Memorial Service for Victims of the Shootings in Tucson, Arizona, January 12, 2011. Online by Gerhard Peters and John T. Woolley, The American Presidency Project. http://www.presidency.ucsb.edu/ws/index.php?pid=88893

Page 151 **skyrocketed to $1.4 trillion** Summary of Receipts, Outlays, and Surpluses or Deficits (-): 1789-2023, Office of Management and Budget. https://www.white-house.gov/omb/historical-tables/

Page 151 **It proposed to slash $4 trillion** Jackie Calmes, "Panel Seeks Social Security Cuts and Higher Taxes," *The New York Times*, November 10, 2010. https://www.nytimes.com/2010/11/11/us/politics/11fiscal.html

Page 152 **a plan to cut $38 billion** Carl Hulse, "Budget Deal to Cut $38 Billion Averts Shutdown," *The New York Times*, April 8, 2011. https://www.nytimes.com/2011/04/09/us/politics/09fiscal.html

Page 152 **"largest real-dollar spending"** Ibid.

Page 153 **"I thought we should have let"** Baker, "Obama's First Term."

Page 153 **"Try to tell the president!"** Jackie Calmes, "Obama's Deficit Dilemma," *The New York Times*, February 27, 2012. https://www.nytimes.com/2012/02/27/us/politics/obamas-unacknowledged-debt-to-bowles-simpson-plan.html

Page 153 **"It's not going to happen"** Barack Obama, Remarks at George Washington University, April 13, 2011. Online by Gerhard Peters and John T. Woolley, The American Presidency Project. http://www.presidency.ucsb.edu/ws/index.php?pid=90246

Page 154 **"I can't believe you poisoned"** Bob Woodward, *The Price of Politics*, p. 105.

Page 154 **"We made a mistake"** Ibid., p. 107.

Page 154 **"had jeopardized"** James Comey, *A Higher Loyalty*, pp. 172-73.

Page 154 **"severe shock" to the global** Glenn Somerville, "U.S. Must Hike Debt Limit Soon to Avoid 'Shock' – IMF," Reuters, June 29, 2011. https://www.reuters.com/article/idINIndia-57992120110629

Page 155 **"Why do they need so much"** Joe Biden, *Promise Me, Dad*, p. 67.

Page 155 **"his most conspicuous weakness"** Leon Panetta, *Worthy Fights*, p. 442.

Page 156 **"Obama really doesn't have"** Woodward, *Price of Politics*, p. 82.

Page 156 **"condescending" and "annoying"** Mitch McConnell, *The Long Game*, p. 215.

Page 156 **"He's like the kid in your class"** Ibid., p. 185.

Page 156 **"the single most important"** "Top GOP Priority: Make Obama a One-Term President," *National Journal*, October 23, 2010. https://www.nationaljournal.com/member/magazine/top-gop-priority-make-obama-a-one-term-president-20101023

Page 157 **"if he's willing to meet us"** Ibid.

Page 157 **"Why don't you get a drink"** Barack Obama, Remarks at the White House Correspondents' Association Dinner, April 27, 2013. Online by Gerhard Peters and John T. Woolley, The American Presidency Project. http://www.presidency.ucsb.edu/ws/index.php?pid=103539

Page 157 **"He reminds me a lot of the guys"** Axelrod, *Believer*, p. 7.

Page 157 **"sneak into the White House"** Sabrina Eaton, "Newly Retired Boehner Reflects on Politics, President Obama," Cleveland.com, November 20, 2015. https://www.cleveland.com/open/index.ssf/2015/11/newly_retired_john_boehner_ref.html

Page 158 **"There's no point in dying"** Matt Bai, "Obama vs. Boehner: Who Killed the Debt Deal?" *The New York Times Magazine*, March 28, 2012. https://www.nytimes.com/2012/04/01/magazine/obama-vs-boehner-who-killed-the-debt-deal.html

Page 159 **"All you need to know about"** Woodward, *Price of Politics*, p. 159-60.

Page 159 **"This may bring my presidency"** Andy Sullivan, "Obama Says Has Reached His Limit in Debt Talks – Aide," Reuters, July 13, 2011. https://www.reuters.com/article/usa-debt-meeting-limit/obama-says-has-reached-his-limit-in-debt-talks-aide-idUSWEN537520110713

Page 160 **plan to reduce $3.7 trillion** "President Obama: Gang of Six Deficit Reduction Plan is 'Good News,'" *PBS NewsHour*, July 19, 2011. https://www.pbs.org/newshour/politics/gang-of-six-shakes-up-debt-limit-drama

Page 160 **"I can't have the Gang of Six"** Woodward, *Price of Politics*, p. 276.

Page 161 **"He had to have known that"** Bai, "Obama vs. Boehner."

Page 161 **"We can't go forward with"** Woodward, *Price of Politics*, p. 297.

Page 161 **"He was spewing coals"** Ibid., p. 299.

Page 162 **"I couldn't get a phone call"** Barack Obama, "Remarks on the Federal Budget and an Exchange With Reporters," July 22, 2011. Online by Gerhard Peters and John T. Woolley, The American Presidency Project. http://www.presidency.ucsb.edu/ws/index.php?pid=90653

Page 162 **"The White House moved the"** Bai, "Obama vs. Boehner."

Page 162 **"Let's not do this again"** p. 355.

Page 162 **"That was a searing experience"** Peter Baker, "4 Years Later, Scarred but Still Confident," *The New York Times*, September 6, 2012. https://www.nytimes.com/2012/09/06/us/politics/obama-seeking-re-election-asks-for-patience.html

Page 163 **"You're never going to"** Ibid.

Page 163 **"I don't think I like the look"** Brian Abrams, *Obama: An Oral History 2009-2017*, pp. 243-44.

Chapter Seven: 'Justice Has Been Done'

Page 165 **"The minutes passed like days"** Mark Mazzetti, Helene Cooper and Peter Baker, "Behind the Hunt for Bin Laden," *The New York Times*, May 2, 2011. https://www.nytimes.com/2011/05/03/world/asia/03intel.html

Page 165 **"They've reached the target"** Ibid.

Page 166 **"Justice has been done"** Barack Obama, Remarks on the Death of Al Qaida Terrorist Organization Leader Usama bin Laden, May 1, 2011. Online by Gerhard Peters and John T. Woolley, The American Presidency Project. http://www.presidency.ucsb.edu/ws/index.php?pid=90315

Page 166 **Obama's poll numbers shot up** His approval rating jumped from 44 percent at the end of April to 51 percent immediately after the raid, a significant rise although still overall a relatively weak number for an incumbent who had just scored an unalloyed foreign policy victory. Gallup Poll. https://news.gallup.com/poll/116479/barack-obama-presidential-job-approval.aspx

Page 167 **"a hell of a lot of risks"** Peter Baker, "Leon E. Panetta, in His Own Words," *The New York Times*, October 23, 2011. https://www.nytimes.com/2011/10/24/us/leon-panetta-in-his-own-words.html

Page 168 **"hiding in plain sight"** Mazzetti, Cooper and Baker, "Behind the Hunt for Bin Laden."

Page 168 **"He would go out and he'd walk"** Leon Panetta, author interview.

Page 169 **"It was a divided room"** Tom Donilon, author interview.

Page 170 **"It's a go"** Mazzetti, Cooper and Baker, "Behind the Hunt for Bin Laden."

Page 170 **nearly 25 percent of Americans"** Michael D. Shear, "With Document, Obama Seeks to End 'Birther' Issue," *The New York Times*, April 27, 2011. https://www.nytimes.com/2011/04/28/us/politics/28obama.html

Page 171 **"look what I found out there"** Mark Halperin and John Heilemann, *Double Down*, p. 11.

Page 171 **"I bet you don't love my idea"** Dan Pfeiffer, *Yes We (Still) Can*, p. 122.

Page 171 **"We're not going to be able"** Shear, "With Document, Obama Seeks to End 'Birther' Issue."

Page 171 **"Today, I'm very proud of myself"** Jeff Zeleny, "On Trail, Trump Basks in Spotlight," *The New York Times*, April 27, 2011. https://www.nytimes.com/2011/04/28/us/politics/28trump.html

Page 171 **"Fuck the White House"** This was reported in several places. In her memoir, Hillary Clinton said she did not remember exactly what she said, but noting that she had been quoted "using a four-letter word," she added, "I have not sought a correction." Hillary Clinton, *Hard Choices*, p. 194.

Page 172 **"Obviously something was"** David Axelrod, author interview.

Page 172 **"Oh, poor Tim Pawlenty"** Ibid.

Page 172 **"It wasn't until the next night"** Ibid.

Page 173 **"America's Cool Guy in Chief"** Laura Bradley, "Barack Obama Reflected on His Legacy, Slow-Jammed the News on *Fallon*," *Vanity Fair*, June 10, 2016. https://www.vanityfair.com/hollywood/2016/06/barack-obama-tonight-show-jimmy-fallon

Page 173 **"the first alt-comedy president"** Emily Heil, "Barack Obama, the First Alt-Comedy President," *The Washington Post*, April 25, 2016. https://www.washingtonpost.com/news/reliable-source/wp/2016/04/25/barack-obama-the-first-alt-comedy-president/?utm_term=.9b7b3602990e

Page 173 **"Despite our differences, we"** Barack Obama, Remarks at the White House Correspondents' Association Dinner, April 25, 2015. Online by Gerhard Peters and John T. Woolley, The American Presidency Project. http://www.presidency.ucsb.edu/ws/index.php?pid=110073

Page 174 **"People think bin Laden is"** Daniel Kurtzman, "Seth Meyers White House Correspondents' Dinner" speech. https://www.thoughtco.com/seth-meyers-white-house-correspondents-dinner-2734785

Page 174 **"Now, I know that he's taken"** Barack Obama, Remarks at the White House Correspondents' Association Dinner, April 30, 2011. Online by Gerhard Peters and John T. Woolley, The American Presidency Project. http://www.presidency.ucsb.edu/ws/index.php?pid=90314

Page 174 **"Our view was lifting Trump"** Brian Abrams, *Obama: An Oral History 2009-2017*, p. 217.

Page 175 **"All kidding aside"** Obama, "Remarks at the White House Correspondents' Association Dinner."

Page 175 **"As I'm coming in, the cast"** Peter Baker, "Obama's First Term: A Romantic Oral History," *The New York Times Magazine*, Jan. 16, 2013. https://www.nytimes.com/2013/01/20/magazine/obamas-first-term-oral-history.html

Page 176 **"I need to watch this"** Peter Bergen, *Manhunt*, p. 218.

Page 176 **"it was kind of a big gulp"** Michael Morell, author interview.

Page 176 **"He basically was drinking"** Panetta interview.

Page 177 **"If he is naked with his hands"** Mark Owen, *No Easy Day*, p. 177. Owen was the pseudonym for Mark Bissonnette, one of the Navy Seals on the mission. Bissonnette's account varied from the official version. According to the Pentagon, the commandos found bin Laden in the second-floor bedroom unarmed but not surrendering and then opened fire. Bissonnette wrote that they saw a man pop his head out of the room as they Seals were rushing up the stairs and they fired at his head. By this account, they then entered the bedroom, saw the man "twitching and convulsing" on the floor and shot him in the chest. (Owen, *No Easy*, p. 236.) Two unloaded weapons, an AK-47 rifle and a Makarov pistol, were found near the bedroom door.

Page 177 **"This was the longest forty"** "One Year After Osama bin Laden Raid, Pres. Obama Details Tense Moments," *Rock Center with Brian Williams*, NBC News, May 1, 2012. http://rockcenter.nbcnews.com/_news/2012/05/01/11484425-one-year-after-osama-bin-laden-raid-pres-obama-details-tense-moments?lite

Page 177 **"Mr. President, I can't be"** Peter Bergen, "Architect of bin Laden Raid: The Anxious Moments," CNN, May 2, 2016. https://www.cnn.com/2016/05/02/politics/osama-bin-laden-raid-architect-mcraven-bergen/index.html

Page 178 **"We got him"** Michelle Obama, *Becoming*, p. 363.

Page 179 **"and tell him he owes me"** Peter Baker, "Panetta's Pentagon, Without the Blank Check," *The New York Times*, October 23, 2011. https://www.nytimes.com/2011/10/24/us/at-pentagon-leon-panetta-charts-change-of-course.html

Page 179 **"There's just two guys slowly"** Baker, "Obama's First Term."

Page 179 **"It cannot ease our pain"** Peter Baker, Helene Cooper and Mark Mazzetti, "Bin Laden Is Dead, Obama Says," *The New York Times*, May 1, 2011. https://www.nytimes.com/2011/05/02/world/asia/osama-bin-laden-is-killed.html

Page 179 **"This is full circle for our"** Ibid.

Page 181 **"there is no straight line"** Barack Obama: Remarks in Cairo, June 4, 2009. Online by Gerhard Peters and John T. Woolley, The American Presidency Project. http://www.presidency.ucsb.edu/ws/index.php?pid=86221

Page 181 **"It all may work out fine"** Clinton, *Hard Choices*, p. 341.

Page 182 **"What was Wisner doing"** Mark Landler, *Alter Egos*, p. 156.

Page 182 **"He took me to the woodshed"** Clinton, *Hard Choices*, p. 345.

Page 182 **"Mubarak is on"** Helene Cooper and Robert F. Worth, "In Arab Spring, Obama Finds a Sharp Test," *The New York Times*, September 25, 2012. https://www.nytimes.com/2012/09/25/us/politics/arab-spring-proves-a-harsh-test-for-obamas-diplomatic-skill.html

Page 182 **"This is my country"** Ibid.

Page 182 **"That's not going to cut it"** Ibid.

Page 182 **"transition must begin now"** Ibid.

Page 183 **"Now started yesterday"** Robert Gibbs, "Press Briefing by Press Secretary Robert Gibbs," February 2, 2011. Online by Gerhard Peters and John T. Woolley, The American Presidency Project. http://www.presidency.ucsb.edu/ws/index.php?pid=88957

Page 184 **"one of the things"** Ben Rhodes, *The World As It Is*, p. 108.

Page 185 **"The Most Dangerous Man"** The cover ran in July 1981. Chrisopher Dickey, "What Libya's Kaddafi Can Teach World Leaders," *Newsweek*, September 16, 2009. https://www.newsweek.com/what-libyas-kaddafi-can-teach-world-leaders-79619

Page 185 **"rats" and "cockroaches"** Kareem Fahim, "Qaddafi's Grip on the Capital Tightens as Revolt Grows," *The New York Times*, February 22, 2011. https://www.nytimes.com/2011/02/23/world/africa/23libya.html Also Jo Becker and Scott Shane, "Hillary Clinton, 'Smart Power' and a Dictator's Fall," *The New York Times*, February 27, 2016. https://www.nytimes.com/2016/02/28/us/politics/hillary-clinton-libya.html

Page 186 **"You are not going to drag"** Becker and Shane, "Hillary Clinton, 'Smart Power' and a Dictator's Fall."

Page 186 **"We have a moral responsibility"** Ben Rhodes, *The World As It Is*, p. 113.

Page 186 **"been a minor character"** Ibid.

Page 186 **"impressive and polished"** Clinton, *Hard Choices*, p. 369.

Page 186 **"Can I finish the two wars"** Becker and Shane, "Hillary Clinton, 'Smart Power' and a Dictator's Fall."

Page 187 a **"51-49" decision** Ibid.

Page 187 **"all necessary measures"** United Nations Security Council Resolution 1973, passed on a vote of 10 to 0 with five abstentions (Brazil, China, Germany, India and Russia), March 17, 2011. https://www.un.org/press/en/2011/sc10200.doc.htm#Resolution

Page 187 **"We in Libya are confronting"** Rhodes, *World As It Is*, p. 115.

Page 188 **"leading from behind"** Ryan Lizza, "The Consequentialist: How the Arab Spring Remade Obama's Foreign Policy," *The New Yorker*, May 2, 2011. https://www.newyorker.com/magazine/2011/05/02/the-consequentialist

Page 188 **"When people were being"** Barack Obama, "Address to the Nation on the Situation in Libya," March 28, 2011. Online by Gerhard Peters and John T. Woolley, The American Presidency Project. http://www.presidency.ucsb.edu/ws/index.php?pid=90195

Page 188 **"We came, we saw, he died!"** Scott Shane and Jo Becker, "A New Libya, With 'Very Little Time Left,'" *The New York Times*, February 27, 2016. https://www.nytimes.com/2016/02/28/us/politics/libya-isis-hillary-clinton.html

Page 189 **"It turns out that I'm really good"** Scott Shane, *Objective Troy*, p. 306.

Page 189 **"a continued and imminent threat"** Ibid., p. 221.

Page 190 **"This is an easy one"** Ibid., p. 224.

Page 190 **"I would have detained and"** Barack Obama, Remarks at National Defense University, May 23, 2013. Online by Gerhard Peters and John T. Woolley, The

American Presidency Project. http://www.presidency.ucsb.edu/ws/index. php?pid=103625

Page 191 **"To my frustration"** Leon Panetta, *Worthy Fights*, p. 393.

Page 191 **"We really didn't want to be"** Peter Baker, "Relief Over U.S. Exit From Iraq Fades as Reality Overtakes Hope," *The New York Times*, June 22,2014. https:// www.nytimes.com/2014/06/23/world/middleeast/relief-over-us-exit-from-iraq-fades-as-reality-overtakes-hope.html

Page 192 **"Thank you for giving me"** Baker, "Relief Over U.S. Exit From Iraq Fades as Reality Overtakes Hope."

Page 192 **"We're leaving behind a"** Barack Obama, Remarks at Fort Bragg, North Carolina, December 14, 2011. Online by Gerhard Peters and John T. Woolley, The American Presidency Project. http://www.presidency.ucsb.edu/ws/index.php?pid=97764

CHAPTER EIGHT: 'Fought Our Way Back'

Page 193 **"I still believe in you"** Barack Obama, Remarks at an Obama Victory Fund 2012 Fundraiser in Redwood City, California, May 23, 2012. Online by Gerhard Peters and John T. Woolley, The American Presidency Project. http://www.presidency.ucsb.edu/ws/index.php?pid=100916

Page 194 ***Out of Hope, Ready for Change*** Peter Baker, "Obama Finds Campaigning Rules Clock," *The New York Times*, May 27, 2012. https://www.nytimes.com/2012/05/28/us/politics/campaigning-tests-obamas-staying-power.html

Page 194 **"never be a perfect president"** One example: Barack Obama, Remarks at an Obama Victory Fund 2012 Fundraiser in Bellevue, Washington, February 17, 2012. Online by Gerhard Peters and John T. Woolley, The American Presidency Project. http://www.presidency.ucsb.edu/ws/index.php?pid=99409

Page 194 **"I know we're probably underdogs"** David Axelrod, *Believer*, p. 442.

Page 194 **"Is Obama Toast"** Nate Silver, "Is Obama Toast? Handicapping the 2012 Election," *The New York Times Magazine*, November 3, 2011. https://www.nytimes.com/2011/11/06/magazine/nate-silver-handicaps-2012-election.html

Page 195 **"He seemed intellectual enough"** John Kerry, *Every Day Is Extra*, p. 343.

Page 197 **"severely conservative"** Jeff Zeleny, "Romney's Record as Governor Resumes Central Role in Nomination Fight," *The New York Times*, February 10, 2012. https://www.nytimes.com/2012/02/11/us/politics/romneys-record-as-governor-resumes-central-role-in-nomination-fight.html

Page 197 **"There have been times where"** Barack Obama, Remarks at a Town Hall Meeting and a Question-and-Answer Session in Strasbourg, April 3, 2009. Online by Gerhard Peters and John T. Woolley, The American Presidency Project https:// www.presidency.ucsb.edu/node/286180

Page 197 **"the United States will be willing"** Barack Obama, Remarks to the Summit of the Americas in Port of Spain, Trinidad and Tobago, April 17, 2009. Online by Gerhard Peters and John T. Woolley, The American Presidency Project https:// www.presidency.ucsb.edu/node/286618

Page 197 **"we went off course"** Barack Obama, Remarks at the National Archives and Records Administration, May 21, 2009. Online by Gerhard Peters and John T.

Woolley, The American Presidency Project https://www.presidency.ucsb.edu/node/286247

Page 198 **"breathtaking greed"** Barack Obama, Remarks at Osawatomie High School in Osawatomie, Kansas, December 6, 2011. Online by Gerhard Peters and John T. Woolley, The American Presidency Project. http://www.presidency.ucsb.edu/ws/index.php?pid=97685

Page 199 **"This is a make-or-break"** Ibid.

Page 199 **received $500 million** Matthew L. Wald, "Solar Firm Aided by Federal Loans Shuts Doors," *The New York Times*, August 31, 2011. https://www.nytimes.com/2011/09/01/business/energy-environment/solyndra-solar-firm-aided-by-federal-loans-shuts-doors.html

Page 199 **"the private sector is doing fine"** Barack Obama, Remarks on the National Economy and an Exchange With Reporters, June 8, 2012. Online by Gerhard Peters and John T. Woolley, The American Presidency Project. http://www.presidency.ucsb.edu/ws/index.php?pid=100997

Page 199 **"If you've got a business"** Barack Obama, Remarks at a Campaign Rally in Roanoke, Virginia, July 13, 2012. Online by Gerhard Peters and John T. Woolley, The American Presidency Project. http://www.presidency.ucsb.edu/ws/index.php?pid=101347

Page 200 **"I hate being sloppy"** Axelrod, *Believer*, p. 455.

Page 201 **"Should come up as a question"** Jo Becker, *Forcing the Spring*, p. 293.

Page 201 **"I am absolutely comfortable"** Transcript, *Meet the Press*, NBC News, May 6, 2012. http://www.nbcnews.com/id/47311900/ns/meet_the_press-transcripts/t/may-joe-biden-kelly-ayotte-diane-swonk-tom-brokaw-chuck-todd/?hasFlash=true&#.W8023i-ZOgQ

Page 202 **"I think you may have just"** Becker, *Forcing the Spring*, p. 290.

Page 202 **"I was really angry about this"** Brian Abrams, *Obama: An Oral History 2009-2017*, p. 262.

Page 202 **"There was a little apoplexy"** Peter Baker, "Obama's First Term: A Romantic Oral History," *The New York Times Magazine*, Jan. 16, 2013. https://www.nytimes.com/2013/01/20/magazine/obamas-first-term-oral-history.html

Page 202 **"a 30 percent chance we're"** Remarks by Vice President Joseph Biden at the House Democratic Issues Conference, Kingsmill Resort, Williamsburg, Virginia, February 6, 2009. Federal News Service.

Page 202 **"I don't remember exactly"** Barack Obama, The President's News Conference, February 9, 2009. Online by Gerhard Peters and John T. Woolley, The American Presidency Project. http://www.presidency.ucsb.edu/ws/index.php?pid=85728

Page 203 **"wrong on nearly every major"** Robert Gates, *Duty*, p. 289.

Page 203 **"In the Situation Room, Biden"** Ben Rhodes, *The World As It Is*, p. 65.

Page 203 **"President Obama would have a"** James Comey, *A Higher Loyalty*, p. 213.

Page 204 **"Joe, in that sense, can help"** Mark Leibovich, "Speaking Freely, Biden Finds Influential Role," *The New York Times*, March 28, 2009. https://www.nytimes.com/2009/03/29/us/politics/29biden.html

Page 204 **"You know what has surprised"** Joe Biden, *Promise Me, Dad*, p. 68.

Page 204 **"you are my brother"** Barack Obama, Eulogy at the Funeral Service for Joseph R. "Beau" Biden III in Wilmington, Delaware, June 6, 2015. Online by Gerhard Peters and John T. Woolley, The American Presidency Project. http://www.presidency.ucsb.edu/ws/index.php?pid=110276

Page 204 **"I've got to put Jay out of his"** Mark Halperin and John Heilemann, *Double Down*, p. 299.

Page 205 **"At a certain point"** Barack Obama, Interview with Robin Roberts of ABC News, May 9, 2012. Online by Gerhard Peters and John T. Woolley, The American Presidency Project. http://www.presidency.ucsb.edu/ws/index.php?pid=115643

Page 205 **Where just 27 percent of** Frank Newport, "Half of Americans Support Legal Gay Marriage," Gallup, May 8, 2012. https://news.gallup.com/poll/154529/half-americans-support-legal-gay-marriage.aspx

Page 206 **"You know what?"** Peter Baker, "Democrats Embrace Once Pejorative 'Obamacare,' Tag" *The New York Times*, August 3, 2012. https://www.nytimes.com/2012/08/04/health/policy/democrats-embrace-once-pejorative-obamacare-tag.html

Page 207 **mouthed the words "not true"** Adam Liptak, "Supreme Court Gets a Rare Rebuke, in Front of a Nation," *The New York Times*, January 28, 2010. https://www.nytimes.com/2010/01/29/us/politics/29scotus.html

Page 207 **"very troubling"** "Justice Criticizes Scene at State of Union," Associated Press, March 10, 2010. https://www.nytimes.com/2010/03/10/us/10brfs-JUSTICECRITI_BRF.html

Page 208 **"It is not our job"** John G. Roberts Jr., *National Federation of Independent Business et al v. Sebelius, Secretary of Health and Human Services et al*, June 28, 2012. https://www.supremecourt.gov/opinions/11pdf/11-393c3a2.pdf

Page 208 **"It seemed that a weight"** Rhodes, *World As It Is*, p. 317.

Page 209 **just 34 percent of Americans** Peter Baker, "For Obama, a Signature Issue That the Public Never Embraced Looms Large," *The New York Times*, June 29, 2012. https://www.nytimes.com/2012/06/30/us/politics/health-care-overhaul-is-still-no-hit-with-public.html

Page 209 **supported by 73 percent of** Ibid.

Page 209 **opponents spent $235 million** Ibid.

Page 210 **"You know there's something"** Jeff Zeleny, "Romney Vows to Deliver Country From Economic Travails," *The New York Times*, August 30, 2012. https://www.nytimes.com/2012/08/31/us/politics/romney-vows-to-deliver-country-from-economic-travails.html

Page 210 **Unemployment that August** Bureau of Labor Statistics. https://data.bls.gov/timeseries/LNS14000000

Page 211 **a meager 1.3 percent in the** Annie Lowery, "Last Quarter's Is Revised Down Sharply," *The New York Times*, September 27, 2012. https://www.nytimes.com/2012/09/28/business/economy/last-quarters-growth-is-revised-down-sharply.html

Page 211 **still over $1 trillion a year** Jackie Calmes, "Test for Obama as Deficit Stays Over $1 Trillion," *The New York Times*, September 25, 2012. https://www.nytimes.com/2012/09/26/us/politics/obama-faces-test-as-deficit-stays-above-1-trillion.html

Page 211 **Fully 87 percent** "For Voters, It's Still the Economy," Pew Research Center, September 24, 2012. From survey taken from September 12-16, 2012. http://www.people-press.org/2012/09/24/for-voters-its-still-the-economy/

Page 211 **only 37 percent** Lydia Saad, "Americans Continue to Give Obama Low Marks on the Economy," Gallup , August 16, 2012. From survey taken August 9-12, 2012. http://news.gallup.com/poll/156698/americans-continue-give-obama-low-marks-economy.aspx

Page 211 **"What do you want me to tell"** Clinton Eastwood, Republican National Convention, Tampa, Florida, August 30, 2012. Transcript published by *The Washington Post*. https://www.washingtonpost.com/politics/rnc-2012-clint-eastwoods-speech-to-the-republican-convention-in-tampa-full-text/2012/08/30/4247043c-f314-11e1-a612-3cfc842a6d89_story.html?utm_term=.4b4c3c27acbf

Page 212 **"Clinton's Bermuda Triangle"** Axelrod, *Believer*, p. 461.

Page 212 **"They want to go back"** Peter Baker, "Clinton Was a Bipartisan President, Except When He Wasn't," *The New York Times*, Sept. 6, 2012. https://thecaucus.blogs.nytimes.com/2012/09/06/clinton-was-a-bipartisan-president-except-when-he-wasnt/?module=ArrowsNav&contentCollection=Politics&action=keypress&region=FixedLeft&pgtype=Blogs

Page 213 **"I won't pretend the path"** Peter Baker, "Obama Makes the Case for 2nd Term; 'Harder' Path to 'Better Place,'" *The New York Times*, September 6, 2012. https://www.nytimes.com/2012/09/07/us/politics/obama-in-democratic-convention-speech-asks-for-more-time.html

Page 214 **"red line" and "change my calculus"** Barack Obama, Remarks and an Exchange With Reporters Following a Press Briefing by White House Press Secretary James F. "Jay" Carney, August 20, 2012. Online by Gerhard Peters and John T. Woolley, The American Presidency Project. http://www.presidency.ucsb.edu/ws/index.php?pid=101939

Page 214 **to move "now versus later"** Mark Landler, *Alter Egos*, pp. 218-19.

Page 214 **thought it was a "stupid idea"** Ibid.

Page 214 **"farmed out to the working level"** Scott Shane and Jo Becker, "A New Libya, With 'Very Little Time Left,'" *The New York Times*, February 27, 2016. https://www.nytimes.com/2016/02/28/us/politics/libya-isis-hillary-clinton.html

Page 215 **In a memo he titled "The Guns of"** Ibid.

Page 216 **"Two of our officers were killed"** Anne Gearan, "Latest State Release: Clinton Emails With Chelsea After Benghazi Attacks and More," *The Washington Post*, January 8, 2016. https://www.washingtonpost.com/news/post-politics/wp/2016/01/08/with-2-a-m-state-department-email-trove-82-percent-of-clinton-emails-now-released/?utm_term=.21aea7b77b27

Page 216 **"No acts of terror will ever"** Barack Obama, Remarks on the Attack on the United States Mission in Benghazi, Libya, September 12, 2012. Online by Gerhard Peters and John T. Woolley, The American Presidency Project. http://www.presidency.ucsb.edu/ws/index.php?pid=102024

Page 216 **"Well, it's too early to know"** Barack Obama, interview with Steve Kroft, *60 Minutes*, CBS News, September 12, 2012. https://www.cbsnews.com/video/obama-suspects-libya-attack-targeted-americans-2/

Page 217 **would call it a "terrorist attack"** Josh Rogin, "Obama Official: Benghazi Was a Terrorist Attack," *Foreign Policy*, September 19, 2012. https://foreignpolicy.com/2012/09/19/obama-official-benghazi-was-a-terrorist-attack/

Page 217 **"Instead of Obama being the"** Peter Baker and Mark Landler, "U.S. Is Preparing for a Long Siege of Arab Unrest," *The New York Times*, September 15, 2012. https://www.nytimes.com/2012/09/16/world/middleeast/us-is-preparing-for-a-long-siege-of-arab-unrest.html

Page 218 **They were, he said, "a drag"** Mark Landler, "Stark Backdrop as President Prepares to Debate," *The New York Times*, October 2, 2012. https://www.nytimes.com/2012/10/03/us/politics/in-struggling-nevada-the-president-prepares.html

Page 218 **"There are 47 percent of the people"** David Corn, "SECRET VIDEO: Romney Tells Millionaire Donors What He REALLY Thinks of Obama Voters," *Mother Jones*, September 17, 2012. https://www.motherjones.com/politics/2012/09/secret-video-romney-private-fundraiser/

Page 219 **"He understood its significance"** Abrams, *Obama*, p. 279.

Page 219 **"Man, we'd better not lose"** Axelrod, *Believer*, p. 462.

Page 220 **"She said, 'I don't know if Mitt'"** David Litt, *Thanks Obama*, p. 117.

Page 220 **"Too much defense throughout"** Axelrod, *Believer*, p. 464.

Page 220 **"Motherfucker's never happy"** Ibid., p. 466.

Page 220 **"I'll be there on game day"** Adam Nagourney, Ashley Parker, Jim Rutenberg and Jeff Zeleny, "How a Race in the Balance Went to Obama," *The New York Times*, November 8, 2012. https://www.nytimes.com/2012/11/08/us/politics/obama-campaign-clawed-back-after-a-dismal-debate.html

Page 221 **"Boy, he's good"** Mark Halperin and John Heilemann, *Double Down*, p. 423.

Page 221 **her husband had "bombed"** Michelle Obama, *Becoming*, p. 374.

Page 221 **"This was a terrific debate"** Barack Obama, Presidential Debate in Denver, Colorado, October 3, 2012. Online by Gerhard Peters and John T. Woolley, The American Presidency Project. http://www.presidency.ucsb.edu/ws/index.php?pid=102317

Page 221 **"I guess the consensus is that"** Nagourney, Parker, Rutenberg and Zeleny, "How a Race in the Balance Went to Obama."

Page 221 **"No one had ever lost a debate"** Abrams, *Obama*, p. 282-83.

Page 222 **"Who knows who those 11 percent"** Ibid.

Page 222 **"This is on me"** Nagourney, Parker, Rutenberg and Zeleny, "How a Race in the Balance Went to Obama."

Page 222 **"Please take a look at"** Hillary Clinton, *What Happened*, p. 66.

Page 222 **"faced his own political mortality"** Peter Baker, "A President's Last Race, Win or Lose," *The New York Times*, November 4, 2012. https://www.nytimes.com/2012/11/05/us/politics/obama-takes-frenetic-final-campaign-days-in-stride.html

Page 222 **"If I give up a couple of points"** Nagourney, Parker, Rutenberg and Zeleny, "How a Race in the Balance Went to Obama."

Page 222 **"*Advocate (don't explain)*"** Halperin and Heilemann, *Double Down*, p. 434.

Page 223 **"If we don't fix this"** Ibid., p. 4.

Page 223 **"I am wired in a different"** Ibid., p. 439.

Page 223 **"Fast and hammy!"** Ibid., p. 443.

Page 224 **"What Governor Romney said"** Barack Obama, Presidential Debate in Hempstead, New York, October 16, 2012. Online by Gerhard Peters and John T. Woolley, The American Presidency Project. http://www.presidency.ucsb.edu/ws/index.php?pid=102343

Page 224 **"Punch, Punch, Punch"** Peter Baker, "Punch, Punch, Punch," *The New York Times*, October 17, 2012. https://www.nytimes.com/2012/10/17/us/politics/in-second-debate-obama-strikes-back.html (The online headline was: "For the President, Punch, Punch, Another Punch.")

Page 225 **"The 1980s are now calling to"** Obama, Presidential Debate in Hempstead, New York.

Page 225 **"The world is watching and I'm"** Quoted by Brandon Hurlbut, Abrams, *Obama*, p. 285.

Page 225 **"He gave me his personal phone"** Chris Christie, author interview.

Page 225 **"I never felt good about the"** Abrams, *Obama*, p. 286.

Page 226 **"Terrible since you got here"** Peter Baker, "A President's Last Race, Win or Lose."

Page 226 **"I got a wife who loves me"** Abrams, *Obama*, p. 287.

Page 226 **"There was this moment where"** Dan Pfeiffer, author interview.

Page 226 **"Let's wait and see when Fox"** Baker, "Obama's First Term."

Page 226 **Obama garnered 51 percent** Federal Election Commission. https://transition.fec.gov/pubrec/fe2012/2012pres.pdf

Page 227 **"In some ways, this one is sweeter"** Rhodes, *World As It Is*, p. 191.

CHAPTER NINE: 'Governing By Crisis'

Page 228 **"how broken they'd left him"** Michelle Obama, *Becoming*, p. 377.

Page 228 **"I had never seen him like that"** Peter Baker, "Obama's First Term: A Romantic Oral History," *The New York Times Magazine*, Jan. 16, 2013. https://www.nytimes.com/2013/01/20/magazine/obamas-first-term-oral-history.html

Page 229 **"I won't be able to get through"** Brian Abrams, *Obama: An Oral History 2009-2017*, pp. 292-93

Page 229 **"He was having real trouble"** Joe Biden, author interview.

Page 229 **"They had their entire lives"** Barack Obama, Remarks on the Shootings in Newtown, Connecticut, December 14, 2012. Online by Gerhard Peters and John T. Woolley, The American Presidency Project https://www.presidency.ucsb.edu/node/303118

Page 230 **"No single law, no set of laws"** Barack Obama, Remarks at the Sandy Hook Interfaith Prayer Vigil in Newtown, Connecticut, December 16, 2012. Online by Gerhard Peters and John T. Woolley, The American Presidency Project https://www.presidency.ucsb.edu/node/303179

Page 230 **"I will put everything I've got"** Barack Obama, Remarks on Gun Violence, January 16, 2013. Online by Gerhard Peters and John T. Woolley, The American Presidency Project https://www.presidency.ucsb.edu/node/303737

Page 232 **"Progress does not compel us"** Barack Obama, Inaugural Address, January 21, 2013. Online by Gerhard Peters and John T. Woolley, The American Presidency Project https://www.presidency.ucsb.edu/node/303425

Page 233 **"I want to take a look, one more"** Peter Baker, "Obama Offers Liberal Vision: 'We Must Act,'" *The New York Times*, January 21, 2013. https://www.nytimes.com/2013/01/22/us/politics/obama-inauguration-draws-hundreds-of-thousands.html

Page 233 **and cried out, "Boo!"** Ibid.

Page 233 **"Our journey is not complete"** Obama, Inaugural Address.

Page 233 **"I would have liked to see a"** Baker, "Obama Offers Liberal Vision: 'We Must Act.'"

Page 235 **"No matter how much you think"** Barack Obama, Remarks at the Dedication Ceremony for the George W. Bush Presidential Library and Museum in Dallas, Texas, April 25, 2013. Online by Gerhard Peters and John T. Woolley, The American Presidency Project https://www.presidency.ucsb.edu/node/304064

Page 235 **"To know the man is to like"** Ibid.

Page 236 **"Nothing the president is"** Peter Baker and Michael D. Shear, "Obama to 'Put Everything I've Got' Into Gun Control," *The New York Times*, January 16, 2013. https://www.nytimes.com/2013/01/17/us/politics/obama-to-ask-congress-to-toughen-gun-laws.html

Page 236 **"The only thing that stops a bad"** Eric Lichtblau and Motoko Rich, "N.R.A. Envisions 'a Good Guy With a Gun' in Every School," *The New York Times*, December 21, 2012. https://www.nytimes.com/2012/12/22/us/nra-calls-for-armed-guards-at-schools.html

Page 237 **failed to garner the sixty votes** The Senate voted 54 to 46 for the amendment, six votes short of the sixty votes needed to overcome a filibuster. Three Republicans voted to advance the measure while four Democrats voted to block it. United States Senate. https://www.senate.gov/legislative/LIS/roll_call_lists/roll_call_vote_cfm.cfm?congress=113&session=1&vote=00097

Page 237 **"Shame on you!"** Jonathan Weisman, "Senate Blocks Drive for Gun Control," *The New York Times*, April 17, 2013. https://www.nytimes.com/2013/04/18/us/politics/senate-obama-gun-control.html

Page 237 **"We got an F"** Abrams, *Obama*, p. 297.

Page 237 **"I've heard some say that blocking"** Barack Obama, Remarks on Senate Action on Gun Control Legislation, April 17, 2013. Online by Gerhard Peters and John T. Woolley, The American Presidency Project https://www.presidency.ucsb.edu/node/303954

Page 238 **"an aider, abettor and/or"** Brian Stelter and Michael D. Shear, "Justice Dept. Investigated Fox Reporter Over Leak," *The New York Times*, May 20, 2013. https://www.nytimes.com/2013/05/21/us/politics/white-house-defends-tracking-fox-reporter.html

Page 238 **terms "Tea Party" or "patriots"** Jonathan Weisman, "I.R.S. Apologizes to Tea Party Groups Over Audits of Applications for Tax Exemption," *The New York Times*, May 10, 2013. https://www.nytimes.com/2013/05/11/us/politics/irs-apologizes-to-conservative-groups-over-application-audits.html

Page 238 **"progressive," "occupy" and** Alan Rappeport, "In Targeting Political Groups, I.R.S. Crossed Party Lines," *The New York Times,* October 5, 2017. https://www. nytimes.com/2017/10/05/us/politics/irs-targeting-tea-party-liberals-democrats. html

Page 239 **"going Bulworth"** Peter Baker, "Onset of Woes Casts Pall Over Obama's Policy Aspirations," *The New York Times,* May 15, 2013. https://www.nytimes. com/2013/05/16/us/politics/new-controversies-may-undermine-obama.html

Page 240 **compared him unfavorably to** Maureen Dowd, "No Bully in the Pulpit," *The New York Times,* April 20, 2013. https://www.nytimes.com/2013/04/21/opinion/ sunday/dowd-president-obama-is-no-bully-in-the-pulpit.html

Page 240 **"Michael, what's your secret"** Barack Obama, Remarks at the White House Correspondents' Association Dinner, April 27, 2013. Online by Gerhard Peters and John T. Woolley, The American Presidency Project https://www.presidency.ucsb. edu/node/304052

Page 240 **"As Mark Twain said"** Barack Obama, The President's News Conference, April 30, 2013. Online by Gerhard Peters and John T. Woolley, The American Presidency Project https://www.presidency.ucsb.edu/node/304110

Page 241 **publishing a series of explosive** Barton Gellman and Laura Poitras, "U.S., British Intelligence Mining Data From Nine U.S. Internet Companies in Broad Secret Program," *The Washington Post,* June 7, 2013. https://www.washingtonpost.com/ investigations/us-intelligence-mining-data-from-nine-us-internet-companies-in-broad-secret-program/2013/06/06/3a0c0da8-cebf-11e2-8845-d970ccb04497_story. html?utm_term=.4b7c087624c1 Glenn Greenwald, "NSA Collecting Phone Records of Millions of Verizon Customers Daily," *The Guardian,* June 6, 2013. https://www.theguardian.com/world/2013/jun/06/nsa-phone-records-verizon-court-order

Page 242 **"That means no more illegal"** Barack Obama, Remarks in Washington, DC: "The War We Need to Win," August 1, 2007. Online by Gerhard Peters and John T. Woolley, The American Presidency Project. http://www.presidency.ucsb.edu/ws/ index.php?pid=77040

Page 242 **"When you get the package"** Peter Baker, "Obama's Path From Critic to Overseer of Spying," *The New York Times,* January 15, 2014. https://www.nytimes. com/2014/01/16/us/obamas-path-from-critic-to-defender-of-spying.html

Page 242 **"this war, like all wars, must"** Barack Obama, Remarks at National Defense University, May 23, 2013. Online by Gerhard Peters and John T. Woolley, The American Presidency Project https://www.presidency.ucsb.edu/node/304467

Page 242 **"Things seem to have grown"** Baker, "Obama's Path From Critic to Overseer of Spying."

Page 244 **"As long as I am president"** Barack Obama, Remarks on the Federal Government Shutdown and the Patient Protection and Affordable Care Act, October 1, 2013. Online by Gerhard Peters and John T. Woolley, The American Presidency Project https://www.presidency.ucsb.edu/node/304269

Page 244 **"We fought the good fight"** "Boehner: 'We Fought the Good Fight,'" NBC News, October 16, 2013. http://firstread.nbcnews.com/_ news/2013/10/16/20993759-boehner-we-fought-the-good-fight

Page 244 **"the Washington establishment"** Jonathan Weisman, "Cruz Won't Block Senate Deal," *The New York Times*, October 16, 2013. https://www.nytimes.com/news/fiscal-crisis/2013/10/16/cruz-wont-block-senate-deal/

Page 244 **"We've got to get out of the habit"** Barack Obama, Remarks on Legislation Continuing Appropriations and Increasing the Public Debt Limit and an Exchange With Reporters, October 16, 2013. Online by Gerhard Peters and John T. Woolley, The American Presidency Project https://www.presidency.ucsb.edu/node/304140

Page 245 **"This is real simple"** Barack Obama, Remarks at Prince George's Community College in Largo, September 26, 2013, Maryland Online by Gerhard Peters and John T. Woolley, The American Presidency Project https://www.presidency.ucsb.edu/node/304368

Page 245 **"Today, there were more problems"** "From Jon Stewart to Jay Leno: Late-Night Hosts Roast Obamacare Website," *The Hollywood Reporter*, October 24, 2013. https://www.hollywoodreporter.com/live-feed/obamacare-best-late-night-jokes-650658

Page 246 **"The web page cannot be found"** *The Colbert Report*, Comedy Central, October 24, 2013.

Page 246 **"Sorry, our system is down"** Susan Levine, "Sebelius Watches Website Crash," *Politico*, November 20, 2013. https://www.politico.com/story/2013/11/kathleen-sebelius-obamacare-website-crash-100152

Page 246 **"No matter how we reform"** Barack Obama, Remarks to the American Medical Association National Conference in Chicago, Illinois, June 15, 2009. Online by Gerhard Peters and John T. Woolley, The American Presidency Project https://www.presidency.ucsb.edu/node/286837

Page 247 **"Lie of the Year"** Angie Drobnic Holan, "Lie of the Year: 'If You Like Your Health Care Plan, You Can Keep It," *Politifact*, December 12, 2013. https://www.politifact.com/truth-o-meter/article/2013/dec/12/lie-year-if-you-like-your-health-care-plan-keep-it/

Page 247 **"No one is madder than me"** Barack Obama, Remarks on the Patient Protection and Affordable Care Act, October 21, 2013. Online by Gerhard Peters and John T. Woolley, The American Presidency Project https://www.presidency.ucsb.edu/node/305217

Chapter Ten: 'Red Line'

Page 248 **"not yet a "slam dunk"** Ben Rhodes, *The World As It Is*, pp. 228-29.

Page 249 **"no one asked you if it was a"** Ibid.

Page 250 **"It's the day after Qaddafi is"** Thomas L. Friedman, "Obama on the World," *The New York Times*, August 8, 2014. https://www.nytimes.com/2014/08/09/opinion/president-obama-thomas-l-friedman-iraq-and-world-affairs.html

Page 251 **"This idea that we could provide"** Ibid.

Page 251 **"I set a red line"** Mark Landler, *Alter Egos*, pp. 227-28.

Page 252 **"history would judge us all"** Peter Baker and Michael R. Gordon, "Kerry Becomes Chief Advocate for U.S. Attack," *The New York Times*, August 30, 2013. https://www.nytimes.com/2013/08/31/world/middleeast/john-kerry-syria.html

Page 252 **"We don't have good options"** Max Fisher, "Read and Watch: Obama Discusses His Current Thinking on Syria," *The Washington Post*, August 29, 2013. https://www.washingtonpost.com/news/worldviews/wp/2013/08/29/read-and-watch-obama-discusses-his-current-thinking-on-syria/?utm_term=.1b816154dc87

Page 252 **Six in ten Americans opposed** Mark Landler and Megan Thee-Brenan, "Survey Reveals Scant Backing for Syria Strike," *The New York Times*, September 9, 2013. https://www.nytimes.com/2013/09/10/world/middleeast/poll-majority-of-americans-oppose-military-strike.html

Page 253 **"I'm well aware of what"** Landler, *Alter Egos*, p. 205.

Page 253 **"I have a pretty big idea"** Other versions provided by aides included, "I've got a crazy idea I want to talk about."

Page 254 **"'It is too easy for a president'"** Rhodes, *World As It Is*, p. 235.

Page 254 **"Congress is never going to"** Ibid., p. 236.

Page 255 **"I'm prepared to give that order"** Barack Obama, Remarks on the Situation in Syria, August 31, 2013. Online by Gerhard Peters and John T. Woolley, The American Presidency Project https://www.presidency.ucsb.edu/node/304717

Page 255 **"They may have heard the word"** John Kerry, *Every Day is Extra*, p. 535.

Page 255 **"Obama hasn't got a chance to"** Peter Baker and Jonathan Weisman, "Obama Seeks Approval by Congress for Strike in Syria," *The New York Times*, August 31, 2013. https://www.nytimes.com/2013/09/01/world/middleeast/syria.html

Page 255 **"an actual or imminent threat"** Charlie Savage, "Barack Obama's Q&A," *The Boston Globe*, December 20, 2007. http://archive.boston.com/news/politics/2008/specials/CandidateQA/ObamaQA/

Page 256 **"wearing the jacket"** Kerry, *Every Day is Extra*, p. 534.

Page 257 **"I don't agree with his arguments"** Peter Baker and Steven Lee Myers, "Obama Falls Short on Wider Backing for Syria Attack," *The New York Times*, September 6, 2013. https://www.nytimes.com/2013/09/07/world/middleeast/obama-syria-strike.html

Page 258 **"He could turn over every single"** Michael R. Gordon and Steven Lee Myers, "Obama Calls Russia Offer on Syria 'Possible Breakthrough,'" *The New York Times*, September 9, 2013. https://www.nytimes.com/2013/09/10/world/middleeast/kerry-says-syria-should-hand-over-all-chemical-arms.html

Page 258 **"required the most political"** Barack Obama, Interview with Jack Schlossberg at the John F. Kennedy Presidential Library and Museum in Boston, Massachusetts. May 7, 2017. Online by Gerhard Peters and John T. Woolley, The American Presidency Project. http://www.presidency.ucsb.edu/node/331724

Page 259 **"a blow to American credibility"** Leon Panetta, *Worthy Fights*, p. 450.

Page 259 **"There's absolutely no question"** Peter Baker, "A Rare Public View of Obama's Pivots on Policy in Syria Confrontation," *The New York Times*, September 11, 2013. https://www.nytimes.com/2013/09/12/world/middleeast/Obamas-Pivots-on-Syria-Confrontation.html

Page 260 **But Obama himself surprised aides** David Kirkpatrick, *Into the Hands of the Soldiers*, pp. 241-44.

Page 261 **"The administration is trying to"** Michael R. Gordon and Mark Landler, "In Crackdown Response, U.S. Temporarily Freezes Some Military Aid to Egypt," *The*

New York Times, October 9, 2013. https://www.nytimes.com/2013/10/10/world/middleeast/obama-military-aid-to-egypt.html

Page 263 **"Just because we have the best"** Rhodes, *World As It Is*, p. 346.

Page 263 **"The analogy we use around here"** The first part of the quote was included in the magazine piece. David Remnick, "Going the Distance: On and Off the Road with Barack Obama," *The New Yorker*, January 7, 2014. https://www.newyorker.com/magazine/2014/01/27/going-the-distance-david-remnick The rest of the exchange was later disclosed in a transcript of the interview provided to *The Washington Post*'s fact-checking columnist. Glenn Kessler, "Spinning Obama's Reference to Islamic State as a 'JV' Team," *The Washington Post*, September 3, 2014. https://www.washingtonpost.com/news/fact-checker/wp/2014/09/03/spinning-obamas-reference-to-isis-as-a-jv-team/?utm_term=.a18d9b5194f7

Page 264 **"probably will attempt to take"** Peter Baker and Eric Schmitt, "Many Missteps in Assessment of ISIS Threat," *The New York Times*, September 29, 2014. https://www.nytimes.com/2014/09/30/world/middleeast/obama-fault-is-shared-in-misjudging-of-isis-threat.html

Page 264 **"I am haunted by those deaths"** Barack Obama, Commencement Address at the United States Military Academy in West Point, New York, May 28, 2014. Online by Gerhard Peters and John T. Woolley, The American Presidency Project https://www.presidency.ucsb.edu/node/305525

Page 266 **"kind of a slouch"** Barack Obama, The President's News Conference, August 9, 2013. Online by Gerhard Peters and John T. Woolley, The American Presidency Project https://www.presidency.ucsb.edu/node/304552

Page 267 **"We're not going to send in"** Joe Biden, *Promise Me, Dad*, p. 100.

Page 267 **"Russia is once again isolating"** Barack Obama, Remarks on the Situation in Ukraine and an Exchange With Reporters, July 29, 2014. Online by Gerhard Peters and John T. Woolley, The American Presidency Project https://www.presidency.ucsb.edu/node/306022

Chapter Eleven: 'Don't Do Stupid ... '

Page 269 **"The bear is loose!"** Pat Cunnane, *West Winging It*, p. 85.

Page 269 **"C'mon guys, give me some space"** Ibid.

Page 270 **"I am eager to work with all"** Barack Obama, Address Before a Joint Session of the Congress on the State of the Union, January 28, 2014. Online by Gerhard Peters and John T. Woolley, The American Presidency Project https://www.presidency.ucsb.edu/node/305034

Page 271 **"perhaps the most substantively"** Noam Scheiber, "As His Term Wanes, Obama Champions Workers' Rights," *The New York Times*, August 31, 2015. https://www.nytimes.com/2015/09/01/business/economy/as-his-term-wanes-obama-restores-workers-rights.html

Page 272 **passed, 68 to 32, in 2013** Fourteen Republicans joined every Democrat in voting yes. June 27, 2013. United States Senate. https://www.senate.gov/legislative/LIS/roll_call_lists/roll_call_vote_cfm.cfm?congress=113&session=1&vote=00167

Page 273 **"deporter-in-chief"** Michael D. Shear, "Obama, Citing a Concern for Families,

Orders a Review of Deportations," *The New York Times*, March 13, 2014. https://www.nytimes.com/2014/03/14/us/obama-orders-review-of-deportations.html

Page 274 **"It is incredible to me that"** Peter Baker, "Obama's Odds With Congress: Bad to Worse," *The New York Times*, June 12, 2014. https://www.nytimes.com/2014/06/13/us/obamas-odds-with-congress-bad-to-worse.html

Page 275 **"Ever competitive, Obama was"** Dan Pfeiffer, *Yes We (Still) Can*, p. 220.

Page 275 **"I've got to go with Han Solo"** Peter Baker, "Dog Pants? Show a Little More Fur, Obama Says," *The New York Times*, January 15, 2016. https://www.nytimes.com/politics/first-draft/2016/01/15/dog-pants-show-a-little-more-fur-obama-says/

Page 276 **"Ultimately, what all of this"** Julie Hirschfeld Davis, "A Digital Team Is Helping Obama Find His Voice Online," *The New York Times*, November 8, 2015. https://www.nytimes.com/2015/11/09/us/politics/a-digital-team-is-helping-obama-find-his-voice-online.html

Page 276 **saw a 40 percent increase** Aaron Blake, "'Between Two Ferns' Video Leads to 40 Percent More Visits to HealthCare.Gov," *The Washington Post*, March 12, 2014. https://www.washingtonpost.com/news/post-politics/wp/2014/03/12/between-two-ferns-video-leads-to-40-percent-more-visits-to-healthcare-gov/?utm_term=.f3d8406125ad

Page 278 **"The United States has always"** Barack Obama, The President's News Conference With President Bronislaw Komorowski of Poland in Warsaw, Poland, June 3, 2014. Online by Gerhard Peters and John T. Woolley, The American Presidency Project https://www.presidency.ucsb.edu/node/305653

Page 279 **"Ben and I have been talking"** Mark Landler, *Alter Egos*, pp. xi-xiii.

Page 280 **"Now what's my foreign policy"** Ibid.

Page 280 **"targeted, clear actions"** Barack Obama, The President's News Conference With President Benigno S. Aquino III of the Philippines in Manila, Philippines, April 28, 2014. Online by Gerhard Peters and John T. Woolley, The American Presidency Project https://www.presidency.ucsb.edu/node/306104

Page 280 **"And that may not always be sexy"** Barack Obama, Joint News Conference with President Benigno Aquino III of the Philippines, Malacañang Palace, Manila, April 28, 2014, White House transcript. https://obamawhitehouse.archives.gov/the-press-office/2014/04/28/remarks-president-obama-and-president-benigno-aquino-iii-philippines-joi

Page 282 **"Dry hole," came the dispiriting** Peter Baker and Eric Schmitt, "Many Missteps in Assessment of ISIS Threat," *The New York Times*, September 29, 2014. https://www.nytimes.com/2014/09/30/world/middleeast/obama-fault-is-shared-in-misjudging-of-isis-threat.html

Page 283 **"I know that many of you are"** Barack Obama, Remarks on the Situation in Iraq, August 7, 2014. Online by Gerhard Peters and John T. Woolley, The American Presidency Project https://www.presidency.ucsb.edu/node/307088

Page 284 **declared himself "heartbroken"** Barack Obama, Remarks on the Death of James W. Foley in Syria From Edgartown, Massachusetts, August 20, 2014. Online by Gerhard Peters and John T. Woolley, The American Presidency Project https://www.presidency.ucsb.edu/node/307291

Page 284 **"We will not get dragged into"** Barack Obama, Address to the Nation on

United States Strategy To Combat the Islamic State of Iraq and the Levant Terrorist Organization (ISIL), September 10, 2014. Online by Gerhard Peters and John T. Woolley, The American Presidency Project https://www.presidency.ucsb.edu/node/307345

Page 285 **Nearly six out of ten voters** Exit Polls, NBC News. https://www.nbcnews.com/politics/elections/2014/US/house/exitpoll

Page 285 **nearly 1,000 state legislative** Robert Draper, "A Post-Obama Democratic Party in Search of Itself," *The New York Times Magazine*, November 1, 2017. https://www.nytimes.com/2017/11/01/magazine/a-post-obama-democratic-party-in-search-of-itself.html

Page 286 **"This is probably the worst"** Peter Baker, "President Obama Left Fighting for His Own Relevance," *The New York Times*, November 4, 2014. https://www.nytimes.com/2014/11/05/us/president-obama-left-fighting-for-his-own-relevancy.html

Page 288 **"I'd get the hell beat out of"** Dan De Luce, "Hagel: The White House Tried to 'Destroy' Me," *Foreign Policy*, December 18, 2015. https://foreignpolicy.com/2015/12/18/hagel-the-white-house-tried-to-destroy-me/

Page 289 **"brazen power grab"** Michael D. Shear, "Obama, Daring Congress, Acts to Overhaul Immigration," *The New York Times*, November 20, 2014. https://www.nytimes.com/2014/11/21/us/obama-immigration-speech.html

Page 289 **"The actions I'm taking are"** Barack Obama, Address to the Nation on Immigration Reform, November 20, 2014. Online by Gerhard Peters and John T. Woolley, The American Presidency Project https://www.presidency.ucsb.edu/node/308498

Page 290 **"By ignoring the will of the"** Shear, "Obama, Daring Congress, Acts to Overhaul Immigration."

Chapter Twelve: 'Could Have Been Me'

Page 291 **"When I get to the second part"** Peter Baker, "When The President Decided to Sing 'Amazing Grace,'" *The New York Times*, July 6, 2015. https://www.nytimes.com/politics/first-draft/2015/07/06/obamabaker/

Page 293 **"Obama is plagued by inescapable"** Michael Eric Dyson, *The Black Presidency*, p. xv.

Page 293 **"palpable discomfort with race"** Ibid., p. 193.

Page 293 **"For many people, it feels worse"** Peter Baker and Julie Hirschfeld Davis, "Urging Persistence on Racial Gains, Obama Recalls Sacrifice in Selma," *The New York Times*, March 6, 2015. https://www.nytimes.com/2015/03/07/us/politics/obama-backs-justice-departments-decision-not-to-indict-ferguson-officer.html

Page 294 **"Cops need to stop shooting"** Ben Rhodes, *The World As It Is*, pp. 257-58.

Page 294 **"President Obama, when he was"** Peter Baker, "Obama Finds a Bolder Voice on Race Issues," *The New York Times*, May 4, 2015. https://www.nytimes.com/2015/05/05/us/politics/obama-my-brothers-keeper-alliance-minorities.html

Page 295 **"His candidacy suggested we had"** Baker and Davis, "Urging Persistence on Racial Gains, Obama Recalls Sacrifice in Selma."

Page 295 **Indeed, 1.7 million more blacks** Ibid.

Page 295 **"By breaking through that"** Ibid.

Page 296 **"While other black politicians"** Dyson, *Black Presidency*, p. 56.

Page 296 **"I can't sound like Martin"** Peter Wallsten, "Obama Struggles to Balance African Americans' Hopes With Country's as a Whole," *The Washington Post*, October 28, 2012. https://www.washingtonpost.com/politics/decision2012/obama-after-making-history-has-faced-a-high-wire-on-racial-issues/2012/10/28/d8e25ff4-1939-11e2-bd10-5ff056538b7c_story.html?utm_term=.10ca18d17bc8

Page 297 **"In the same way that some"** Dyson, *Black Presidency*, p. xvi.

Page 297 **"a nation of cowards"** Attorney General Eric Holder at the Department of Justice African American History Month Program, February 18, 2009. Remarks as prepared for delivery. https://www.justice.gov/opa/speech/attorney-general-eric-holder-department-justice-african-american-history-month-program?loc=interstitialskip

Page 298 **"It's fair to say that if I had"** Transcript, "Obama's Interview Aboard Air Force One," *The New York Times*, March 7, 2009. https://www.nytimes.com/2009/03/08/us/politics/08obama-text.html

Page 298 **"There's no longer any room"** Barack Obama, Commencement Address at Morehouse College in Atlanta, Georgia, May 19, 2013. Online by Gerhard Peters and John T. Woolley, The American Presidency Project https://www.presidency.ucsb.edu/node/304432

Page 298 **"scold of 'black America'"** Ta-Nehisi Coates, "How the Obama Administration Talks to Black America," *The Atlantic*, May 20, 2013. https://www.theatlantic.com/politics/archive/2013/05/how-the-obama-administration-talks-to-black-america/276015/

Page 298 **police had "acted stupidly"** Barack Obama, The President's News Conference, July 22, 2009. Online by Gerhard Peters and John T. Woolley, The American Presidency Project https://www.presidency.ucsb.edu/node/286533

Page 299 **"If I had a son, he'd look like"** Barack Obama, Remarks on the Nomination of Jim Yong Kim To Be President of the World Bank and an Exchange With Reporters, March 23, 2012. Online by Gerhard Peters and John T. Woolley, The American Presidency Project https://www.presidency.ucsb.edu/node/300587

Page 299 **"a black mascot of Wall Street"** Chris Hedges, "The Obama Deception: Why Cornel West Went Ballistic," Truthdig, May 16, 2011. https://www.truthdig.com/articles/the-obama-deception-why-cornel-west-went-ballistic/

Page 299 **"If you're not going to address"** Peter Baker, "President, Not Preacher, but Speaking More on Race," *The New York Times*, August 27, 2013. https://www.nytimes.com/2013/08/28/us/politics/president-not-preacher-but-speaking-more-on-race.html

Page 299 **"Still Waiting for Our First"** Fredrick Harris, "Still Waiting for Our First Black President," *The Washington Post*, June 1, 2012. https://www.washingtonpost.com/opinions/still-waiting-for-our-first-black-president/2012/06/01/gJQARsT16U_story.html?utm_term=.7ab65420e89c

Page 299 **"A President for Everyone"** Kevin Johnson, "A President for Everyone, Except Black People," *The Philadelphia Tribune*, April 14, 2013. http://www.phillytrib.

com/news/a-president-for-everyone-except-black-people/article_164f06d9-abf2-5f29-a531-10ff57edf5f2.html

Page 299 **"I'm not the president of"** Derek T. Dingle, "Oval Office Interview With President Barack Obama," *Black Enterprise*, August 2012. https://www.blacken-terprise.com/president-obama-interview-small-business-unemployment-exclusive/

Page 300 **"Trayvon Martin could have"** Barack Obama, Remarks on the Verdict in State of Florida v. George Zimmerman, July 19, 2013. Online by Gerhard Peters and John T. Woolley, The American Presidency Project https://www.presidency.ucsb.edu/node/304775

Page 301 **"There is no blood flowing"** Peter Baker and Matt Apuzzo, "Shared Vision, Varying Styles," *The New York Times*, August 19, 2014. https://www.nytimes.com/2014/08/20/us/holder-and-obama-differ-in-approach-to-underlying-issues-of-missouri-unrest.html

Page 301 **"I can't breathe"** Joseph Goldstein and Nate Schweber, "Man's Death After Chokehold Raises Old Issue for the Police," *The New York Times*, July 18, 2014. https://www.nytimes.com/2014/07/19/nyregion/staten-island-man-dies-after-he-is-put-in-chokehold-during-arrest.html

Page 301 **"criminals and thugs"** Barack Obama, The President's News Conference With Prime Minister Shinzo Abe of Japan, April 28, 2015. Online by Gerhard Peters and John T. Woolley, The American Presidency Project https://www.presidency.ucsb.edu/node/310549

Page 302 **"Maybe we now realize the"** Barack Obama, Eulogy at the Funeral Service for Pastor Clementa C. Pinckney of the Emanuel African Methodist Episcopal Church in Charleston, South Carolina, June 26, 2015. Online by Gerhard Peters and John T. Woolley, The American Presidency Project https://www.presidency.ucsb.edu/node/310874

Page 302 **"Dear Mr. President"** Rhodes, *World* pp. 320-21.

Page 303 **"It's a shame that those nine"** Ibid.

Page 303 **"a broken system"** Barack Obama, Remarks at the NAACP Annual Convention in Philadelphia, Pennsylvania, July 14, 2015. Online by Gerhard Peters and John T. Woolley, The American Presidency Project https://www.presidency.ucsb.edu/node/311387

Page 305 **"There but for the grace of"** Barack Obama, Remarks Following a Visit at Federal Correctional Institution El Reno and an Exchange With Reporters in El Reno, Oklahoma, July 16, 2015. Online by Gerhard Peters and John T. Woolley, The American Presidency Project https://www.presidency.ucsb.edu/node/311405

Page 305 **"If you're asking me, 'Was there'"** Peter Baker, "Kenya Trip Takes Obama Back to a Complex Part of Himself," *The New York Times*, July 22, 2015. https://www.nytimes.com/2015/07/23/world/africa/africa-trip-takes-obama-back-to-a-complex-part-of-himself.html

Page 306 **fill "a great emptiness" he felt** Barack Obama, *Dreams from My Father*, p. 302.

Page 306 **"Obviously, this is personal"** Barack Obama, Remarks During a Panel Discussion at the Global Entrepreneurship Summit in Nairobi, Kenya, July 25, 2015. Online by Gerhard Peters and John T. Woolley, The American Presidency Project https://www.presidency.ucsb.edu/node/310307

Page 306 **"Part of the challenge that I've"** Barack Obama, The President's News Conference With President Uhuru Kenyatta of Kenya in Nairobi, Kenya, July 25, 2015. Online by Gerhard Peters and John T. Woolley, The American Presidency Project https://www.presidency.ucsb.edu/node/310338

Page 307 **"Nobody should be president"** Barack Obama, Remarks at African Union Headquarters in Addis Ababa, Ethiopia, July 28, 2015. Online by Gerhard Peters and John T. Woolley, The American Presidency Project https://www.presidency.ucsb.edu/node/310442

Page 307 **"Because they marched"** Barack Obama, Remarks at the "Let Freedom Ring" Ceremony Commemorating the 50th Anniversary of the March on Washington for Jobs and Freedom, August 28, 2013. Online by Gerhard Peters and John T. Woolley, The American Presidency Project https://www.presidency.ucsb.edu/node/304643

Page 307 **"If you say that's not the"** Peter Baker and Sheryl Gay Stolberg, "Saluting a Dream, and Adapting It for a New Era," *The New York Times*, August 28, 2013. https://www.nytimes.com/2013/08/29/us/politics/where-king-stood-obama-reframes-a-dream-for-a-new-era.html

Page 307 **"Who would have guessed fifty"** Ibid.

Page 307 **"We don't need the Ferguson report"** Peter Baker and Richard Fausset, "Obama, at Selma Memorial, Says 'We Know the March Is Not Over Yet,'" *The New York Times*, March 7, 2015. https://www.nytimes.com/2015/03/08/us/obama-in-selma-for-edmund-pettus-bridge-attack-anniversary.html

Page 308 **"I don't know whether"** Michael S. Schmidt and Matt Apuzzo, "F.B.I. Chief Links Scrutiny of Police With Rise in Violent Crime," *The New York Times*, p. Oct. 23, 2015. https://www.nytimes.com/2015/10/24/us/politics/fbi-chief-links-scrutiny-of-police-with-rise-in-violent-crime.html

Page 309 **"What are you seeing"** James Comey, *A Higher Loyalty*, pp. 148-51.

Page 310 **the sentences of 1,715 prisoners** Clemency Statistics, Office of the Pardon Attorney, Department of Justice. https://www.justice.gov/pardon/clemency-statistics

Page 310 **"Malachi and I shared the fact"** Barack Obama, Remarks Announcing the "My Brother's Keeper" Alliance at Lehman College in New York City, May 4, 2015. Online by Gerhard Peters and John T. Woolley, The American Presidency Project https://www.presidency.ucsb.edu/node/310876

Page 310 **"This will remain a mission"** Ibid.

CHAPTER THIRTEEN: 'Never Fear to Negotiate'

Page 312 **"These fifty years have shown"** Barack Obama, Address to the Nation on United States Policy Toward Cuba, December 17, 2014. Online by Gerhard Peters and John T. Woolley, The American Presidency Project https://www.presidency.ucsb.edu/node/308223

Page 312 **"irresponsible and frankly naïve"** Patrick Healy, "Clinton and Obama Campaigns Spar Over Debate," *The New York Times*, July 25, 2017. https://www.nytimes.com/2007/07/25/us/politics/25debate.html

Page 313 **"inexperience and reckless judgment"** John Sullivan, "Obama and McCain Spar Over Iran," *The New York Times*, May 20, 2008. https://www.nytimes.com/2008/05/20/us/politics/19cnd-campaign.html

Page 313 **"We are powerful enough to be"** Thomas L. Friedman, "Iran and the Obama Doctrine," *The New York Times*, April 5, 2015. https://www.nytimes.com/2015/04/06/opinion/thomas-friedman-the-obama-doctrine-and-iran-interview.html

Page 314 **"This deal won't be a farewell"** Peter Baker, "In Congress, Netanyahu Faults 'Bad Deal' on Iran Nuclear Program," *The New York Times*, March 3, 2015. https://www.nytimes.com/2015/03/04/world/middleeast/netanyahu-congress-iran-israel-speech.html

Page 314 **"a speech that hit below the belt"** John Kerry, *Every Day Is Extra*, p. 504.

Page 316 **"Eight years, no daylight"** Peter Baker and Jodi Rudoren, "Obama and Netanyahu: A Story of Slights and Crossed Signals," *The New York Times*, November 8, 2015. https://www.nytimes.com/2015/11/09/us/politics/obama-and-netanyahu-a-story-of-slights-and-crossed-signals.html

Page 316 **"This is as annoyed as I've been"** Ben Rhodes, *The World As It Is*, pp. 146-47.

Page 317 **"I came out of the Jewish"** Ibid.

Page 317 **"You're fed up with him"** Isabel Kershner, "In Overheard Comments, Sarkozy Calls Netanyahu a 'Liar,'" *The New York Times*, November 8, 2011. https://www.nytimes.com/2011/11/09/world/middleeast/in-overheard-comments-nicolas-sarkozy-calls-benjamin-netanyahu-a-liar.html?module=inline

Page 317 **"Part of our goal here has been"** Peter Baker, "Obama's Iran Deal Pits His Faith in Diplomacy Against Skepticism," *The New York Times*, July 15, 2015. https://www.nytimes.com/2015/07/16/world/middleeast/obama-diplomacy-iran-nuclear-deal.html

Page 318 **"something big on Cuba"** Julie Hirschfeld Davis and Peter Baker, "A Secretive Path to Raising U.S. Flag in Cuba," *The New York Times*, August 13, 2015. https://www.nytimes.com/2015/08/14/world/americas/a-secretive-path-to-raising-us-flag-in-cuba.html

Page 319 **"If you take in Snowden"** Rhodes, *World As It Is*, p, 263.

Page 320 **"At that point, you're on the hook"** Davis and Baker, "A Secretive Path to Raising U.S. Flag in Cuba."

Page 320 **"As Joe Biden would say, this is"** Rhodes, *World As It Is*, p. 307.

Page 320 **"Señor Presidente!" he declared** Ibid.

Page 320 **"It's been a long time since they've"** Ibid.

Page 320 **"This entire policy shift"** Peter Baker, "U.S. to Restore Full Relations With Cuba, Erasing a Last Trace of Cold War Hostility," *The New York Times*, December 14, 2015. https://www.nytimes.com/2014/12/18/world/americas/us-cuba-relations.html

Page 321 **"You shake our conscience from"** Barack Obama, Remarks at a Welcoming Ceremony for Pope Francis, September 23, 2015. Online by Gerhard Peters and John T. Woolley, The American Presidency Project https://www.presidency.ucsb.edu/node/310621

Page 322 **"Boehner, man, I'm going to miss"** "John Boehner Gives Emotional Exit Interview to Bill Hemmer," Fox News, October 30, 2015. http://insider.foxnews.com/2015/10/30/john-boehner-gives-emotional-exit-interview-bill-hemmer?page=2&amp%3Bfb_comment_id=945399168864888_945554785515993

Page 324 **"Susan, this is a goddamn good"** Rhodes, *World As It Is*, p. 253.

Page 324 **"John, don't go overselling it"** Senior administration official, author interview.

Page 324 **"the world's most complex"** Wendy Sherman, *Not for the Faint of Heart*, p. x.

Page 325 **"a high level of pain"** Brian Abrams, *Obama: An Oral History: 2009-2017*, pp. 369-70.

Page 325 **"John, I've already got my legacy"** Rhodes, *World As It Is*, p. 328.

Page 326 **"It's not our job to question him"** Senior administration official, author interview.

Page 326 **"The president suffers when he"** Robert Gates, author interview.

Page 326 **disclosed by the *Wall Street*** Jay Solomon and Carol E. Lee, "U.S. Sent Cash to Iran as Americans Were Freed," *The Wall Street Journal*, August 3, 2016. https://www.wsj.com/articles/u-s-sent-cash-to-iran-as-americans-were-freed-1470181874

Page 327 **"was like a scene out of *Argo*"** Peter Baker, "14 Testy Months Behind U.S. Prisoner Swap With Iran," *The New York Times*, January 17, 2016. https://www.nytimes.com/2016/01/18/us/politics/14-testy-months-behind-us-prisoner-swap-with-iran.html

Page 327 **"I am desperate to feed my"** Michael R. Gordon and David E. Sanger, "Deal Reached on Iran Nuclear Program; Limits on Fuel Would Lessen With Times," *The New York Times*, July 14, 2015. https://www.nytimes.com/2015/07/15/world/middleeast/iran-nuclear-deal-is-reached-after-long-negotiations.html

Page 327 **"a historic mistake"** Ibid.

Page 330 **"We have contained them"** Barack Obama, Interview with George Stephanopoulos of ABC, September 12, 2015. Online by Gerhard Peters and John T. Woolley, The American Presidency Project https://www.presidency.ucsb.edu/node/326799

Page 330 **"half-baked ideas"** Barack Obama, The President's News Conference, October 2, 2015. Online by Gerhard Peters and John T. Woolley, The American Presidency Project https://www.presidency.ucsb.edu/node/311290

Page 331 **the word "shall" for "should"** Melissa Eddy, "The Road to a Paris Climate Deal," *The New York Times*, December 14, 2015. https://www.nytimes.com/interactive/projects/cp/climate/2015-paris-climate-talks/at-climate-talks-three-letters-almost-sunk-the-deal

Chapter Fourteen: 'A Personal Insult'

Page 333 **"We have to understand an"** Barack Obama, Remarks at the Islamic Society of Baltimore in Catonsville, Maryland, February 3, 2016. Online by Gerhard Peters and John T. Woolley, The American Presidency Project https://www.presidency.ucsb.edu/node/311781

Page 334 **"It's apparently open mike day"** David Axelrod, Twitter message, June 16, 2015. https://twitter.com/davidaxelrod/status/610833937573769216

Page 334 **there was a 100 percent chance** "David Plouffe on Why Donald Trump Can't Get to 270," *With All Due Respect*, Bloomberg, September 27, 2016. https://www.bloomberg.com/news/videos/2016-09-27/david-plouffe-on-why-donald-trump-can-t-get-to-270

Page 334 **"a great publicity-seeker"** Barack Obama, Interview with Steve Kroft of CBS, October 11, 2015. Online by Gerhard Peters and John T. Woolley, The American Presidency Project https://www.presidency.ucsb.edu/node/332160

Page 334 **"I like people who weren't"** Jonathan Martin and Alan Rappeport, "Donald Trump Says John McCain Is No War Hero, Setting Off Another Storm," *The New York Times*, July 18, 2015. https://www.nytimes.com/2015/07/19/us/politics/trump-belittles-mccains-war-record.html

Page 334 **"to scapegoat fellow citizens"** Barack Obama, Address Before a Joint Session of the Congress on the State of the Union, January 12, 2016. Online by Gerhard Peters and John T. Woolley, The American Presidency Project https://www.presidency.ucsb.edu/node/313186

Page 336 **only 26 percent thought so** Sarah Dutton, Jennifer De Pinto, Fred Backus and Anthony Salvanto, "Negative Views of Race Relations Reach All-Time High – CBS/NYT Poll," July 13, 2016. https://www.cbsnews.com/news/negative-views-of-race-relations-reach-all-time-high-cbsnyt-poll/

Page 336 **"Democracy breaks down when"** Obama, State of the Union.

Page 337 **"won just 50.5 percent"** Lee Epstein and Eric Posner, "The End of Supreme Court Deference to the President?" January 20, 2017. http://epstein.wustl.edu/research/PresWinRate.pdf

Page 337 **"It's fair to say he's had a more"** Peter Baker, "Obama's Tangled History With Supreme Court Sets Stage for Nominee Fight," *The New York Times*, February 28, 2016. https://www.nytimes.com/2016/02/29/us/politics/obamas-tangled-history-with-supreme-court-sets-stage-for-nominee-fight.html

Page 339 **"The judgment is affirmed by"** *United States v. Texas*, June 23, 2016. https://www.supremecourt.gov/opinions/15pdf/15-674_jhlo.pdf

Page 339 **Cubans called out "Obama!"** Julie Hirschfeld Davis, "Obama Family Spring Break: Making History and Doing the Tango," *The New York Times*, March 25, 2016. https://www.nytimes.com/2016/03/26/world/americas/obama-argentina-tango.html

Page 339 **"It seemed an apt metaphor"** Ben Rhodes, *The World As It Is*, p. 355.

Page 340 **"What political prisoners?"** Barack Obama, The President's News Conference With President Raúl Castro Ruz of Cuba in Havana, Cuba, March 21, 2016. Online by Gerhard Peters and John T. Woolley, The American Presidency Project https://www.presidency.ucsb.edu/node/315738

Page 340 **"Cuba's destiny will not be"** Ibid.

Page 340 **"Seventy-one years ago, on a"** Barack Obama, Remarks With Prime Minister Shinzo Abe of Japan at Hiroshima Peace Memorial Park in Hiroshima, Japan, May 27, 2016. Online by Gerhard Peters and John T. Woolley, The American Presidency Project https://www.presidency.ucsb.edu/node/318118

Page 341 **"When incidents like this"** Barack Obama, Remarks on the Deaths of Alton Sterling and Philando Castile in Warsaw, Poland, July 7, 2016. Online by Gerhard Peters and John T. Woolley, The American Presidency Project https://www.presidency.ucsb.edu/node/318182

Page 342 **"Let me be clear"** Barack Obama, Remarks Following a Meeting With President Donald Franciszek Tusk of the European Council and President Jean-Claude

Juncker of the European Commission in Warsaw, Poland, July 8, 2016. Online by Gerhard Peters and John T. Woolley, The American Presidency Project https://www.presidency.ucsb.edu/node/318207

Page 342 **"led directly to the climate"** Mark Landler and Michael D. Shear, "Obama's Delicate Balance on Issue of Race and Policing," *The New York Times*, July 8, 2016. https://www.nytimes.com/2016/07/09/us/politics/obama-balance-race-police-dallas-shooting.html

Page 343 **"I consider Hillary a strong"** Barack Obama, Interview of President Obama and Secretary of State Clinton with Steve Kroft of CBS's *60 Minutes*, January 27, 2013. Online by Gerhard Peters and John T. Woolley, The American Presidency Project https://www.presidency.ucsb.edu/node/309834

Page 344 **"I think he was just a tiny"** Hillary Clinton, *What Happened*, p. 52.

Page 344 **"The president was not"** Joe Biden, *Promise Me, Dad*, p. 233.

Page 344 **"Great nations need organizing"** Mark Landler, "A Rift in Worldviews Is Exposed as Clinton Faults Obama on Policy," *The New York Times*, August 11, 2014. https://www.nytimes.com/2014/08/12/world/middleeast/attacking-obama-policy-hillary-clinton-exposes-different-worldviews.html

Page 345 **Clinton "made a mistake"** Barack Obama, Interview with Steve Kroft of CBS, October 11, 2015. Online by Gerhard Peters and John T. Woolley, The American Presidency Project https://www.presidency.ucsb.edu/node/332160

Page 346 **"a very small number"** Mark Landler and Eric Lichtblau, "F.B.I. Director James Comey Recommends No Charges for Hillary Clinton on Email," *The New York Times*, July 5, 2016. https://www.nytimes.com/2016/07/06/us/politics/hillary-clinton-fbi-email-comey.html

Page 346 **"extremely careless"** Ibid.

Page 346 **"Don't try to be hip"** Clinton, *What Happened*, p. 67.

Page 347 **"No matter how daunting the"** Barack Obama, Remarks at the Democratic National Convention in Philadelphia, Pennsylvania, July 27, 2016. Online by Gerhard Peters and John T. Woolley, The American Presidency Project https://www.presidency.ucsb.edu/node/317855

Page 347 **approval rating at 51 percent** Gallup Poll. https://news.gallup.com/poll/116479/barack-obama-presidential-job-approval.aspx

Page 347 **"No, Obama has not been"** David Brooks, "I Miss Barack Obama," *The New York Times*, February 9, 2016. https://www.nytimes.com/2016/02/09/opinion/i-miss-barack-obama.html

Page 347 **"This is not me going through"** Barack Obama, Remarks at a Campaign Rally for Democratic Presidential Nominee Hillary Rodham Clinton in Philadelphia, Pennsylvania, September 13, 2016. Online by Gerhard Peters and John T. Woolley, The American Presidency Project https://www.presidency.ucsb.edu/node/318808

Page 348 **"My name may not be on the"** Barack Obama, Remarks at the Congressional Black Caucus Foundation Phoenix Awards Dinner, September 17, 2016. Online by Gerhard Peters and John T. Woolley, The American Presidency Project https://www.presidency.ucsb.edu/node/318840

Page 349 **"President Barack Obama was"** David Jackson, "Trump Finally Says Obama Born in U.S., Blames Clinton for Controversy," *USA Today*, September 16, 2016.

https://www.usatoday.com/story/news/politics/elections/2016/2016/09/16/donald-trump-barack-obama-hillary-clinton-presidential-campaign-birtherism/90471868/ *The New York Times* took the extraordinary step of calling Trump's birther assertions a "lie" at the top of the front page. Michael Barbaro, "Donald Trump Clung to Birther Lie for Years, and Still Isn't Apologizing," *The New York Times,* September 16, 2016. https://www.nytimes.com/2016/09/17/us/politics/donald-trump-obama-birther.html

Page 349 **"an extra spring in my step"** Obama, Remarks at Congressional Black Caucus Foundation Phoenix Awards Dinner.

Page 349 **"President Obama will go down"** Donald Trump, Twitter message, August 2, 2016. https://twitter.com/realdonaldtrump/status/760552601356267520?lang=en

Page 350 **"At least I'll go down as a president"** Dave Itzkoff, "It's Late Night With President Obama," *The New York Times,* November 7, 2016. https://www.nytimes.com/2016/11/08/arts/television/its-late-night-with-president-obama.html

Page 350 **"All the progress we've made"** Barack Obama, Remarks at a Campaign Rally for Democratic Presidential Nominee Hillary Rodham Clinton in Jacksonville, Florida, November 3, 2016. Online by Gerhard Peters and John T. Woolley, The American Presidency Project https://www.presidency.ucsb.edu/node/319550

Page 350 **"cleaning his room"** Barack Obama, Remarks at a Campaign Rally for Democratic Presidential Nominee Hillary Rodham Clinton in Miami, Florida, November 3, 2016. Online by Gerhard Peters and John T. Woolley, The American Presidency Project https://www.presidency.ucsb.edu/node/319404

Page 350 **"con artist and a know-nothing"** Barack Obama, Remarks at a Campaign Rally for Democratic Presidential Nominee Hillary Rodham Clinton in Chapel Hill, North Carolina, November 2, 2016. Online by Gerhard Peters and John T. Woolley, The American Presidency Project https://www.presidency.ucsb.edu/node/319410

Page 350 **"Come on," he said. "This guy?"** Barack Obama, Remarks at a Campaign Rally for Democratic Presidential Nominee Hillary Rodham Clinton in Columbus, Ohio, November 1, 2016. Online by Gerhard Peters and John T. Woolley, The American Presidency Project https://www.presidency.ucsb.edu/node/319416

Page 350 **"If your closest advisers don't"** Barack Obama, Remarks at a Campaign Rally for Democratic Presidential Nominee Hillary Rodham Clinton in Ann Arbor, Michigan, November 7, 2016. Online by Gerhard Peters and John T. Woolley, The American Presidency Project https://www.presidency.ucsb.edu/node/319532

CHAPTER FIFTEEN: 'Backed the Wrong Horse'

Page 351 *We know what you're up to* Barack Obama, The President's News Conference, December 16, 2016. Online by Gerhard Peters and John T. Woolley, The American Presidency Project https://www.presidency.ucsb.edu/node/320647

Page 351 **"we've had problems with cyber"** Barack Obama, "Press Conference by President Obama After G20 Summit," White House, September 5, 2016. https://obamawhitehouse.archives.gov/the-press-office/2016/09/05/press-conference-president-obama-after-g20-summit

Page 352 **"use any opportunity to criticize"** Matt Apuzzo and Sharon LaFraniere, "13 Russians Indicted as Mueller Reveals Effort to Aid Trump Campaign," *The New*

York Times, February 16, 2018. https://www.nytimes.com/2018/02/16/us/politics/russians-indicted-mueller-election-interference.html

Page 352 **"information that would incriminate"** Jo Becker, Adam Goldman and Matt Apuzzo, "Russian Dirt on Clinton? 'I Love It,' Donald Trump Jr. Said," *The New York Times*, July 11, 2017. https://www.nytimes.com/2017/07/11/us/politics/trump-russia-email-clinton.html

Page 353 **"That's when the hairs"** Victoria Nuland, interview with Susan Glasser, *The Global Politico*, February 5, 2018. https://www.politico.com/magazine/story/2018/02/05/victoria-nuland-the-full-transcript-216936

Page 353 **"we for our part will do everything"** Jan M. Lodal, "Brezhnev's Secret Pledge to 'Do Everything We Can' to Reelect Gerald Ford," *The Atlantic*, July 26, 2017. https://www.theatlantic.com/international/archive/2017/07/ford-brezhnev-note/534798/

Page 354 **meddled in eighty-one elections** Dov H. Levin, "Partisan Electoral Interventions By The Great Powers," *Conflict Management and Peace Science*, September 19, 2016. http://journals.sagepub.com/doi/abs/10.1177/0738894216661190

Page 355 **"Save Islamic Knowledge"** Scott Shane and Mark Mazzetti, "The Plot to Subvert an Election: Unraveling the Russia Story So Far," *The New York Times*, September 20, 2018. https://www.nytimes.com/interactive/2018/09/20/us/politics/russia-interference-election-trump-clinton.html

Page 355 **"Hillary is a Satan"** Alicia Parlapiano and Jasmine C. Lee, "The Propaganda Tools Used by Russians to Influence the 2016 Election," *The New York Times*, February 16, 2018. https://www.nytimes.com/interactive/2018/02/16/us/politics/russia-propaganda-election-2016.html

Page 355 **"I created all these pictures"** Ibid.

Page 355 **created 2,700 Facebook** Shane and Mazzetti, "The Plot to Subvert an Election."

Page 355 **"exactly what buttons to"** Ibid.

Page 355 **"doing a great job in rebuilding"** Donald Trump, interview with Larry King, CNN, aired on October 15, 2007. http://www.cnn.com/TRANSCRIPTS/0710/15/lkl.01.html

Page 355 **his "new best friend"** Donald Trump, Twitter message, June 18, 2013. https://twitter.com/realdonaldtrump/status/347191326112112640?lang=en

Page 356 **"Russia, if you're listening, I hope"** Ashley Parker and David E. Sanger, "Donald Trump Calls on Russia to Find Hillary Clinton's Missing Emails," *The New York Times*, July 27, 2016. https://www.nytimes.com/2016/07/28/us/politics/donald-trump-russia-clinton-emails.html

Page 356 **no "hard evidence" of collusion** James Clapper, *Facts and Fears*, p. 349.

Page 357 **"Our first goal was to"** Lisa Monaco, interview with Susan Glasser, *The Global Politico*, April 3, 2017. https://www.politico.com/magazine/story/2017/04/lisa-monaco-the-full-transcript-214974

Page 358 **"There were a number of us"** Nuland interview with Glasser, *Global Politico*.

Page 358 **"He didn't want to be seen"** Clapper, *Facts and Fears*, p. 350.

Page 359 **"dismissive, disparaging"** Greg Miller, *The Apprentice*, p. 161.

Page 359 **"If I speak out more, he'll just"** Ben Rhodes, *The World As It Is*, p. 399.

Page 359 **"voice of inoculation" message** James Comey, *A Higher Loyalty*, p. 190.

Page 359 **"We were very conscious"** Monaco interview with Glasser, *Global Politico*.

Page 359 **"He backed the wrong horse"** Comey, *Higher Loyalty*, p. 19.

Page 359 **"There was a real reticence"** Adam Schiff, interview with Susan Glasser, *The Global Politico*, February 20, 2017. https://www.politico.com/magazine/story/2017/02/adam-schiff-house-intel-trump-russia-investigation-214800

Page 360 **"we have concluded that"** Dianne Feinstein and Adam Schiff, Statement on Russian Hacking, September 22, 2016. https://www.feinstein.senate.gov/public/index.cfm/press-releases?ID=A04D321E-5F86-4FD6-AD8E-7F533E1C2845

Page 360 **"The U.S. Intelligence Community"** Joint Statement from the Department of Homeland Security and Office of the Director of National Intelligence on Election Security, October 7, 2016. https://www.dhs.gov/news/2016/10/07/joint-statement-department-homeland-security-and-office-director-national

Page 361 **"We believe, based on the scope"** Ibid.

Page 361 **Early drafts of the statement** Greg Miller, Ellen Nakashima and Adam Entous, "Obama's Secret Struggle to Punish Russia for Putin's Election Assault," *The Washington Post*, June 23, 2017. https://www.washingtonpost.com/graphics/2017/world/national-security/obama-putin-election-hacking/?utm_term=.04834ccc2344

Page 361 **posted online a video of Trump** David A. Fahrenthold, "Trump Recorded Having Extremely Lewd Conversation About Women in 2005," *The Washington Post*, October 8, 2016. https://www.washingtonpost.com/politics/trump-recorded-having-extremely-lewd-conversation-about-women-in-2005/2016/10/07/3b9ce776-8cb4-11e6-bf8a-3d26847eeed4_story.html?utm_term=.0a067363282e

Page 361 **"I did try and fuck her"** "Transcript: Donald Trump's Taped Comments About Women," *The New York Times*, October 8, 2016. https://www.nytimes.com/2016/10/08/us/donald-trump-tape-transcript.html

Page 361 **"locker room banter"** Alexander Burns, Maggie Haberman and Jonathan Martin, "Donald Trump Apology Caps Day of Outrage Over Lewd Tape," *The New York Times*, October 8, 2016. https://www.nytimes.com/2016/10/08/us/politics/donald-trump-women.html?module=Uisil

Page 362 **"Anyone who knows me"** Ibid.

Page 362 **"I have to tell you that I can't"** "Michelle Obama: Trump's 2005 Revelations Has 'Shaken Me to My Core," NBC News. https://www.nbcnews.com/video/michelle-obama-trump-s-2005-revelations-has-shaken-me-to-my-core-785238595789?v=raila&

Page 362 **"that appear to be pertinent"** James Comey, letter to congressional leaders, October 28, 2016. https://www.nytimes.com/interactive/2016/10/28/us/politics/fbi-letter.html?module=inline

Page 363 **"we have not changed our"** Matt Apuzzo, Michael S. Schmidt and Adam Goldman, "Emails Warrant No New Action Against Hillary Clinton, F.B.I. Director Says," *The New York Times*, November 6, 2016. https://www.nytimes.com/2016/11/07/us/politics/hilary-clinton-male-voters-donald-trump.html

Page 363 **"international law, including the"** William M. Arkin, Ken Dilanian and Cynthia McFadden, "What Obama Said to Putin on the Red Phone About the Election

Hack," NBC News, December 19, 2016. https://www.nbcnews.com/news/us-news/what-obama-said-putin-red-phone-about-election-hack-n697116

Page 365 **"We're going to have to rework"** Brian Abrams, *Obama: An Oral History 2009-2017*, p. 392.

Page 365 **"I'm sorry for letting you down"** Hillary Clinton, *What Happened*, pp. 385-86.

Page 366 **"This stings," he said. "This hurts"** David Remnick, "Obama Reckons With a Trump Presidency: Inside a Stunned White House, the President Considers His Legacy and America's Future," *The New Yorker*, November 28, 2016. https://www.newyorker.com/magazine/2016/11/28/obama-reckons-with-a-trump-presidency

Page 366 **"There are more stars in the"** Rhodes, *World As It Is*, p. xiii.

Page 366 **"Never been as wrong on anything"** Brent Griffiths, "Plouffe: 'Never Been as Wrong on Anything in My Life," *Politico*, November 9, 2016. https://www.politico.com/story/2016/11/david-plouffe-wrong-2016-election-231045

Page 367 **98 percent chance of winning** Natalie Jackson, "HuffPost Forecasts Hillary Clinton Will Win With 323 Electoral Votes: Democrats Stand A Strong Chance of Taking Control of the Senate As Well," *The Huffington Post*, November 7, 2016. (*The Huffington Post* formally renamed itself *HuffPost* in 2017.) https://www.huffingtonpost.com/entry/polls-hillary-clinton-win_us_5821074ce4b0e80b02cc2a94

Page 367 **Clinton victory at 71 percent** "Who Will Win the Presidency?" FiveThirtyEight.com, November 8, 2016. https://projects.fivethirtyeight.com/2016-election-forecast/

Page 367 **her chances at 85 percent** Josh Katz, "Who Will Be President?" *The New York Times*, November 8, 2016. https://www.nytimes.com/interactive/2016/upshot/presidential-polls-forecast.html

Page 367 **"Maybe 15 percent of that gets"** Remnick, "Obama Reckons With a Trump Presidency."

Page 368 **"I feel like Michael Corleone"** Rhodes, *World As It Is*, p. xix.

Page 368 **"excellent conversation"** Barack Obama, Remarks Following a Meeting With President-Elect Donald J. Trump, November 10, 2016. Online by Gerhard Peters and John T. Woolley, The American Presidency Project https://www.presidency.ucsb.edu/node/319434

Page 368 **"I'm trying to place him"** Rhodes, *World As It Is*, pp. 404-05.

Page 369 **"Maybe this is what people want"** Ibid., p. 405.

Page 369 **"heralding economic progress"** Stanley Greenberg, "The Democrats' 'Working-Class Problem': It's Not Only With Whites. It Reaches Well Into the Party's Base," *The American Prospect*, June 1, 2017. http://prospect.org/article/democrats'-'working-class-problem'

Page 370 **tested eighty-five slogans** Matt Flegenheimer, "When Hillary Clinton Tested New Slogans – 85 of Them," *The New York Times*, October 19, 2016. https://www.nytimes.com/2016/10/20/us/politics/hillary-clinton-campaign-slogans.html

Page 370 **"I just want to tell you something"** Comey, *Higher Loyalty*, pp. 209-10.

Page 371 **"What if we were wrong?"** Rhodes, *World As It Is*, p. xvi.

Page 371 **He had read a column** He probably meant the Sunday Review piece headlined "The End of Identity Liberalism" by Mark Lilla, a Columbia University professor, in *The New York Times*, November 18, 2016. https://www.nytimes.com/2016/11/20/opinion/sunday/the-end-of-identity-liberalism.html

Page 371 **"They'd succeeded beyond their"** Clapper, *Facts and Fears*, p. 3.

Page 372 **"These are the same people that"** David E. Sanger, "Trump, Mocking Claim That Russia Hacked Election, at Odds with G.O.P.," *The New York Times*, December 10, 2016. https://www.nytimes.com/2016/12/10/us/politics/trump-mocking-claim-that-russia-hacked-election-at-odds-with-gop.html

Page 372 **"Great move on delay (by V. Putin)"** Donald Trump, Twitter message, December 30, 2016. https://twitter.com/realdonaldtrump/status/814919370711461890?lang=en

Page 372 **"Putin and the Russian government"** "Background to 'Assessing Russian Activities and Intentions in Recent US Elections': The Analytic Process and Cyber Incident Attribution," Office of the Director of National Intelligence, January 6, 2017. https://www.dni.gov/files/documents/ICA_2017_01.pdf

Page 372 **the collective evidence was "staggering"** Clapper, *Facts and Fear*, pp. 366-37.

Page 373 **"Are we living in Nazi Germany?"** Donald Trump, Twitter message, January 11, 2009. https://twitter.com/realDonaldTrump/status/819164172781060096?ref_src=twsrc%5Etfw%7Ctwcamp%5Etweetembed%7Ctwterm%5E81916417278106 0096&ref_url=https%3A%2F%2Fwww.nytimes.com%2F2017%2F01%2F11%2Fus%2Fdonald-trump-nazi-comparison.html

Page 373 **"I feel like we sort of choked"** Greg Miller, Ellen Nakashima and Adam Entous, "Obama's Secret Struggle to Punish Russia for Putin's Election Assault," *The Washington Post*, June 23, 2017. https://www.washingtonpost.com/graphics/2017/world/national-security/obama-putin-election-hacking/?utm_term=.04834ccc2344

Page 373 **"I do wonder sometimes about"** Clinton, *What Happened*, p. 356.

Page 374 **"Stay strong Israel"** Donald Trump, Twitter message, December 28, 2016. https://twitter.com/realdonaldtrump/status/814114980983427073?lang=en

Page 374 **"I'm confident that if I had run"** Barack Obama, Interview with David Axelrod on CNN's "The Axe Files" Online, December 26, 2016. by Gerhard Peters and John T. Woolley, The American Presidency Project https://www.presidency.ucsb.edu/node/331720

Page 374 **"President Obama said that he"** Donald Trump, Twitter message, December 26, 2016. https://twitter.com/realdonaldtrump/status/813498739923054593?lang=en

Page 375 **"There's a difference between"** Michael D. Shear and Peter Baker, "In Farewell, Obama Sets Red Lines That Would Pull Him Back Into Fray," *The New York Times*, January 18, 2017. https://www.nytimes.com/2017/01/18/us/politics/obama-last-news-conference-as-president.html

Page 375 **"This is not a period, this is a comma"** Brent Griffiths, "Full Text: Obama Farewell Speech Transcript," *Politico*, January 20, 2017. https://www.politico.com/story/2017/01/full-text-obama-farewell-speech-transcript-233916

EPILOGUE: 'Forever President'

Page 376 **"threat to our democracy"** Peter Baker, "Obama Lashes Trump in Debut 2018

438

Speech. President's Response: 'I Fell Asleep,'" *The New York Times*, September 2018. https://www.nytimes.com/2018/09/07/us/politics/obama-2018-campaign-trump.html

Page 377 **"It did not start with Donald Trump"** Ibid.

Page 378 **"But what we have not seen"** Campaign 2018 Former President Barack Obama Wisconsin Rally, Federal News Service, October 26, 2018.

Page 380 **More than 11 million new jobs** Obama and his team prefer to say that more than 15 million new jobs were created, measured from the point in 2010 when the recession he inherited bottomed out and the economy began growing again. Brad Tuttle, "Here's What Really Happened to Jobs During the Obama Years," *Money*, January 18, 2017. http://time.com/money/4636761/jobs-barack-obama-presidency/

Page 381 **drop to 3.7 percent under Trump** "The Employment Situation – October 2018," News Release, Bureau of Labor Statistics, November 2, 2018. https://www.bls.gov/news.release/pdf/empsit.pdf

Page 381 **added 4.9 million new jobs** Bureau of Labor Statistics. https://data.bls.gov/timeseries/CES0000000001?output_view=net_1mth

Page 382 **59 percent of Americans** Presidential Approval Ratings – Barack Obama, Gallup. https://news.gallup.com/poll/116479/barack-obama-presidential-job-approval.aspx

Page 383 **66 percent of Americans** Ryan Struyk, "George W. Bush's Favorable Rating Has Pulled a Complete 180," CNN, January 22, 2018. https://www.cnn.com/2018/01/22/politics/george-w-bush-favorable-poll/index.html

Page 383 **"beat the hell" out of Trump** Eileen Sullivan, "Trump Threatens Joe Biden, Saying He 'Would Go Down Fast and Hard' if They Fought," *The New York Times*, March 22, 2018. https://www.nytimes.com/2018/03/22/us/politics/trump-biden-threat.html

Page 383 **"when they go low, we kick"** Peter Baker, "Trump's Contradiction: Assailing 'Left-Wing Mob' as Crowd Chants 'Lock Her Up,'" *The New York Times*, October 10, 2018. https://www.nytimes.com/2018/10/10/us/politics/trump-rally-opponents.html

Page 383 **"There are well-meaning folks"** Baker, "Obama Lashes Trump in Debut 2018 Speech. President's Response: 'I Fell Asleep.'"

Page 384 **the party's "forever president"** Peter Baker, "Once Reluctant to Speak Out, an Energized Obama Now Calls Out His Successor," *The New York Times*, November 2, 2018. https://www.nytimes.com/2018/11/02/us/politics/obama-trump-campaign-trail.html

INDEX

449

451

453

454

Obama: The Call of History
has been produced by Callaway Arts & Entertainment
in collaboration with the New York Times.

The book is typeset in Trump roman and italic,
with typography and layout by Jerry Kelly.
The type is named for the German calligrapher
& type designer Georg Trump (1896–1985).

FOR CALLAWAY ARTS & ENTERTAINMENT

Nicholas Callaway, *President and Publisher*
Manuela Roosevelt, *Editorial Director*
Danielle Sweet, *Managing Editor*
Ivan Wong, *Production Manager*
Jason Gill, *Chief Operating Officer*

FOR THE NEW YORK TIMES

Alex Ward, *Editor*
Phyllis Collazo, *Photo Editor*
David Stout, *Copy Editor*
Lisa Kleinholz, *Indexer*